50 Hikes in Maryland

50 Hikes in Maryland

Walk, Hikes & Backpacks from the Allegheny Plateau to the Atlantic Ocean

Third Edition

LEONARD M. ADKINS

THE COUNTRYMAN PRESS
A division of W. W. Norton & Company
Independent Publishers Since 1923

AN INVITATION TO THE READER

Over time trails can be rerouted and signs and landmarks altered. If you find that changes have occurred on the routes described in this book, please let us know so that corrections may be made in future editions. The author and publisher also welcome other comments and suggestions. Address all correspondence to:

Editor, 50 Hikes Series
The Countryman Press
P.O. Box 748
Woodstock, VT 05091

Third Edition

50 Hikes in Maryland
978-1-58157-173-8

Maps by Erin Greb Cartography,
© The Countryman Press
Book design by Glenn Suokko
Text composition by PerfecType, Nashville, TN
Interior photographs by the author

Published by The Countryman Press,
www.countrymanpress.com

A division of W. W. Norton & Company, Inc.,
500 Fifth Avenue, New York, NY 10110
Printed in the United States of America

10 9 8 7 6 5 4 3

Nature must be left undisturbed in ever-widening circles, so that she can heal the wounds of civilization and re-create the wonders of God's wilderness.

William O. Douglas

Dedicated to the employees of agencies and organizations, and to the many volunteers, whose hard work enables us to continue to enjoy and appreciate the natural world. Your efforts are appreciated and do not go unnoticed.

OTHER BOOKS BY LEONARD M. ADKINS

Maryland: An Explorer's Guide

50 Hikes in Northern Virginia: Walks, Hikes, and Backpacks from the Allegheny Mountains to the Chesapeake Bay

50 Hikes in Southern Virginia: From the Cumberland Gap to the Atlantic Ocean

50 Hikes in West Virginia: Walks, Hikes, and Backpacks from the Allegheny Mountains to the Ohio River

Explorer's Guide West Virginia

Hiking and Traveling the Blue Ridge Parkway: The Only Guide You Will Ever Need, Including Maps, GPS, and More

Wildflowers of the Blue Ridge and Great Smoky Mountains

The Appalachian Trail: A Visitor's Companion

Wildflowers of the Appalachian Trail

The Best of the Appalachian Trail Day Hikes (with Victoria and Frank Logue)

The Best of the Appalachian Trail Overnight Hikes (with Victoria and Frank Logue)

Images of America: Along the Appalachian Trail: Georgia, North Carolina, and Tennessee

Images of America: Along Virginia's Appalachian Trail

Postcards of America: Along Virginia's Appalachian Trail

Acknowledgments

Without the full support of the following, this book would never have been possible, and would have been less complete and accurate. My sincere thanks to each of you for your help:

Renee Barrett and Craig Peddicord, Baltimore County Convention and Visitors Bureau; Kevin Berry, John Burns, David Chrest, Rachelle Daigneault, Dave Davis, Nate Finney, Kim Haly, Robert Hansen, Rebecca Harriett, Rita L. Knox, Melissa D. McCormick, J. Mel Poole, Rod Sauter, Brent Steury, Faye Walmsley, National Park Service;

Mark Beals, Samuel J. Bennett, Walter F. Brown, Gary Burkett, Harry Cage, Bob Cantin, Eric Creter, Dave Davis, Mary Ellen Dorn, Paul Durham, Cindy Ecker, Mike Gregory, Steve Hamilton, Chuck Harris, Kenny Hartman, April Havens, Jessica Helmbold, Karen Jarboe, Dorothy Kengla, Barbara Knisely, Amy Lutsko, Amelia Matos, John Ohler, D. Clark Old, Craig Patterson, Leslie Porter, Dave Powell, Noah Rawe, R. Smith, Adam Stachowiak, Joe Ward, Julia Weiners, Maryland Department of Natural Resources;

Terry Gardner, Little Bennett Regional Park; Tina Brown and Joanne Roland, Charles County Office of Tourism; Lisa Challenger, Worcester County Tourism; Laurie Crossley, Kent County Office of Tourism; Debbie Dodson, Talbot County Office of Tourism; Susan Durn, Stronghold, Inc.; Wanda Dyson, Prince George's County Conference and Visitors Bureau; Ish Ennis, Chincoteague National Wildlife Refuge; Steve Green, High Mountain Sports; Don Hershfeld, Streams and Dreams B&B; Julie Horner, Somerset County Tourism; Randy and Alice Ift, Chanceford Hall Inn B&B; Diane Molner, Discover Hartford County Tourism Council; Margaret Niland, American Chestnut Land Trust; Jan and Jim Quick, Holland House; Beth Rhoades, Tourism Council of Frederick County; Wini Roche, Dorchester County Tourism; Herman Schieke Jr., Calvert County Department of Economic Development;

Peg and Bill Sites, Lauretum Inn B&B; Marlene and Len Slavin, Loblolly Landings and Lodge; Nell Baldacchino, Susan Talbott, US Fish and Wildlife Service; Sandy Turner, Cecil County Office of Tourism; Colleen Wilcoxon, Maryland National Capital Park and Planning Commission; Ken Wishnick, Garrett County Chamber of Commerce; Connie Yingling, Maryland Office of Tourism Development;

Dr. Stephen Lewis, Caroline Charonko, Terri and Susie, there is no doubt where I would be without your help; Nancy Adkins, my mother and friend; Laurie, thanks for making life so much fun.

50 Hikes in Maryland at a Glance

HIKE	REGION
1. Meadow Mountain and Deep Creek Lake	Western Maryland
2 Muddy Creek and Swallow Falls	Western Maryland
3. Herrington Manor State Park	Western Maryland
4. New Germany State Park	Western Maryland
5. Garrett State Forest	Western Maryland
6. Big Savage Mountain	Western Maryland
7. Lostland Run	Western Maryland
8. Evitt's Mountain and Rocky Gap Gorge	Western Maryland
9. Green Ridge	Western Maryland
10. Paw Paw Bends and Paw Paw Tunnel	Western Maryland
11. Antietam	Western Maryland
12. Maryland Heights	Western Maryland
13. Appalachian Trail	Western Maryland
14. Catoctin Mountain	Capital Region
15. Gambrill State Park	Capital Region
16. Cunningham Falls	Capital Region
17. Catoctin Mountain Park	Capital Region
18. Deerfield Nature Center and Owens Creek	Capital Region
19. Sugarloaf Mountain	Capital Region
20. Edwards Ferry to the Monocacy River Aqueduct	Capital Region
21. Schaeffer Farm	Capital Region
22. Little Bennett Regional Park	Capital Region
23. Rock Creek Regional Park and Lake Frank	Capital Region
24. Potomac River at Carderock	Capital Region
25. Great Falls Recreation Area	Capital Region

M = Mountain views W = Water views
B = Backcountry camping D = Developed camping available within park

DISTANCE (miles)	VIEWS	GOOD FOR KIDS	WATERFALLS	CAMPING	NOTES
4.9	M			D	Old coal mine and mountaintop wetlands
1.3		★	★	D	51-foot waterfall
6.0				D	Maryland's first managed timberlands
6.1				D	Popular with cross-country skiers
7.0				B	High-altitude ponds are populated by beavers and muskrats
17.2	M			B	Rough and rocky, but great isolation
4.5 or 8.4			★	B	All downhill if done as one-way; cascades & pools
9.9	M			D	Old homesite from early 1700s
18.1	M			B	Almost always by a stream; great swimming holes
15.5	W			B	0.6-mile tunnel on the C&O Canal
4.5		★			Site of deadliest single day in Civil War
5.1	M				A view T. Jefferson said was "worth a voyage across the Atlantic"
39.3	M			B	A hike across the full height of the state
27.2	M			D	Rugged backcountry hike; optional trip to Cunningham Falls
6.0	M			D	Great vista; popular with locals
1.2		★	★	D	78-foot waterfall; 200-year-old hemlocks
8.1	M			D	Four great views, each of different terrain
3.0		★		D	Easy walk, leaves directly from campground
7.5	M				Maryland's only monadnock; grand vistas
11.7	W	★*		B	Chance to take last remaining ferry across Potomac
9.8					Very popular with mountain bikers
9.6				D	Great variety: streams, woods, meadows
4.3					Complete circumambulation of Lake Frank
5.8	W				Excellent introduction to the Potomac River
5.8	W		★		Best view of Great Falls; isolated hillside hiking

50 Hikes in Maryland at a Glance

HIKE	REGION
26. Billy Goat Trail	Capital Region
27. Greenbelt Park	Capital Region
28. Patuxent Research Refuge	Capital Region
29. Merkle Wildlife Sanctuary	Southern Maryland
30. Zekiah Swamp Run and Wolf Den Branch	Southern Maryland
31. Myrtle Grove Wildlife Management Area	Southern Maryland
32. Calvert Cliffs	Southern Maryland
33. American Chestnut Land Trust	Southern Maryland
34. The Cascade and Buzzard Rock	Central Maryland
35. Patapsco River	Central Maryland
36. Soldiers Delight	Central Maryland
37. Oregon Ridge	Central Maryland
38. Big Gunpowder Falls	Central Maryland
39. Northern Central Railroad Trail	Central Maryland
40. Sweet Air	Central Maryland
41. Gunpowder Falls State Park	Central Maryland
42. Susquehanna State Park	Central Maryland
43. Turkey Point on Elk Neck	Eastern Shore
44. Eastern Neck	Eastern Shore
45. Wye Island	Eastern Shore
46. Tuckahoe State Park	Eastern Shore
47. Blackwater National Wildlife Refuge	Eastern Shore
48. Janes Island	Eastern Shore
49. Bald Cypress Nature Trail	Eastern Shore
50. Assateague Island	Eastern Shore

M = Mountain views
B = Backcountry camping
W = Water views
D = Developed camping available within park

DISTANCE (miles)	VIEWS	GOOD FOR KIDS	WATERFALLS	CAMPING	NOTES
3.8	W				Like playing on a giant rock jungle gym
7.0					1,078-acre urban oasis
3.1	W	★			Easy walking
3.5	W				Refuge for Canada Geese
5.6				D	Some very isolated hiking in Southern Maryland
4.0					Has a short bushwhacking section
5.2	W				A chance to hunt for fossilized sharks' teeth
5.4					Protected land in one of Maryland's fastest growing counties
5.7	M		★		Challenging hike over rugged terrain and maze of pathways
4.3		★	★		With only slight ups and downs, great for kids with a bit of stamina
6.0	M				Largest remaining serpentine grasslands in Maryland
4.3					Small pond, quiet stream valley, and interesting view
12.8	W		★		Miles of riverside walking; great hike, do not miss it
18.8			★		Best rail-trail in Maryland
6.0					Two stream fords; very little used
9.25			★		Great swimming hole
4.9	W			D	Open meadows and deep forests
2.0	W	★		D	Easy hike to lighthouse and commanding view of Chesapeake
1.7		★			Views of Chesapeake Bay and Chester River
6.6					Short drive from Annapolis; 250- to 300-year-old holly tree
3.7				D	Chance to become acquainted with swamplands
2.9	W				Thousands of waterfowl; home to endangered Delmarva fox squirrel
3.2	W	★		D	You need a boat to get to the trailhead!
0.9		★			Near the northern limit of bald cypress tree
25.0	W			B	Two days of isolated beach walking

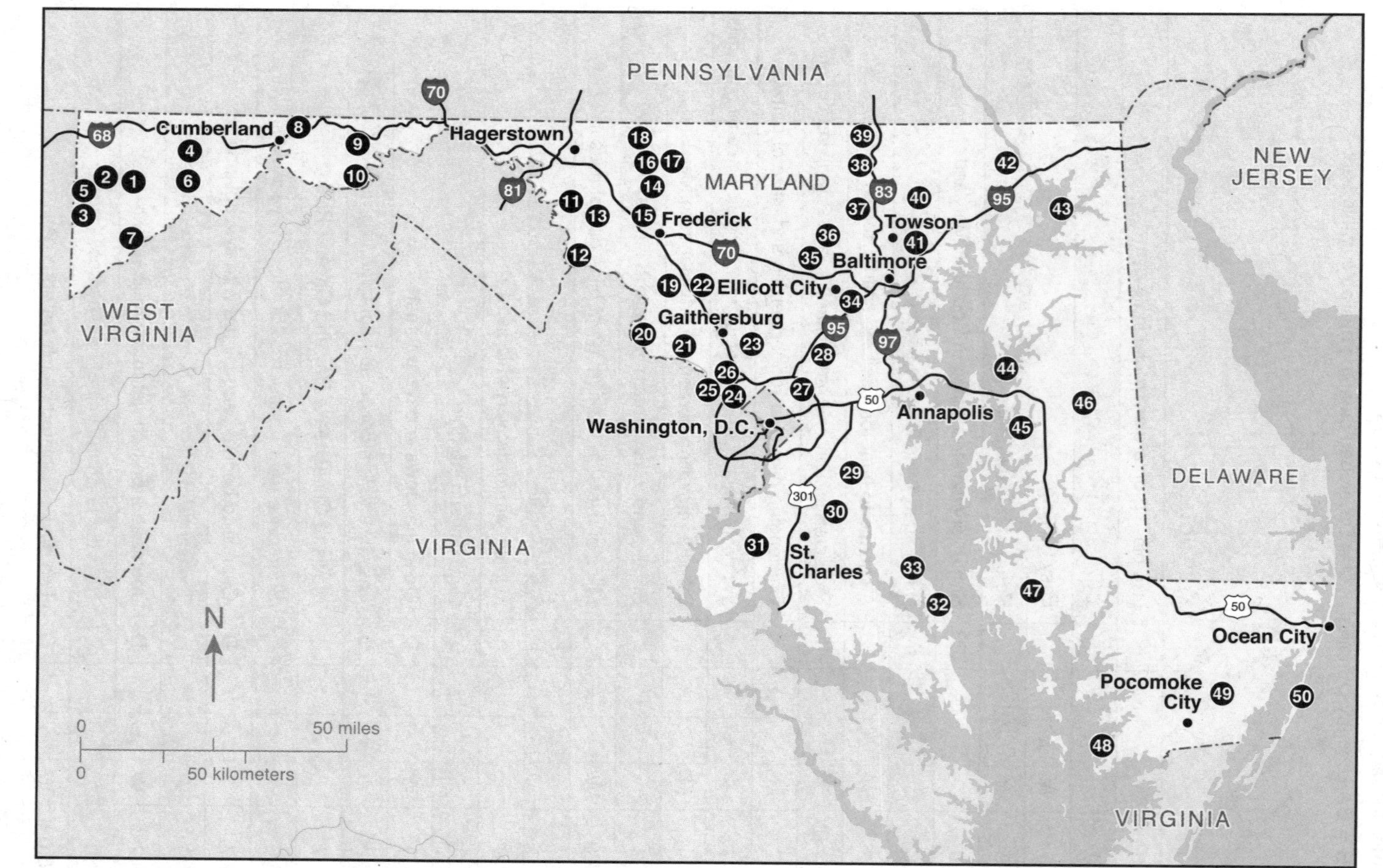

PENNSYLVANIA
NEW JERSEY
MARYLAND
DELAWARE
WEST VIRGINIA
VIRGINIA
VIRGINIA
Cumberland
Hagerstown
Frederick
Towson
Baltimore
Ellicott City
Gaithersburg
Annapolis
Washington, D.C.
St. Charles
Ocean City
Pocomoke City
N
0
50 miles
0
50 kilometers

Contents

IV. CENTRAL MARYLAND

V. EASTERN SHORE

Introduction

"So many things to do. So close together." As a general rule, the tourist-bureau-inspired slogan for a state can be written off as so much hype, but not so in the case of Maryland. With a topography that ranges from the lofty peaks of the Blue Ridge and Allegheny Mountains to the wave-swept sands of the Atlantic coast, the state has just about everything you could expect to find in the eastern part of the United States.

Barely above sea level in many places, the Eastern Shore is the place to go for easy, nearly level walks into tall pine forests, through dark swamps, and onto isolated beaches to watch the seasonal migrations of, literally, tens of thousands of waterfowl and other birds. The shallow water of the marshes, where land meets water, is a reminder of the primordial ooze from which all life emerged.

The hikes within the Central Region, which contains both the state's capital, Annapolis, and its most populated city, Baltimore, are characterized by low ridgelines created by numerous streams cutting through the coastal plain. The state has wisely seen fit to protect many of these watersheds, enabling you to discover hidden valleys thick with vegetation and hardwood forests, many bordered by fields of cultivated crops.

Somewhat reminiscent of the Eastern Shore, the low-lying landscape of Southern Maryland is also influenced by the waters of the Chesapeake Bay. Slow-moving, tannin-stained streams dotted by the colorful plumage of wading great blue herons; fossils to be found below 100-foot sand cliffs; and an introduction into the human manipulations of the environment to improve wildlife habitats await those who come to walk here.

Without a doubt the most populated portion of the state, the Capital Region is where the mountains meet the piedmont, which results in the most diverse topography. Here you may walk through grassy meadows with extensive views just as often as you meander a narrow pathway through dense woodlands. The western part of the region contains the eastern rampart of the Blue Ridge Mountains, where connecting plots of municipal, state, and federal land enable visitors to walk a 25-mile ridgeline, complete with miles of connecting side routes.

The mountains of Western Maryland are the least populated, and it is here that you will find the longest, most isolated, rugged, and quiet hikes. The Appalachian Trail provides the opportunity to walk the height of the state, while a number of state forest pathways offer backcountry camping beside hemlock-lined mountain streams. Black bears, deer, and other wildlife are most abundant here.

True to the aforementioned slogan, all of these things are within a few hours' drive of each other. The best part, though, is that no matter where you happen to be in the state at any given moment, you will never be more than a 30-minute drive away from one of the hikes in this guidebook.

Part of the mid-Atlantic region, Maryland can have a wide range of temperatures and conditions. Winters can be unpredictably cold or relatively mild, while summers can become hot and humid or may be rather temperate. Spring and autumn can be the most pleasant times of the year to be outdoors, as days warm up to a comfortable temperature, nights cool down for easy sleeping, and crowds are fewer.

Snow is common in the mountains, moderate in the Capital and Central Regions, and quite infrequent in Southern Maryland and the Eastern Shore. When heat and humidity have taken the joy and fun out of outdoor activities in the eastern portion of the state, the mountains will beckon with temperatures that can be 10 or more degrees lower.

Therefore, be willing to visit an area more than once, and do not limit your outings in Maryland to just one or two seasons. Outdoor adventuring here can be a year-round activity.

It is my sincere hope that this book will inspire you to visit, appreciate, and learn more about the best that Maryland has to offer. I only have one final thing to say: Go take a hike!

HOW TO USE THIS BOOK

50 Hikes in Maryland contains a variety of hikes that range from easy walks on level ground to ambitious, multiday backpacking excursions across rough territory. Therefore, no matter what your level of outdoor experience or physical fitness, you can choose an excursion that best fits your abilities, time restraints, or need for adventure. The headings at the beginning of each hike provide you with a quick overview of what to expect.

The total distance was determined by walking with a surveyor's measuring wheel on each hike. There may be some differences if you look to other sources for additional information, such as trail signs, handout brochures from the park or agency, or other books. Many of these merely measure distance from the trailhead and do not take into account how far you must walk to reach it. To be as accurate as possible, I measured the hike from the point you leave your automobile to where you are able to return to it and have included the distance of any side trail(s) the hike description tells you to take.

A one-way hike ends at a different point from where you started, necessitating a car shuttle. A round trip is an out-and-back excursion that follows the same route in both directions. You will take a circular journey on a circuit hike, re-walking very little, if any, of the same trail or trails.

Keep in mind that the hiking time is the minimum amount of time it would take a person of average ability to do a trip at a leisurely pace. Some of you may go faster, a few of you slower. When planning the hike, remember that the hiking time does not take into account rest breaks or time out for sightseeing and nature study.

Taking a good look at the vertical rise will probably give you the best indication of how strenuous a hike will be. It is the sum total of all the uphill hiking you will do, not just the difference in elevation between the lowest and highest points of a hike. This rise was determined by using information on US Geological Survey (USGS) maps.

The specific USGS maps that contain the topographic features of the hike are included in the map heading. The hike route is traced on these maps and reproduced for you in this book and should be all you need. Obviously, you are only getting a partial view, and if you wish more, the entire map can help identify various features, such as nearby peaks or waterways, and can help you become proficient in orienteering. They may be obtained through outfitters or from the United States Geological Survey, 1201 Sunrise Valley Drive, Reston, VA 20191, 703-648-5953. You may need several maps to complete just one hike, and the price of each is now in the multiple-dollars range. Of course, there are many map software programs available, and you'll need to decide which one will best suit your needs and hardware. If you do decide to go that way, be sure to first check the USGS website, www.usgs.gov, as some maps are now available free of charge if downloaded.

The other maps identified can be obtained, often free of charge, at the appropriate contact stations, visitors centers, or agency offices.

There are, of course, a number of different routes you could drive to reach each hike's trailhead, but the ones described are designed to keep you on four-lane highways as much as possible and, hopefully, to take the least amount of time.

Do not reject a hike or an area because the length, time, or vertical rise appears to be beyond your abilities. I feel that once you are out there, you might as well enjoy the experience for as long as possible. Therefore, I have often chosen the most circuitous and longest possible hike to be taken in a particular area. Yet, many places have numerous side trails or alternate routes you could take in order to shorten a hike. A good example is Catoctin Mountain Park (see Hike 17). I describe a trip of almost 9 miles with a vertical rise of nearly 1,500 feet, but there are so many interconnecting trails in the park that you could take a rewarding circuit hike of only 1 or 2 miles with very little elevation change. Study your maps and the descriptions in this book, and you will find that this is the case in many places.

You do not have to be in the best physical shape to enjoy a walk, but do take into account the difficulty of the terrain, the weather report, and your conditioning. Allow enough time to complete your outing before dark, and always let someone know where you are hiking.

Be aware that fees are charged for you to gain access to many of the hikes in this book. Since the imposition and amount of these fees seem to constantly change, they are not identified in the text of each individual hike. Just know that you will pay them at a large percentage of the state parks as well as some of the national parks. Whenever it is possible to start a hike at a trailhead where a fee is not charged, I did so.

ADVICE AND PRECAUTIONS

Water

If you are going to be hiking for much more than an hour, it is a wise idea to bring along some water. All of us know how thirsty we can become on hot summer days; what many people do not realize is that in the cool temperatures of winter your body needs even greater amounts of water to keep from becoming dehydrated. On overnight trips you are going to have to depend on a stream or spring, but the rise in the number of people visiting the natural areas of Maryland has brought about a corresponding increase in the appearance of *Giardia,* a waterborne parasite. Water can also become tainted by viruses, bacteria, and synthetic pollutants.

This water could be made potable by boiling, or by using iodine tablets, although using a portable water purifier is more convenient and probably as effective. Consult trusted friends or your local outfitter to help you decide which purifier is best for you. Always look for one that removes viruses as well as bacteria.

Note: For your convenience, water sources have been identified in a number of the hike descriptions, but this is not an endorsement of their purity. All sources should be treated before drinking!

Your choice of a campsite can help assure that you are not the cause of any further water pollution. Select a site a minimum of 200 feet away from any source of water, such as springs, streams, lakes, ponds, and even wet meadows. Carry water to some other point so that you can do all of your washing, including dishes, clothes, and yourself, well away from the source.

Snakes

With a wide variety and large number of snakes living in Maryland, encountering one is a possibility. Only two, the copperhead and the rattlesnake, are poisonous. It would be wise to learn how to identify them.

There are a number of things you can do to reduce the possibility of an encounter:

- Stay on authorized pathways
- Avoid rocky areas
- Do not put your hands in places you cannot see
- Step on a log first instead of stepping over it
- Walk with a group

Do remember that the outdoors is a snake's natural habitat and that it has as much right, if not more, to be there as you do. Please refrain from killing one; just walk around it, give it a wide berth, and continue on your way. This advice, of course, should be followed whenever you meet any animal in the wild.

Important: All snakebites–even from nonpoisonous snakes–may contain bacteria, so seek medical attention as soon as possible for any type of bite.

Black Bears

Western Maryland is home to an estimated 300 black bears. Your chance of seeing one or more, especially on the longer and more remote trails, is very real. The best time of day to catch a glimpse of one is in early morning or early evening, but they are also known to roam about throughout the day.

Seeing a bear in its natural setting is definitely exciting. This experience, though, brings some responsibility with it. Although it is exceedingly rare for a black bear to attack a human, you must remember that they are wild animals and do not like to be approached at close range. Do not try to feed a bear. Not only does this endanger you, it also endangers the bear. Once a bear becomes used to close human contact, it may begin wandering into campsites or housing developments looking for free handouts. This often results in the bear having to be destroyed by the authorities.

Insects

Warm weather brings no-see-ums, gnats, fleas, sand fleas, deerflies, mosquitoes, ticks, and more. Although the mountains have their fair share, the lowlands, marshes, and beaches of the eastern part of the state, especially Southern Maryland and the Eastern Shore, can be nearly swarming with them at times. Bring lots of repellent on any hike from late spring to midfall. (And remember that one of the pleasures of hiking during the colder months of the year is the absence of insects.)

Recent years have seen a rise in the reported cases of Lyme disease, a bacterial infection transmitted by the bite of a deer tick. Preliminary research indicates that commercially prepared insect repellents may not work well against ticks, so as a precaution some people tuck their pant legs into socks or boots and wear long-sleeved shirts and caps. Check yourself for ticks after each outing, remembering that the thing you are looking for could be as small as the period at the end of this sentence.

Jellyfish

Jellyfish numbers increase as the summer temperatures rise. In some years, they are so plentiful by late August as to preclude swimming in the Chesapeake Bay (and to a lesser extent in the Atlantic Ocean). Obviously, the best defense is to stay out of the water when they are present. If stung, use alcohol, vinegar, baking soda, or meat tenderizer to help relieve the pain. A few people have a severe allergic reaction, which requires medical attention.

Plants

Poison ivy is found just about everywhere in Maryland. Learn how to identify it, as it can grow in a number of forms. The most common is a woody shrub of up to 2 feet high that grows in large patches, often lining or overtaking pathways. It also grows as a hairy, root-covered vine that clings to the trunk of a tree, climbing far up into the branches. All parts of the plant contain the poison; and this is true even in winter when it appears to be dead.

Not as prevalent, but certainly present, poison oak is most often found in sandy soil habitats. As its name suggests, its leaflets resemble the leaves of an oak tree, but they are fuzzy.

Considered by some to be one of the most dangerous plants in the United States, poison sumac occurs in Maryland, most extensively in the eastern part of the state. Unlike the low-standing poison ivy, it can grow to be 25 feet in height and has compound leaves with an odd number of leaflets. The upper side of a leaflet is shiny green, while the bottom side is lighter with small hairs.

Trumpet creeper, or vine, is most often found in the lowlands. Also known as cow itch, it can cause contact dermatitis.

Stinging nettle will grow in large carpets and encroach upon pathways that are not well maintained. Brushing up against the plant may cause your skin to itch for the rest of the day.

Sun

By now we have all heard of the dangerous effects of the sun, especially with the continued deterioration of Earth's atmosphere. More and more doctors are suggesting that you apply a high-strength sunblock lotion whenever you will be outdoors for extended periods of time—summer or winter.

Hunting

Due to the abundance of wildlife, hunting is extremely popular in Maryland, even in the more populated counties. The usual season runs from early fall into January, and then there is a season again in the spring. Since dates do vary from year to year and place to place, you should check with local authorities. During the season, it may be best to hike in a group. In any case, do not venture forth without wearing some kind of blaze orange clothing. If you are hunting (or fishing), be sure to obtain the proper licenses and check about local regulations.

Mountain Bikes

Mountain biking is very popular in Maryland, especially in the populated areas around Baltimore and Washington, D.C., where many state and regional parks permit riders to use the trails. Although most devotees of the activity I have met have been courteous, you should be prepared to quickly step aside at any moment as an unannounced biker goes zipping by you at a high rate of speed. If you are a mountain biker, you may find this guidebook useful, as it points out many places where you may ride. Please remember to stay on the trail, and alert anyone of your approach.

Unattended Vehicles

There has been a continuous rise in theft and vandalism to cars left unattended at trailheads, so it is wise to leave your valuables at home. Place whatever valuables you do have out of sight and lock the car.

If you are going to leave a car overnight, be sure to give a ranger or the proper authority your vehicle's make and license number, the length of time you will be leaving it, and the name of each person in your party.

A way to avoid a car shuttle on a one-way hike, and the problems associated with leaving an automobile overnight, is to have someone drop you off at the beginning and pick you up when you have finished.

Proper Clothing and Equipment

As with any outdoor pursuit, you must be ready for abrupt fluctuations in the weather. Warm and sunny summer days may become cold and rainy in just a matter of minutes. Additionally, do not be surprised if a pleasant spring or fall day changes to one with sleet or snow.

Because people are caught off guard on days such as this, when the temperature dips into the low 60s and 50s, hypothermia may strike. A condition in which the body loses heat faster than it can produce it, hypothermia is one of the leading causes of hiker and camper deaths. Be prepared by carrying rain gear and an insulating layer of clothing, such as a wool sweater or synthetic jacket, in your day pack. Because layering is a more effective means of keeping warm than wearing just one thick layer, carry several warm items of clothing for winter travel.

In addition to rain gear and extra layers of clothes, your pack should include a first-aid kit, flashlight, knife, compass, toilet paper, and some waterproof matches. If you are camping, be prepared for possible cool nights, even in the summer.

It is not necessary to subject your feet to the tortures of heavy-duty, mountaineering-type boots in order to enjoy hiking in Maryland. Excluding those who have ankle or foot problems, people can wear comfortable tennis, walking, or running shoes for most of the hikes—especially the shorter ones in the eastern half of Maryland. Lightweight hiking boots or shoes should be sufficient for hikes in the mountains and on overnight backpacking trips.

In order to reduce friction and rubbing on your feet, you should wear a thick sock over a thinner one. Immediately applying moleskin (available at most pharmacies and outdoor outfitters) at the first sign of a "hot spot" on your feet will go a long way toward preventing blisters from developing.

The aforementioned are just the basics you should know about foot travel in areas removed from the mainstream. Obviously it is not the intent of this guidebook to be a hiking or backpacking equipment "primer," so I suggest that you solicit the advice of backpacking acquaintances, trail club members, and outdoor outfitters. I am a firm believer, especially if you are a novice hiker, in supporting your neighborhood backpack shop instead of mail-order companies. Not only will the local folks help fit and adjust your equipment and be there to help you if you have any questions, many shops rent hiking and camping equipment—enabling you to try something before you decide to buy it.

A number of books are available if you feel the need for further information. Currently, two of the most complete books on the subject of outdoor travel are *Backpacking and Hiking* by Karen Berger and *Hiking and Backpacking: Essential Skills, Equipment, and Safety* by Victoria Logue.

Trail Life: Ray Jardine's Lightweight Backpacking contains some debatable, yet very innovative information. *The Complete*

Walker IV by Colin Fletcher and Chip Rawlins is not only informative but also makes for some entertaining reading.

HIKING AND CAMPING ETIQUETTE

Endorsed by almost every organization connected with the outdoors, the Leave No Trace principles have been developed to protect a fragile natural world from increased usage. (This copyrighted information has been reprinted with permission from the Leave No Trace Center for Outdoor Ethics. For more information or materials, please visit www.LNT.org or call 1-800-332-4100.)

Plan Ahead and Prepare

- Know the regulations and special concerns for the area you'll visit.
- Prepare for extreme weather, hazards, and emergencies.
- Schedule your trip to avoid times of high use.
- Visit in small groups. Split larger parties into groups of four to six.
- Repackage food to minimize waste.
- Use a map and compass to eliminate the use of marking paint, rock cairns, or flagging.

Travel and Camp on Durable Surfaces

- Durable surfaces include established trails and campsites, rock, gravel, dry grasses, or snow.
- Protect riparian areas by camping at least 200 feet from lakes and streams.
- Good campsites are found, not made. Altering a site is not necessary.

In popular areas:

- Concentrate use on existing trails and campsites.
- Walk single file in the middle of the trail, even when wet or muddy.
- Keep campsites small. Focus activity in areas where vegetation is absent.

In pristine areas:

- Disperse use to prevent the creation of campsites and trails.
- Avoid places where impacts are just beginning.

Dispose of Waste Properly

- Pack it in, pack it out. Inspect your campsite and rest areas for trash or spilled foods. Pack out all trash, leftover food, and litter.
- Deposit solid human waste in catholes dug 6 to 8 inches deep at least 200 feet from water, camp, and trails. Cover and disguise the cathole when finished.
- Pack out toilet paper and hygiene products.
- To wash yourself or your dishes, carry water 200 feet away from streams or lakes and use small amounts of biodegradable soap. Scatter strained dishwater.

Leave What You Find

- Preserve the past: examine, but do not touch, cultural or historic structures and artifacts.
- Leave rocks, plants, and other natural objects as you find them.
- Avoid introducing or transporting nonnative species.
- Do not build structures, furniture, or dig trenches.

Minimize Campfire Impacts

- Campfires can cause lasting impacts to the backcountry. Use a lightweight stove for cooking and enjoy a candle lantern for light.
- Where fires are permitted, use established fire rings, fire pans, or mound fires.
- Keep fires small. Only use sticks from the ground that can be broken by hand.
- Burn all wood and coals to ash, put out campfires completely, then scatter cool ashes.

Respect Wildlife

- Observe wildlife from a distance. Do not follow or approach them.
- Never feed animals. Feeding wildlife damages their health, alters natural behaviors, and exposes them to predators and other dangers.
- Protect wildlife and your food by storing rations and trash securely.
- Control pets at all times, or leave them at home.
- Avoid wildlife during sensitive times: mating, nesting, raising young, or winter.

Be Considerate of Other Visitors

- Respect other visitors and protect the quality of their experience.
- Be courteous. Yield to other users on the trail.
- Step to the downhill side of the trail when encountering pack stock.
- Take breaks and camp away from trails and other visitors.
- Let nature's sounds prevail. Avoid loud voices and noises.

Backwoods Ethics by Laura and Guy Waterman is an excellent resource, not only providing details on the "how" of making little or no impact on the environment, but also the "why."

SUGGESTED READINGS AND FIELD GUIDES

Abercrombie, Jay. *Weekend Walks on the Delmarva Peninsula: Walks and Hikes in Delaware and the Eastern Shore of Maryland and Virginia.* Woodstock, VT: The Countryman Press, 2006.

Adkins, Leonard M. *The Appalachian Trail: A Visitor's Companion.* Birmingham, AL: Menasha Ridge Press, 1998.

---. *50 Hikes in Northern Virginia: Walks, Hikes, and Backpacks from the Allegheny Mountains to the Chesapeake Bay.* Woodstock, VT: The Countryman Press, 2006.

---. *Explorer's Guide Maryland.* Woodstock, VT: The Countryman Press, 2013.

---. *50 Hikes in West Virginia: From the Allegheny Mountains to the Ohio River.* Woodstock, VT: The Countryman Press, 2005.

---. *Wildflowers of the Appalachian Trail.* Birmingham, AL: Menasha Ridge Press, 1999.

---. *Wildflowers of the Blue Ridge and Great Smoky Mountains.* Birmingham, AL: Menasha Ridge Press, 2005.

Borland, Hal. *A Countryman's Flowers.* New York: Knopf, 1981.

Brill, David. *As Far as the Eye Can See: Reflections of an Appalachian Trail Hiker.* Harpers Ferry, WV: Appalachian Trail Conservancy, 2004.

Burn, Barbara. *North American Mammals.* New York: Random House Value Publishing, 1991.

---. *North American Trees.* New York: Random House Value Publishing, 1987.

---. *North American Wildflowers.* New York: Random House Value Publishing, 1992.

Busch, Phyllis. *Wildflowers and the Stories Behind Their Names.* New York: Charles Scribner's Sons, 1977.

Byrd, Nathan, ed. *A Forester's Guide to Observing Animal Use of Forest Habitat in the South.* Atlanta, GA: US Department of Agriculture, Forest Service, 1981.

Chambers, Kenneth A. *A County-Lover's Guide to Wildlife: Mammals, Amphibians, and Reptiles of the Northeastern United States.* Baltimore, MD: Johns Hopkins University Press, 1979.

Dana, William S. *How to Know the Wildflowers.* Boston: Houghton Mifflin, 1991.

Douglas, William O. *My Wilderness: East to Katahdin*. San Francisco: Comstock Editions, 1989.

Eastman, John. *The Book of Forest and Thicket: Trees, Shrubs, and Wildflowers of Eastern North America*. Mechanicsburg, PA: Stackpole Books, 1992.

Grimm, William. *The Illustrated Book of Trees: The Comprehenseive Field Guide to More than 250 Trees in Eastern North America*. Mechanicsburg, PA: Stackpole Books, 2001.

---. *The Illustrated Book of Wildflowers and Shrubs: The Comprehensive Field Guide to More than 1,300 Plants in Eastern America*. Mechanicsburg, PA: Stackpole Books, 1993.

Halliday, Tim, and Kraig Adler, eds. *The New Encyclopedia of Reptiles and Amphibians*. New York: Oxford University Press, 2002.

Johnson, Hugh. *Hugh Johnson's Encyclopedia of Trees*. New York: Gallery Books, 1984.

Murie, Olaus J. *Peterson Field Guide to Animal Tracks*. Boston: Houghton Mifflin, 2005.

Peterson, Roger Torey. *A Field Guide to the Birds of Eastern and Central North America*. Boston: Houghton Mifflin, 2002.

Peterson, Roger T., and Margaret McKenny. *A Field Guide to Wildflowers of Northeastern and North-Central North America*. Boston: Houghton Mifflin, 2002.

Petrides, George A. *A Field Guide to Trees and Shrubs*. Boston: Houghton Mifflin, 1988.

Rue, Leonard Lee III. *Pictorial Guide to Mammals of North America*. New York: Thomas Y. Crowell Company, 1967.

Reid, Fiona. *Field Guide to Mammals of North America*. Boston: Houghton Mifflin, 2006.

Stokes, Donald W. *The Natural History of Wild Shrubs and Vines: Eastern and Central America*. New York: Harper and Row, 1981.

ADDRESSES

Hike 1:

Deep Creek Lake State Park
898 State Park Road
Swanton, MD 21561
301-387-5563
www.dnr.state.md.us/publiclands/western/deepcreek.asp

Hike 2:

Swallow Falls State Park
c/o Herrington Manor State Park
222 Herrington Lane
Oakland, MD 21550
301-387-6938
www.dnr.state.md.us/publiclands/western/swallowfalls.asp

Hike 3:

Herrington Manor State Park
222 Herrington Lane
Oakland, MD 21550
301-334-9180
www.dnr.state.md.us/publiclands/western/herrington.asp

Hike 4:

New Germany State Park
349 Headquarters Lane
Grantsville, MD 21536
301-895-5453
www.dnr.state.md.us/publiclands/western/newgermany.asp

Hike 5:

Potomac-Garrett State Forest
1431 Potomac Camp Road
Oakland, MD 21550
301-334-2038
www.dnr.state.md.us/publiclands/western/garrett.asp

Hike 6:

Savage River State Forest
127 Headquarters Lane
Grantsville, MD 21536
301-895-5759
www.dnr.state.md.us/publiclands/western/savageriver.asp

Hike 7:

Potomac-Garrett State Forest
1431 Potomac Camp Road
Oakland, MD 21550
301-334-2038
www.dnr.state.md.us/publiclands/western/potomacforest.asp

Hike 8:

Rocky Gap State Park
12500 Pleasant Valley Road
Flintstone, MD 21530
301-722-1480
www.dnr.state.md.us/publiclands/western/rockygap.asp

Hike 9:

Green Ridge State Forest
28700 Headquarters Drive NE
Flintstone, MD 21530-9525
301-478-3124
www.dnr.state.md.us/publiclands/western/greenridge.asp

Hike 10:

Chesapeake and Ohio Canal
Hancock Visitor Center
326 E. Main Street
Hancock, MD 21750
301-678-5463
www.nps.gov/choh

Hike 11:

Antietam National Battlefield
P.O. Box 158
Sharpsburg, MD 21782
301-432-7648
www.nps.gov/anti

Hike 12:

Harpers Ferry National Historical Park
P.O. Box 65 Harpers Ferry, WV 25425
304-535-6029
www.nps.gov/hafe

Hike 13:

Appalachian Trail Conservancy
799 Washington Street
P.O. Box 807
Harpers Ferry, WV 25425-0807
304-535-6331
www.appalachiantrail.org

Hike 14:

Potomac Appalachian Trail Club
118 Park Street, S.E.
Vienna, VA 22180-4609
703-242-0315
www.patc.net

Hike 15:

Gambrill State Park
c/o Cunningham Falls State Park
8602 Gambrill Park Road
Thurmont, MD 21702
301-271-7574
www.dnr.state.md.us/publiclands/western/gambrill.asp

Hike 16:

Cunningham Falls State Park
14039 Catoctin Hollow Road
Thurmont, MD 21788
301-271-7574
www.dnr.state.md.us/publiclands/western/cunningham.asp

Hikes 17 and 18:

Catoctin Mountain Park
6602 Foxville Road
Thurmont, MD 21788
301-663-9330
www.nps.gov/cato

Hike 19:

Stronghold, Inc.
7901 Comus Road

Dickerson, MD 20842
301-874-2024
www.sugarloafmd

Hike 20:

Chesapeake & Ohio Canal
Brunswick Visitor Center
40 West Potomac Street
Brunswick, MD 21716
301-834-7100
www.nps.gov/choh

Hike 21:

Seneca Creek State Park
11950 Clopper Road
Gaithersburg, MD 20878
301-924-2127
www.dnr.state.md.us/publiclands
/central/seneca.asp

Hike 22:

Little Bennett Regional Park
23701 Frederick Road
Clarksburg, MD 20871
301-528-3450
www.montgomeryparks.org/facilities
/regional_parks/little_bennett/

Hike 23:

Rock Creek Regional Park
6700 Need Wood Road
Rockville, MD 20855
301-948-5053
www.montgomeryparks.org/facilities
/regional_parks/rockcreek

Hikes 24, 25, and 26:

Chesapeake & Ohio Canal
Great Falls Tavern Visitor Center
11710 MacArthur Boulevard
Potomac, MD 20854
301-767-3714
www.nps.gov/choh

Hike 27:

Greenbelt Park
6565 Greenbelt Road
Greenbelt, MD 20770
301-344-3948
www.nps.gov/gree

Hike 28:

Patuxent Research Refuge
10901 Scarlet Tanager Loop
Laurel, MD 20708-4027
301-497-5761
www.fws.gov/northeast/patuxent

Hike 29:

Merkle Wildlife Sanctuary
11704 Fenno Road
Upper Marlboro, MD 20772
301-888-1410
www.dnr.state.md.us/publiclands
/southern/merkle.asp

Hike 30:

Southern Maryland Recreational Complex
Cedarville State Forest
10201 Bee Oak Road
Brandywine, MD 20613
301-888-1410
www.dnr.state.md.us/publiclands
/southern/cedarville.asp

Hike 31:

Myrtle Grove WMA
5625 Myrtle Grove Road
LaPlata, MD 20646
301-743-5161
www.dnr.state.md.us/wildlife/public
lands/southern/myrtlegrove.asp

Hike 32:

Calvert Cliffs State Park
c/o Smallwood State Park
2750 Sweden Point Road
Marbury, MD 20658
301-743-7613
www.dnr.state.md.us/publiclands
/southern/calvertcliffs.asp

Hike 33:

American Chestnut Land Trust
P.O. Box 2363
Prince Frederick, MD 20678

410-414-3400
www.acltweb.org

Hikes 34 and 35:

Patapsco Valley State Park
8020 Baltimore National Pike
Ellicott City, MD 21043
410-461-5005
www.dnr.state.md.us/publiclands/central/patapsco.asp

Hike 36:

Soldiers Delight Natural Environment Area
5100 Deer Park Road
Owings Mills, MD 21117
410-461-5005
www.dnr.state.md.us/publiclands/central/soldiersdelight.asp

Hike 37:

Oregon Ridge Nature Center
13555 Beaver Dam Road
Cockeysville, MD 21030
410-887-1815
www.oregonridge.org

Hikes 38, 40, and 41:

Gunpowder Falls State Park
PO Box 480
Jerusalem Road
Kingsville, MD 21087
410-592-2897
www.dnr.state.md.us/publiclands/central/gunpowder.asp

Hike 39:

Northern Central Railroad Trail
c/o Gunpowder Falls State Park
PO Box 480 Jerusalem Road
Kingsville, MD 21087
410-592-2897
www.dnr.state.md.us/greenways/ncrt_trail.html

Hike 42:

Susquehanna State Park
4122 Wilkonson Road
Havre de Grace, MD 21708
410-557-7994
www.dnr.state.md.us/publiclands/central/susquehanna.asp

Hike 43:

Elk Neck State Park
4395 Turkey Point Road
North East, MD 21901
410- 287-5333
www.dnr.state.md.us/publiclands/central/elkneck.asp

Hike 44:

Eastern Neck National Wildlife Refuge
1730 Eastern Neck Road
Rock Hall, MD 21661
410-639-7056
www.fws.gov/northeast/easternneck

Hike 45:

Wye Island Natural Resources Management Area
632 Wye Island Road
Queenstown, MD 21658
410-827-7577
www.dnr.state.md.us/publiclands/eastern/wyeisland.asp

Hike 46:

Tuckahoe State Park
13070 Crouse Mill Road
Queen Anne, MD 21657
410-820-1668
www.dnr.state.md.us/publiclands/eastern/tuckahoe.asp

Hike 47:

Blackwater National Wildlife Refuge
2145 Key Wallace Drive
Cambridge, MD 21613
410-229-2677
www.fws.gov/blackwater

Hike 48:

Janes Island State Park
26280 Alfred Lawson Drive
Crisfield, MD 21817
410-968-1565

www.dnr.state.md.us/publiclands
/eastern/janesisland.asp

Hike 49:

Pocomoke River State Forest and Park
3461 Worcester Highway
Snow Hill, MD 21863
410-632-2566
www.dnr.state.md.us/publiclands
/eastern/pocomokeriver.asp

Hike 50:

Assateague Island National Seashore
7206 National Seashore Lane
Berlin, MD 21811
Maryland District Visitor Information
410-641-1441
Virginia District Visitor Information
757-336-6577
www.nps.gov/asis

and

Assateague State Park
7307 Stephen Decatur Highway
Berlin, MD 21811
410-641-2120
www.dnr.state.md.us/publiclands
/eastern/assateague.asp

and

Chincoteague National Wildlife Refuge
8231 Beach Road
Chincoteague, VA 23336
757-336-6122
www.fws.gov/northeast/chinco

I Western Maryland

1

Meadow Mountain and Deep Creek Lake

Total distance (circuit): 4.9 miles

Hiking time: 2 hours, 45 minutes

Vertical rise: 820 feet

Maps: USGS 7½' McHenry; park map

Swelling up like the wave of a ripple on Western Maryland's Allegheny Plateau, Meadow Mountain rises to 3,000 feet above sea level and forms part of the divide that determines if water falling in Garrett County, Maryland, ends up in the Atlantic Ocean or the Gulf of Mexico. Running in a northeast to southwest direction, it stretches from the Maryland/Pennsylvania border to the waters of Deep Creek Lake–almost the full width of the county.

Situated within a wide valley of the plateau, the lake was formed in the 1920s when Deep Creek was dammed as part of a hydroelectric project to provide power to the residents of Pennsylvania. As on most large artificial lakes, motorboating, water-skiing, sailing, fishing, and other outdoor pursuits are popular activities. Yet, it seems like the idea for such lakes comes from real-estate developers as much as it does from the need for electric power. Deep Creek Lake covers 6 square miles and has approximately 65 miles of shoreline, but out of all of this, Deep Creek Lake State Park is the only bit of land on which the general public is permitted. Although you are permitted to walk along the shoreline around the lake, nearly every other inch of land beyond it has been turned into housing developments, private home lots, or commercially operated enterprises such as restaurants, motels, marinas, and bait and tackle shops. The only public swimming area on the entire lake is in the state park, a beach all of 700 feet long.

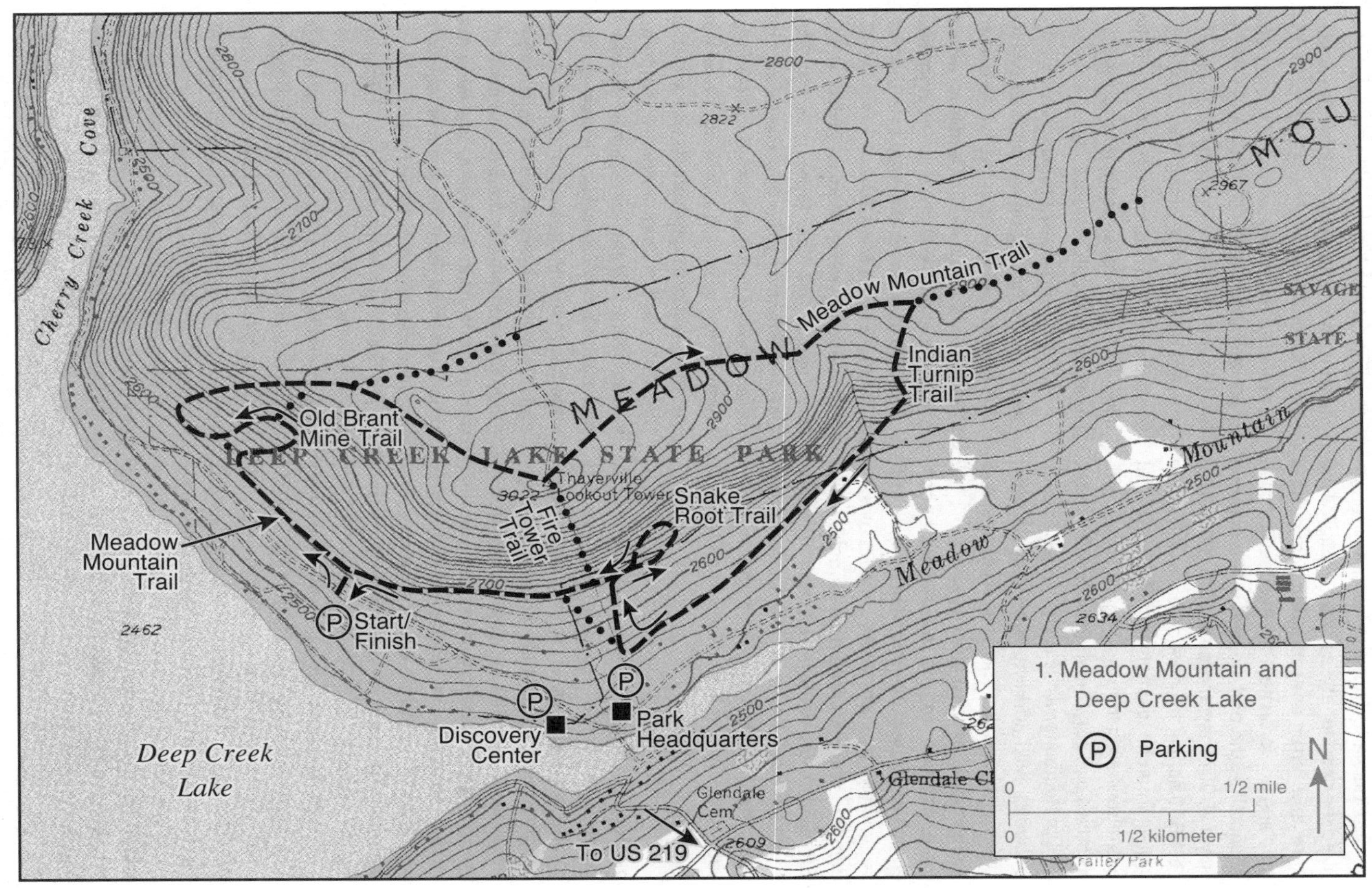
1. Meadow Mountain and Deep Creek Lake
Parking
0
1/2 mile
0
1/2 kilometer
N
Meadow Mountain Trail
Indian Turnip Trail
Old Brant Mine Trail
Thayerville Lookout Tower
Fire Tower Trail
Snake Root Trail
Meadow Mountain Trail
Start/ Finish
Discovery Center
Park Headquarters
To US 219
Glendale Cem
Deep Creek Lake
Cherry Creek Cove
DEEP CREEK LAKE STATE PARK
MEADOW
Meadow
Mountain
2822
2967
3022
2462
2634
2609

The Maryland General Assembly recognized the need for at least a bit of public land here and, after appropriating money and reaching an agreement for the use of 1 mile of shoreline, the park opened to the public in July 1959. Today, more than 95 percent of its 1,800 acres (this may increase with pending land purchases) consists of a forest that has regenerated from the original timber, with hickories and oaks being the dominant trees. This protected terrain is home to black bears, bobcats, wild turkeys, white-tailed deer, skunks, chipmunks, squirrels, raccoons, and numerous other small mammals.

In addition to the swimming beach, amenities in the park include more than 100 campsites, hot showers, mini-cabins, a dumping station, and a boat-launch facility. Stocked trout, walleye, bass, and yellow perch keep anglers busy. Ranger naturalists lead interpretive programs throughout the year, and the excellent Discovery Center is open year-round.

This hike along the slopes and crest of Meadow Mountain is an opportunity to get away from the crowds of the lake and campground, visit an old mining site, enjoy a couple of vistas, and study mountaintop wetlands. Be aware that hunting is permitted in the park's backcountry area during regular hunting seasons, and that some of the trails are open to mountain bikes. The Meadow Mountain Trail is open to snowmobiles during the winter.

The park is reached by driving west from Cumberland on I-68 for approximately 30 miles. At Keysers Ridge, take exit 14 onto US 219 south. Follow this roadway through the commercial section of the resort area, cross the bridge over the lake, and, in Thayerville, make a left onto Glendale Road. Keep left after you cross a second bridge over the lake, pass by waterfront cottages, and make another left onto State Park Road. After stopping at the park office to obtain a brochure keyed to stops along the Snake Root Nature Trail, follow signs past the beach area to leave your car at the far end of Parking Lot 3. If you find the road to Parking Lot 3 closed (as it usually is in winter), you may park your car at the Discovery Center and walk the road to the beginning of the hike. This adds less than a mile to the outing's overall length.

The hike begins by crossing State Park Road and ascending on a connector trail for 300 feet to turn left onto the white-blazed Meadow Mountain Trail. Continue with a gradual rise until you come to the right turn you need to make at 0.4 mile onto the red-blazed Old Brant Mine Trail.

Ascending more quickly, arrive at the mine site at 0.7 mile. Opened in 1923 by Delphia Brant and George Beckman, the mine supplied the coal needed to heat local homes. The operation was a success, but the men worked themselves so hard that they both died of lung disease within three years. Eventually the mine caved in, and it has never been reworked. However, the state has reconstructed a portion of the site, and it is worth spending some time here to study the old tram car, tracks, and mine entrance. (Interpretive hikes to the mine are scheduled throughout the summer; check at the park office for dates and times.)

Do not take the trail that heads uphill to the right when you are ready to leave; rather, you should descend the pathway to the left. At 0.8 mile, turn right onto the white-blazed Meadow Mountain Trail and begin to ascend along a woods road, soon making a switchback to the right.

Reach the ridgeline at 1.2 miles and avoid the trail to the right, which leads back to the mine site. In addition, do not turn onto the road coming in from the left. Continue straight, with easy walking and little change

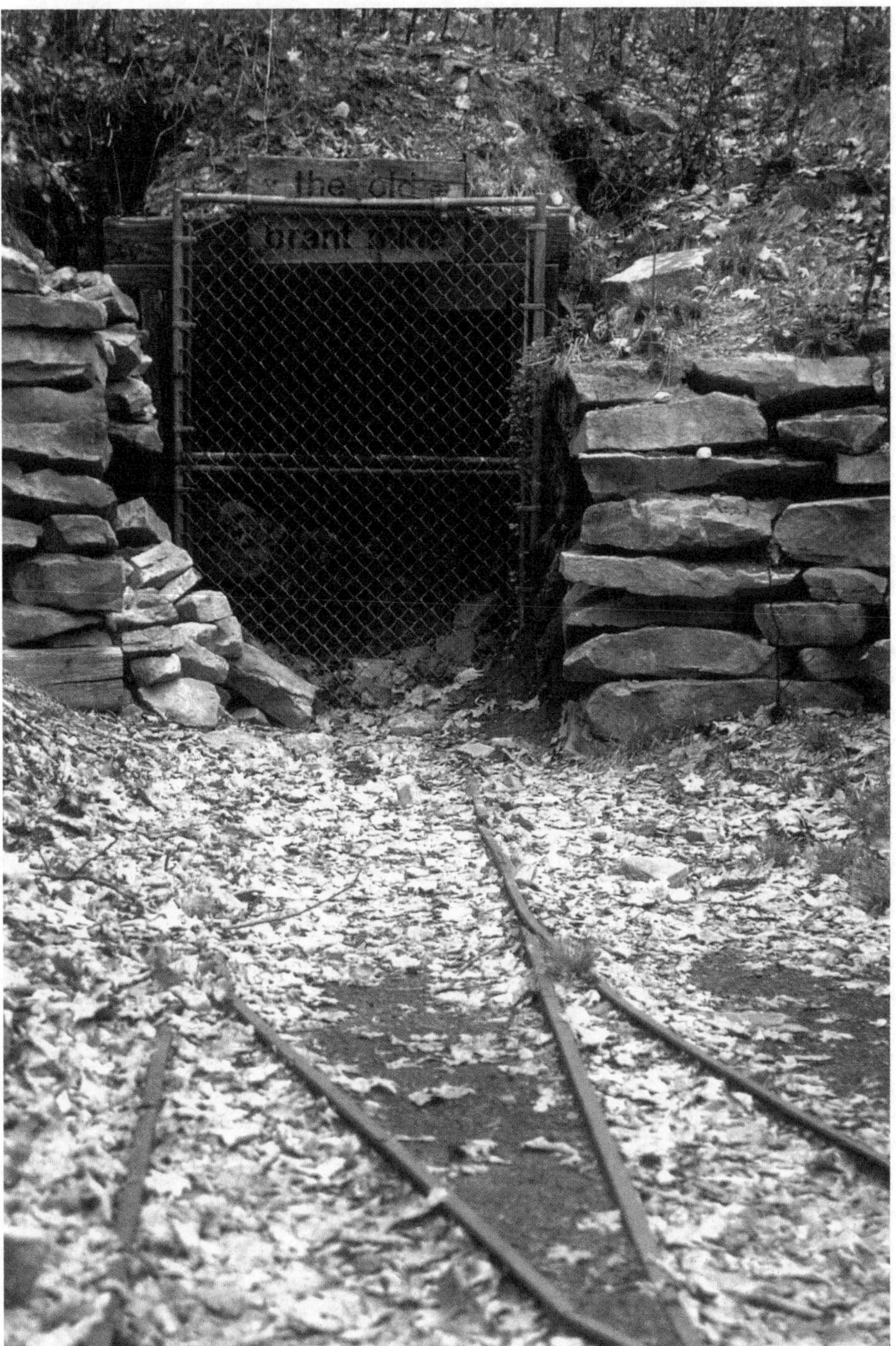

Old Brant Mine

in elevation. Take the side trail to the right at 1.7 miles to enjoy a view of Deep Creek Lake with Roman Nose Hill rising up behind it. Unless this overlook has been recently maintained, you may not have much of a view, but you only expended a little bit of energy and have walked through a part of the park you would have otherwise missed. Return to the main trail and bear right.

Pass by a communications facility at 2.1 miles and turn right at the fire tower, which is not open to the public. You can gain another perspective onto the lake and the surrounding countryside from the power-line right-of-way. (If you wish to shorten this hike by 1.9 miles, you can follow the steep and rocky Fire Tower Trail down the right-of-way to rejoin this description at the 4.4-mile point.)

Return to the main trail and bear right, now following a route marked by blue and white blazes. Railroad ties in the "corduroy" road at 2.7 miles enable you to negotiate a mountain wetland area without getting wet feet. Be sure and slow down to appreciate this spot, whose vegetation of arrowhead-shaped leaves is more often thought of as being associated with the marshlands of eastern Maryland.

Be alert soon after the planks come to an end at 2.9 miles. Do not continue to the left along the white-blazed Meadow Mountain Trail; rather, make a hard right onto the narrower and blue-blazed Indian Turnip Trail to descend steeply.

Cross a wooden bridge at 3.3 miles. Some of the water of the small stream underneath you may end up taking a long journey. Heading downhill into Meadow Mountain Run, it mixes with the waters of Deep Creek Lake, which empties into the Youghiogheny River. Flowing northward, the Youghiogheny meets the Monongahela River just south of Pittsburgh, Pennsylvania. This, in turn, joins the Allegheny River to form the Ohio River. Now moving to the west and south, the water from the small stream on Meadow Mountain mingles with drops of rain that fell upon the Rocky Mountains and the Great Plains, all of this liquid coursing down the route of the Mississippi River to finally end up in salt water at the Gulf of Mexico.

In early spring you might find wood anemone growing around the bridge over the stream. Like they do with a number of flowers that bloom at this time of year, ants help disseminate the wood anemone's seeds. Attracted to oils and possibly other nutrients found in the bulges–known as elaiosomes–on the plant's seed casing, the ants bring the seeds back to their tunnels and eat the elaiosomes. Because the rest of the casing is too hard to open, the ants discard the seed–which is then able to germinate and sprout within the safety of the tunnel.

An old road comes in from the left at 4 miles; keep to the right. There is another intersection in 200 more feet. The trail to the left descends to the campground; keep to the right and ascend the black-blazed Fire Tower Trail along the power line. Turn right onto the green-blazed Snake Root Nature Trail at 4.2 miles and right again at the circuit trail intersection, using the brochure you obtained at the park office to learn a bit of the natural history of the area.

Having walked your way back to the Fire Tower Trail at 4.4 miles, go across it to follow the white-blazed Meadow Mountain Trail. Slabbing the hillside above the campground, come to the connector trail you began this journey on, turn left, and return to your car at 4.9 miles.

2

Muddy Creek and Swallow Falls

Total distance (circuit): 1.3 miles

Hiking time: 40 minutes

Vertical rise: 100 feet

Maps: USGS 7½' Oakland (MD/WV); USGS 7½' Sang Run (MD/WV); park map

What is it about waterfalls that so draws us to them? Are we in awe of the unbridled power of hundreds of gallons of liquid rushing down the face of water-carved rock sculptures? Do we look forward to swimming in the pool at the base of a falls, enjoying the rainbow created by the mist floating down onto us like wispy raindrops? Do our eyes become mesmerized by the ever-changing water patterns, as they do when we watch the dancing flames of a campfire? Or is it simply the overall natural beauty of the scenery in which most waterfalls exist?

A walk in Swallow Falls State Park provides you with not just one, but four distinctly different waterfalls to help you decide just what it is that attracts you to them. An added enticement is a shaded, 37-acre hemlock and white pine forest.

The park is reached by taking I-68 exit 14A at Keysers Ridge and following US 219 South for 19.5 miles. Turn right onto Mayhew Inn Road, continue another 4.5 miles, and turn left onto Oakland Sang Road. Driving an additional 0.3 mile brings you to a right turn onto Herrington Manor/Swallow Falls Road; follow this road for 1.3 miles to the entrance to the state park on the right. Leave your car in the day-use parking lot. Pets must be leashed. Pets may be off-leash and under voice control while swimming; see park signs for additional information.

Begin the hike by taking the trail behind the information kiosk. Within a few feet, you'll enter a 37-acre stand of hemlock and white pine; bear left in 250 feet to take the pathway toward Muddy Creek Falls.

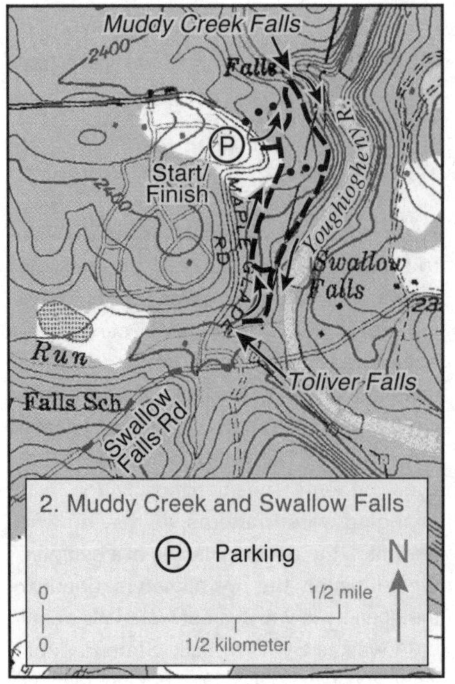

At the intersection at 0.15 mile, descend to the right. Make a right onto a side trail in an additional 250 feet, passing by the spot used as a campsite in 1918, and again in 1921, by industrialists Henry Ford and Harvey Firestone, inventor Thomas Edison, and naturalist John Burroughs. As it is today, Western Maryland was a popular destination in the early 20th century. In those days before air-conditioning, many people came to the region not only to enjoy the scenery, but to escape the heat of summers in the cities, valleys, and coastal areas.

Arrive at an overlook at 0.25 mile, which provides a perspective into the rocky gorge carved out of the Allegheny Plateau by the rushing waters of Muddy Creek. After enjoying the view for a few minutes, return to the main trail and turn right to stand at the top of the wooden stairs beside Muddy Creek Falls.

Stained by the tannin of decaying material in Cranesville Swamp–the source of the creek, about 3 miles to the west–Muddy Creek tumbles down a 51-foot (some sources claim it's more than 60 feet; see the waterfall discussion in Hike 16) ledge into the canyon below. At one time, a saw-mill made use of the power of the falls to work locally harvested timber. Descend the steps to the base of the falls, the best place to view it and appreciate the beauty of the scene as sunlight sparkles onto the white water of the cascade, framed by rock walls and the evergreen leaves of an abundant growth of rhododendron.

As you continue the hike downstream, the pathway becomes narrower, rougher, and rockier. This is all right, because it means that you are forced to slow your pace somewhat so that you can take in and enjoy the true glory of this place. The trunks of the hemlock trees you are walking next to rise more than 100 feet toward the sky. Although there is some question as to whether or not this is a virgin forest, many of these trees are known to be more than 300 years old.

Walking below the steep cliffs of the gorge, you'll come to the confluence of two streams, where the waters of Muddy Creek mix with those of the Youghiogheny River. Keep a sharp eye out, and you'll discover that some of the boulders beside the trail bear fossil imprints.

Pass by the Lower Falls of the Youghiogheny, continue upstream by ascending steps, and keep left when a pathway comes in from the right. Keep left at the next intersection and arrive at Swallow Falls. You are now about halfway through the hike, so this is the logical point to take a break. Flat rocks above and below the 25-foot falls are great places to warm up and sunbathe. Although you may witness a number of people swimming, park personnel discourage this due to

Resting along the Youghiogheny River

swift currents, underwater hydraulics, submerged hazards, and varying water levels. Some foolhardy people have even been observed taking running jumps into the water from surrounding rock ledges.

Local lore says that the area was named in the early pioneer days for the large flocks of cliff swallows that nested in the nooks of the gorge walls. As has been known to happen in other areas, the swallows probably abandoned the cliffs and instead built their nests under the protective eaves of cabins and barns as more settlers moved into western Maryland. Famed pioneer hunter Meshach Browning roamed throughout western Maryland in the mid- to late 1700s and vividly described these early days of Garrett County in his book, *Forty-Four Years in the Life of a Hunter.*

When ready to resume the hike, continue upstream through hemlocks and copious amounts of rhododendron, whose white blossoms would make this a beautiful walk in June.

You may be tempted to take a dip when you swing to the right at 0.75 mile and come to an inviting sandy beach below the tumbling waters of Toliver Falls. You could ascend a pathway from the falls and intercept this hike at the 1 mile point; however, this description retraces the route back to Swallow Falls and takes the pathway ascending left via stairs.

The deep shade of the hemlocks makes for cool walking, even on warm summer days. However, every once in a while—where an older tree has fallen, thereby opening a break in the canopy—sunlight reaches the ground and you find the shamrock-shaped leaves and the pretty pink and white blossoms of the wood sorrel. This plant's genus name of *Oxalis* is from the Greek language, and roughly translates to mean "sharply acid." The stalks and leaves of the plant do have an acidic, lemonlike taste and can be a refreshing treat when chewed or added to a fresh salad. Native Americans made a drink from the leaves that was said to taste a bit like lemonade. Although they did not know that the plant contains a high concentration of vitamin C, they also ate large amounts of it raw because they had learned that it helped to prevent "winter sickness" (known to us today as scurvy). Please remember not to pick any plants in the park.

Keep to the right when the old trail from Toliver Falls comes in from the left at 1 mile; be wary of the stinging nettle lining the pathway. Noises coming from the crowds at the parking lot become audible where you keep left at the intersection at 1.1 miles. The next left returns you to your automobile and concludes the hike at 1.3 miles.

3

Herrington Manor State Park

Total distance (circuit): 6.0 miles

Hiking time: 3 hours

Vertical rise: 540 feet

Maps: USGS 7½' Oakland (MD/WV)

Near the turn of the 20th century, America's forests were so vast that most people felt they could be extensively timbered and still provide an inexhaustible supply of lumber. Born in Connecticut and trained at L'Ecole Nationale Forestière in France, Gifford Pinchot disagreed with this common attitude. Unless something changed, he foresaw a day when the United States would experience a timber crisis such as the one that occurred in Europe in the late 1800s.

Under his direction as the first forester of the United States–appointed by President Theodore Roosevelt in 1898–more than 200 million acres of national forest lands came under scientific management, or in Pinchot's own words, "the greatest good of the greatest number in the long run." This philosophy of obtaining the greatest total crop eventually evolved into the multiple-use policy that governs the management of all national forests and most state forest lands.

Maryland's development of scientific forestry began in 1906, when John and Robert Garrett, two brothers from Baltimore, donated close to 2,000 acres to the state. The land was given with the understanding that a state forestry division would be established to help protect woodlands and further the science of silviculture.

In the same year, the Maryland General Assembly complied with the brothers' wishes by creating a board of forestry to manage the donated timberlands. Going through several bureaucratic changes, the board eventually evolved into today's Park

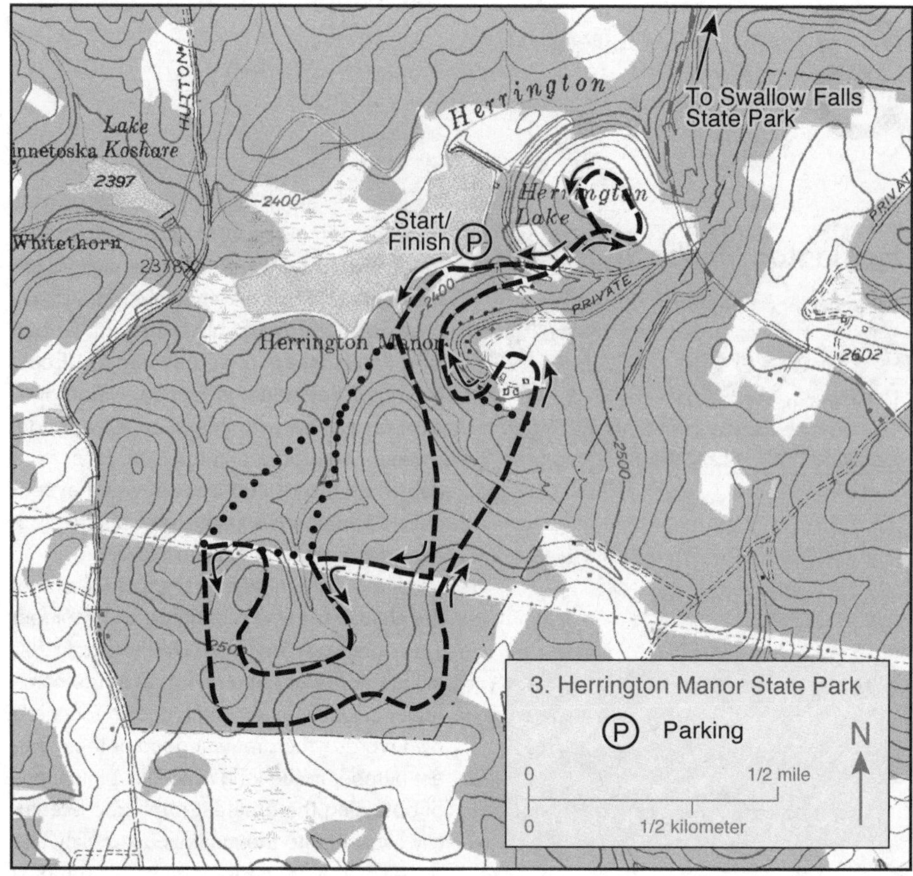

Service, Forest Service, and Wildlife and Heritage Service.

In 1917, the state purchased a 600-acre tract containing Herrington Manor. (The foundation of the large frame manor house, built in the mid-1800s, can be found behind the park office.) This 600 acres and the original 2,000 donated acres were combined with several other tracts in 1930 to form Garrett State Forest. It was during this decade of the Great Depression (and into the first years of World War II) that members of the Civilian Conservation Corps (CCC) worked on developing the park by fabricating cabins and bathhouses, building roads, and creating a 53-acre lake by damming Herrington Creek. Herrington Manor was designated a state park in 1964.

Today, the state park's blend of recreational opportunities makes use of many of the still-standing CCC constructions, such as cabins 1 through 10. The park offers interpretive programs during the usual heavy-use months, rental cabins, a concession stand, swimming, boat rentals, picnic tables and shelters, and a volleyball and tennis area. Herrington Lake is stocked with trout and other game and panfish. Be aware that anglers must comply with Maryland's fishing laws and regulations. Pets must be leashed.

Pets may be off-leash and under voice control while swimming; see park signs for additional information.

A system of trails, some of them wide, nearly level old roads from former logging days, winds through the park's 365 acres. Because of their relatively easy ups and downs, and due to the fact that park personnel sometimes groom the snow in winter, the trails are popular with cross-country skiers.

The park is reached by taking I-68 exit 14A at Keysers Ridge and following US 219 South for 19.5 miles. Turn right onto Mayhew Inn Road, continue another 4.5 miles, and turn left onto Oakland Sang Road. Driving an additional 0.3 mile brings you to a right turn onto Herrington Manor/Swallow Falls Road; follow this road approximately 4 miles to turn right into Herrington Manor State Park. Follow the signs to the boat launching ramp.

Begin the hike to the left of the boat ramp by following the hiking and skiing trail lined with small yellow flowers in late summer and fall. Avoid the unmarked trail to the left at 0.2 mile, keep right, and make a slight descent on a blue-blazed pathway. A few hundred yards later, cross a stream lined with false hellebore, ascend to make a left, and continue to follow the blue blazes to enter the Potomac-Garrett State Forest Hunting Area.

Level out and avoid the unmarked trail to the left. Stay right as you walk under towering maple trees.

Bear right onto an unmarked trail at the four-way intersection 0.7 mile into the hike. Begin a gradual descent to where the unmarked trail comes to an end at a T intersection 500 feet later. Turn left onto a red-blazed pathway (a right leads back to the lake), cross another stream lined with false hellebore at 1 mile, and ascend for a short distance.

Primarily found in damp environments—such as wet meadows, the edges of swamps and bogs, along streambanks, or on moist wooded slopes—false hellebore is best observed from a distance. Coming into contact with the plant can cause a severe skin irritation, and its foliage and rootstock have proved to be fatal to grazing livestock. One of its other common names, Indian poke, may refer to the story that some chiefs of Native American tribes were permitted to ascend to the position only after they had survived eating the plant.

Some people feel that false hellebore is at its most charming a short time before the flowers actually develop. It is at this time that the large leaves begin to uncurl from around the stem and their undefiled yellowish green adds a welcome bit of color to the early-spring forest. After the flowers have bloomed, the leaves begin to deteriorate, turning brown and ragged looking.

Continuing along the red-blazed route, pass under utility lines at 1.4 miles. Avoid the trail to the right at 1.6 miles, and keep to left on the red-blazed trail (blazes may be faint) to cross a stream. Be alert at 1.8 miles, as you need to turn left onto a blue-blazed route, which has occasional jack-in-the-pulpits next to it. (The red- and blue-blazed trail to the right returns to the boat ramp.)

You are walking next to the state park boundary line, and private homes are visible through the vegetation to the right as you descend at 2.4 miles. Avoid unmarked trails to the right and keep left, continuing to follow the blue blazes. There are scattered mayapples along the trail, while ferns are abundant at 2.9 miles, where open meadows and farmhouses add a bucolic air to the hike.

Mayapples make their appearance in March, at about the same time bloodroot is blooming. Wrapped tightly around the stem when the plant is pushing its way out of the ground, the umbrellalike leaves soon open up to form huge carpets that spread out across the forest floor.

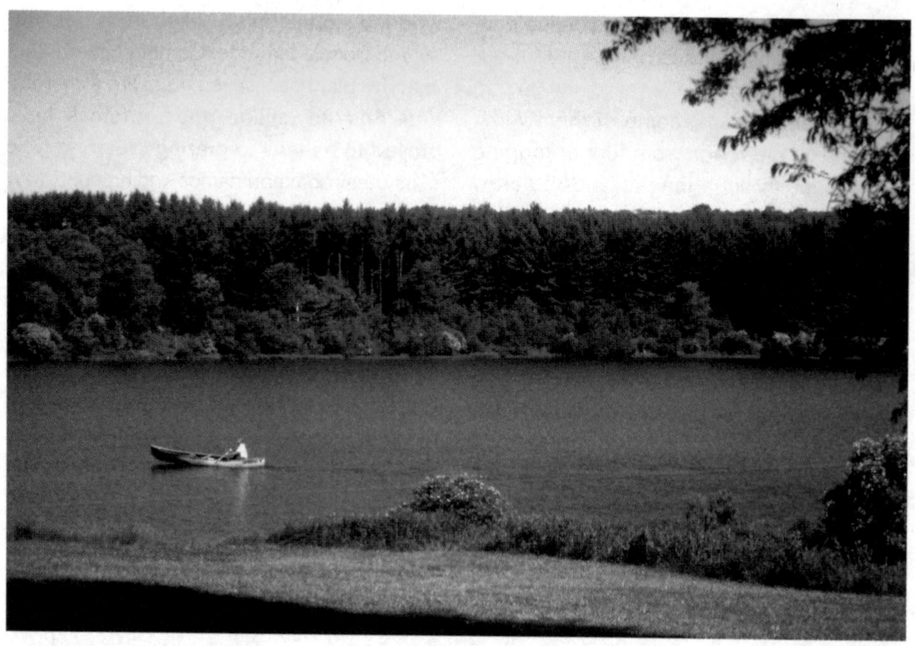

Herrington Lake

The plant was used in the past as a treatment for warts, but even today two of the drugs that are found in mayapple are used for medicinal purposes–podophyllin is used as a purgative and, along with peltatine, has been used for the treatment of cancer and venereal disorders. Researchers have found that the latter substance affects DNA and RNA synthesis and discourages the growth of cells.

Walk under utility lines at 3.4 miles, soon returning to the four-way intersection you passed 0.7 mile into the hike. Take the unmarked route that heads off to the right. Leave the hunting area at 3.6 miles and keep right so as to avoid the trail to the left. If you have not seen any white-tailed deer so far in this hike, you have a good chance of spotting one or more in the small clearing here, especially in the early morning or early evening.

Stay to the right again when you come to the next intersection at 3.8 miles, and look for more jack-in-the-pulpits when you cross a small swale in a few hundred more feet. If you have ever wondered what kind of trees you are walking by, small signs placed by park personnel will help you to identify white oak, red maple, hawthorn, and others.

Come to the edge of an open field at 4.3 miles. There are no markings or blazes to indicate which way to go, but you want to turn to the right along the edge of the field. In a few hundred more feet, make a left along the park road, walking by tennis courts and a water fountain. Continue to bear left until you come to the sign for Herrington Manor Shop Road, where you need to cross the pavement and reenter the woods on a pathway. Pay attention, for you need to turn right almost immediately onto a yellow-blazed route lined with crow's foot.

Do not take the unmarked trail to the left at 4.7 miles; keep right on the yellow-blazed route, soon passing by an old homesite. Cross a paved road at 5 miles, soon keeping to the right when you come to a loop trail intersection where the trail encircles a white pine plantation.

Stands of trees such as this are typical of Pinchot's scientific management of forests. After the original timber is cut, foresters will usually replant a species of pine, as the evergreens are some of the fastest-growing trees. Many environmentalists are against this practice, saying it robs the forest of its diversity, displaces animals dependent on a variety of trees, and makes the forests more susceptible to damage from diseases and insects.

Be alert at 5.3 miles, as the trail makes an abrupt left turn. However, before you leave the area, take a few minutes to explore the old cemetery to the right. I found a number of gravestones dating from the early 1800s.

Follow the pathway as it swings left several times to return to the loop trail intersection, where you descend to the right. Upon reaching the paved road, head toward the boat ramp, ending the hike at your automobile at 6 miles.

If you are looking for an additional hiking opportunity while in the area, there is a 5-mile (one-way) trail that connects Herring-ton Manor State Park with Swallow Falls State Park (see Hike 2). The well-marked route is fairly level and easy to follow, makes use of an old roadbed much of the way, parallels Herrington Run for a distance, and weaves in and out of lush growths of rhododendron. The trail begins near the lake in Herrington Manor and emerges from the woods at the entrance to the campground in Swallow Falls.

4

New Germany State Park

Total distance (circuit): 6.1 miles

Hiking time: 3 hours, 15 minutes

Vertical rise: 840 feet

Maps: USGS 7½' Barton; USGS 7½' Bittinger; USGS 7½' Grantsville (MD/PA); USGS 7½' Avilton (MD/PA)

Whereas Deep Creek Lake State Park (see Hike 1) is situated at the southern extremity of Meadow Mountain, New Germany State Park occupies lands along the slopes of the mountain's northern regions. In contrast to 3,900-acre Deep Creek Lake, New Germany's lake is all of 13 acres. The lake was formed in the early 1800s when John Swauger dammed Poplar Lick Run to obtain waterpower for a sawmill and gristmill.

A hike in the park will not deliver you to any spectacular waterfalls or open up any grand vistas of the surrounding countryside, but it does provide you with the opportunity to meander through a quiet woodland, surveying the different small parts of the forest that come together to make up the whole.

The park's trail system was designed with cross-country skiers in mind (who come to the park in large numbers when snow is on the ground; ski and snowshoe rentals available), so the routes are generally wide and for the most part rise and fall at a moderate grade. Other attractions here include rental cabins (open year-round) with modern amenities, a campground with hot showers, a snack bar, a picnic area, a sandy beach swimming area, fishing in the trout-stocked lake, geocaching, a nature center, and rowboat and kayak rentals during the summer season. Pets must be leashed. Pets may be off-leash and under voice control while swimming; see park signs for additional information.

You can reach New Germany State Park by driving westward from Cumberland on I-68. Take exit 22 (about 20 miles from Cumberland), head southward on Chestnut Ridge Road for

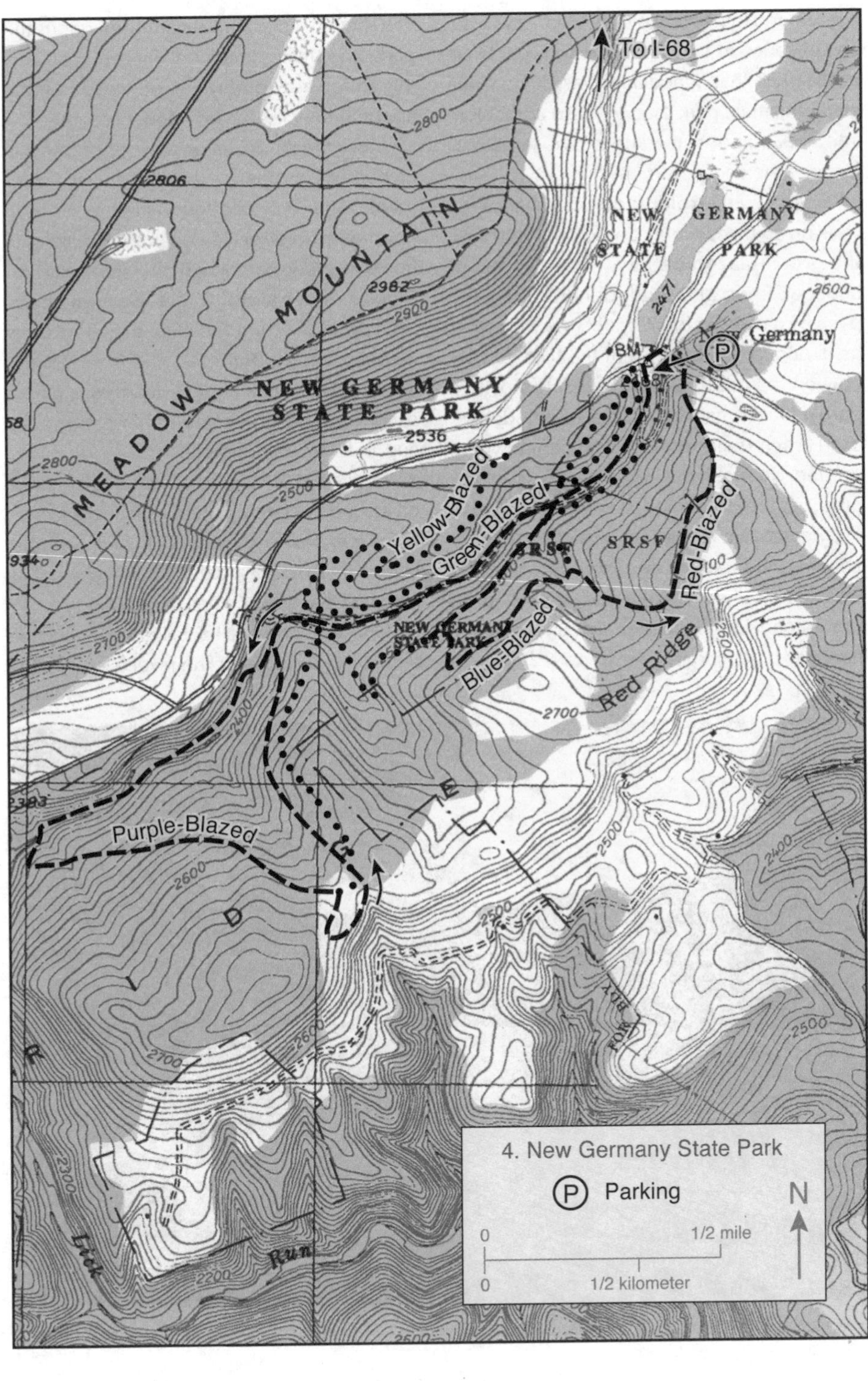

To I-68
MEADOW MOUNTAIN
NEW GERMANY STATE PARK
New Germany
Yellow-Blazed
Green-Blazed
Blue-Blazed
Red-Blazed
Red Ridge
Purple-Blazed
4. New Germany State Park
Parking
N
0
1/2 mile
0
1/2 kilometer

2 miles, and turn left onto New Germany Road. The entrance to the park will be on your left in a little more than 2 additional miles. Continue along the main park road to make a right turn into Parking Lot 5, marked by two large millstones at its entrance.

Begin your exploration of the park by walking to the bulletin board and following the green-blazed pathway into a forest of hemlock trees and rhododendron. You will pass by a number of intersections with other trails during the first mile of the hike; always stay on the green-blazed route. The pink to purple blossoms of the Catawba rhododendron reach their northern limits somewhere around Shenandoah National Park in Virginia, yet the great rhododendron you find in Maryland has a range that stretches from Alabama and Georgia into New England. Its clusters of white flowers appear in time to grow alongside those of the mountain laurel, normally blooming in June or early July.

Chipmunks are abundant throughout the park, and their cheeping calls and scampering antics may entertain you as you amble about in the mixed hardwood forest here.

More than a dozen species of chipmunks inhabit North America, but the eastern chipmunk is the only one found in Maryland. An aggressive digger, the chipmunk makes its home in a long, winding tunnel that could extend for more than 30 feet. Several chambers open out from the main tunnel to serve as bedrooms, bathrooms, and food storage areas. Inside the sleeping quarters is a nest of leaves and grasses with an emergency supply of food underneath.

Be alert at 1.1 miles so as not to continue on the green-blazed route, which now ascends to the left. You need to stay right on the purple-blazed trail, bypassing the other section of its loop trail that soon comes in from the left.

Cross a bridge at 1.2 miles and swing left onto an old roadbed. The level terrain of the

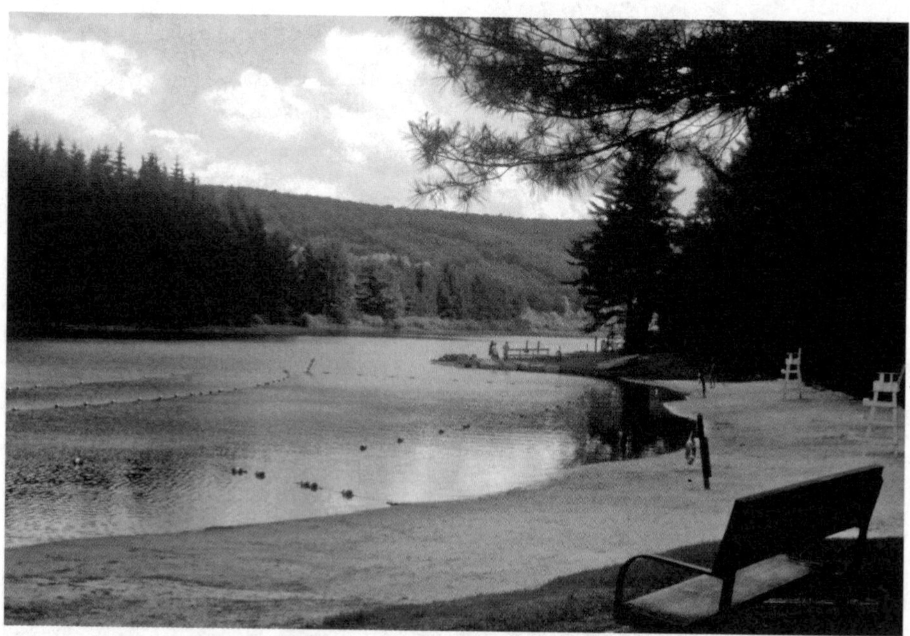

The beach and lake may be hard to resist after the hike

abandoned narrow-gauge railroad, the deep shade of hemlock trees, and the soft gurgle of small cascades and ripples make for easy and pleasurable walking for the next 0.5 mile. Cross another bridge at 1.6 miles, and one more at 1.7 miles.

The effortless walking comes to an end when you come to a road gate to the right at 1.9 miles. Swing left, crossing another bridge, and begin a steady ascent. As you rise from the moist bottomland, the hemlock trees give way to a mixed hardwood forest, and mountain laurel makes an appearance. Mountain laurel can be an important link in returning a forest to health after a fire. Even if the plant is burned all the way to the ground, its roots will survive to quickly grow new stems. Living longer than much of the vegetation growing in a forest's understory, some mountain laurel bushes have been found to be more than a century old.

Soon after the trail levels out at 2.7 miles, make sure you stay on the purple-blazed trail. Be alert here, as the blazes may be difficult to distinguish. Club moss, looking like a miniature version of the evergreens that tower above it, lines both sides of the trail as you swing around a damper part of the forest.

There may be some confusing intersections, but always stay on the purple-blazed route. Eventually, where you begin to descend–steeply in spots–hemlock trees begin to reappear, and clusters of star moss and club moss grow in the moist soil beside the trail. Mosses do not flower but reproduce by spores borne in capsules–known as sporangia–which rise above the rest of the plant on long stalks. Late in the summer the capsule breaks open, and the slightest bit of a breeze picks up the spores and scatters them about.

Return to the loop trail intersection, turn right, and in a short distance continue by retracing your steps following the green blazes along Poplar Lick Run, soon bypassing the yellow-blazed trail coming in from the left.

You have an option when you come to the intersection at 4.2 miles. If you are tired or running out of time, the parking lot and your car are less than 0.5 mile straight ahead. However, if you wish to extend your time in the woods as much as possible, make a hard right and ascend the blue-blazed pathway. Less than 200 feet later, stay right on the blue-blazed trail, and rise at an almost imperceptible rate. The deep shade provided by the abundant leaves of the deciduous trees helps to keep the temperature a few degrees cooler than that found at the park's lake in the summer.

An orange-blazed route is encountered at 4.6 miles; stay left on the blue-blazed trail, walking along a route lined by striped maple. This tree can grow up to 30 feet tall but is most often seen as part of the forest understory. Its green-and-white-striped bark–a favorite food of deer, rabbits, and other woodland creatures–makes it easy to identify.

Arriving at a T intersection at 5.1 miles, turn right and ascend a red-blazed trail. (Do not worry about going against the flow of the one-way sign; it applies to cross-country skiers when snow is on the ground.)

Steer clear of the small trail to the right at 5.3 miles. Keep left, soon reaching the top of the knob and beginning the final descent. Avoid another faint trail at 5.6 miles.

Pass by block outbuildings at 5.7 miles and turn right onto a paved road. Within a few feet, turn left downhill along the main park road, soon making a left into the parking lot across from the lake and returning to your car at 6.1 miles.

5

Garrett State Forest

Total distance (circuit): 7.0 miles

Hiking time: 4 hours

Vertical rise: 740 feet

Maps: USGS 7½' Oakland (MD/WV)

Within the borders of 7,400-acre Garrett State Forest is a network of old logging roads, pathways, and dirt and gravel roads open to hikers, mountain bikers, cross-country skiers, and snowmobilers. The hike described here winds through hardwood forests of varying ages, into hemlock groves, and beside ridgetop wetlands. The route also makes use of a portion of the Swallow Falls–Herrington Manor Trail (see the last paragraph of Hike 3), which runs for more than 5 miles to connect the two state parks.

An additional attraction of Garrett State Forest is the opportunity to do some overnight camping. Although there are designated sites and a trail shelter along one of the dirt roads, you could also pitch your tent at a backcountry site anywhere along the route. A permit and payment of a fee are required for any overnight camping; you can make arrangements at the Potomac-Garrett State Forest office, or by self-registration at all designated sites.

The park is reached by taking I-68 exit 4 (about 40 miles west of Cumberland) and driving south on MD 42. Nearly 8 miles later, keep to the right and follow US 219 for 7.4 miles through the commercial area of Deep Creek Lake. Be watching, as the right turn you need to make onto Mayhew Inn Road may be a bit obscure. Bear left onto Oakland–Sang Run Road in another 4.3 miles. An additional 0.3 mile brings you to a right turn onto Herrington Manor/Swallow Falls Road; follow this road until you come to a Y intersection in 1.4 miles and make a hard right onto Cranesville Road. Continue on this road for just about a mile to make a left turn onto the gravel and dirt Snaggy Mountain Road. An additional 0.5 mile of driving brings you to the small parking lot on the left. There may be several small parking areas along the road, so be sure that you are leaving your automobile in the one that has an obvious green-blazed trail connecting with it.

Begin the journey by walking out of the parking lot, turning left along Snaggy Mountain Road, and descending slightly to pass by a high-altitude wetland area. Just beyond, goldenrod and Queen Anne's lace line the roadway.

Most botanists believe that Queen Anne's lace is named for England's ruler from 1702 to 1714. The story goes that she was fond of fancy lace on her dresses and used the plant as a model. One day while sewing some lace she pricked her finger, and the one dark

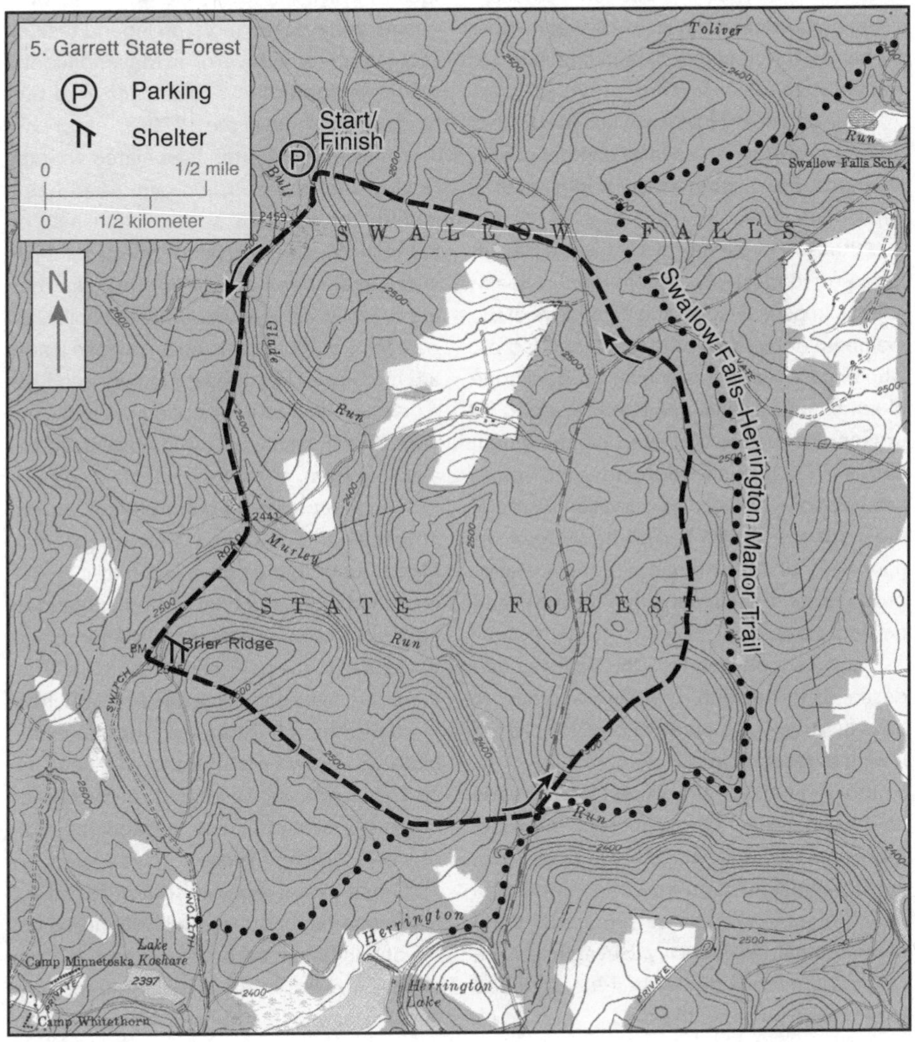

red floret in the middle of the flower's umbel is where the drop of blood landed. Other reference books emphatically deny this origin of the name, stating instead that the plant honors the wife of James I, Anne of Denmark, also an admirer of fine lace.

Avoid the road coming in from the right at 0.1 mile. At 0.3 mile you will begin to pass by the state forest's designated campsites, each with a picnic table and fire grate. Stay on the main route when another road comes in from the right, walking through a pleasant forest of mixed hardwood trees that hosts a profusion of tent caterpillars in late summer and early fall.

After ascending to a small rise at 0.8 mile, descend gradually to pass by another scenic wetlands area, where you might spot a beaver or a muskrat.

At the top of the rise at 1.7 miles, bear left to the Adirondack-style shelter in the designated campsite. Inspect the handiwork of the members of the Youth Conservation Corps, who originally built this shelter on Backbone Mountain and which was later moved to its present site by the Maryland Conservation Corps. Both groups were patterned somewhat after the Civilian Conservation Corps of the 1930s and 1940s and have been responsible for improvements to trails, campgrounds, and other facilities in state and national parks.

Facing the shelter, take the pathway that descends to the right. (There are a number of trails here, so make sure the one you are following is green-blazed.)

It is pleasing to be walking close to trees after having walked for so long on the wide, gravel roadbed. The songs of the birds seem more immediate, and you might hear the snorts of a deer or two as you startle them along the narrow pathway. Several species of ferns grow beside the trail—as opposed to the one type along the road.

Swing around a low ridge at 2.6 miles and make a quick descent to where a trail comes in from the right; keep left and continue to descend. Cross Herrington Creek at 3 miles where joe-pye weed towers above the undergrowth. The plant is named for a Native American herbalist who supposedly roamed the New England countryside at about the time of the American Revolution. Using parts of the plant (mixed with liquor), he treated the locals for a variety of ailments, including typhus fever. Although the story seems to be based more on legend than on fact, there is a tavern in Massachusetts whose ledgers show that a Joe Pye purchased rum there in the 1770s.

A flower most often associated with the heat of late summer, joe-pye weed has a number of different species that may be found in Western Maryland. Spotted joe-pye weed has a deep purple or purple-spotted stem, while joe-pye weed has a similar appearance but is a smaller plant whose leaves are more rounded. Sweet joe-pye weed has a greenish stem with bits of purple and black near the leaf joints; hollow joe-pye weed has a hollow stem.

Within a couple of hundred feet you will intersect the Swallow Falls–Herrington Manor Trail. (To the right it is 0.5 mile to Herrington Manor.) You need to turn left and diagonally cross Herrington Manor Road. Once across the pavement, it is time to leave the green-blazed snowmobile trail, which ascends to the left. Keep right on the white-blazed Swallow Falls–Herrington Manor Trail as it initially passes through a couple of evergreen groves and begins to follow the route of an old logging railroad.

Cross over a wooden footbridge at 3.3 miles. Another bridge just a few hundred feet beyond is bordered by jewelweed and bee balm. Growing in moist woods and along small streams, bee balm colonies are conspicuous in the forest; their 3- to 4-foot-tall stems, which rise above most other undergrowth, are topped by tubular flowers of the deepest, richest scarlet to be found on any wildflower. Although bees are attracted to the flower, the long floral tubes—which make it hard for insects to reach the nectar—are more suited to the bills of hummingbirds, which are attracted by the blossoms' brilliant red color.

As part of a group negotiating a treaty in 1743 with the Oswego Indians of New York, naturalist John Bartram learned that the Native Americans made a tea from bee balm that helped alleviate the discomforts of fevers or chills. The drink soon became popular with colonists, who used it as a substitute for imported tea and earned the plant one of its other common names, Oswego tea.

Having dipped down to cross a third wooden bridge at 3.6 miles, begin to rise on a route that is rockier and looks more like the old railroad bed that it is. Cross the snowmobile trail at 3.9 miles.

After a short, quick descent, cross a fourth wooden bridge at 4.9 miles, where crow's foot and running cedar keep the banks above the trail green throughout most of the year. A fifth wooden bridge is crossed just before walking under utility lines at 5.1 miles. You need to be alert here. The Swallow Falls–Herrington Manor Trail continues straight, but you want to make an abrupt (and not all that obvious) left turn uphill to follow the green-blazed snowmobile trail.

Cross paved Swallow Falls Road at 5.4 miles. Ascend into a younger forest than you have been walking through on most of this hike before dropping down to cross the

A high-altitude wetlands area

paved Cranesville Road at 5.7 miles. Continue with minor ups and downs through a forest of red maples, passing by a few hemlock trees. Until now, hemlocks were rare on this hike, but they soon become abundant as you walk into a thick grove of them at 6.2 miles. After making a short, easy rise into a younger forest, descend, and come to your car to end the hike at 7 miles.

For an additional outdoor diversion before heading home after the hike, take the short drive over to The Nature Conservancy's Cranesville Swamp. Actually located more in West Virginia than in Maryland, it is a relic of the Ice Age, having changed little since the glaciers receded. Situated within a depression, the swamp is a "frost pocket," a place in which cold air is trapped by the surrounding mountains. When the rest of Western Maryland is experiencing a relatively mild spring or fall day, there may be a heavy frost in the swamp.

Because of its microclimate, the plants that inhabit Cranesville Swamp are more typical of those found far to the north in boreal Canada. Spiny woodfern, rose pogonia, hoary alder, creeping snowberry, yellow-fringed orchids, and the carnivorous round-leaf sundew all make their homes here. In addition, the swamp is where the tamarack tree (also commonly called the American larch) reaches its southernmost point.

A 1-mile trail, part of which is a boardwalk across wet areas, permits you to explore the area by foot. Cranesville Swamp can be reached by turning right out of the parking area in which you ended the Garrett State Forest hike. Drive Snaggy Mountain Road back to Cranesville Swamp Road, turn left, and continue for approximately 3 miles to make a left onto Lake Ford Road, which soon becomes dirt. In an additional 0.3 mile, bear right at an intersection. A few hundred feet later, make another right and come to the trailhead parking lot.

6

Big Savage Mountain

Total distance (one-way): 17.2 miles

Hiking time: 9 hours or overnight hike

Vertical rise: 1,300 feet

Maps: USGS 7½' Frostburg (MD/PA); USGS 7½' Avilton (MD/PA); USGS 7½' Barton; USGS 7½' Bittinger; Savage River State Forest map

The Big Savage Hiking Trail must be one of the best-kept outdoor secrets in Maryland. With a fine sense of isolation, relatively minor changes in elevation, several viewpoints, and an abundance of deer and other wildlife, the route traverses the crest of Big Savage Mountain for 17 miles. In addition, visitors may set up a backcountry camp wherever they wish—yet the trail shows very few signs of use.

There are no worn-out areas from too many people camping in the same spot, fire rings are almost nonexistent, and the trail's treadway is narrow and shallow.

The hike could be accomplished as a long day trip, but to best appreciate it, you should make it an overnighter. In the spirit of keeping the area looking as pristine as possible—and of letting you meet this challenge on your own—I am not going to recommend any particular camping spot. I will suggest that the amazing amounts of rocks on the ground make it hard to find a suitable site for the first half of the hike. Many of the water sources may be dry in summer and fall. Also, I ask that you carry a stove so you don't have to build any fires (which are prohibited, more or less, on at least half of the hike). In addition, there is a resident bear population, so take proper precautions.

The required backcountry camping permit (and payment of a fee) may be obtained at the office of Savage River State Forest, 127 Headquarters Lane, Grantsville, MD 21536, accessible from I-68 exit 22 (about 12 miles west of Frostburg).

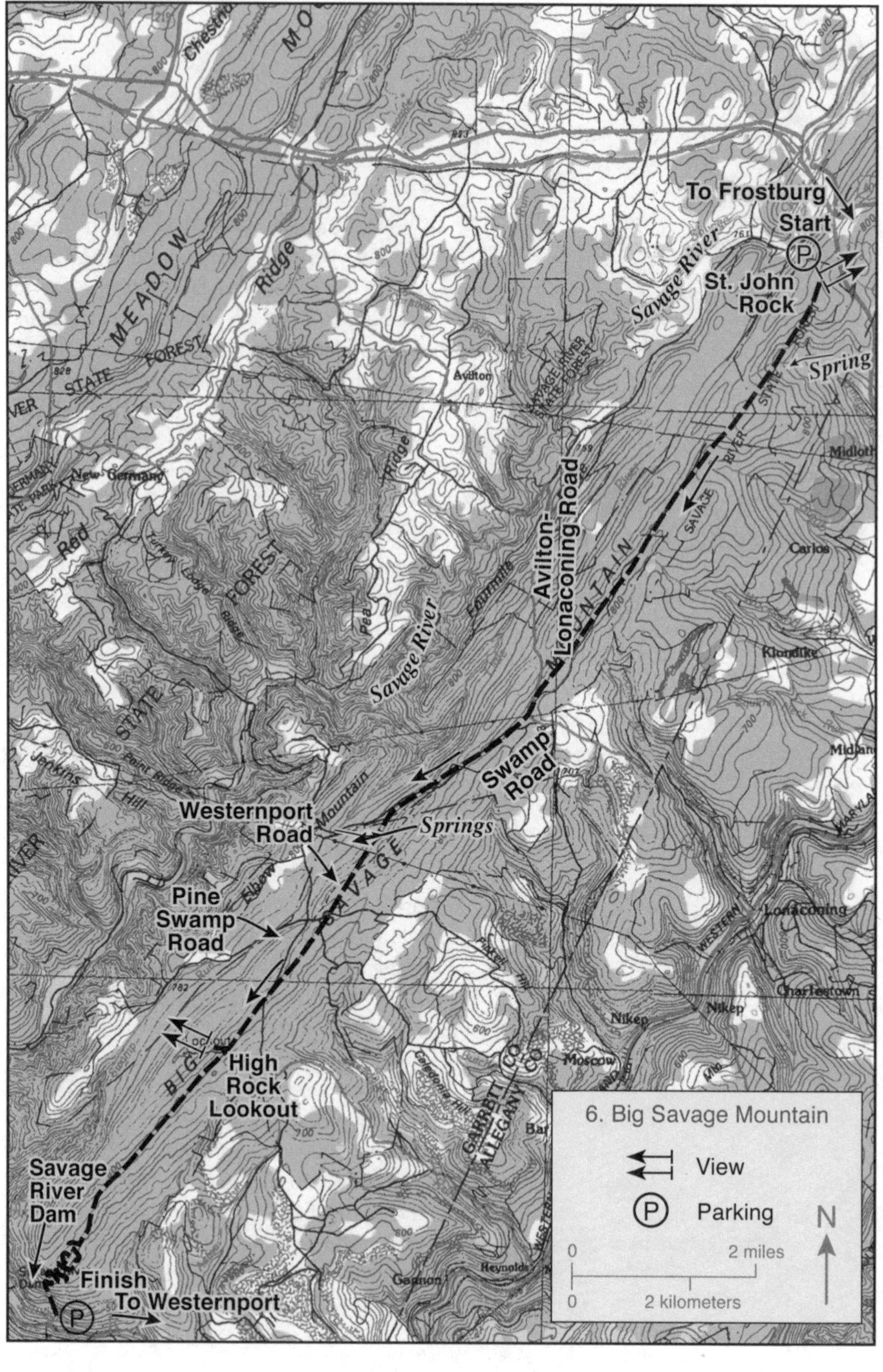

To Frostburg
Start
St. John Rock
Savage River
Spring
Avilton-Lonaconing Road
Swamp Road
Westernport Road
Springs
Pine Swamp Road
High Rock Lookout
Savage River Dam
Finish
To Westernport
MEADOW
STATE FOREST
Ridge
Savage River
BIG SAVAGE MOUNTAIN
6. Big Savage Mountain
View
Parking
N
0
2 miles
0
2 kilometers

Since this is a one-way hike, a car shuttle will be necessary. The shuttle involves many miles of driving, so allow ample time. At the eastern edge of Frostburg, take I-68 exit 34 and drive southward on MD 36. Arrive in Westernport about 14 miles later and turn right onto MD 135. Just after passing through the small town of Luke, turn uphill onto Savage River Road. Close to 4 miles later, turn right into the parking area and leave your car.

Re-drive the route back to Frostburg in the second car and proceed westward on I-68. Approximately 7 miles later, take exit 29 and drive southward on Beall School Road for 1.2 miles to make a left onto Old Beall School Road. After several hundred yards, turn right onto a fairly new road–which may or may not be signed–heading uphill. A few hundred yards later there will be a dirt road ascending left. Follow this to the crest of the mountain and the beginning of the Big Savage Hiking Trail.

Walk into the woods on a gently ascending pathway lined by wild oats. Following the Doctrine of Signatures, herbalists once used this plant for the treatment of throat ailments–as the drooping flowers reminded them of the uvula, the flap of tissue that hangs from the soft palate at the back of mouth. This also gave rise to the wild oats' genus name of *Uvularia*. Its species name, *sessilifolia,* arises from the fact that its leaves are sessile, or without stems.

Cross a rock field at 0.25 mile. You might as well get used to loose footing and twisted ankles, as rocks remain underfoot for a large portion of the hike. Studying the flat layers of the strata of the large rock facing at 0.9 mile can help you understand why–even though you are in the mountains–most of the terrain you will be traversing on this hike is relatively level. Unlike the Blue Ridge Mountain region to the east, which attained its appearance through pressure and heat, or the Ridge and Valley Province, shaped by being folded and angled, the entire Allegheny Plateau upon which you are walking was lifted up as one continuous mass. Continue along the crest of the ridgeline.

The scent from the wild azalea's pink blossoms in late May and early June can be so strong that you might feel as if you have been spritzed by an employee of the perfume section of a department store. In late spring you may notice a growth at the end of a twig of azalea that is about the size of a golf ball. This gall-like form is not produced by an insect, but rather a bacterium or fungus, and, surprisingly, is quite tasty–with a crisp texture and juicy flavor. In fact, this little sweet was so highly prized in earlier times that it was preserved and saved as a treat for later in the year.

Pass under utility lines at 2.8 miles and continue to follow the obvious route identified by white paint blazes. A faint woods road is crossed at 4.6 miles where crow's foot lines the trail; be alert at 6 miles, as you need to bear right onto a woods road and cross Avilton-Lonaconing Road.

Hemlock trees are most often found along the moist slopes of a mountainside or close to lower-elevation streams, but you pass a few of them on top of the ridge at 6.5 miles. The work that the utility company has done to keep vegetation from growing under its power lines at 7.1 miles furnishes a viewpoint. Closest to you is the gap that the Little Savage River has cut between Fourmile Ridge and Elbow Mountain. Forming the western horizon, Meadow Mountain (see Hikes 1 and 4) rises behind the narrow valleys created by Blue Lick Run, West Branch, and Blacklick Run.

Be alert at 7.6 miles. Do not keep to the left; the route you want to follow makes a

Fog rolls across the ridge of Big Savage Mountain.

right turn onto what may be a less obvious pathway and soon begins a steep descent.

(Although the track to the left is a former route of the Big Savage Hiking Trail that rises onto spine of the ridgeline, it is worthwhile to follow it for several hundred feet if you are here in April to June. Scores of columbines grow among the rocks at that time. Look closely at the spurs, and you may see tiny holes in the tips. Most bees and many other insects are too large to gain access to the nectar by crawling into the spurs; they simply nip the tip and steal the nectar without collecting any pollen. But the flowers' red color entices hummingbirds, whose needlelike bills and long tongues enable them to reach the nectar at the base of the spurs, making them the columbine's most efficient pollinators. In the past, the juice from a fresh plant was given to those suffering from jaundice to help reduce the size of a swollen liver. The leaves and flowers were also believed to be a cure for measles and smallpox. It may not have cured these ills, but since the plant does contain prussic acid, it may have had a narcotic and soothing effect that helped ease sufferers' pains.)

Along the proper route of the Big Savage Hiking Trail, pass two small springs at 8.1 miles as the steep descent comes to an end and you begin slabbing the hillside. Bear left onto a woods road at 8.6 miles, coming to the paved Swamp Road a few hundred feet later. Do not cross the road, but bear right, paralleling it as you descend into a grove of planted red pines. Passing through the site of an old homestead, there is a partially hidden boxed spring on the left side of the trail at 8.8 miles. (The water flow is a bit better below the trail.)

Rise gradually to cross paved Swamp Road, pass by a small water run, and begin following a woods road. There are several springs and small rills along this flat route, enticing some people to set up camp here. However, I have always found the ground to be too moist and the sites too close to the road to suit my tastes.

Pass under another set of utility lines at 9.3 miles, and cross Westernport Road at 10 miles. You are again at the boundary edge of the state forest when you begin walking beside a barbed-wire fence at 10.3 miles. Make a right onto Pine Swamp Road at 10.5 miles, but walk less than 200 feet before turning left into the woods and climbing steadily for 600 feet to the main crest of Big Savage Mountain. The small rocks and boulders underfoot are now much fewer in number than they have been on this broad ridgeline, so you should have little trouble finding a place to pitch your tent from this point to the end of the hike.

False hellebore grows around the edges of a small swampy area at 11.2 miles. Your heart may skip a beat or two soon after crossing a woods road at 11.8 miles if several grouse suddenly come flapping upward from the underbrush. It is likely they have been feasting on the wintergreen berries beside the trail.

Ruffed grouse are common throughout Western Maryland and are the source of the pulsation that sounds like a tractor is starting up in the distant woods. In order to attract a mate, the male grouse drums his wings against his body, and the resulting low, muffled sound often feels like it is resonating within your chest. During the spring, a female grouse may burst out of the brush and go running down the trail as if she has a broken wing. The act is designed to lead a potential predator away from a nest or nearby chicks. If the display fails, she turns around and, hissing loudly, charges the intruder.

For an excellent view of the surrounding mountains, turn right to ascend High Rock Fire Tower Road at 12.2 miles. At 12.5 miles reach the ridgeline and your reward for having walked up here–one of the best views in Garrett County. To the west, and forming a backdrop for the lower hills in front of it, is Meadow Mountain. The ridgeline visible farther west is that of Negro Mountain. To the southwest is Backbone Mountain, which contains the highest point in Maryland, 3,360 feet above sea level. Turn to the east, and you will see the western slopes of Dan's Mountain rising above George's Creek Valley.

Walk down High Rock Fire Tower Road to make a right turn back onto the Big Savage Hiking Trail, slabbing the eastern side of the mountain. The large rocks beside that trail at 12.6 miles are covered with lichens, those stalwart little plants that are able to grow and survive in some of the most unlikely and harshest of environments. They are actually two living entities that have combined into one plant to overcome adversity. Alga is the food producer for the fungus, which is unable make its own nourishment. The fungus, for its part, is able to absorb and hold water, at times even from moist air or fog, keeping the alga alive during hot, dry spells.

Cross over to the west side of the ridge at 14 miles. With ferns spreading throughout the forest floor, return to the east side at 14.5 miles, where the flat terrain yields a profusion of good tent sites.

The final downward trend of the journey begins at 15 miles, soon providing a view of the Savage River Reservoir and making use of long switchbacks to ease the rate of descent. Walk along a wire fence above the reservoir spillway at 16.5 miles. Bear left onto an access road at 17 miles, parallel the Savage River, and arrive next to your waiting automobile at 17.2 miles.

7

Lostland Run

Total distance: 4.5 miles one-way; 8.4 miles round-trip

Hiking time: 2 hours one-way; 4 hours, 25 minutes round-trip

Vertical rise: less than 100 feet one-way; 840 feet round-trip

Maps: USGS 7½' Deer Park; USGS 7½' Goorman (MD/WV); USGS 7½' Mount Storm (MD/WV); Potomac State Forest map

Without a doubt, Lostland Run Trail is the showpiece pathway of the Potomac State Forest. Volunteers, members of the Maryland Conservation Corps, and personnel of the forest service have lavished much attention onto the route, keeping it well maintained and building a number of bridges–both simple and complex–to enable you to hike with greater ease and enjoyment.

The attention is well deserved, as the Lostland Run area is one of the most attractive in Western Maryland. The hike begins in a hemlock grove, soon coming into contact with three lively and gurgling mountain streams as it drops to the calmer waters of the Potomac River. Along the way are an abundance of wildflowers, numerous cascades, ripples, and waterfalls, and the possibility of seeing bobcats, opossums, deer, groundhogs, weasels, minks, and black bears. An additional draw is the possibility of a night of backcountry camping in this beautiful setting. Because of the proximity of the forest service road, you also have the option of shuttling a car to make this a one-way hike. A short relocation may have been completed by time you hike here, but it will not make a major change in the route or its length.

Lostland Run Trail may be reached by driving eastward from Oakland on MD 135. Make a right turn onto MD 560 in 1.5 miles, following it for a little more than 2 miles to turn left onto Bethlehem Road. Continue for 3.5 miles (there are a couple of tricky intersections; be sure to stay on Bethlehem Road) to bear left onto Combination Road.

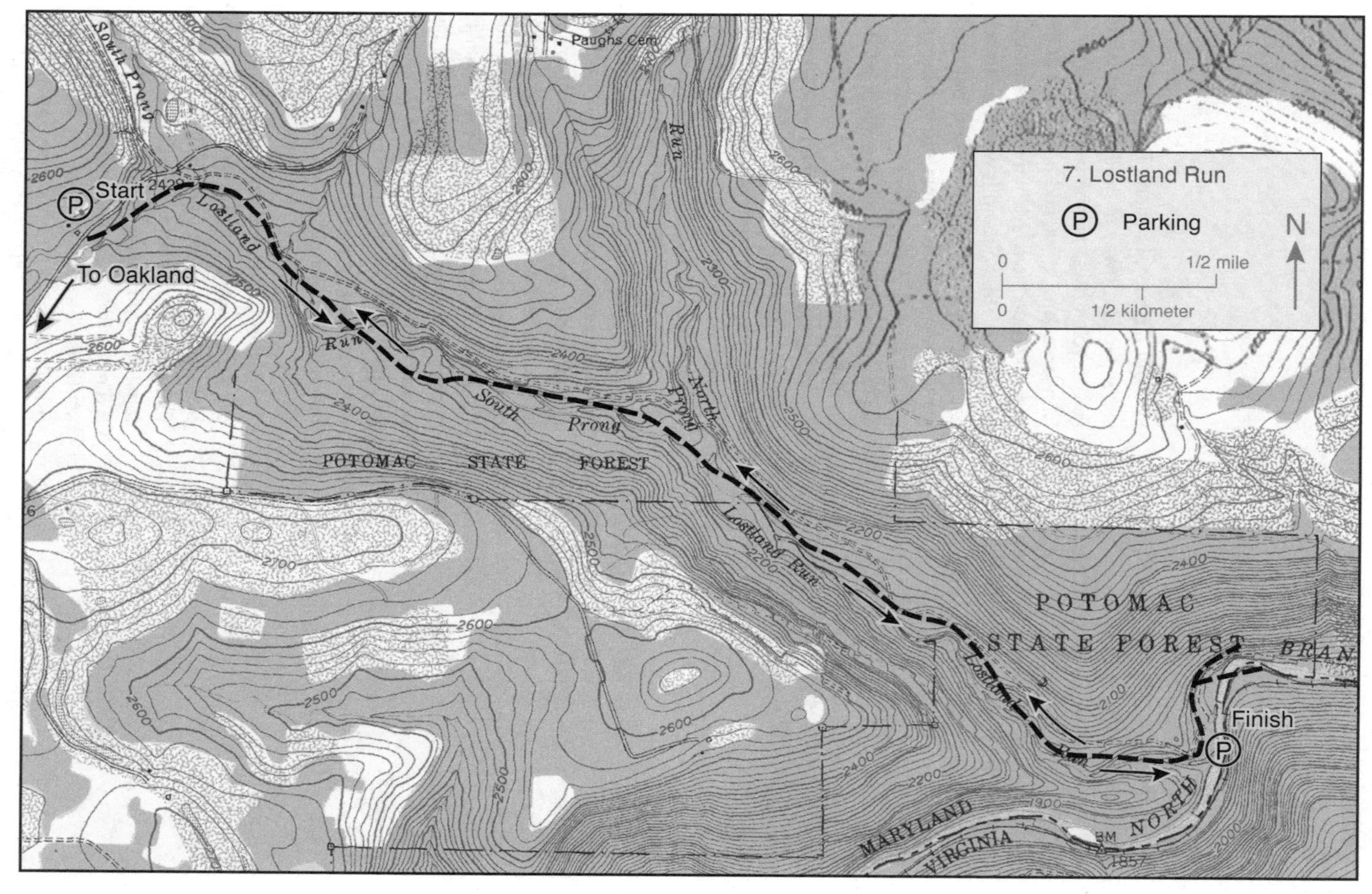
7. Lostland Run
P Parking
0
1/2 mile
0
1/2 kilometer
N
Start
To Oakland
Finish
Paughs Cem
South Prong
Lostland
Run
South
Prong
North
Prong
Run
Lostland Run
Lostland
POTOMAC STATE FOREST
POTOMAC
STATE FOREST
BRAN
NORTH
MARYLAND
VIRGINIA
BM
1857

An additional 0.5 mile brings you to a left onto Potomac Camp Road. The Potomac State Forest office and parking area are reached 0.7 mile later. If shuttling a car, continue past the office to make a right at the first intersection. Drop for several miles on Lostland Run Road to the Potomac River, where you will leave one car in the parking area before driving the other back to the forest service office.

Personnel in the office can supply you with a small map of the hike–and the required permit if you are camping overnight. There is also a self-registration booth at the beginning of the trail. Lostland Run Trail starts across Potomac Camp Road and enters a dark grove of hemlock trees. Swing right at 0.1 mile, and begin to descend and parallel a stream for a few feet as the hemlocks fade and the forest becomes dominated by red maple trees.

The trail makes an abrupt turn to the left at 0.4 mile. Areas such as this are what make walking in a deep woodland so much of a relaxing change from our everyday lives. The narrow needles of the hemlocks mix with the broad leaves of hardwood trees. Sunlight passing through this canopy of disparate shades of green dapples the understory, while luxuriant growths of moss soften the appearance of boulders scattered across the ground. The soft burble of the South Prong of Lostland Run and the chirrups of several different songbirds add to the atmosphere of serenity.

At 0.6 mile, rhododendron branches arch over the stream, whose small pools may prove to be too tempting to pass up on a hot summer day. The strange-looking contraption along the creek was placed there by the forest service to gradually release lime into the creek, thereby helping to reduce the effects of acid rain.

Use a footbridge to cross the South Prong for the first time at 0.8 mile. Mountain laurel is now part of the understory, while running cedar creeps along the forest floor. Jewelweed makes an appearance in the moist ground along a swampy area at 1 mile. Cross the South Prong twice again on bridges, but be alert for a trail relocation after the latter one. Do not continue straight and ford the stream; rather, bear left to ascend a bit, only to drop steeply on wooden steps to cross the South Prong on a log bridge.

Although you have only hiked 1.3 miles when you come to a small falls, it is time to take a break and maybe a swim in the pool at the base of the falls. If you don't feel like getting wet, just enjoy your surroundings. Shrubs of rhododendron make up the understory, while hemlock trees are overshadowed by taller maple trees. Water spiders drift over of the surface of the pool, and deer tracks and, possibly, bear paw prints are outlined in the soft mud.

Black bears abounded in Maryland when settlers from Europe began to arrive in the New World. The great forest of eastern North America, stretching from Canada to Florida and westward to the Great Plains, was the perfect habitat for the bears, providing an abundance of food and no major predators. Within a few years of their arrival, Maryland's early settlers hunted and killed so many bears that the mammal almost became extinct. The population was so decimated that as late as the mid–20th century it was estimated there were no more than 10 to 12 bears within the state's borders.

Alarmed, Maryland conservationists were able to have bear hunting banned in 1949 and had the animal declared endangered in the early 1970s. Once protected–and supplemented with bears imported from neighboring states–the population stabilized and

The Potomac in midsummer as seen from the Potomac Overlook

began to grow. In 1980, the bears were removed from the endangered list, and it is believed that close to 300 black bears currently reside within Western Maryland.

When you are ready to resume walking, do not ford the stream to follow the old route of the trail. Instead, make a sharp right away from the falls to a short, steep ascent. Soon, drop back to the South Prong and walk through a bottomland of stinging nettle, Solomon's seal, false Solomon's seal, twisted stalk, and partridgeberry.

A suspension bridge constructed by the Maryland Conservation Corps in 1994 enables you to cross the South Prong without getting wet. Because the trail may be faint in a rocky area, pay close attention to the blazes once you rise high above the stream at 1.7 miles. Dropping back down, avoid the trail that heads left to Lostland Run Road.

Be alert at 2.1 miles where the trail splits. You want to bear left to cross the North Prong of Lostland Run on a suspension bridge. After rising a short distance, be sure to take the switchbacked trail that descends and continues downstream. Avoid the old trail coming in from the left at 2.8 miles.

The wooden stairway at 2.9 miles takes you to an observation deck overlooking Cascade Falls. Ascend from the falls, continuing your downstream journey. At the top of the rise, keep right to avoid the blue-blazed trail that heads left to Lostland Run Road. Rhododendron forms a tunnel over the trail at 3.6 miles, where you will soon come to a bridge over Lostland Run. Do not make this right turn, as it leads to a short pathway that ends at a private-property boundary. Keep left, and come to the day-use parking area beside the Potomac River at 3.9 miles.

Even if you have shuttled a car here earlier, do not end the hike just yet. After grabbing the lunch or snacks stashed in the car (or your pack), continue by taking the pathway that leads from the far side of the parking area.

Less than 200 feet later, keep left on the route that rises gradually on a wide pathway, arriving at the Potomac Overlook at 4.1 miles. The Potomac River is certainly smaller and narrower here than it is in eastern Maryland, yet it is still powerful enough to have cut a deep gorge through the mountains of the Allegheny Plateau.

Retrace your steps back to the intersection and turn to the left, soon walking under the cliffs upon which you were standing a few moments ago. From this vantage point you can appreciate the erosive power of the river even more. The water has cut deeply into the face of the cliff, causing large chunks of rock to break off and fall to the riverbank.

From the river, return to the day-use parking area, 4.5 miles after beginning your journey. If you have not shuttled an automobile here, make your way back to your car at the forest service office by renegotiating Lostland Run Trail, completing the hike at 8.4 miles. Even though you will be covering the same ground, you may be surprised at how different it looks and feels ascending, instead of descending, the mountainside.

8

Evitt's Mountain and Rocky Gap Gorge

Total distance (circuit): 9.9 miles

Hiking time: 6 hours

Vertical rise: 1,440 feet

Maps: USGS 7½' Evitts Creek (PA/MD/WV); Rocky Gap State Park map

Like the more famous Cumberland Gap along the Virginia/Kentucky/Tennessee border, Rocky Gap has been used for centuries by humans as an access route through the mountains of eastern North America. Following the tracks made by game animals, Native Americans were the first to pass through. As settlers from the Old World began pushing into Western Maryland, the course was enlarged into the Old Hancock Road, a wagon route connecting Hancock in the east with Fort Cumberland to the west.

The powerful engines of today's automobiles make it easy to forget what a formidable obstacle the mountains once were. Yet, as you drive westward on I-68 to the hike in Rocky Gap State Park, there is a vividly powerful reminder that, even today, we must contend with the vagaries of the topography.

At the Washington County/Allegany County line, the four-lane highway makes a long climb over 1,600-foot Sideling Hill. In order to reduce the length and grade of the ascent, highway workers spent more than two years making a cut 360 feet deep into the mountain's ridgeline (the deepest road cut in Maryland).

The cut is also a great place to learn about the geology of the mountains, so you should take a few minutes' break from driving to stop at the Sideling Hill rest area, accessed directly from the interstate. Take the short trail that emanates from the restrooms and find that the road cut reveals fossilized plants and seashells from 350 million years ago, when the site was at the bottom of an ancient ocean. The cut also shows how the

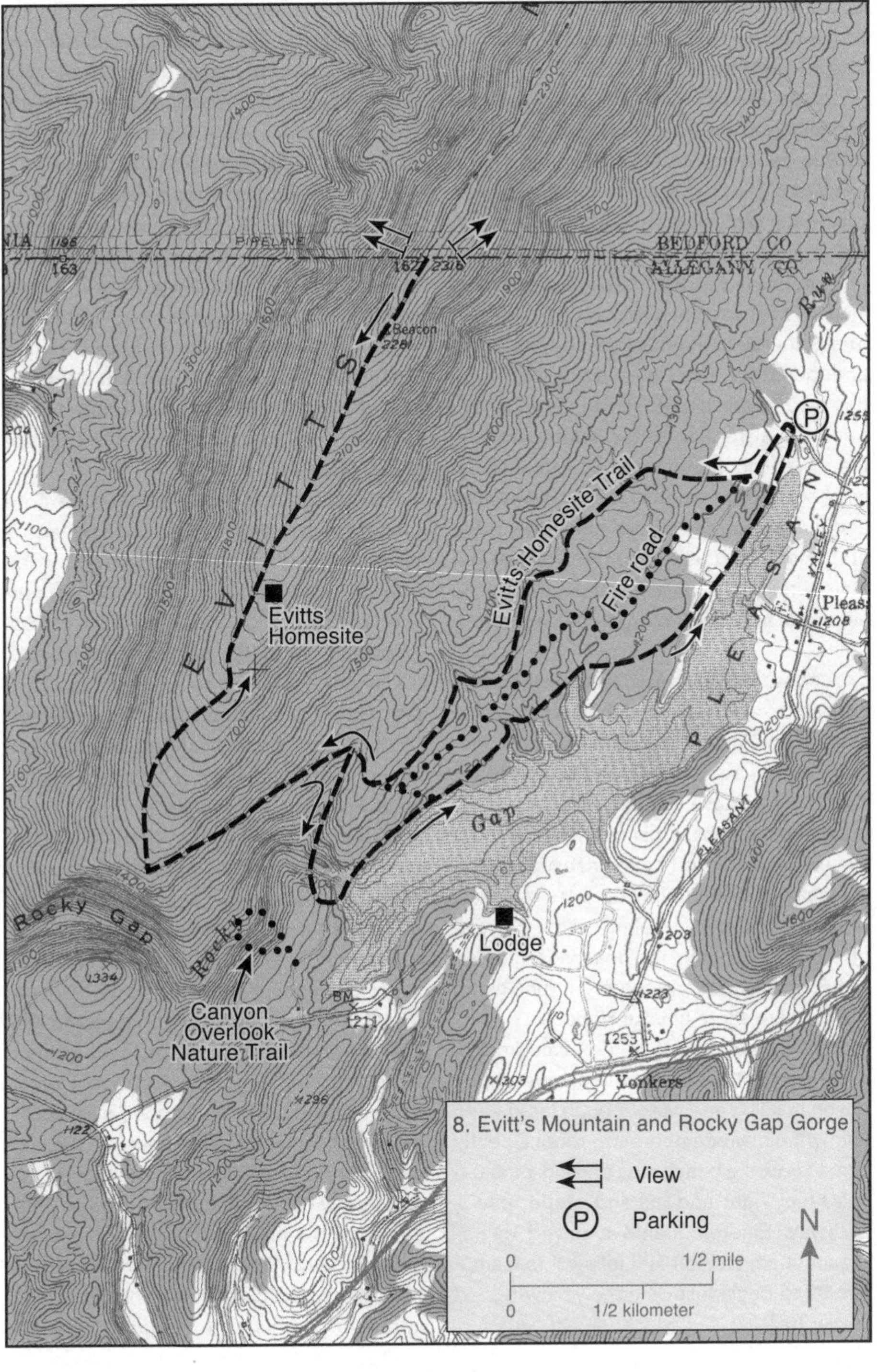

BEDFORD CO
ALLEGANY CO
Beacon 2281
Evitts Homesite
Evitts Homesite Trail
Fire road
Rocky Gap
Lodge
Canyon Overlook Nature Trail
Yonkers
8. Evitt's Mountain and Rocky Gap Gorge
View
Parking
N
0
1/2 mile
0
1/2 kilometer

layers of sedimentary rock were folded as Africa collided with North America about 230 million years ago.

Rocky Gap State Park is reached by continuing to drive west on I-68 to exit 50. As you descend Martin's Mountain on the interstate, the first thing to catch your eye will be the park's massive 220-room resort lodge and conference center, built along the southern shore of Lake Habeeb. The manicured greens of a Jack Nicklaus Signature golf course stretch between the lodge and the interstate. There is no doubt that this type of development adds another aspect and attraction to the state park, but there was much debate and protest in the local community (and throughout Maryland) about changing the natural character of the state park–and as to the propriety of the state turning such a large amount of public land over to a private, profit-making corporation.

Also within the boundaries of the state park are a campground with hot showers, a camp store, laundry, beaches with modern bathhouses, a snack bar, and boat rentals. The 243-acre Lake Habeeb attracts anglers with largemouth bass, panfish, and trout. The excursion described below rises along the southeastern-facing slope of Evitt's Mountain to traverse its fairly level ridgeline. Coming off the mountain, the hike descends into narrow Rocky Gap Gorge before it runs along the northern shore of Lake Habeeb.

If you're not staying in the campground, leave your automobile at the camper registration building and walk through the gate to follow the main campground road. Directly across from the beach area parking lot at 0.5 mile, turn right and ascend steps onto a pathway. Emerging onto a paved campground road, turn left and follow it to Campsite 92 to begin following the yellow-blazed Rocky Trail.

Ascend along a rough and rocky old fire road, lined by mountain laurel, blueberry bushes, and oak trees. The fire road, now purple-blazed and called the Settler's Path, heads off to the left at 0.9 mile; keep right and continue to ascend on the Rocky Trail, now a narrower pathway. A couple of short ups and downs bring you to a marked intersection at 1.8 miles. Bear right onto the blue-blazed Shortcut Trail and stay to the right again just a short distance later, so that you will be following the white-blazed Evitt's Homesite Trail to the low point at 2.2 miles that marks the start of a long, steady ascent of close to 500 feet to the main crest of Evitt's Mountain.

Having gained the ridgeline, turn right onto the side trail to Evitt's Homesite at 3.5 miles. Although no one seems to know the true story, local belief holds that Mr. Evitt arrived in Allegany County in the early 1730s. Hoping to escape the memories and pains of a lost love, he built a cabin on what is now his namesake mountain and never returned to the eastern part of the state. Today, a caved-in well and some old stone walls are mute evidence of his life here.

When done exploring the homesite, return to the main trail and turn right. You may note that most people return to the campground after visiting the homesite, as the pathway soon becomes narrower and obviously less used. After walking by an occasional patch of mayapple and a bit of black cohosh that line the trail, pass an aviation beacon at 4.4 miles. Black cohosh, which blooms from June to September, is also commonly known as bugbane because the malodor it emits is repellent to certain bugs.

The low-cut vegetation of a pipeline right-of-way at 4.6 miles marks the end of state park property. Although you can legally walk no farther, you have come to one of the most interesting views in Allegany County.

Stretching out to both the eastern and western horizons, the wide pipeline swath climbs over ridgelines and descends into valleys, following the Maryland/Pennsylvania border as delineated by the course of the Mason-Dixon Line.

To settle a dispute between the followers of William Penn and the descendants of George Calvert, first Lord of Baltimore, British astronomers and surveyors Charles Mason and Jeremiah Dixon were commissioned in 1765 to firmly establish the boundary between the two colonies. Because the Mason-Dixon Line later became the dividing point between slaveholding and free states, many people believe it was the impetus for calling the South "Dixie." The name actually came from ten-dollar bills printed by a bank in Louisiana; much of the population in that state traces its ancestry back to France, and they referred to the money as *dix,* French for ten. The bills became so extensively distributed that the entire South became known as Dixie. The term became even more widely used when minstrel Daniel Emmett wrote and popularized the song "Dixie" while in New York City in 1859.

From the pipeline, retrace your steps, passing by the side trail to Evitt's Homesite at 5.7 miles. Be alert at the intersection at 7.1 miles, as you want to bear right and descend into a forest of hemlock trees along the rough and rocky route of the Evitt's Homesite Trail. Come to Rocky Gap Run at 7.4 miles, and pay close attention to the white blazes that mark the route of the Evitt's Homesite Trail; you need to cross a footbridge over the stream and begin a steep ascent.

Do not go left onto the unauthorized trail when you reach the top of the rise at 7.6 miles, where small patches of wintergreen add color to the forest floor. You need to be alert again just a few hundred feet later. The trail makes an abrupt turn to the left; do not continue right on the unauthorized pathway.

Turn left onto a paved park road at 7.8 miles and walk by a wastewater treatment facility. You might want to take a break to enjoy the scenery when you come to the dam that impedes the flow of Rocky Gap Run and created Lake Habeeb. The sounds of children laughing and playing on the beach area of the opposite shore are audible on warm summer days. The 220 rooms of the resort lodge loom above the green links of the golf course, while anglers try their luck from the lakeside and from small boats upon the water.

Continue the hike by crossing the dam and ascending the steps of the orange-blazed Lakeside Trail to enter the woods. Deep shade and breezes coming off the lake help cool your skin as you walk above the shoreline. Leave the Lakeside Trail at 8.6 miles and bear left onto the red-blazed route, referred to by park personnel as the "alternate trail." Continuing through the woods with basically no change in elevation, you will soon pass through a recreation field and begin to follow the main paved campground road. Cold liquids and high-calorie snacks may be purchased by heading to the camp store at 9.3 miles. After slaking your thirst and filling the emptiness in your stomach, continue along the campground road to finish your hike and return to your car at 9.9 miles.

If the camp store snacks did not suffice, drive over to the restaurant in the lodge for a complete three-course meal. Before leaving the park, you could take another short walk along the Canyon Overlook Self-Guided Nature Trail, accessed beyond the lodge. A brochure available from park personnel is keyed to numbered stops along the pathway to help enlighten you about the area's natural history.

Green Ridge

Total distance (one-way): 18.1 miles

Hiking time: 10 hours, 30 minutes, or overnight hike

Vertical rise: 2,120 feet

Maps: USGS 7½' Artemas (MD/PA); USGS 7½' Paw Paw (MD/WV); Oldtown (MD/WV)

A hike in Green Ridge State Forest is one of the best backpacking outings in Maryland at any time of year, but to get the most fun out of it, wait for a hot weekend in June or July. The majority of the hike is along one creek or another, each with miles of small ripples and cascades—and a profusion of wading and swimming holes. Even if you don't want to take advantage of these mountain streams to cool off a bit, you will still need to ford them more than 60 times, so it may be best to wait until the summer weather has had a chance to raise the water temperature a few degrees. Abundant possible tent sites and three Adirondack-style shelters make this a good choice for two, or even three, days' enjoyment in the woods. Pets must be on a leash and hunting is permitted during the season, so take proper precautions.

The Great Eastern Trail joins the hike for about 2 miles in the middle of this journey. The route is an exciting long-distance trail project that is currently under construction. Stretching for close to 2,000 miles, it runs from Alabama to New York. More information may be obtained at www.greateasterntrail.net.

Since this is a one-way hike, a car shuttle will be necessary. In addition, the shuttle involves many miles of dirt-road driving, so allow ample time. Backcountry camping is permitted, but because you need to pay a fee and obtain a permit, take I-68 Exit 64 (approximately 20 miles west of Hancock), and drive just a very short distance southward on M. V. Smith Road to the Forest Service Headquarters. Be sure to tell the personnel you will be leaving a car overnight close to the trail's northern terminus.

Return to I-68 and continue west to take Exit 62, where you turn southward along Fifteenmile Creek Road, which soon becomes gravel and dirt. A little more than 2 miles later, keep to the right onto Green Ridge Road when Fifteenmile Creek Road swings to the left. Bypassing all side roads, stay on this mountaintop route for approximately 11 miles to turn left onto paved MD 51. Pay close attention, for within a very short distance you need to turn right onto an unmarked dirt access road to the C&O Canal Towpath. Leave one car, making sure not to block traffic.

Drive the second automobile back to I-68. About 0.3 mile after crossing back over the interstate, turn left and follow the dirt and gravel Fifteenmile Creek Road for 1 mile before bearing left onto Double Pine Road. An additional 2 miles will bring to the intersection with Old Cumberland Road. Leave your car at the parking area and walk southward onto the Pine Lick Blue Trail. (Following the trail north for about 0.8 mile would bring you to the Mason-Dixon Line, where the pathway connects with the Pennsylvania Mid-State Trail.)

Gradually descend into a wildlife clearing dotted by a few birdsfoot violets and bluets. Favoring deciduous forests, grassy hillsides, open meadows, and sunny fields and clearings, a number of species of bluets may be found in Maryland. Long-leaved bluets have terminal clusters of two to three white to pale purple flowers. Large, or mountain, bluets have ribbed leaves that grow oppositely on a 4- to 18-inch stem and white or pink flowers that grow in terminal clusters. Because of its size, many observers believe it lacks the daintiness of the common bluet, the one most frequently observed in the mountains. It has four light blue to almost

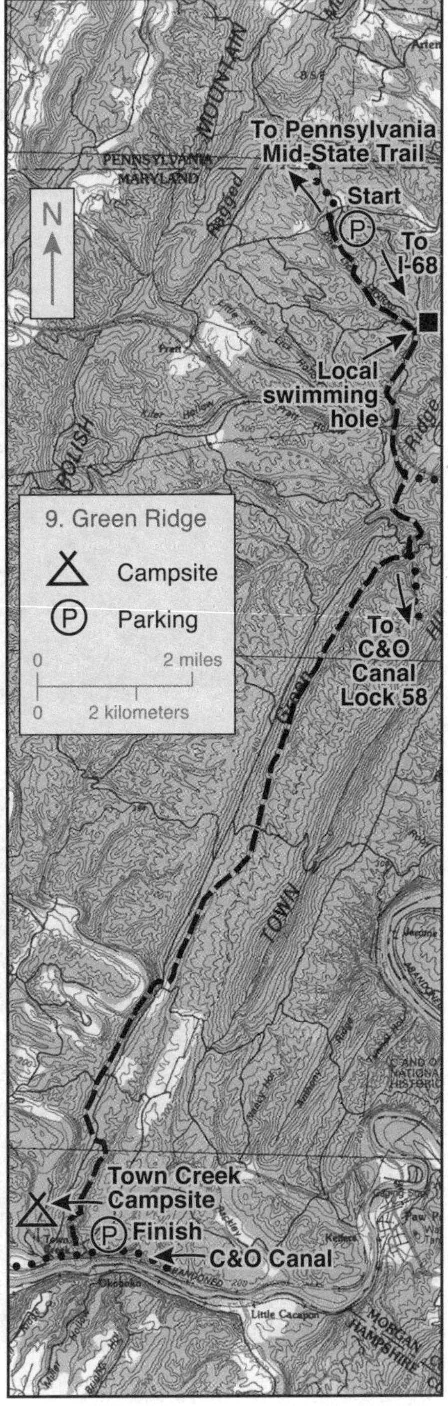

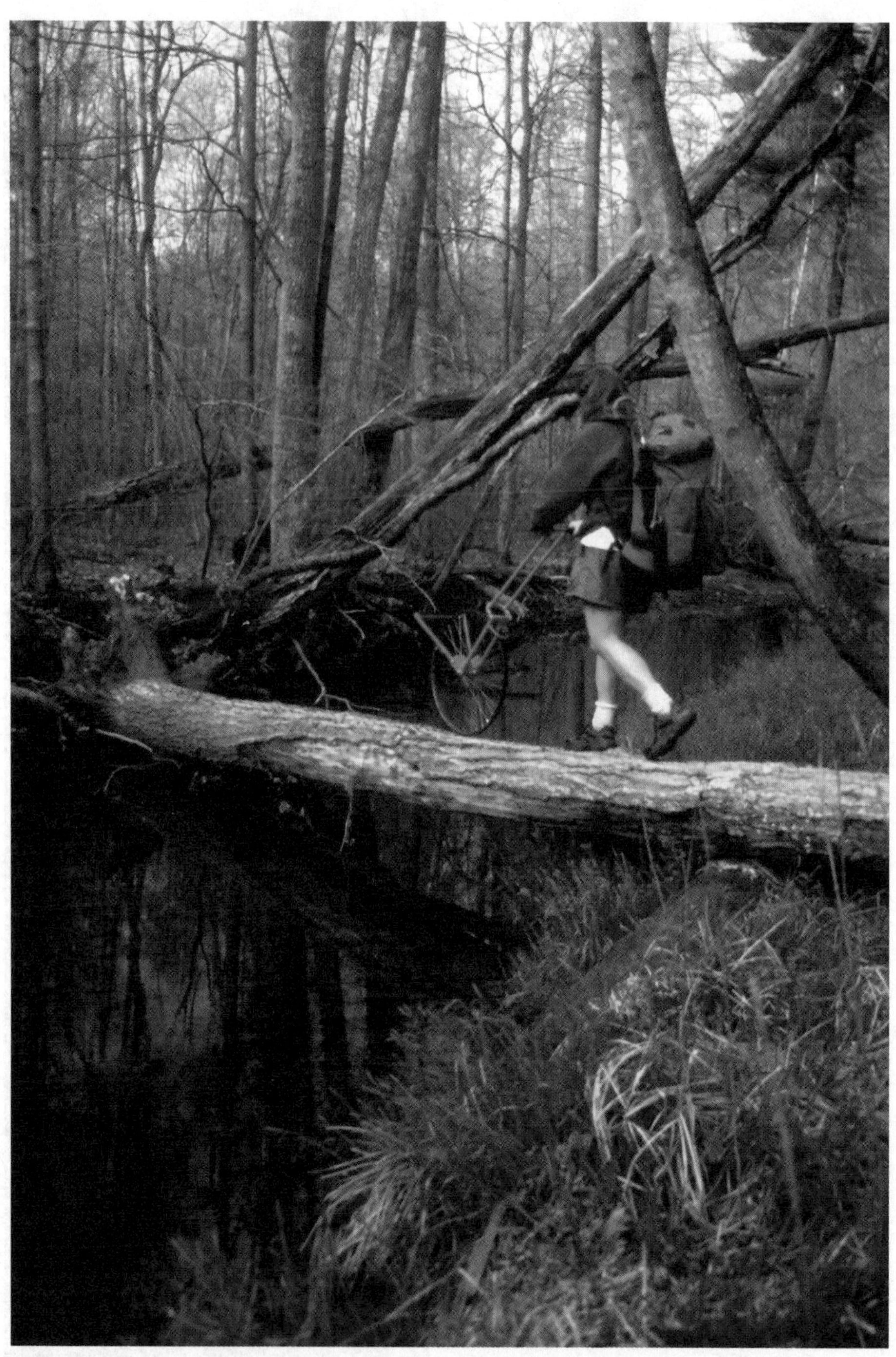

Crossing Fifteenmile Creek while measuring the trail

white petals that are joined together with a slightly yellow center; each stem has a solitary flower.

Continuing through a forest of dogwood, redbud, and serviceberry, the descent steepens at 0.5 mile. In early summer, the serviceberry's flowers give way to berries of 0.5 inch in diameter, which are a favorite food of ruffed grouse, wild turkeys, deer, bears, raccoons, and other wildlife. At one time the fruits were widely harvested and eaten fresh or cooked into puddings, pies, and preserves. The Cree Indians made a long-lasting pemmican by mixing the dried berries with cured meat and animal fat. Unknowingly, most hikers of today overlook this very sweet treat that nature provides to them within an arm's reach of the trail. A member of the rose family, serviceberry is also variously known as sarvisberry, shadbush, and juneberry.

Walk through a bottomland forest at 0.7 mile, and make the first few of what will be many stream crossings while on this hike. At 0.9 mile is the first of the three trailside shelters on this hike. The ford at 1.3 miles may be easier to accomplish if you go upstream a bit from where the trail encounters the creek. The umbrellalike leaves of mayapple form a carpet along the forest floor beside the Pine Lick crossing at 1.4 miles.

Turn right onto Fifteenmile Creek Road at 1.8 miles to cross Pine Lick on the road bridge. The large pool beside the road, where Pine Lick and Fifteenmile Creek meet, is so deep that it has become a popular local swimming hole (complete with swinging rope). You have probably worked up a good sweat in the hour you have been walking, so why not take a break and wander in?

When ready to resume the hike, continue along Fifteenmile Creek Road for less than 200 feet before turning left into the woods. Cross a footbridge, parallel Fifteenmile Creek, walk through the lush vegetation of a bottomland forest, and cross Fifteenmile Creek Road at 2.5 miles.

The trail crosses the creek twice more before crossing paved US 40 at 3 miles, but there are no bridges, so you will need to ford the stream. You may notice that easy road access makes this portion of the stream popular with trout anglers. Use a constructed walkway to pass under I-68, after which you need to be alert to follow the trail close to the interstate spillway and not take the angler's trail along the creek.

Begin a steep climb at 3.5 miles, reaching a ridgeline at 3.9 miles, only to descend gradually along an old woods road. The trail to the left at 4.2 miles leads to the Green Ridge State Forest Headquarters in 1 mile. Keep right and descend very steeply on a rough and rocky treadway that probably should be rerouted to prevent any additional erosion.

Those of you who decide to make camp next to where a footbridge crosses Firfteenmile Creek at 4.5 miles will be serenaded by a host of restful sounds. As the light of day begins to fade, the gobbling of turkeys and honking of ducks may bounce off the narrow valley's walls. The call of a barred owl and the cheeps of spring peepers start about the time you crawl into your sleeping bag, while the lonesome cry of a train whistle sounds in the distance.

Be alert at 4.8 miles; to avoid the creek, the trail makes a steep uphill climb to the right, dropping back down to the stream at 5 miles. Arrive at a trail intersection at 5.1 miles, where you need to bear right so as to now follow the Deep Run/Big Run Green Trail and ford that pathway's namesake. (The route to the left goes for several miles to connect with the C&O Canal; see Hike 10.)

Cross the creek again at 5.2 miles (nice wading pool); 5.27 miles; 5.3 miles (good campsite shaded by hemlocks); and 5.4 miles. Turn right onto Fifteenmile Creek Road at 5.6 miles, cross the bridge, and turn left into the woods onto an old railroad grade.

Are your feet still dry? If yes, they probably won't be after you ford Dry Run 19 more times within the next 2.5 miles. In some places the trail may not be well defined, so keep a close watch on the blazes. During some of those crossings, slow down to watch minnows dart around in the shallow water and observe a crayfish or two crawling from hiding place to hiding place. Among the many claws and legs on the crayfish are three pairs of very short, diminutive legs tipped with single claws. Known as jaw-feet, these legs are almost constantly shoveling bits of food into the invertebrate's three pairs of jaws.

A trail comes in from the left at 9.1 miles; keep right on the Deep Run/Big Run Green Trail, cross a side stream before fording Deep Run three more times, and pass by the second trailside shelter of the hike at 9.6 miles. Walk under utility lines at 9.8 miles, cross Mertens Avenue a few hundred feet later, and ford Deep Run two more times.

You will cross Deep Run for the final time at 10.5 miles. Leave its drainage area by rising to a brier-covered ridgeline, which is no fun to walk along if the trail has not been recently maintained. Turn right at 11.1 miles, descend along a woods road, and cut across a small clearing.

Swing left and rise above a small stream at 11.9 miles, beginning a series of short ups and downs along the creek before sidehill trail brings the route to Kirk Road at 12.8 miles.

Turn right and ascend steeply along the roadway to the top of Green Ridge and the T intersection with Green Ridge Road at 13 miles. Before continuing the hike, bear right for a few feet for an impressive vista from Log Roll Overlook. To the far north are the mountains of Pennsylvania, to the west is Maryland, and to the south is West Virginia. Directly in front of you, the mountainside drops 500 to 600 feet at a dramatic rate, revealing the U-shaped bend Town Creek has carved out of the landscape below. At one time, timber was rolled down the mountain to the creek and was floated to a nearby sawmill.

Staying on Green Ridge Road, walk back past Kirk Road, looking for the sign (or blazes) for the Log Roll Orange Trail marking your route's entry into the woods on the right. The builders of this pathway deserve a round of applause for the work done here. The narrow trail is carved out of the steep mountainside, which angles precipitously toward the creek. Bear left and ascend a woods road at 14.2 miles, soon turning right back onto a trail and crossing a paved road a few hundred feet later.

At 14.5 miles, make a right and descend along a woods road, only to turn off it to the left in a short distance. There are a couple of possible small campsites at 15.2 miles—just as you begin the descent to recross Green Ridge Road. Continue to descend, and you'll come to the first water you have seen for almost 3 miles at 15.5 miles. Swing right and parallel the stream on an old woods road, crossing Big Run for the first time at 16 miles.

The next 2 miles of downstream walking are perhaps the highlight of the journey. Not only will you cross Big Run 25 more times, but you will pass through the lush vegetation of hemlock and mountain laurel groves, go by many suitable sites to set up a tent close to the stream, and have ample opportunities to take a dip in the shadow of a large rock outcropping. The final trailside shelter of the hike is located at 16.75 miles.

A few hundred feet after the final ford, the trail rises slightly to come to an end next to MD 51 at 18.1 miles. Your shuttled automobile and the C&O Canal Towpath are waiting for you on the other side of the road.

If you wish to spend another night in your tent before returning home, the National Park Service's free Town Creek Campsite (with chemical toilets and water available in season) is about 0.3 mile to the right (westward) along the towpath. See Hikes 10, 20, 24, 25, and 26 for more information and additional outings along the canal towpath.

10

Paw Paw Bends and Paw Paw Tunnel

Total distance (one-way): 15.5 miles

Hiking time: 7 hours or overnight hike

Vertical rise: less than 70 feet

Maps: USGS 7½' Artemas (MD/PA/WV); USGS 7½' Paw Paw (MD/WV)

Around the turn of the 19th century, individual canals afforded access around waterfalls and rapids, providing an easy water route between a young America's populated eastern coastline and the newly settled areas west of the Blue Ridge Mountains. Taking a cue from ideas expressed by George Washington and Thomas Jefferson, construction of the Chesapeake and Ohio Canal began on July 4, 1828.

Originally projected to extend 360 miles from Georgetown to Pittsburgh on the Ohio River, the canal never quite lived up to its investors' dreams. Although sections opened for navigation as they were completed, construction was beset by labor shortages and unrest, unreliable delivery of needed building materials, and unforeseen difficulties in excavation. Mounting costs, coupled with the other problems, caused financial backers to decide in 1850 that enough was enough, and that Cumberland was the farthest west the canal would be constructed–a distance of 184.5 miles.

Although it may have never reached Pittsburgh, the canal was a marvel of human engineering and labor. Averaging 40 to 60 feet wide and 6 feet deep, it had 74 lift locks to adjust for the water-level difference between near sea level at Georgetown and the 605-foot elevation at Cumberland. Hand-carved (and hand-laid) stone aqueducts carried the water over intersecting streams, and seven dams were built to divert water from the Potomac River to the canal.

In its heyday, barges pulled by teams of horses or mules plied the waters of the

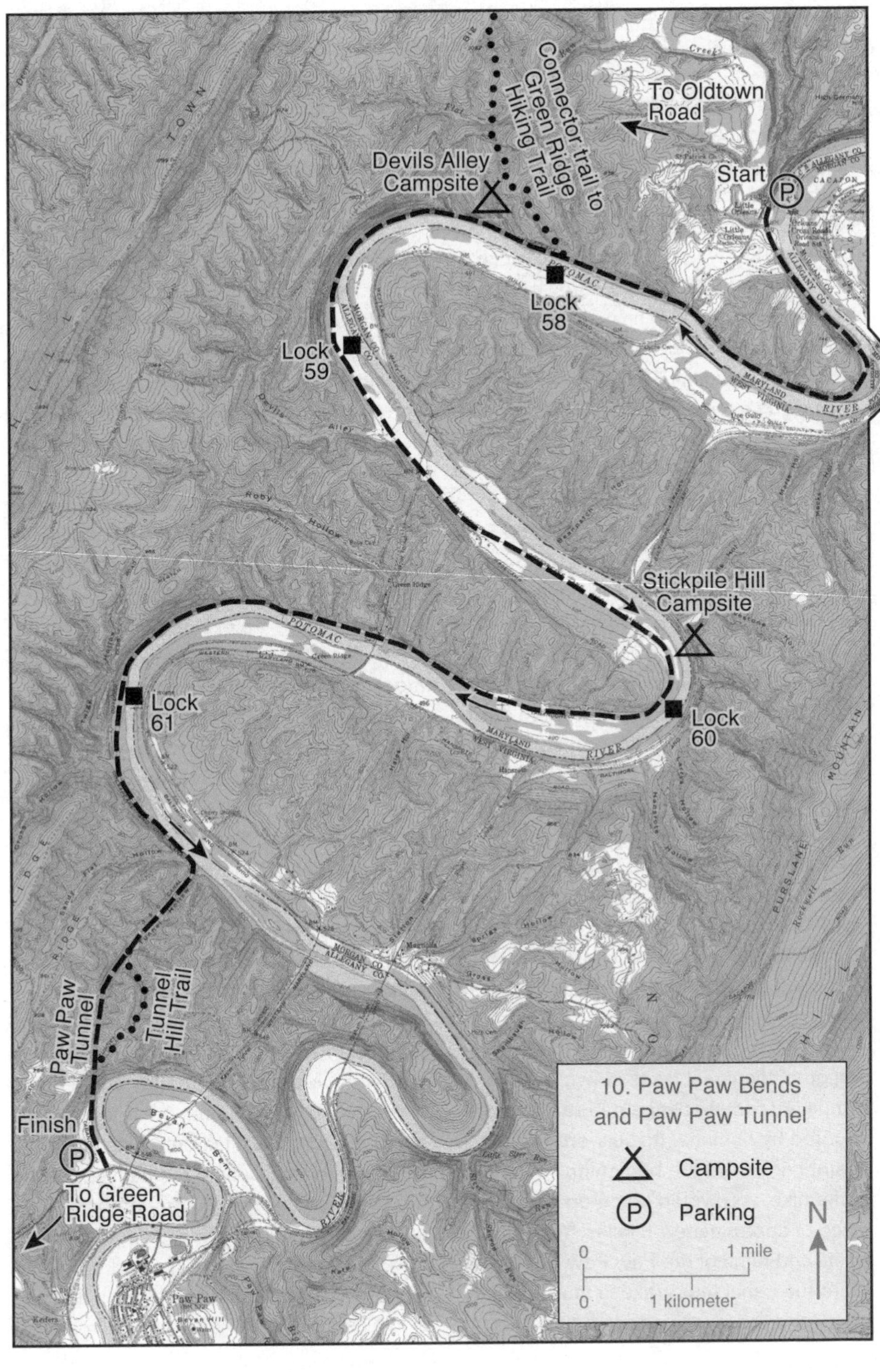

Connector trail to
Green Ridge
Hiking Trail
To Oldtown
Road
Devils Alley
Campsite
Start
Lock
58
Lock
59
Stickpile Hill
Campsite
Lock
61
Lock
60
Paw Paw
Tunnel
Tunnel
Hill Trail
Finish
To Green
Ridge Road
10. Paw Paw Bends
and Paw Paw Tunnel
Campsite
Parking
N
0
1 mile
0
1 kilometer

canal, transporting people and goods in both directions—most of the goods being coal hauled downstream from Cumberland. Yet dry spells, floods, winter freezes, and competition from the B&O Railroad (which coincidentally began construction on the very same day) kept the canal from ever operating at a profit. The final blow was a tremendous flood in 1924, which destroyed so much of the infrastructure that the canal never reopened. Burdened with financial woes, canal owners turned it over to the federal government for $2 million in 1938.

The canal was proclaimed a national monument in 1961 and named a national historical park in 1971. Today, the towpath is open to hikers, bikers, and (except for a short section) horseback riders, and the park service operates visitors centers at Georgetown, Great Falls Tavern, Williamsport, Hancock, and Cumberland. Camping is permitted at designated sites, and you may picnic anywhere you wish (with fires permitted only where fireplaces are provided). If you desire more information about the canal, the park service has an abundance of handout sheets, while Mike High's book, *The C&O Canal Companion,* covers the subject in great detail. *184 Miles of Adventure: Hiker's Guide to the C&O Canal,* published by the Mason-Dixon Council of the Boy Scouts of America, is probably the best resource to consult when considering a long-distance trek along the canal.

This 15.5-mile outing along the western portion of the canal takes in two of its most significant features—one natural, one constructed by humans. If you were to draw a straight line from the beginning to the end of the hike, you would come up with a distance of approximately 6 miles. Yet, with the twists and turns of the Paw Paw Bends, the route the canal must take is more than 15 miles—and this is with saving 5 to 6 miles of river bends by making use of the Paw Paw Tunnel.

Like so many other things associated with the canal, construction of the 3,118-foot tunnel faced difficulties and miscalculations from the onset. Intense friction among camps of Irish, English, and German laborers—in conjunction with a cholera epidemic—compounded the problems. Originally estimated to be built within two years at a cost of $33,500, it took 14 years and more than $600,000 to complete. Once finished, though, the tunnel—lined with close to 6 million bricks in layers of 7 to 11 deep—was used from 1850 until the canal's demise in 1924.

Since this is a one-way hike, a car shuttle will be necessary. In addition, the shuttle involves many miles of dirt-road driving, so allow ample time. About 20 miles west of Hancock, take I-68 exit 62 and drive southward along Fifteenmile Creek Road. A little more than 2 miles later, keep to the right onto Green Ridge Road when Fifteenmile Creek Road swings to the left. Bypassing all side roads, stay on this mountaintop route for approximately 11 miles to turn left onto paved MD 51. Roughly 5 miles later, turn left to leave one car in the Paw Paw Tunnel Parking Area.

Retrace your route along MD 51 for 0.9 mile to make a right onto Malcolm Road. Make another right onto Oldtown Road 3.1 miles later; keep straight at the four-way intersection with Mertens Avenue 2.4 miles farther on. Making sure to stay on Oldtown Road, continue for another 6.2 miles to cross a bridge and make a left onto Orleans Road, which will bring you into the hamlet of Little Orleans. Go through the underpass to the canal's Fifteenmile Creek Campground.

The adventure starts by walking westward along the canal towpath, using the single-arch, flintstone aqueduct to cross over

Fifteenmile Creek. You may notice the shells of snails, Asiatic clams, and freshwater mussels along the banks of the creek and the Potomac River. The mussels are a member of the mollusk family, related to clams, snails, slugs, and squids. These bottom dwellers pump water through their gills, filtering out and retaining microscopic algae and organic debris.

The female mussel carries thousands of eggs in her gills; if a nearby male happens to release sperm, the eggs are fertilized as the female filters the water. When the eggs hatch about two weeks later, the female releases the larvae into the water, where they attach themselves to a host fish. (Each species of mussel requires specific host fish species.) Eventually, the juvenile mussels detach from the host and sink to the bottom; some species' lives may span a full century.

The walking is easy on the canal towpath, so in less time than it would take you to hike 2.5 miles through the mountains, you will be walking under the Western Maryland Railroad trestle over the Potomac River. Unlike most of the locks built of stone along the rest of the canal, Lock 58 at 3.1 miles made use of timber and rock in its construction—due to a lack of quality stone available in the local area. You won't notice the wood today, as it has deteriorated and been replaced with concrete. The pathway that ascends to the right at this point is a connector section of the Green Ridge Hiking Trail (see Hike 9).

Devils Alley Campsite is beside the towpath at 3.6 miles; pass milepost 145 at 4.1 miles. Some of the wood still remains in Lock 59, 4.6 miles into the hike. The trestle at 6.2 miles brings the Western Maryland Railroad back onto the Maryland side of the river.

As you continue upstream to curve around another bend, you may have noticed the pattern by now. Whenever the river swings to the southeast, the flat land along the Maryland

Paw Paw Tunnel

side becomes wider and the hillside less steep, while just the opposite occurs on the West Virginia side: When the river swings to the northwest, the strip of Maryland's flat land becomes narrower, and the mountains rise above the river at a faster rate.

Pass the Stickpile Hill Campsite, named for the ridge you are swinging around, at 8.4 miles, and walk beside Lock 60 just a few hundred yards beyond. A third trestle sends the Western Maryland Railroad to the West Virginia side of the river at 10.3 miles. The railroad crosses the river three more times before coming to the end of the bends, but none of the trestles is visible from the towpath because the Paw Paw Tunnel circumvents the areas of crossing.

The deteriorating Lock 61 is at 12.2 miles, Twigg Hollow and an access road to Outdoor Club Road are at 12.4 miles, and Sorrel Ridge Campsite and Lock 62 are at 13.2 miles.

Swinging away from the river and rising almost imperceptibly toward the tunnel, Locks 63⅓ and 64⅔, curiously numbered, are passed at miles 13.6 and 13.7. Historians have decided the locks apparently were given these strange numbers as a way to fudge on bookkeeping. Also, note that there is no Lock 65 when you next walk by Lock 66 at 13.8 miles. The pathway that ascends to the left is the Tunnel Hill Trail, which goes over the ridgeline to rejoin the towpath at the tunnel's south portal.

Break out your flashlight and enter the Paw Paw Tunnel at 14.3 miles. Even after its completion, the tunnel proved to be a source of contention. Since heavily laden boats were headed downstream from Cumberland, they were given the right-of-way in the main body of the canal. However, at the tunnel, the rule of thumb was that the first boat to either portal had the right to go through first. Although this was general knowledge, some boat captains would refuse to yield. Local lore tells of an occasion when two barges stayed in place for several days because neither captain would give way. Canal workers finally built a fire to smoke them out.

The pathway inside the tunnel is usually wet and slippery, so use the provided handrail. Some of the boards are the original lumber, and you can feel the grooves worn into it from years of tow ropes sliding across.

Emerge from the tunnel at 14.9 miles and come to a picnic area and the Tunnel Hill Trail a few hundred feet later. (The hike is almost over, but just for the fun of it, consider taking the Tunnel Hill Trail up and over the ridgeline and walking through the tunnel once more. This would add less than 2 miles to your journey.)

Turn left onto a short connector trail at 15.4 miles, returning to your shuttled car at 15.5 miles. See Hikes 9, 20, 24, 25, and 26 for additional outings along the C&O Canal.

11

Antieram

Total distance (circuit): 4.5 miles

Hiking time: 2 hours

Vertical rise: 350 feet

Maps: USGS 7½' Keedysville (MD/WV); National Park Service Antietam brochure; National Park Service Sherrick Farm Trail map

In August 1862, Union and Confederate forces met at the Second Battle of Manassas in Virginia. General Robert E. Lee, in command of the Confederates and aided by the forces of General Stonewall Jackson, employed brilliant military tactics to force General John Pope's Union army to withdraw from the area and return to Washington, D.C. This opened the way for Lee's first drive into Northern territory and a possible recognition of the Confederate States of America by major European powers.

As the Confederates marched into Maryland, General George B. McClellan moved his Federal Army of the Potomac westward to stop the advance. Meeting the rebels on South Mountain on September 14 in Turners, Fox, and Crampton Gaps (all of which today are crossed by the Appalachian Trail—see Hike 13), the Federal army forced its way through. By the next day, both sides had established battle lines west and east of Antietam Creek near Sharpsburg.

Having secured Harpers Ferry on September 15, Jackson's troops reached Sharpsburg the following day, at which time Lee consolidated his position along a low ridge that runs north and south of the town. The Battle of Antietam began at dawn on September 17, when Union general Joseph Hooker's artillery began firing on Jackson's men in the Miller Cornfield north of town. Throughout the day, blue and gray met in skirmishes over a battlefield encompassing an area of 12 square miles. One conflict along an old sunken road lasted for nearly four hours, with the fighting so intense that

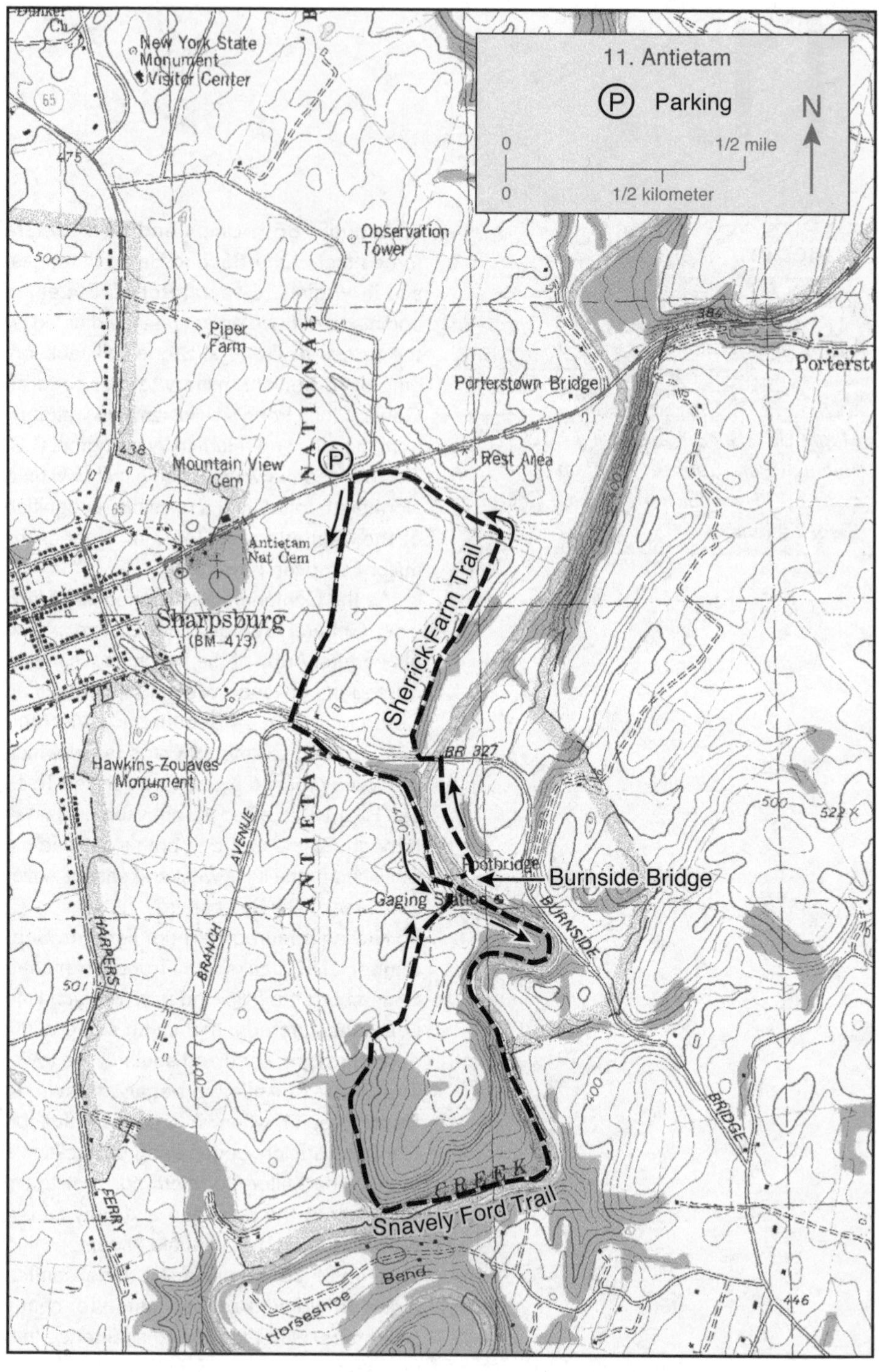
11. Antietam
P Parking
N
0
1/2 mile
0
1/2 kilometer
New York State Monument
Visitor Center
Observation Tower
Piper Farm
Porterstown Bridge
Rest Area
Mountain View Cem
Antietam Nat Cem
Sharpsburg
(BM 413)
NATIONAL
ANTIETAM
Sherrick Farm Trail
Hawkins Zouaves Monument
Footbridge
Burnside Bridge
Gaging Station
BURNSIDE
BRIDGE
HARPERS
FERRY
BRANCH
AVENUE
CREEK
Snavely Ford Trail
Horseshoe
Bend

the road was forever after known as Bloody Lane. More men were killed or wounded at Antietam than on any other single day in United States military history. Union forces lost more than 12,410 men, while the Confederates had 10,700 fatalities.

The next day Lee began to withdraw his armies to the south of the Potomac River. This failure to bring the war into the North's territory resulted in Great Britain refusing to recognize the Confederate government. Soon afterward, President Lincoln issued the Emancipation Proclamation, reinforcing the idea that one of the major reasons the war was being waged was to end slavery.

Antietam National Battlefield Park may be reached by taking exit 29 off I-70 near Hagerstown and driving south on MD 65. Close to 9 miles later, turn left into the park to arrive at the visitors center. The park is open daily except Thanksgiving, Christmas, and New Year's Day; a small admission fee is charged. Relic hunting is prohibited.

To add to your enjoyment of the hike, you should devote at least some time to the exhibits and multimedia programs presented in the center. Several brochures are available that describe the battles, the physical features of the more than 3,000-acre park, and the itinerary for a driving tour of the battlefield.

The circuit hike described here follows a figure-eight route that touches on a number of sites relevant to the battle of Antietam. In addition, it offers a quiet and moderate walk through open fields, wooded forests, quiet country lanes, and along meandering and shallow Antietam Creek. The peace and quiet of this hike is made even more enjoyable when you realize you are barely more than 10 miles from the hustle and bustle of downtown Hagerstown.

To reach the trailhead, drive away from the visitors center and head south along Hagerstown Pike (MD 65). Turn left in 0.9 mile onto Main Street (MD 34) in Sharpsburg. Make a right in an additional 0.6 mile onto Rodman Avenue (the first paved road past the National Cemetery–which contains the remains of 4,776 Federal soldiers, including 1,836 unknowns) and park in the small two-car pullout.

Walk south through the fence on Rodman Avenue, which at the time of the battle was a partially enclosed route known as Sherrick's Lane. The open expanse of the countryside today allows you to enjoy hawks and turkey vultures soaring in the sky above. Reach the high point of the lane at 0.25 mile and pass by the monument to Pennsylvania colonel Benjamin C. Christ; then descend.

Turn left onto the paved road toward the Burnside Bridge at 0.5 mile, passing by the Otto Farmhouse. Be alert at 0.9 mile, as you want to bear left and descend along the gravel and grass service road (also part of a handicapped-accessible route). Arrive at the Burnside Bridge at 1 mile.

After trying to cross the bridge several times during the early-morning hours of the battle, but being repulsed each time by Georgian forces, Union General Ambrose E. Burnside's troops finally made it across at about 1 PM. By late afternoon, the Southerners had been pushed back almost to Sharpsburg. Around 4 PM, Confederate general A. P. Hill's troops joined the fray, driving the Union army back toward the bridge and effectively bringing the battle to a close.

Without crossing the bridge, ascend and descend a few steps and begin to follow the Snavely Ford Trail along Antietam Creek. The slow-moving creek is popular with canoeists and kayakers. A local outfitter runs training trips during the warmer months, and it is a common sight to see a family enjoying an afternoon inner-tube float downstream become interspersed with eight or nine

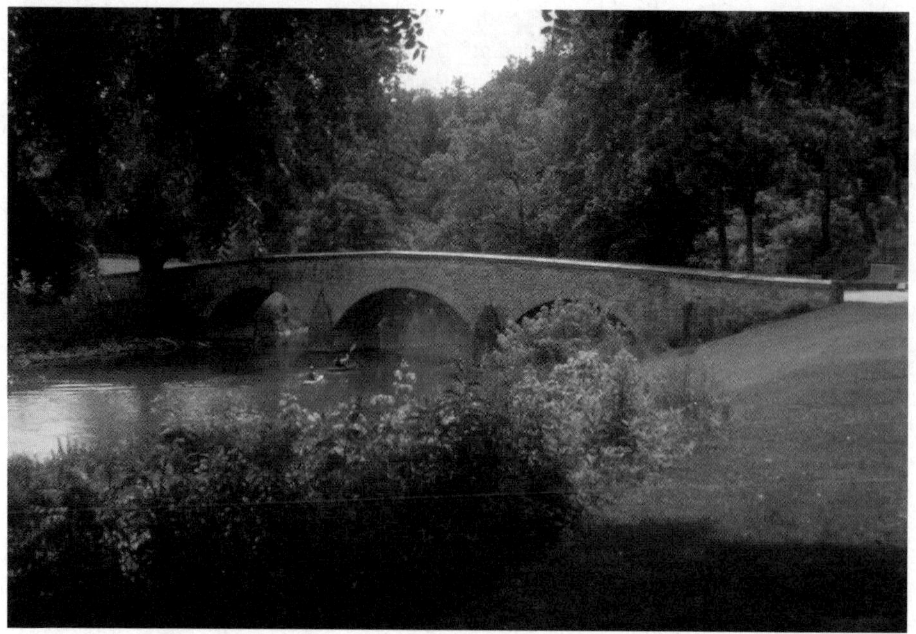

Along the Snavely Ford Trail

kayakers dressed in colorful outfits, being taught how to paddle.

Keep along the creek when you come to an intersection at 1.4 miles; the pathway to the right ascends back to the Burnside Bridge parking area. Big-leaved pawpaw trees, tiny Deptford pinks, and daylilies line the trail in large numbers here. An import from the Old World that has escaped from cultivated gardens and become firmly established in Maryland, the daylily is most often seen in wet meadows and along streams or other bodies of water. Although all parts of the plant are edible, those in the know say that the blossom, when cooked in oil or butter, is the best tasting part.

Mayapple is part of the undergrowth where you begin to rise away from the stream at 2.25 miles. The restful greenery of a few juniper trees adds to the quiet and isolated feeling of this spot. The shallow water is Snavely's Ford, where General Rodman's division crossed Antietam Creek; the general was killed in the fields south of Sharpsburg as the battle was coming to an end.

The ascent steepens for a distance at 2.6 miles before leveling out to turn left onto a roadbed. Just before you reach the parking area, bear right onto the grass and soon follow a paved pathway downhill (the trail that heads right is a short pathway to the Georgians Overlook of Antietam Creek) to the Burnside Bridge.

Cross over the bridge at 3.1 miles and bear left onto the Sherrick Farm Trail to walk upstream beside an old stone wall and open meadow. The stately sycamore tree on this side of the bridge was a mere sapling at the time of the battle. Keep walking along the edge of the meadow when the stone wall ends at 3.2 miles, but be alert at 3.3 miles. You need to bear left to follow the route into the woods, climb up the embankment to Burnside Bridge Road, and turn left to cross the creek on a highway bridge (use caution; watch for automobile traffic). Just a few feet later, turn right through a gate that leads into a field. Rise to the left onto a pathway through a narrow strip of trees that form a windbreak between two cultivated fields. There are a number of places above and below the trail where the ground is dotted by the burrows of groundhogs and other small woodland animals.

Unlike many other creatures, groundhogs dig their own burrows, which can be more than 4 feet deep and 25 feet long. In fact, many other mammals, such as raccoons, foxes, skunks, opossums, and rabbits, will appropriate space for their own homes in groundhog tunnels. True hibernators, groundhogs spend the winter months underground, curled into a tight ball on a mat of grass. Their heart rate drops to only four beats per minute, they take only one breath every six minutes, and their body temperature decreases from 97 degrees to less than 40 degrees Fahrenheit.

The trail passes an old stone wall at 3.6 miles and swings left to emerge into a cultivated field at 3.9 miles. You might happen to spot a sparrow, cardinal, or bluebird resting on the fence you walk next to before you pass through a windrow at 4.1 miles and continue along the edge of the field. The hike ends once you return to your car at 4.5 miles.

See Hike 12 for another walk in an area with Civil War connections.

12

Maryland Heights

Total distance (circuit): 5.1 miles

Hiking time: 3 hours, 30 minutes

Vertical rise: 1,620 feet

Maps: USGS 7½' Harpers Ferry (WV/VA/MD); National Park Service Maryland Heights map

Located at the confluence of the Shenandoah and Potomac Rivers, Harpers Ferry—despite the relatively small size of its population—has played an important role throughout many stages of America's history.

Peter Stephens began a ferry service in 1733, helping to facilitate westward expansion. The business was purchased in 1747 by Robert Harper, who built a gristmill on a low island in the Shenandoah. On his way to Philadelphia in 1783 to serve as a Virginia delegate to the Continental Congress, Thomas Jefferson looked down upon the meeting of the two rivers and declared it to be "perhaps one the most stupendous scenes in Nature." (You will have a chance to form your own opinion while on this hike.)

In his younger years, George Washington was employed as a surveyor in the area, while as president he worked with Congress to establish a federal armory and arsenal in the town. The quality munitions manufactured by the armory attracted the attention of Meriwether Lewis, who traveled to Harpers Ferry in 1803 to obtain supplies before heading westward with William Clark and "The Corps of Discovery" to explore the Louisiana Territory.

Events about a half century later truly thrust the little town into the spotlight. John Brown's failed raid on the federal arsenal in October 1859 was an attempt to seize the 100,000 muskets and rifles stored there. Brown had intended to turn the arms over to slaves, hoping to inspire an insurrection against their owners. In what seems like irony to us now, the federal forces ordered by

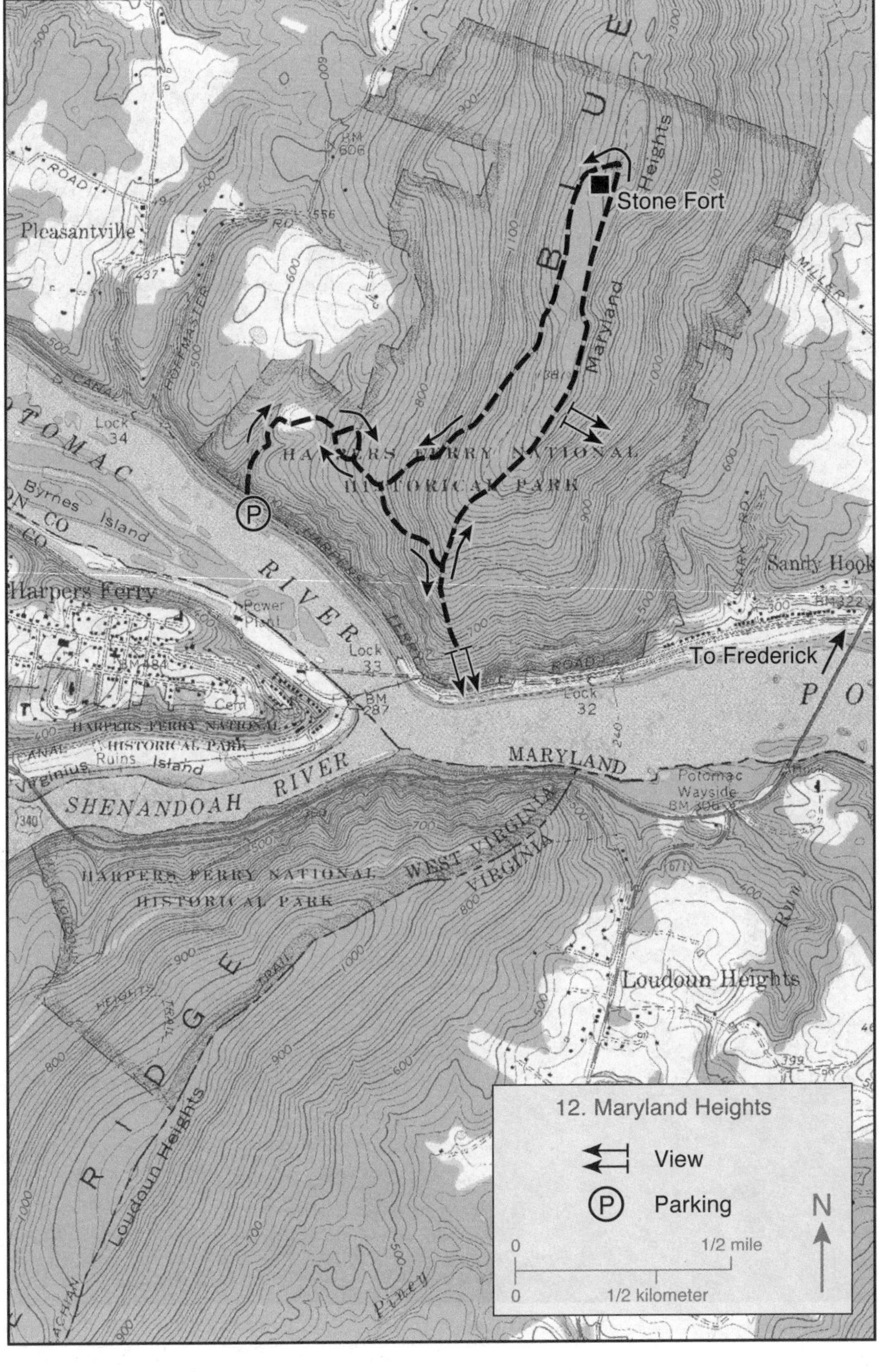

12. Maryland Heights
View
Parking
N
0
1/2 mile
0
1/2 kilometer
Stone Fort
To Frederick
Pleasantville
Harpers Ferry
Sandy Hook
Loudoun Heights
Maryland Heights
POTOMAC RIVER
SHENANDOAH RIVER
HARPERS FERRY NATIONAL HISTORICAL PARK
MARYLAND
WEST VIRGINIA
VIRGINIA
Byrnes Island
Ruins Island
Lock 34
Lock 33
Lock 32
Potomac Wayside

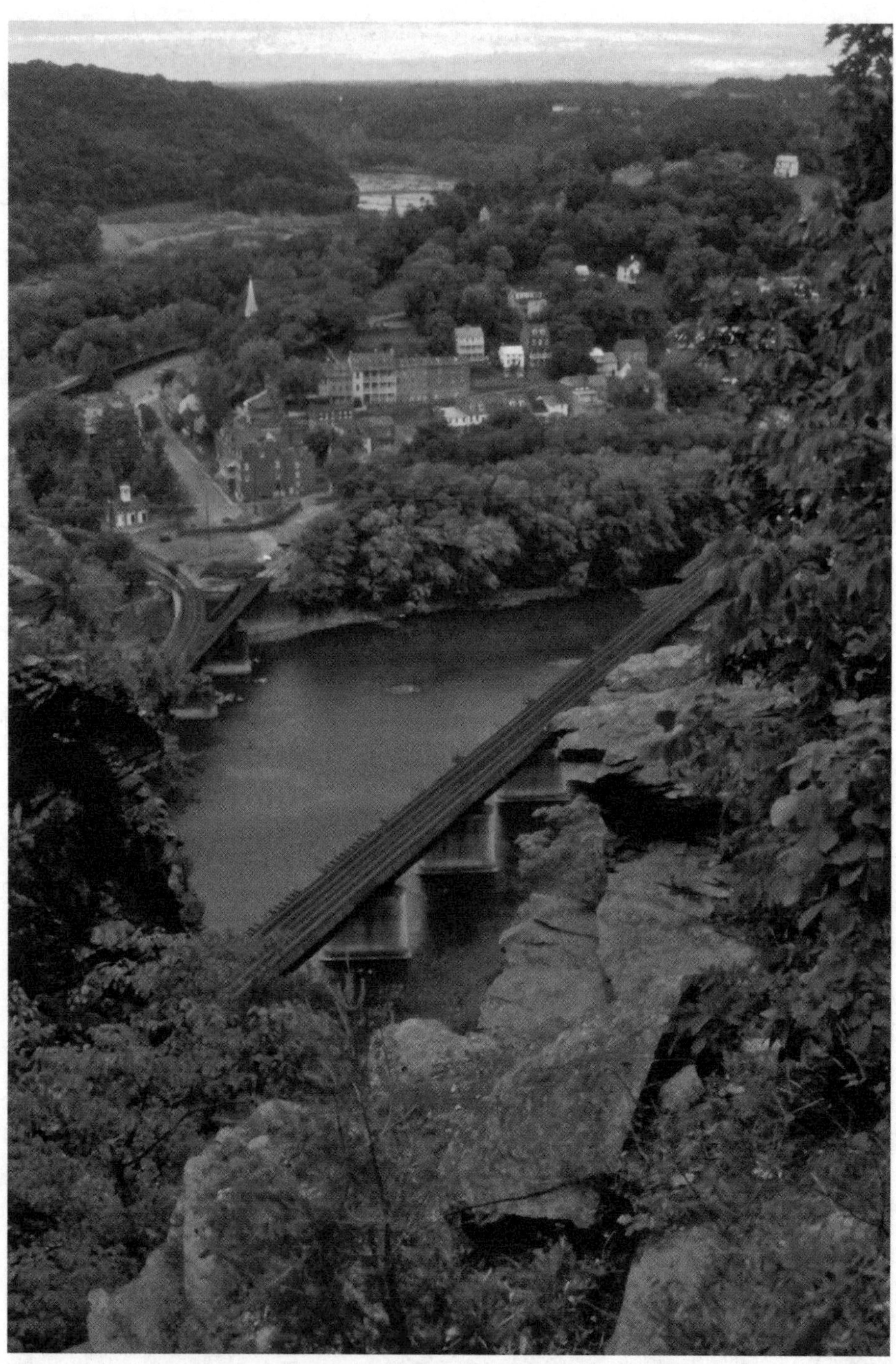

The view of Harpers Ferry from Maryland Heights

President James Buchanan to Harpers Ferry to capture Brown and his followers were under the command of Lt. Col. Robert E. Lee.

Strategically situated as it was near the border between North and South, the town exchanged hands eight times during the Civil War. Immediately following Virginia's secession in 1861, Thomas (later known as "Stonewall") Jackson seized the armory and sent its weapon-producing machinery farther south. By the time he returned to Harpers Ferry in 1862 as part of Lee's first invasion of the North, Maryland Heights–the mountain on the northern side of the Potomac overlooking the town–had begun to be fortified. Yet Jackson's brilliant military tactics forced the surrender of the Federal forces stationed both on Maryland Heights and in town–the largest surrender of US troops during the Civil War.

In spite of Jackson's victory, Confederate forces retreated south following the failed attempt at Antietam to bring the war into Northern territory. Harpers Ferry became a major Union supply base, and the fortifications on Maryland Heights grew in size.

On land that is now part of Harpers Ferry National Historical Park, the hike to Maryland Heights can be a strenuous one, but it affords the opportunity to relive history while taking in the area's natural beauty and a few spectacular views. The hike is reached by taking I-70 exit 52 at Frederick and driving southwest on US 340. About 15 miles later, make a left onto Keep Tryst Road. Turn right onto Sandy Hook Road in an additional 0.3 mile, leaving your car at the trailhead parking on the right 2.1 miles farther.

Walk back along the road a few feet to turn left and ascend along the old military road. This is the same route on which the Union forces retreated on September 12, 1862. There is a partial view of the Potomac River at 0.2 mile. Pass under a utility line at 0.5 mile, making sure to stay on the main route at 0.6 mile by swinging left and leveling out a bit before resuming the ascent. Don't feel too bad if you break out in a sweat and huff and puff as you gain elevation; Abraham Lincoln gave up long before attaining the ridgeline while on an inspection tour in 1862.

Keep to the left when the trail to the naval battery comes in from the right at 0.75 mile. Keep right on the red-blazed route when you come to the major intersection about 200 feet later; avoid trails to the left and right to continue straight at 1 mile and begin a long descent via a series of switchbacks.

All of the effort you have gone through so far is more than amply compensated when you break out into the open at 1.5 miles. Although he was looking upon the confluence of the rivers from the West Virginia side, Jefferson's addition of the words "worth a voyage across the Atlantic" to the aforementioned quote is hard to dispute. More than 300 feet below the top of the rock cliff upon which you are standing, the shimmering ripples and bits of white water in the Shenandoah and Potomac Rivers reflect the light of bright sunny days as they cut their respective ways through the mountains. Spanning the Potomac River upstream from where the two rivers meet is the B&O Railroad bridge. All of Harpers Ferry, West Virginia, is spread out before you. Saint Peter's Catholic Church, with its prominent steeple, sits on the cliffs overlooking the Shenandoah, while Hilltop House Hotel, high above the Potomac, towers over the historic district. To the southeast are the precipitous cliffs of Loudoun Heights in Virginia.

(*Note:* It is possible to do a circuit hike of close to 7 miles that passes through all three states and incorporates parts of the C&O Canal Towpath, Loudoun Heights, the Appalachian Trail, and the historic district of

Harpers Ferry. Check at the park service visitors center in town or consult *50 Hikes in Northern Virginia* for more information.)

After a rest break and a picture-taking session (almost all of the publicity photos of Harpers Ferry you may ever come across are taken from this vantage point), retrace your steps uphill to the previous intersection. This time, turn right and ascend steeply on the narrow, blue-blazed pathway.

The trail swings right at 2.1 miles, but before continuing, spend a few minutes exploring the earthwork remains of the 30-pounder battery. The Parrott rifles placed here in 1862 could fire 29-pound projectiles for a distance of more than a mile, easily able to hit targets on Bolivar Heights (south of Harpers Ferry) and Loudoun Heights.

The blue-blazed trail swings around the battery and soon ascends steeply along a rocky route. There is a wintertime view of the Potomac River where the ascent moderates at 2.3 miles and follows the jagged crest of the ridge. A better view opens up when the trail comes to the site of the 100-pounder battery. A 9-inch gun weighing 9,700 pounds (which required two to three hundred men to haul it up the same road you ascended) and capable of heaving a 100-pound shell more than 2 miles was placed here in 1863. The gun was mounted on a raised earthen platform and could be rotated 360 degrees.

Black cohosh blooms along the trail during the summer as you continue on the ridge. As you walk through this now peaceful forest, it may be hard to imagine what Maryland Heights looked like during the war. The top of the mountain was nearly denuded, scores of men and horses hustled about as they moved tons of earth from one place to the next, plumes of smoke rose from cooking fires, wheel marks were dug deeply in the ground from heavy artillery being set up, and large canvas tents were placed upon any flat spot that could be found.

The parallel stone walls you pass at 3 miles were constructed in 1863 as a defense against a possible attack from the north and once extended more than 500 feet down the mountainside. A few hundred feet later, arrive at the high point of Maryland Heights (1,448 feet) and the site of the Stone Fort. Originally designed as an infantry blockhouse to aid in warding off a Confederate attack, it was never completed, and by September 1863 it was used as a commissary and storage area.

Be alert as you continue across the crumbling foundation; turn left at the signed post and enter the Interior Fort area. (The pathway to the right connects with the Elk Ridge Trail, closed in the 1990s due to private landowners' requests.) Union soldiers labored to raise the line of trenches here by 9 to 10 feet, the largest earthwork project on Maryland Heights. Openings in the construction permitted the placement of 30-pounder Parrott rifles.

Squawroot sticks up from the leaf litter of the forest floor amid these old fortifications. In early spring you may come across a colony of the plants that has been scattered about and looks like it has been trampled upon. Most likely this is the result of black bears feeding upon the plants, as the animals–just having emerged from their winter slumbers–find the squawroot to be some of the most delicious and abundant of plants growing at that time of year.

Keep left at 3.25 miles (a right leads to the Elk Ridge Trail) and descend, passing by crumbling stone walls where you might see a browsing deer. Merge onto an old, grassy woods road at 3.4 miles and descend at a more rapid rate, passing by the remains of a charcoal hearth at 3.9 miles. More than 50 hearths like this one were built on Maryland Heights during the first half of the 19th century. Each one was capable of transforming 30 to 50 cords of wood into approximately 1,800 bushels of charcoal within a 10-day period.

A vista that looks upstream along the Potomac River is passed at 4.1 miles. Keep right to continue to descend upon reaching the major intersection at 4.3 miles. To take a bit of a different route than you did on the way up, turn left onto the trail marked for the naval battery a few hundred yards later. Built in the spring of 1862 as Stonewall Jackson's forces were advancing northward in the Shenandoah Valley, the naval battery at 4.4 miles was the first Union fortification on Maryland Heights. The earthwork was added in mid-1863.

Continuing past the battery, rejoin the main route at 4.5 miles, turn left, and continue to descend. Turn right on paved Sandy Hook Road and return to your car at 5.1 miles.

Before leaving this area, you should walk over the bridge into Harpers Ferry to the historic district and/or hike along the C&O Canal Towpath to the east for about 3.5 miles to turn left and ascend 1 mile along the Appalachian Trail (see Hike 13) for a different view of the rivers from Weverton Cliffs.

13

Appalachian Trail

Total distance (one-way): 39.3 miles

Hiking time: 4 days

Vertical rise: 6,740 feet

Maps: USGS 7½' Harpers Ferry (WV/VA/MD); USGS 7½' Keedysville (MD/WV); USGS 7½' Middletown;USGS 7½' Myersville; USGS 7½' Smithsburg (MD/PA); Potomac Appalachian Trail Club Appalachian Trail Across Maryland maps 5 and 6

There may be no better introduction to backpacking and primitive camping than the Appalachian Trail through Maryland. Shelters and campsites are conveniently spaced so that you don't have to do marathon miles to find a place to spend the night. Deer, squirrels, chipmunks, and other animals are abundant, and wildlife spottings are frequent. The trail crosses numerous roads where help may be available in case of an emergency, and even though the route has a good feeling of isolation, there are four places where it is possible to make use of modern restroom facilities—and one spot that offers free hot showers!

The gentle terrain and great scenery are what makes this the perfect place to bring the kids for overnight hikes or to introduce friends to the pleasures of backpacking without the rigors of a more rugged topography. Other than a couple of climbs of less than 500 feet, the trail stays along the gently undulating crest of South Mountain for nearly the entire distance, neither losing nor gaining much in the way of elevation. On the rare occasions when winter cooperates by bringing in a blanket of snow deep enough to completely cover all of the rocks and boulders, the trail can be a great cross-country skiing or snowshoeing route.

In addition to its natural beauty, South Mountain has been the scene of numerous activities in American history. George Washington crossed the mountain a couple of decades before the colonies broke from England, the first national road coursed its way over it, and skirmishes of the Civil War were waged on its heights.

Trying to get away from the bugs in Pine Knob Shelter

Local lore states the mountain was used by escaped slaves on their flight to freedom as part of the Underground Railroad, and by some of John Brown's men following the failed raid on Harpers Ferry. On September 14, 1862, the battle of South Mountain raged from Crampton Gap to Fox Gap to Turners Gap. The Union prevailed as Lee retreated west to Antietam Creek. About 72 hours later, the two sides fought at that site during the single bloodiest day of the war.

This portion of the A.T.–well built, marked, and maintained by the Potomac Appalachian Trail Club–is heavily traveled, especially in May and June when the bulk of thru-hikers (people hiking the A.T.'s entire length) pass through. It is instructive and entertaining to be on the trail at this time, but no matter what month it is, carry a tent in the event a shelter becomes overcrowded. Water is available near the shelters and from several other sources. Be aware that camping and fires are only permitted at the shelters or in designated campsites. There are planned trail relocations in several heavily used places, but the route will not be significantly altered, nor will any great distance be added or subtracted.

The car shuttle to reach the two ends of this hike involves many miles of driving, so allow ample time. There are, of course, a number of different routes you could take to accomplish the shuttle, but to keep you on four-lane highways as much as possible and, hopefully, take the least amount of time, follow US 15 north from Frederick for close to 20 miles. Turn left near Thurmont onto MD 550, continuing to the entrance to Fort Richie, where, a short distance later, you bear left, cross under railroad tracks, and turn right onto Pen Mar Road. Enter Pennsylvania, cross over the railroad tracks, and leave one car in the small pullout on the right, making sure not to block the gate.

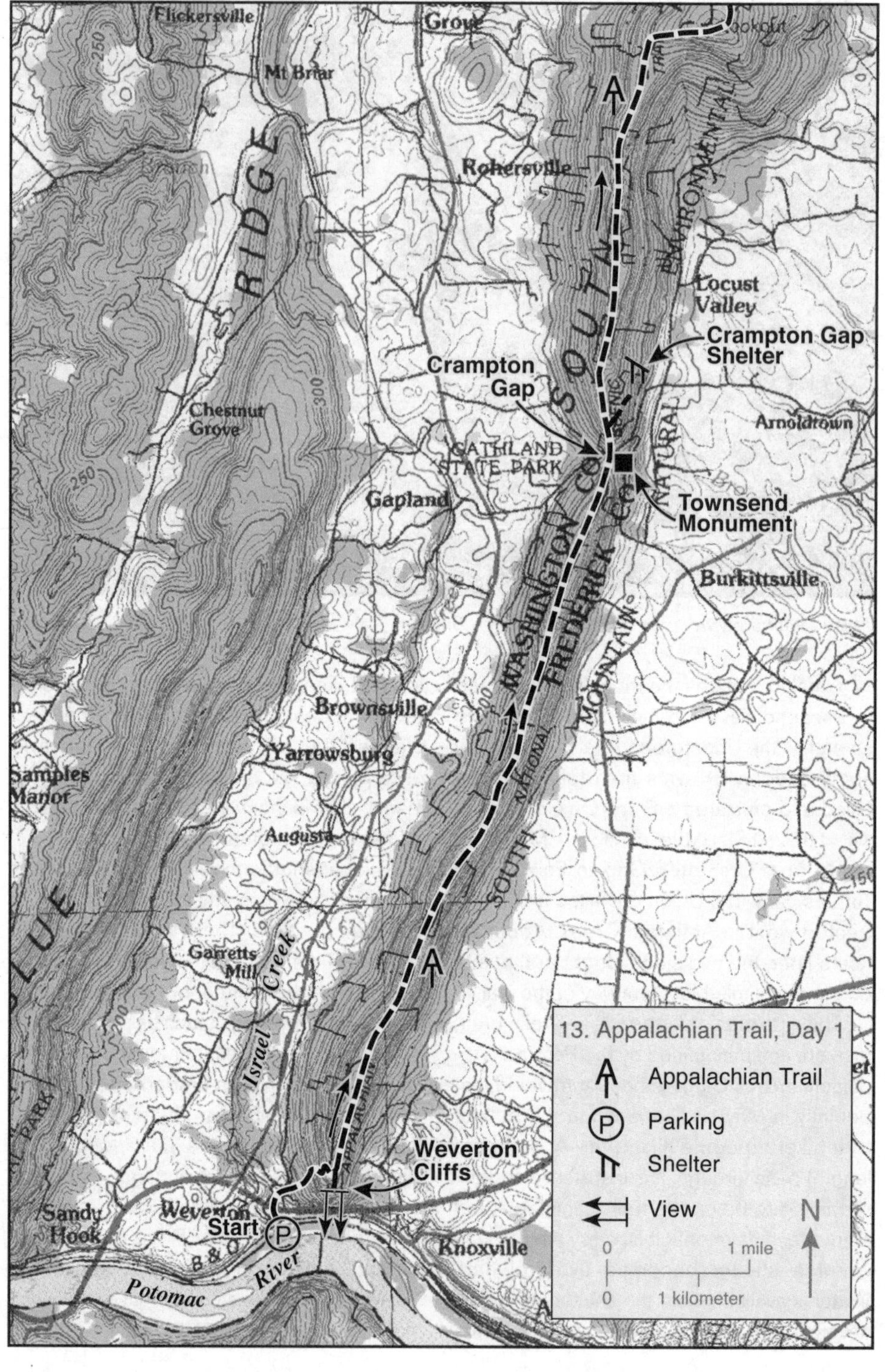

13. Appalachian Trail, Day 1
Appalachian Trail
Parking
Shelter
View
N
0
1 mile
0
1 kilometer
Crampton Gap Shelter
Crampton Gap
Townsend Monument
Weverton Cliffs
Start
Flickersville
Mt Briar
Rohersville
Locust Valley
Arnoldtown
Chestnut Grove
GATHLAND STATE PARK
Gapland
Burkittsville
Brownsville
Yarrowsburg
Samples Manor
Augusta
Garretts Mill
Israel Creek
Sandy Hook
Weverton
Knoxville
Potomac
River
B & O
RIDGE
WASHINGTON CO
FREDERICK CO
SOUTH MOUNTAIN

Drive the second car back to Frederick, where you want to take US 340 to the southwest. Approximately 15 miles later, make a left onto Keep Tryst Road. Keep straight when Sandy Hook Road comes in from the right. Start your journey by leaving the car at the designated area alongside the road.

DAY ONE

Total distance (one-way): 8.0 miles
Hiking time: 4 hours, 30 minutes
Vertical rise: 1,760 feet

Follow the A.T. northward as it enters the woods, cross under the US 340 overpass at 0.2 mile, and walk into a field being reclaimed by nature. Pass through a private lawn and cross Weverton Road at 0.4 mile to begin the nearly 500-foot ascent. Sixteen switchbacks through heavy forest deliver you to an intersection at 1.3 miles. Bear right onto the blue-blazed pathway to come to the Weverton Cliffs.

You will be treated to quite a number of great views while on the A.T., but this may be the most spectacular one, especially at sunrise. From your perch upon jagged, uplifted rocks you can gaze onto three states. Across the Potomac River are the cliffs of Short Hill Mountain in Virginia. Hundreds of feet directly below you, the flat land of the C&O Canal Towpath in Maryland drops down to rows of boulders that are outlined by the white, foamy water of the Potomac River. Upstream a couple of miles, the Shenandoah River empties into the Potomac, shaping the V-shaped piece of land where Harpers Ferry, West Virginia, stands.

Return to the A.T. and follow the white blazes along the eastern side of the ridgeline as the trail rises to the very crest of the mountain and proceeds with slight ups and downs. A short side trail at 3.4 miles leads to the Ed Garvey Shelter, built in 2001 in honor of one of the A.T.'s earliest thru-hikers and the author of *Appalachian Hiker.* The side trail to the left at 4.2 miles leads about 30 yards to a limited view to the west.

There may bit a bit of confusion about which way to go after passing over the clearing for a communication cable at 5.5 miles, so pay particular attention to the white blazes. Cross old Brownsville Gap Road at 5.6 miles, passing by a granite plaque dedicated in March 1976 to the memory of Glenn R. Gaveney, an ardent volunteer maintainer of this section of trail.

You might not wish to know this since you will be camped in the woods this evening, but the forest and mountainside just to the east of the trail in this area are where the 1999 movie *The Blair Witch Project* was filmed.

Beginning a gradual descent at 7.2 miles, pass by a trail to the right, which leads a short distance to the remains of trenches built as defenses during the Civil War. As you continue downhill, enter Crampton Gap and Gathland State Park and pass by stone Gath Hall and a restroom. Be sure to fill your water bottles here, as the spring at the shelter you are staying in this evening is unreliable. If the restroom is closed, you can obtain water (in season) from a hand pump next to the building.

The trail crosses MD 572 (Gapland Road) at 7.3 miles, but before proceeding, bear right a few feet to—as far as has been determined—the only monument in the world to war correspondents. Planned and built by George Alfred "Gath" Townsend, a journalist and columnist from 1866 to 1910, it memorializes more than 150 reporters and artists who covered the Civil War from both sides of the conflict. The off-balance monument contains a large Moorish arch below three smaller ones of Roman design. Taking the time to look at and read the dozens of inscriptions and mythological figures could take up much of an afternoon.

Walk through the stone wall on the north side of the road and ascend along the A.T. to enter the woods. Turn right onto the blue-blazed side trail at 7.7 miles to arrive at your home for the night–Crampton Gap Shelter, at 8 miles. Rather small when compared to shelters being constructed along the A.T. today, Crampton Gap was built by the Civilian Conservation Corps and has been a welcome sight for tired hikers since 1941.

DAY TWO

Total distance (one-way): 12.7 miles
Hiking time: 7 hours
Vertical rise: 1,900 feet

Return to the A.T. and continue northward, rising to the crest of the ridgeline to follow its small ups and downs. Be sure to keep to the left at 2.9 miles when the blue-blazed Bear Spring Cabin Trail comes in from the right. As the A.T. swings below the summit of 1,758-foot Lamb's Knoll, the quartzite cliffs of White Rocks look out across Catoctin Creek Valley, bordered by the long ridgeline of Catoctin Mountain to the east. (See Hikes 14, 15, 16, 17, and 18.)

After reaching the high point, make a descent of approximately a mile and cross a road at 4.7 miles. Unless you are in need of water, you can pass by the blue-blazed trail to the left at 5.2 miles, which descends about 400 yards to Rocky Run Shelter and a seasonal spring. Ascend.

Turn left onto an old woods road at 5.5 miles and descend gradually, passing under a utility line at 5.7 miles. The cleared right-of-way overlooks the rolling lands to the west and, on clear days, the urban sprawl of Hagerstown creeping eastward.

Cross paved Reno Monument Road just a few hundred yards west of Fox Gap at 6.1 miles. During the battle of South Mountain, when Federal forces were trying to break through the Confederate lines to continue their westward march, Union officers Maj. Gen. Jesse L. Reno and Brig. Gen. Samuel Garland were killed here. Future US president Rutherford B. Hayes was wounded during the fighting.

Continue northward through a forest of chestnut oak trees. Although they reach their largest size on moist, lowland sites, chestnut oaks adapt well to the dry, rocky soil of the ridgeline environments. In this harsher environment, the oaks–black, white, scarlet, chestnut, and others–become the dominant trees.

Thriving on open sunshine, oak trees are some of the first to reestablish themselves (from both seeds and stump sprouts) when a woodland has been destroyed by fire or cut for timber. Some of them, such as northern red oak, chestnut oak, and white oak, are also quite tolerant of shade. So, even if a sapling happens to have sprouted underneath a larger tree, it will probably survive long enough to take the place of the larger tree when it dies. Also, the leaves of a sapling are larger and less indented than those of mature oaks, which provide the younger tree with more surface area in which to gather nourishment from the sun.

Turn left onto a woods road at 6.5 miles and descend through woods dotted by the medium-height trunks of dogwood trees. With their early-spring flowers, colorful fruits, and deep red leaves in the fall, dogwoods are some of the most beautiful trees to be found in Maryland, but a disease of unknown origin is removing large numbers of them from the landscape. First discovered in the late 1970s in New York, dogwood anthracnose has now spread throughout most of the Appalachians. By breaking down the tree's living tissues, the fungal disease begins in the lower branches and moves upward. The first signs of infection are tan blotches and purple-rimmed spots on leaves. Moving

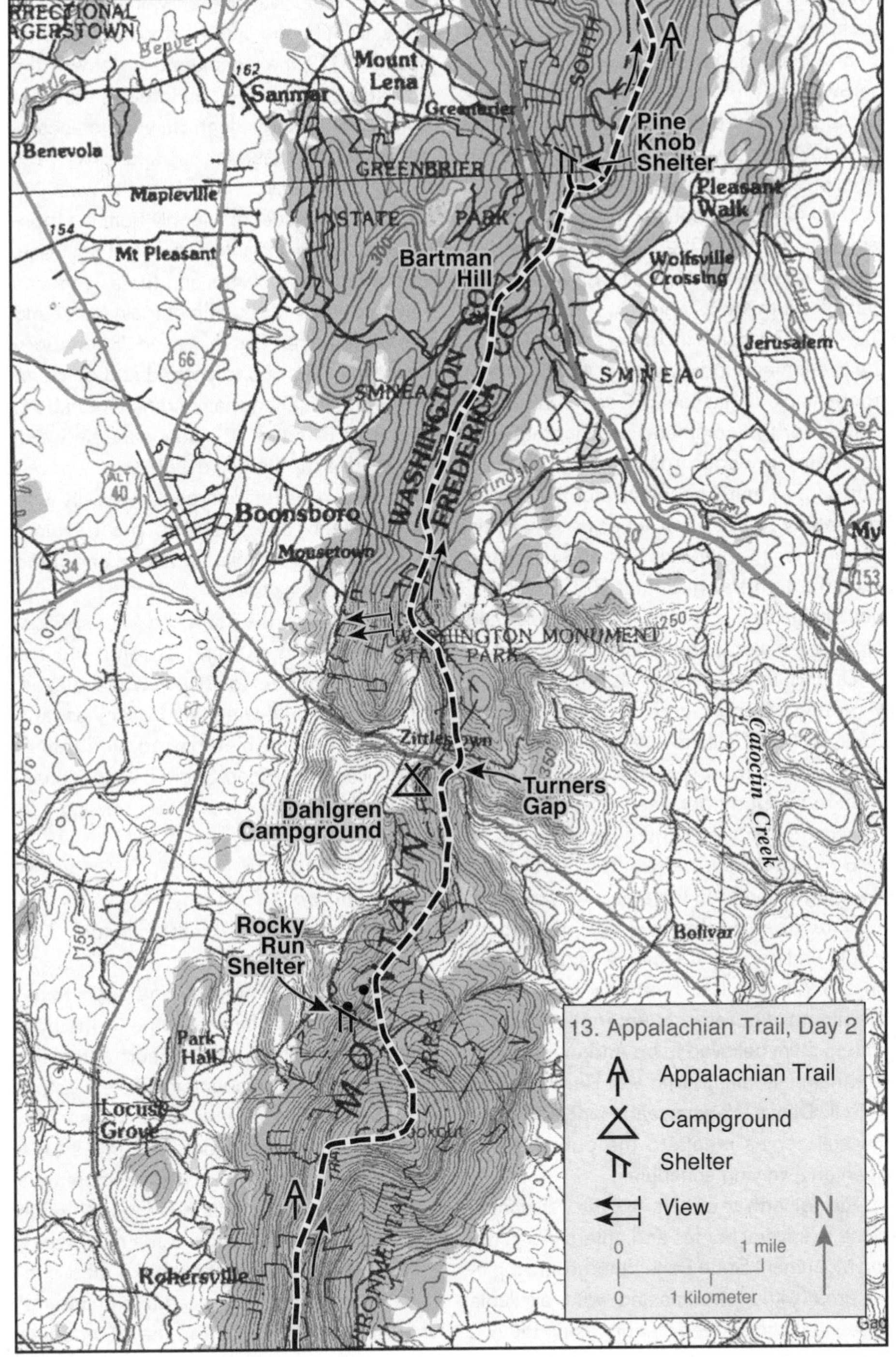

Pine
Knob
Shelter
Bartman
Hill
Turners
Gap
Dahlgren
Campground
Rocky
Run
Shelter
13. Appalachian Trail, Day 2
Appalachian Trail
Campground
Shelter
View
N
0
1 mile
0
1 kilometer
Mount
Lena
Sanmar
Benevola
Mapleville
Mt Pleasant
GREENBRIER
STATE
PARK
Pleasant
Walk
Wolfsville
Crossing
Jerusalem
Boonsboro
Mousetown
WASHINGTON CO
FREDERICK CO
WASHINGTON MONUMENT
STATE PARK
Zittlestown
Catoctin Creek
Bolivar
Park
Hall
Locust
Grove
Rohersville

swiftly into the twigs, branches, and then the trunk, the disease can kill a tree in a shaded area within two to five years.

Swing left into the Dahlgren Back Pack Campground at 6.9 miles. Drop your heavy load, take a break, and head into the restroom building to take a free hot shower (April through October), courtesy of South Mountain State Park and the State of Maryland.

Resume the hike by following the white blazes northward, and cross paved US Alt.-40 at 7.1 miles in Turners Gap. During the French and Indian War in 1755, British troops (including a young George Washington) under the command of General Braddock built a wagon road through Turners Gap as they marched westward. Encountering enemy forces near what is now Pittsburgh, they met with defeat and retreated back through the gap. In 1806, the route was designated part of the national road and became a major thoroughfare to the west.

During the Civil War battle of South Mountain, forces under Union general George B. McClellan were met and delayed by Southern troops in Turners Gap long enough for Confederates under Stonewall Jackson to capture Harpers Ferry.

Built decades before Braddock and Washington entered the area and more than a century before the Civil War, the South Mountain Inn (only 0.1 mile west of the A.T. on US Alt.-40) has hosted a long list of prominent figures of American history, among them believed to be Andrew Jackson, Abraham Lincoln, Martin Van Buren, James K. Polk, Daniel Webster, and Henry Clay. The inn still serves meals to the public but is open on a varying schedule.

Rising north of US Alt.-40, the trail comes close to several homes and enters Washington Monument State Park. Emerge into a picnic area (with restrooms and water available in season) and ascend steadily along the A.T. to come to the Washington Monument at 9.1 miles. Built by the citizens of nearby Boonsboro in 1827, the jug-shaped tower was the first structure to be completed in honor of America's first president. Be sure to ascend the inside staircase for a grand view of the rolling Maryland countryside to the west.

The A.T. descends steeply from the monument, passes under a utility line at 9.4 miles, and, with several twists and turns, works its way through a forest of mountain laurel and chestnut oaks. Cross paved Boonsboro Road at 11.3 miles to ascend and descend Bartman Hill. Diagonally cross Boonsboro Mountain Road at 12 miles, pass between two houses, and cross over I-70 on a paved footbridge. A favorite thru-hiker activity is to sit on the bridge, wave to the travelers whizzing by at 70 miles an hour, and try to get them to honk back.

Turn left from the north end of the bridge, pass under US 40, and ascend into the woods. Continue to follow white blazes, cross under utility lines at 12.5 miles, and turn left onto the blue-blazed side trail at 12.6 miles. Pine Knob Shelter, your destination for the evening, is 500 feet beyond.

DAY THREE

Total distance (one-way): 8.4 miles
Hiking time: 4 hours, 30 minutes
Vertical rise: 1,400 feet

Return to the A.T., turn left, and begin to ascend, steeply in places. Come to the high point at 0.5 mile and descend along the eastern side of the mountain. Make a detour onto the blue-blazed trail at 1.8 miles to descend to Annapolis Rock at 2 miles for a great view to the west and of the impressive escarpment of rock cliffs running both north and south along the edge of the mountain.

Retrace your steps to the A.T. and continue northward to 3.2 miles to a number of short trails that head left to the 180-degree

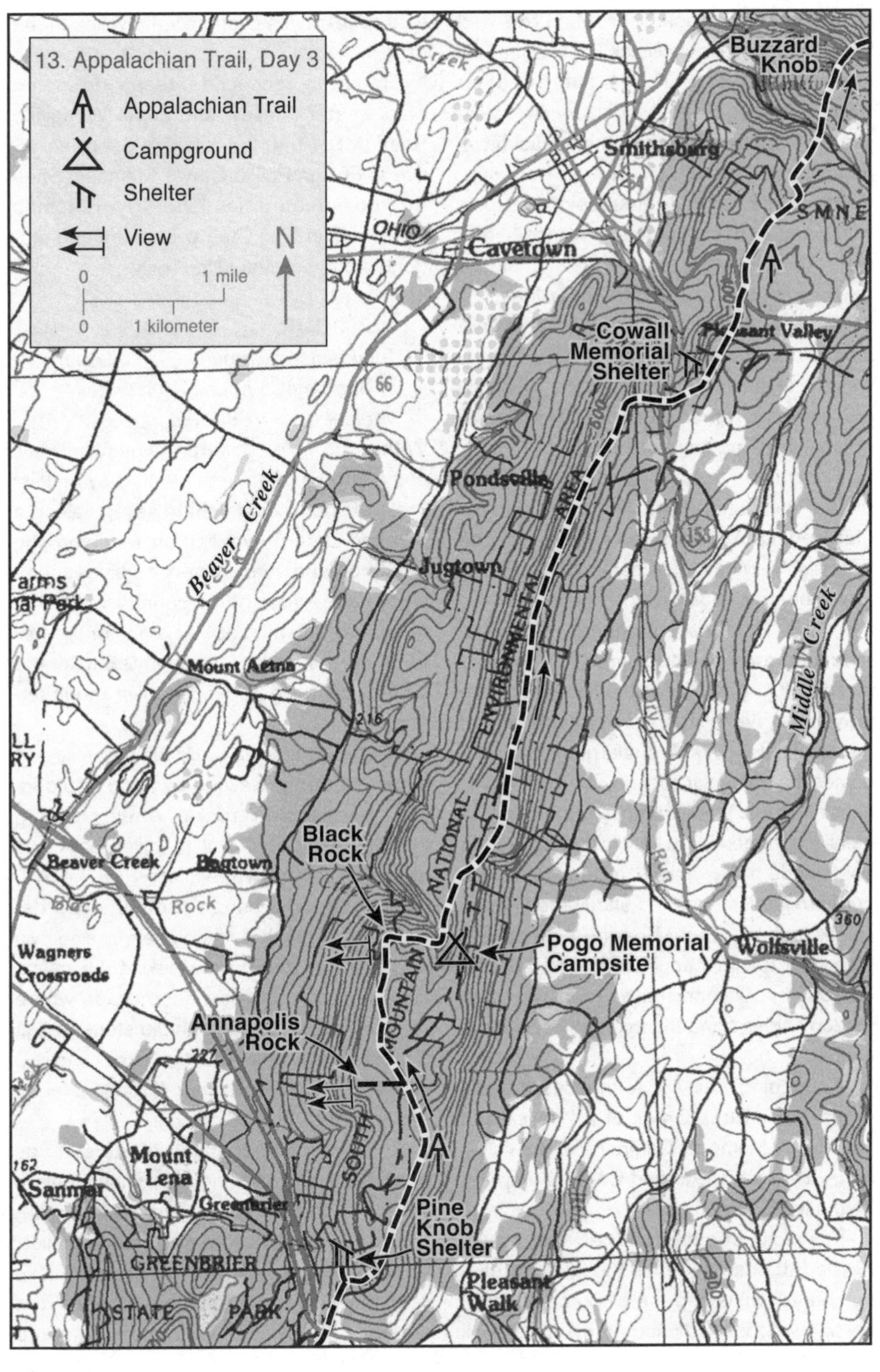
13. Appalachian Trail, Day 3
Appalachian Trail
Campground
Shelter
View
N
0
1 mile
0
1 kilometer
Buzzard Knob
Smithsburg
Cavetown
OHIO
Cowall Memorial Shelter
Pleasant Valley
Pondsville
Jugtown
Beaver Creek
Mount Aetna
SOUTH MOUNTAIN NATIONAL ENVIRONMENTAL AREA
Middle Creek
Black Rock
Pogo Memorial Campsite
Wolfsville
Wagners Crossroads
Annapolis Rock
Mount Lena
Sanmar
Greenbrier
Pine Knob Shelter
GREENBRIER STATE PARK
Pleasant Walk

vista from Black Rock Cliffs. More exposed than Annapolis Rock, Black Rock Cliffs feel much windier as well. This and the other overlooks along South Mountain make great seats from which to watch the annual hawk migration in the fall. Heated air from sun-warmed cliffs and rock outcroppings couples with warm air rising from the lowlands to create forceful drafts, or thermals, that the hawks use to soar upward. In addition, by gliding near the crest of the ridges, they are able to take advantage of the northwesterly winds that strike the Appalachians where air currents are forced across the mountain crests, providing more uplift.

Sometimes as early as mid-August, ospreys, American kestrels, and a few bald eagles begin the procession southward. The migration begins in earnest in the middle of September as broad-winged hawks take to the skies. Peak daily sightings of several thousand are not uncommon. In the early weeks of October, peregrine falcons join the movement, while later in the month, one of the smallest hawks, the sharp-shinned, becomes the dominant migrant. Joining the procession at this time are the larger but less in number Cooper's hawks. Making use of the cold winds of November, red-tailed hawks, northern harriers, and red-shouldered hawks zip by leafless trees. Soaring over an Appalachian Trail that could be covered by December snows, northern goshawks and golden eagles bring the migratory season to a close.

Continuing your A.T. journey northward, cross Black Rock Creek at 3.7 miles and pass Pogo Memorial Campsite at 3.9 miles. It may be possible to find water at a spring on the left side of the trail.

Pay close attention to the white blazes beyond the campsite, as the A.T. makes a number of twists and turns on and off intersecting woods roads and pathways. A rock field at 6.1 miles overlooks the valley to the east.

Begin to descend–steeply in some places–at 7.6 miles, and cross Wolfsville Road (MD 17) at 8.3 miles. At 8.4 miles, arrive at Ensign Phillip Cowall Memorial Shelter, constructed in 1999 by Potomac Appalachian Trail Club volunteers and students from Gallaudet University.

DAY FOUR

Total distance (one-way): 10.2 miles
Hiking time: 5 hours, 45 minutes
Vertical rise: 1,680 feet

Within 0.5 mile of starting your final day, come into an open area created by a utility line and soon swing right to ascend along a pipeline right-of-way. Upon reaching the height of land, make a very quick descent, enjoying the vista of the countryside to the north. Pay attention as you drop, for the trail turns right into the woods at 0.8 mile and continues its steep descent over rough terrain.

Step over a small water run at 1 mile and ascend steeply, walking by large boulders and overhanging rocks. After crossing Foxville Road (MD 77) at 1.2 miles, pay close attention to the white blazes as the A.T. twists and turns before another steep descent at 2.4 miles. Ascend after passing by a spring and crossing a creek at 2.6 miles. Hemlock trees provide deep shade where the trail passes through an old stone wall at 3 miles. Cross Little Antietam Creek and MD 491 at 3.4 miles to ascend through a forest of hardwoods and evergreens.

To experience as much of the state as possible, and to visit one more shelter before the hike comes to an end, turn left and descend the blue-blazed pathway at 4.3 miles. Nestled in a glen with hillsides rising above it is the Devils Racecourse Shelter and spring at 4.6 miles. Although you can drop

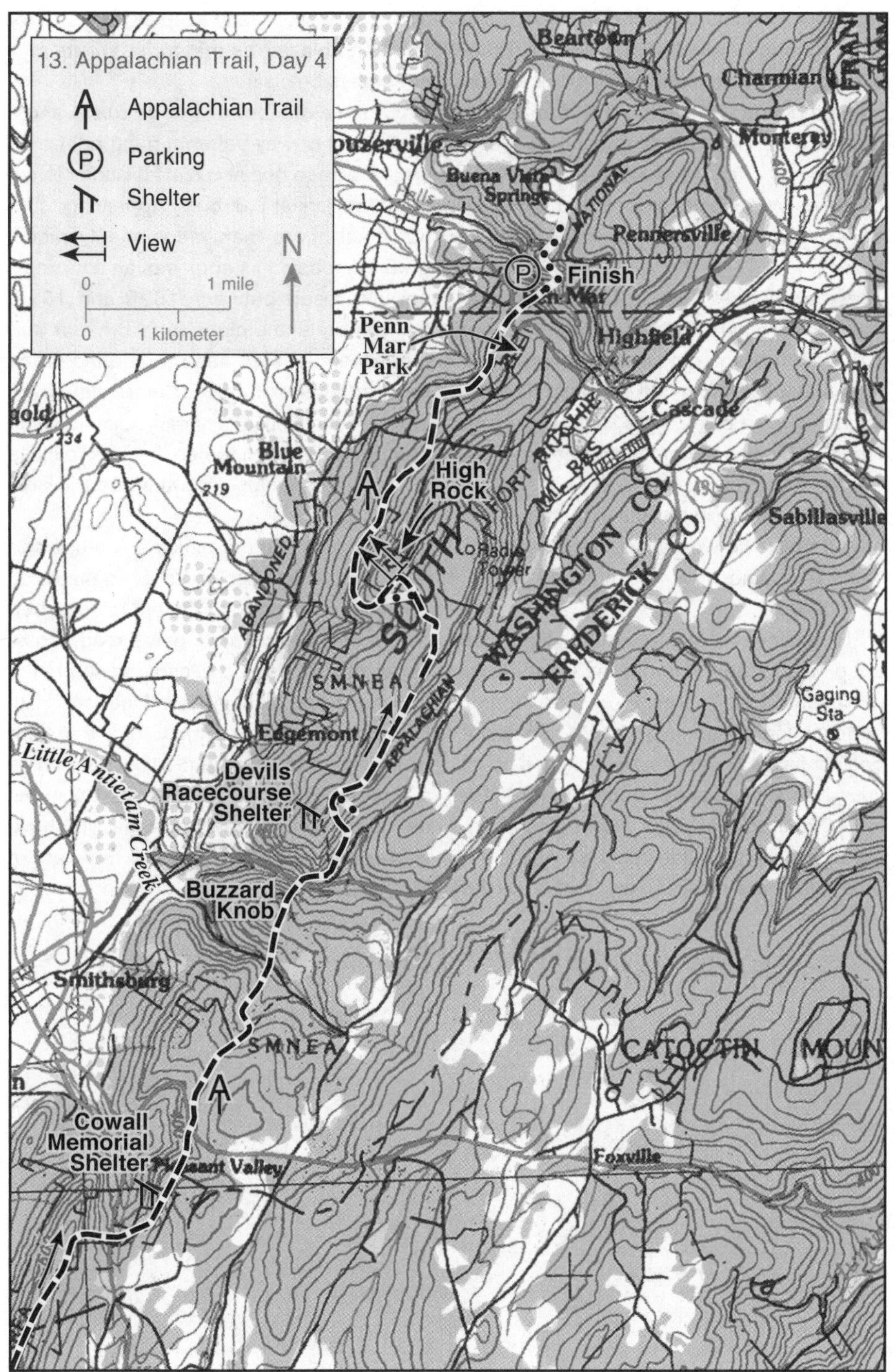
13. Appalachian Trail, Day 4
Appalachian Trail
Parking
Shelter
View
N
0 1 mile
0 1 kilometer
Beartown
Charmian
Monterey
Buena Vista Springs
Pennersville
Finish
Penn Mar Park
Highfield
Cascade
Blue Mountain
High Rock
Sabillasville
Radio Tower
WASHINGTON CO
FREDERICK CO
SMNEA
Edgemont
Little Antietam Creek
Devils Racecourse Shelter
Buzzard Knob
Smithsburg
CATOCTIN MOUN
Gaging Sta
Cowall Memorial Shelter
Foxville

your pack, don't stop descending here. Continue for another 500 feet to Devils Racecourse, a large and interesting boulder field created during the last Ice Age. Large rock sheets were broken into pieces as water seeped into cracks and froze. The resulting boulders were moved around and on top of each other by the upward force of frost heave.

Ascend back to the A.T. and continue northward, reaching the high point (about 1,900 feet) of the day on the western side of Quirauk Mountain, at 6.1 miles. Keep to the right on the blue-blazed High Rock Loop Trail at 6.8 miles to come to a parking area, the stone foundation of a former observation pavilion, a hang-gliding launch platform, and an Olympian view onto Hagerstown Valley. The hike is almost over, so tarry as long you as you like.

To resume walking, follow the High Rock Loop Trail to the left, enter the woods, and rejoin the A.T. at 7 miles. From here the trail begins a long descent across a number of boulder fields. For the next 30 minutes or so, your boots will rarely touch flat ground; rather, your ankles will be twisting and turning as you slip and slide from one rock to the other. Use extra caution if the stones are the slightest bit moist, and keep close watch for the white blazes, as the correct route may not always be clear.

Cross a number of woods roads and a utility right-of-way before turning right onto an old railroad bed at 9.6 miles and entering Pen Mar Park at 9.8 miles. Appearing to be not much more than a community picnic grounds today, this spot was an amazingly popular resort between 1890 and 1920. Seven hotels and close to 100 guest cottages were located nearby, catering to the daily crowds of 5,000 or more that were drawn to the amusement park. Gas rationing during World War II forced the park to close in 1943. Restrooms and water are available in season.

After enjoying the park's amenities and the view of Hagerstown Valley to the west, continue northward on the old railroad bed before turning left onto a gravel road, crossing some railroad tracks, and entering Pennsylvania at the Mason-Dixon Line (see Hike 8 for more information). Cross Pen Mar Road, return to your shuttled car, and come to the end of your A.T. journey at 10.2 miles, delighting in the knowledge that you have walked the complete height of the state of Maryland.

II Capital Region

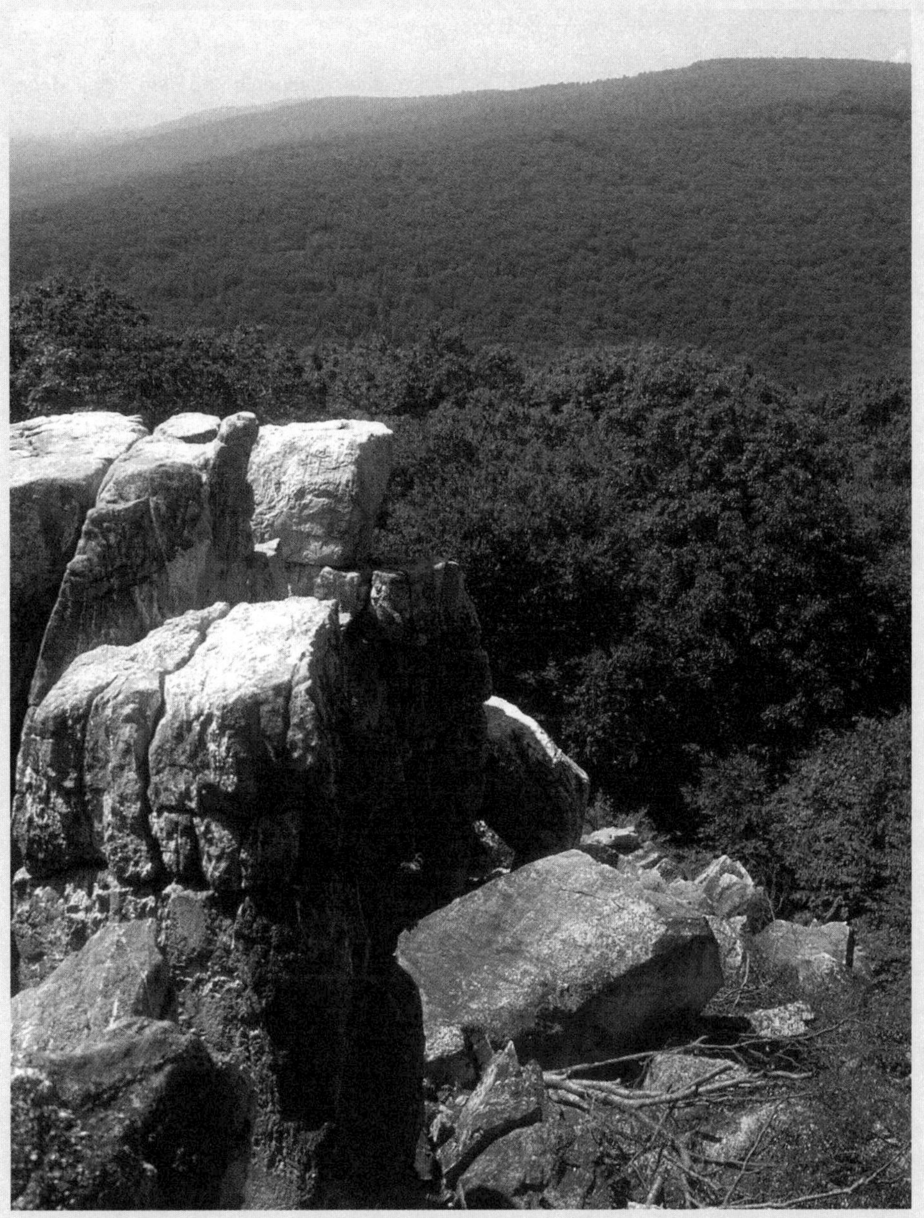

14

Catoctin Mountain

Total distance (one-way): 27.2 miles

Hiking time: 2 days

Vertical rise: 4,600 feet

Maps: USGS 7½' Frederick; USGS 7½' Catoctin Furnace; USGS 7½' Blue Ridge Summit (MD/PA)

The eastern rampart of the Blue Ridge Mountains, Catoctin Mountain stretches almost 40 miles from southern Pennsylvania, across Maryland, and into the northern portion of Virginia. Geologists believe the mountain once attained heights comparable to those of the Andes Mountains in South America, but the power of wind and water over the course of millions of years has eroded Catoctin into a much lower ridgeline. Today, its high point is only about 1,900 feet above sea level, while its low point is a mere 500 feet. The mountain's numerous rock outcroppings are a bit more resistant to erosion, being composed of Catoctin greenstone that developed from lava flows 600 million years ago.

The mountain's name is a derivation of *Kittocton,* from an Algonquian tribe of Native Americans that once lived near the Potomac River. Linguists believe the word translates to "land of the big mountain" or "land of the white-tailed deer."

Public lands occupy much of the mountain north of Frederick, and in the late 1970s and early 1980s volunteers from the Potomac Appalachian Trail Club built several miles of pathways to link up with existing trails to create the 26-mile Catoctin Trail. There are a few places where the trail comes close to roads and signs of civilization, but for the most part it provides a great sense of isolation. Be aware that, in places, the route may be marked with a number of different-colored paint blazes; always follow the blue blazes. Although backcountry camping is not permitted anywhere along its route, you can stay in the Manor Area Campground in Cunningham Falls State Park, making it possible to traverse the trail during a two-day outing.

This is a one-way hike, so a car shuttle involving several miles of driving will be necessary. Drive northward from Frederick on US 15 for close to 20 miles and turn west onto MD 77 near Thurmont. Stop in at the Catoctin Park Visitor Center 4 miles later to inform personnel that you will be leaving an automobile overnight at the parking area outside Owens Creek Campground, across from the old sawmill. (The northern terminus of the Catoctin Trail is actually 2 miles from there on Mount Zion Road, but leaving a car overnight at that point is not recommended.)

Drive Park Central Road northward from the visitors center, following its twists and turns through the park and past several trailheads (see Hike 17). Several miles later, cross Manahan Road, soon making a right turn onto Foxville-Deerfield Road. About a mile later, turn left onto Owens Creek Campground Road to leave one car at the sawmill parking area.

Return to the visitors center and turn right onto MD 77 for just a few yards to make a left onto Catoctin Hollow Road. Passing by the entrance road to the William Houck Area of Cunningham Falls State Park (see Hike 16), keep to the right onto Mink Farm Road–which soon becomes Tower Road–in about 2 miles. Close to 2 miles later, when Tower Road comes to an end, bear right onto Gambrill Park Road. Stay on this route for nearly 10 miles and turn right into the Rock Run Area of Gambrill State Park. Inform park personnel you will be leaving the car overnight. (The Catoctin Trail actually begins at a parking lot along Gambrill Park Road, but overnight parking is not permitted there.)

(A shuttle option that has worked well for a number of hikers is to set up camp and leave one car at the Manor Area of Cunningham Falls State Park–accessible from US 15–before driving to the beginning of the hike in Gambrill State Park. The next morning you can shuttle a car to Owens Creek Campground, where you will end the hike. Using this option allows you to carry only a day pack for both days of hiking.)

DAY ONE

Total distance (one-way): 17.6 miles
Hiking time: 10 hours
Vertical rise: 2,480 feet

From the day-use parking lot in the Rock Run Area of Gambrill State Park, walk the paved road into the campground, keeping right at all intersections. As this main road begins to curve to the left at about 0.2 mile, turn right between two campsites and walk onto the connector path to the Red Trail. A few feet later, turn right onto the Red Trail and begin a gradual rise as you swing around High Knob and cross the paved Gambrill Park Road at 0.5 mile. Coming close to the park's eastern boundary, continue to rise, and arrive at an intersection at 0.9 mile.

The Red Trail continues to the left; you want to bear right to follow the blue blazes of the Catoctin Trail through a forest of hickory. In addition to hickory, chestnut oak, black birch, and sugar maples are found along the ridgeline and upper slopes, while you will walk beside wild cherry, sassafras, hemlock, black locust, ash, yellow poplar, and white oak in the valleys or along creeks.

Avoid the unwanted trail to the right at 1.2 miles and descend quickly on a rocky pathway. A portion of the green-blazed trail comes in from the left at 1.5 miles, but you need to keep right on the pathway marked by blue, black, and green blazes.

Be alert at 1.7 miles, as the trail swings off the old road you have been following and ascends steeply. Come to a four-way intersection at 2.1 miles. An old, unmarked trail

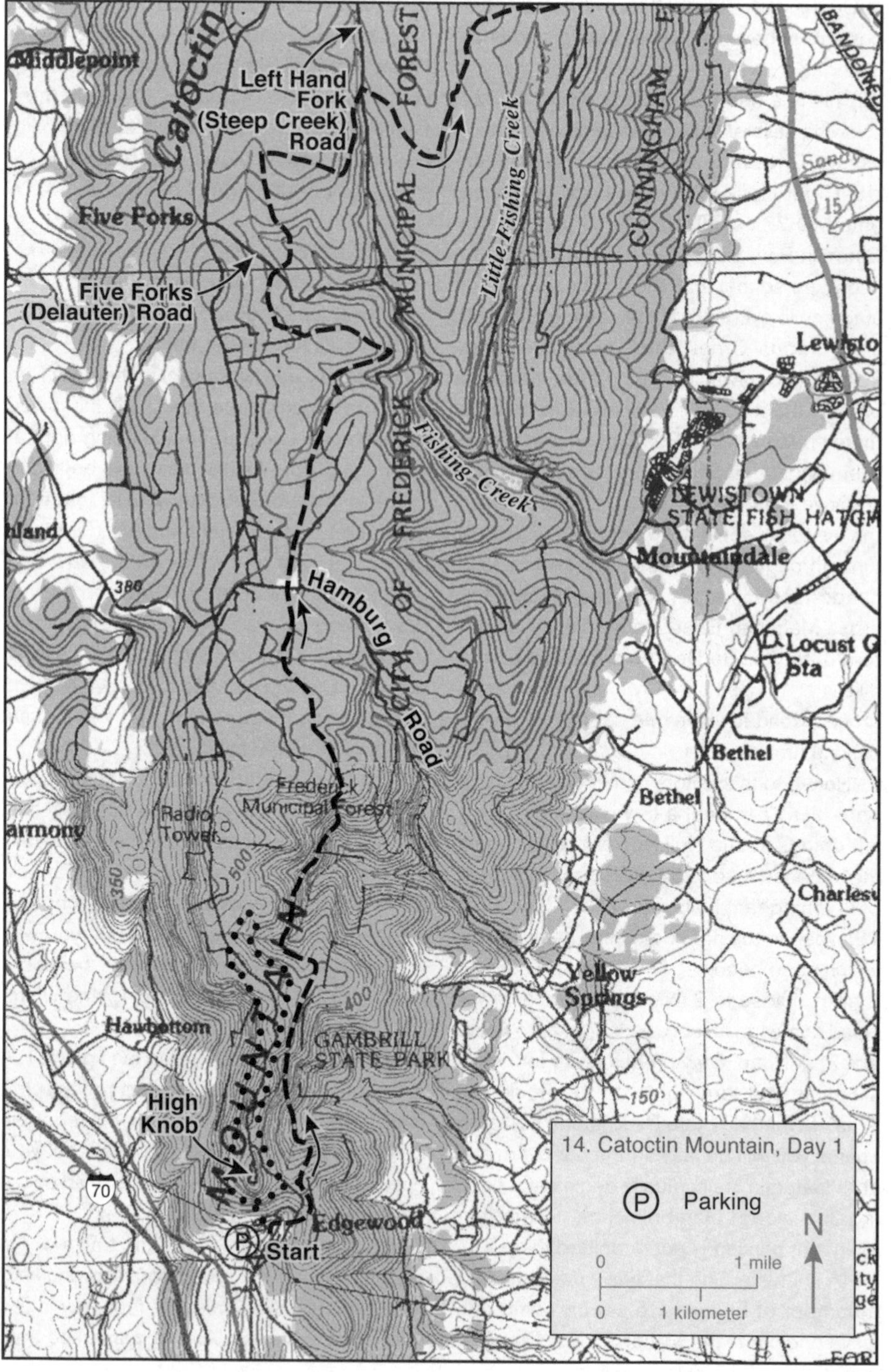

Middlepoint
Catoctin
Left Hand Fork (Steep Creek) Road
FOREST
MUNICIPAL
Little Fishing Creek
CUNNINGHAM
Five Forks
Five Forks (Delauter) Road
15
Lewistown
FREDERICK
Fishing Creek
LEWISTOWN STATE FISH HATCHERY
Mountaindale
OF
CITY
Hamburg Road
Locust Grove Sta
380
Bethel
Frederick Municipal Forest
Radio Tower
Harmony
500
350
Charlesville
MOUNTAIN
400
Yellow Springs
Hamburg
GAMBRILL STATE PARK
150
High Knob
70
Edgewood
Start
14. Catoctin Mountain, Day 1
Parking
N
0
1 mile
0
1 kilometer

bears right, while the green- and black-blazed trail bears left; continue straight and rise through a forest of hickory on blue-blazed Catoctin Trail.

A yellow-blazed pathway comes in from the left at 2.4 miles; keep right. Bear right onto a dirt road at 2.6 miles (yellow blazes head left), only to make a left onto the blue-blazed pathway a few hundred feet later. (Remember, always follow the blue blazes at any intersection.) Mountain laurel and blueberry bushes are a large part of the undergrowth as you descend and negotiate a rock field at 2.9 miles.

Cross a tributary of Tuscarora Creek at 3.1 miles and enter the Frederick City Watershed Area. Hunting is permitted throughout the area. The usual seasons run from September 15 to January 31 and from April 15 to May 20. If you hike here anytime around these dates, be alert and wear blaze orange. (Hunting is prohibited on Sunday.) Cross a stream at 3.3 miles and at 3.4 miles. The *drink-your-tea* song of towhees is often heard breaking the silence of the woods. You might spot one on the ground, scratching through the forest litter in search of a meal. The males have a black head and back, white belly, and patches of brownish red on their sides; females are similar but are dark tan where the males are black. Cross a stream at 3.6 miles.

Pass by an unmarked trail to the right at 3.8 miles and keep descending, but be alert just a few hundred feet later. The blue-blazed Catoctin Trail makes a sudden hard left turn and ascends; do not continue to the right. You must be alert again in an additional 300 feet. The route you need to follow makes a right turn to continue the ascent, steeply at times; do not go left.

Reach the top of the ridge at 4.7 miles, descending to cross a woods road at 4.8 miles and gradually ascending through a pine plantation. At 6 miles, pass by a couple of small ponds constructed to improve the quality of water within the watershed area and provide habitat enhancement for wildlife. Turn right onto a woods road and soon cross a water run, bearing left onto a pathway.

Cross Hamburg Road at 6.6 miles and descend. The deep crimson leaves of the dogwood trees add color to an early-fall forest. The wood of this tree is so hard that it has been used for mallets, pulleys, and industrial spools. Native Americans made a dye from the roots and used the dogwood's bark in the treatment of malaria.

Now following woods roads, you will be coming to a number of intersections, so be alert to follow the blue blazes. Turn right at 7.5 miles, but within a few steps be sure to veer left. The small pond on the left has a few fish and makes for a restful break spot. Come to a T intersection at 7.7 miles and turn left downhill, soon passing by another pond. Swing left at the Y intersection at 8 miles to pass by a large pond on the right. The impressive three-trunked poplar nearby probably sprouted from the stump of a single-trunked poplar harvested for lumber.

Sassafras borders the roads where another T intersection at 8.2 miles requires a right turn. Expect to run into many mountain bikers in this area. Be alert at 8.6 miles, as the road you have been following continues to the right downhill; you need to make a left and follow the route uphill to the top of a knob, where you begin to descend at 8.9 miles.

Merge right onto a woods road at 9.5 miles. Passing by a private residence at 9.7 miles, turn right onto Five Forks Road (some maps identify it as Delauter Road) before turning left to descend into the woods. Pass by a small pond at 10.1 miles, bear right, then bear left to ascend where mountain laurel, blueberry bushes, and other undergrowth may be overtaking the pathway. Whereas blueberries are enjoyed by many woodland creatures, some studies conducted by biologists indicate that blue-berries can account for 25 percent of everything a black bear may eat during the summer months.

Come to a T intersection at 10.8 miles and turn right; make another right 500 feet later at the next intersection. A trail comes in from the left at 11 miles; keep right and descend. A free-flowing spring next to the trail at 11.9 miles could be used to replenish your water supply. Turn right when you come to the T intersection at 12 miles. Cross Left Hand Fork Road (shown on some maps as Steep Creek Road) diagonally to the right to follow a gated road back into the woods, and level out after a short ascent.

There is another T intersection at 12.8 miles; turn left and descend. The sound of your approach may cause frogs to leap into the small pond on the right at 13.6 miles. Although they have well-developed tails that are their exclusive means of movement as tadpoles, frogs and toads can be distinguished from other amphibians by the absence of a tail in the adult stage. Scientists speculate that the tails disappear as frogs and toads mature because they would get in the way of their large hind legs, which are designed for leaping and hopping. Frogs may be differentiated from toads by (generally) longer legs, smoother skin, and greater swimming abilities. Toads are usually plumper than frogs, and they hop more than leap. In addition, their conspicuous warts secrete chemicals that are poisonous to predators.

Jewelweed lines the trail as you come to a pond on the left at 14 miles, which has cardinal flower growing along its banks. Hummingbirds are this plant's main pollinators, as their bills are perfectly suited to reach the nectar located at the end of the flower tube–

Copperhead and rattlesnake

which is too narrow and too long for most insects to reach into. In addition to propagating itself by seeds, the cardinal flower can send out little shoots that rise above the ground as a small cluster of leaves. The following year, the small shoots develop into mature flowering plants and send out their own shoots. This is why, when you are lucky enough to find one, you will probably find a whole colony of the flowers.

Cross Right Hand Fork Road at 14.2 miles and come into a clearing where several routes converge. Be sure to take the one marked with blue blazes, which continues more or less straight ahead.

A viewpoint on the right side of the trail at 14.4 miles looks eastward onto the rolling piedmont farmlands of Frederick County. The small bodies of water almost directly below are part of the Lewistown State Fish Hatchery. Continuing your northward journey, pay close attention to the blue blazes where the trail makes several turns at intersections as you descend, steeply at times: Keep right at 14.7 miles; left at 14.9 miles; right at 15.1 miles; right at 15.5 miles; right at 15.6 miles; right at 15.7 miles; and left at 16.1 miles.

A woods road comes in from the right at 16.4 miles; keep left. Just about the time you can make out a paved road a few feet below you at 16.6 miles, turn left onto the pathway and cross Catoctin Hollow Road about 50 yards later.

Descend to ford Little Hunting Creek, whose extensive populations of brown, brook, and rainbow trout make it popular with anglers. (Although some rocks are strategically placed, this can be a precarious stream crossing–especially when it has been raining. If the water is too high, return to Catoctin Hollow Road and follow it to US 15. Turn left onto 15 for approximately 325 feet to turn left into the Manor Picnic Area and Campground. Continue to the campground, set up your tent, and resume the hike in the morning, following the Day 2 itinerary.)

After crossing Little Hunting Creek, begin an ascent on a rocky and barely defined pathway, coming to an intersection at 17.1 miles, where you need to turn right and descend along the yellow-blazed Bob's Hill Trail. Bear left onto Manor Area Road and walk into the campground at 17.6 miles. Pick your site, set up the tent, and go enjoy a well-deserved hot shower before cooking an evening meal.

DAY TWO

Total distance (one-way): 9.6 miles
Hiking time: 5 hours, 45 minutes
Vertical rise: 2,120 feet

Retrace your steps back to the intersection with the Catoctin Trail at 0.5 mile. Bear right and ascend–steeply in places–along a woods road marked by blue and yellow blazes. The ascent levels out for a short distance before resuming the steep climb at 1.8 miles.

Come to the Bob's Hill Overlook Trails at 1.9 miles. Eschewing the one to the right, whose view is somewhat obscured by vegetation, take the pathway left for 100 yards to the viewpoint. The panorama to the south reveals much of the topography you walked across yesterday, as well as the deep cleft in the landscape created by the erosive action of Little Hunting Creek.

Return to the Catoctin Trail, turn left, and continue, with only minor ups and downs. The white blossoms of mountain laurel make this a very attractive walk in late May and early June. Yellow-blazed Cat Rock Trail comes in from the right at 3.1 miles; keep left.

Be alert at 3.2 miles. The route makes a sudden right onto a much rougher and rockier treadway. There is a T intersection at 3.8 miles; turn left and continue to descend.

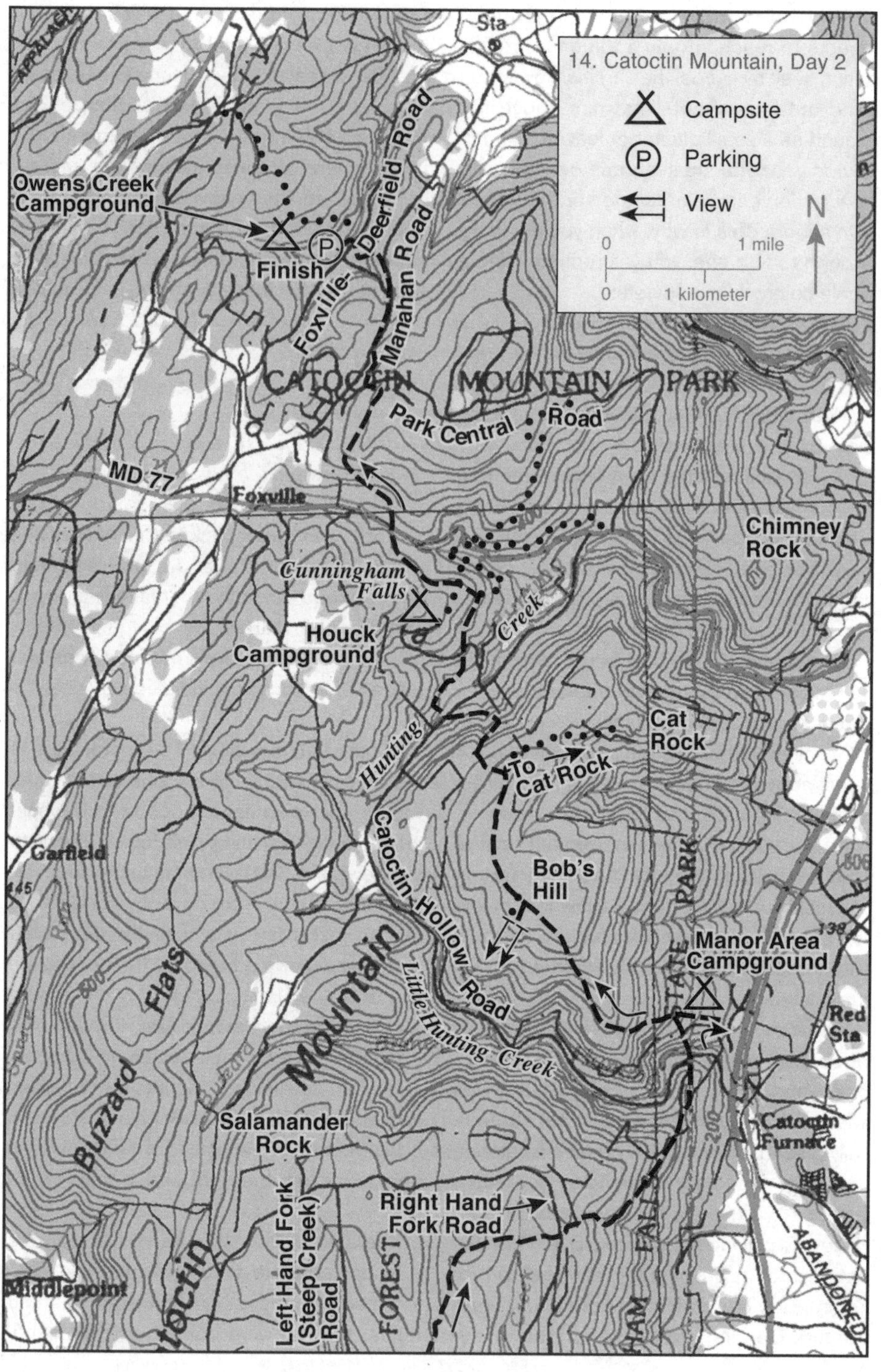
14. Catoctin Mountain, Day 2
Campsite
Parking
View
N
0
1 mile
0
1 kilometer
Owens Creek
Campground
Finish
Foxville-
Deerfield Road
Manahan Road
CATOCTIN MOUNTAIN PARK
Park Central Road
MD 77
Foxville
Chimney
Rock
Cunningham
Falls
Houck
Campground
Creek
Hunting
Cat
Rock
To
Cat Rock
Catoctin Hollow Road
Garfield
Bob's
Hill
Mountain
Little Hunting Creek
Flats
Buzzard
Manor Area
Campground
Red
Sta
Catoctin
Furnace
Salamander
Rock
Right Hand
Fork Road
Left Hand Fork
(Steep Creek)
Road
FOREST
Middlepoint
ABANDONED
PARK
FALLS
Sta

Bear right at 4 miles as the descent steepens and passes over an even rockier area at 4.3 miles.

You might not encounter any here, but terrain such as this is a favorite home for copperheads and timber rattlesnakes, the only two venomous snakes found in Maryland. Although there are variations, the copperhead's tan body has unique darker-colored, hourglass-shaped markings. Basking during the day in the spring and fall and having a tendency to become nocturnal in warm summer temperatures, they can be well camouflaged by leaf litter on the forest floor. Timber rattlesnakes have large, heavy bodies, typically with dark blotches in the front that become fused to form crossbands in the back. Color can range widely from yellow to pinkish gray to black, but the tail is almost always black. In some populations, the identifying features fade and the body color gets darker as the snake matures, making them almost look like black racer snakes. Of course, no matter what color, rattlesnakes will rattle when threatened.

Cross paved Catoctin Hollow Road at 5 miles, and cross Hauver Branch. Passing under a utility line at 5.5 miles, cross Houck Campground Road (the camp store and restrooms are approximately 0.5 mile to the left), take the trail up the road bank, and soon rise steeply.

Amid hemlock trees and giant boulders, the Catoctin Trail stays to the left when you encounter the Cunningham Falls Trail coming in from the right at 6.1 miles. However, you should seriously consider taking this optional side jaunt (see Hike 16). The Cunningham Falls Cliff Trail (which also could lead you to the falls) comes in from the right at 6.3 miles.

Keep to the left at the 6.5-mile and the 6.7-mile intersections. Watching for speeding cars, cross paved MD 77 at 6.8 miles and use the trail's footbridge to cross over Big Hunting Creek. Originating from highland springs, the creek was Maryland's first fly-fishing-only stream and later became the state's first catch-and-return trout stream. Brook, brown, and rainbow trout all spawn in the stream, with the rainbows being the most abundant. A free *Fly Fisherman's Guide to Big Hunting Creek* is available at the Catoctin Mountain Park Visitor Center (about 1 mile east on MD 77).

Begin to rise through a boulder-strewn woodland, passing several springs along the way. Soon after walking by a stone wall at 7.4 miles, turn right onto a pathway and continue to ascend. The buildings you see uphill are part of Greentop Camp, a facility available to organized groups. The forest through this area bears the scars–old roads, dirt piles, and more–of past construction work, so pay close attention to the blue blazes. Turn right onto a woods road at 7.6 miles, only to bear left off it in 500 more feet. Keep left at 7.8 miles, where a trail to the right heads to some cabins.

Cross Park Central Road at 8 miles, coming to Manahan Road at 8.1 miles. Turn right along the road, watching for the left turn you need to make next to the horse trail sign at 8.3 miles. Within just a few steps, turn right onto a narrow pathway.

Cross a tributary of Owens Creek at 8.7 miles and recross it at 8.8 miles. Come to Foxville-Deerfield Road at 9.4 miles and head toward Owens Creek Campground. Just after crossing Owens Creek on the campground road, pass by the sawmill (see Hike 18) and come to your shuttled car and the end of the journey at 9.6 miles.

(If you wish to hike the Catoctin Trail all the way to its northern terminus, ascend from the campground road and follow the blue blazes for 1.8 miles to Mount Zion Road.)

15

Gambrill State Park

Total distance (circuit): 6.0 miles
Hiking time: 3 hours, 15 minutes
Vertical rise: 840 feet
Maps: USGS 7½' Frederick

Gambrill State Park is a gift that a group of conservationists in Frederick County gave to themselves and the other citizens of Maryland. After using private funds to purchase land around the High Knob area of Catoctin Mountain, the group donated the tract to the city of Frederick to be used as a municipal park. In 1934, the city turned the acreage over to the state to develop as a component of the state park system.

Within the park's 1,137 acres are picnic facilities, a campground with modern restrooms and hot showers, a nature center, a ridgeline roadway with designated overlooks, an excellent system of trails, and a small pond popular for the fishing of largemouth bass, bluegill, and channel catfish. Park personnel and volunteers lead nature walks and conduct evening campfire programs periodically throughout the summer season.

Because they are located within a 15-minute drive of Frederick, the park's trails are a popular destination and are extensively used by exercise walkers, hikers, naturalists, and mountain bikers. Fortunately, park personnel are aided in maintaining the pathways by a diverse number of volunteer groups from the area.

Encircling the top of the mountain in a predominantly oak and hickory forest, this hike makes use of almost every one of the park's trails, including a section of the Catoctin Trail (see Hike 14). For the most part, the route has only minor ups and downs, with a few steep but short sections. The route described here makes somewhat of a detour to rise to one of the park's constructed overlooks for a grand view to the east.

The trailhead may be reached by taking I-70, exit 53, at Frederick onto US 15 north. Drive by the US 340 exit and take the next exit onto US 40, heading west. In 4.3 miles, turn right onto Gambrill Park Road and follow it for 1.3 miles to the trailhead parking area on the right.

Facing the bulletin board, begin by taking the Black Locust Trail on the far right, marked by red, black, and blue blazes, and maintained by the Potomac Appalachian Trail–West Chapter. Enter a woods dotted by mountain laurel bushes and, in only 100 yards, come to an intersection where the red blazes continue to the right. You want to bear left to follow the black and blue blazes of the combined Black Locust and Catoctin Trails.

Avoid the unwanted trail to the right at 0.3 mile and stay on the main route to quickly descend the rocky pathway. Nuts falling from the hickory trees and acorns from the oaks provide food—or *mast,* as biologists call it—for the park's population of white-tailed deer, wild turkeys, and chipmunks, squirrels, and other rodents. A section of the green-blazed trail comes in from the left at 0.6 mile; keep right on the pathway marked by blue, black, and green blazes.

Be alert at 0.8 mile, as the trail swings off the old road you have been following and ascends steeply, passing under a utility line at 1.1 miles. Come to a four-way intersection at 1.2 miles. An old, unmarked route bears right, and the blue blazes of the Catoctin Trail continue straight. You need to bear left and ascend along the green- and black-blazed trail. (The green-blazed Green Ash Trail is maintained by Wheel Base, a bicycle shop in Frederick.)

Pass by a well-flowing piped spring at 1.3 miles, and, just beyond a stone structure, leave the green blazes to the left and ascend

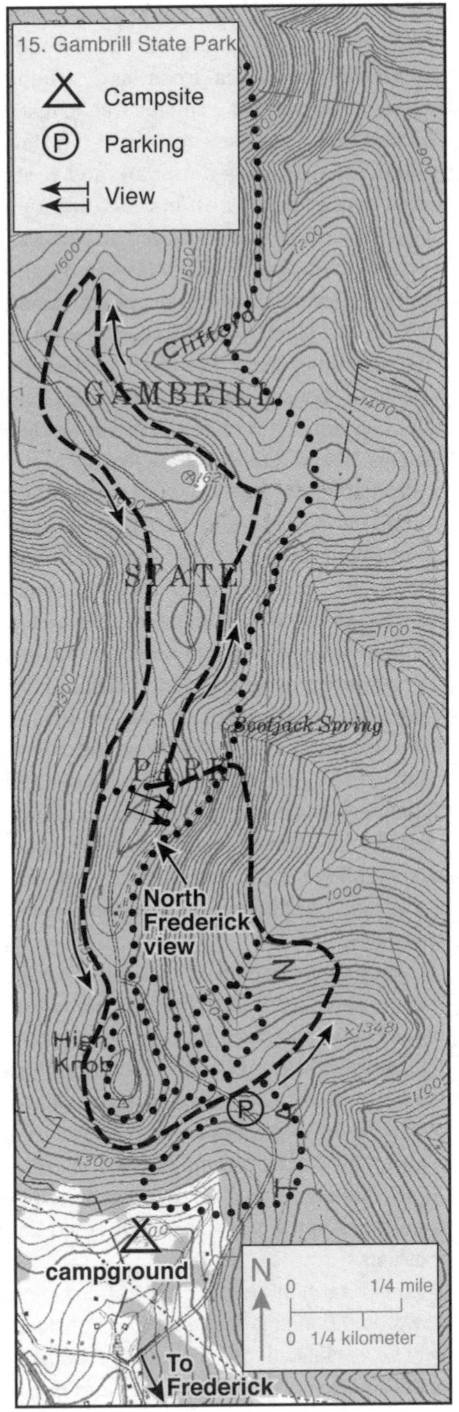

the black blazes to the right at a utility line. Within a few steps, swing left into a woods with small sassafras trees and ascend steeply. In addition to using the tree to make tea and root beer, early settlers of the New World believed sassafras bark and roots could cure all manner of illnesses, and sold large amounts of them to buyers in Europe.

A yellow-blazed trail comes in from the right at 1.5 miles; keep left on the combined yellow- and black-blazed trail. A few yards later, this trail veers off to the right, but you want to continue to the left and ascend along the utility line to come to the North Frederick Overlook on Gambrill Park Road.

If you're lucky, it will be a clear day when you arrive at this grand 180-degree viewpoint. Along the ridgeline to the north you should be able to make out the lushly forested slopes of Catoctin Mountain within the boundaries of the Frederick City Watershed Area. Spreading out to the east and the south, the rolling lands of the Monocacy River Valley can almost look like a patchwork quilt, with squares of green farmland interspersed amid irregularly shaped plots of suburban homes. Turkey vultures are often seen soaring above and below the ridgeline, taking advantage of thermals rising from the valley floor.

When you have soaked in all you can from the overlook, retrace your steps along the utility line. Within a few feet, bypass the first trail heading left to Gambrill Park Road. At the next intersection, take the yellow-blazed trail to the left and cross under the utility line, where tiny Deptford pink flowers line the route. (Yellow-blazed Yellow Poplar Trail is maintained by the Mid-Atlantic Off Road Enthusiasts.)

The beautifully colored Deptford pink flower is 0.5 inch in diameter and speckled with white dots. Its generic name, *Dianthus,* is derived from a coupling of the word *dios*—referring to the Greek god Zeus—with the word *anthos,* for flower. Thus translated, the name means "divine flower" or "God's flower."

Keep right to continue to gradually descend where an unmarked trail comes in from the left at 1.9 miles. The blue-blazed Catoctin Trail comes in from the right at 2.2 miles to join up with your route, so keep left on the now combined yellow- and blue-blazed pathway. Less than 1,000 feet later, the blue-blazed Catoctin Trail heads off to the right where you need to turn left onto a yellow-blazed dirt road.

A number of twists and turns and ups and downs begin at 2.5 miles: Turn right off the dirt road, cross under a utility line, and make another turn to the right. Ascend into a boulder field dotted by mountain laurel, but soon descend—steeply at times.

An unmarked trail comes in from the right at 3 miles, so keep to the left, quickly passing by a small pond where the trail swings left uphill to parallel a utility line. Be alert at 3.3 miles, as the trail swings left onto a grassy roadway.

Cross paved Gambrill Park Road and reenter a woods whose understory is dominated by luxuriant growths of mountain laurel. For some reason, scarlet tanagers are often spotted by hikers along this portion of the ridgeline. During the spring breeding season, the male scarlet tanager is a dazzling shade of deep red with dark black wings, while later in the year his feathers become the same olive green as the female's (the male's wings, however, remain black).

Continue near the crest of the mountain, with little change in elevation, and cross a woods road at 3.7 miles. The trail coming in from the left at 4.7 miles leads to the North Frederick Overlook; keep to the right and gradually descend. Stay right again when the black-blazed trail comes in from the left at

4.8 miles to join up with the route you are following.

You might want to take a short rest break atop a small rock outcrop at 5.1 miles to contemplate why people driving along I-70, visible to the west, are in so much of a hurry while you have been enjoying such a leisurely day in the woods. A short distance later, the yellow-blazed trail continues straight into the High Knob Picnic Area, where water and restrooms are available in season. Keep right and descend steeply along the black-blazed route, soon avoiding a trail that drops off to the right.

Jack-in-the-pulpit grows close to the trail in the spring as you cross under a utility line at 5.7 miles, while black cohosh makes its appearance a month or so later. Come to a four-way intersection at 5.8 miles. The red-blazed Red Maple Trail (maintained by The Trail House, an outdoor outfitter in Frederick) heads right to descend to the park's campground. The yellow-blazed trail goes left to the picnic area; you want to stay straight on the combined black-, red-, and yellow-blazed route. (Be aware that, unless it has been fixed, the signpost here may give incorrect directions.)

This quiet exploration of Catoctin Mountain's High Knob area comes to an end when you cross Gambrill Park Road and return to the trailhead parking at 6 miles.

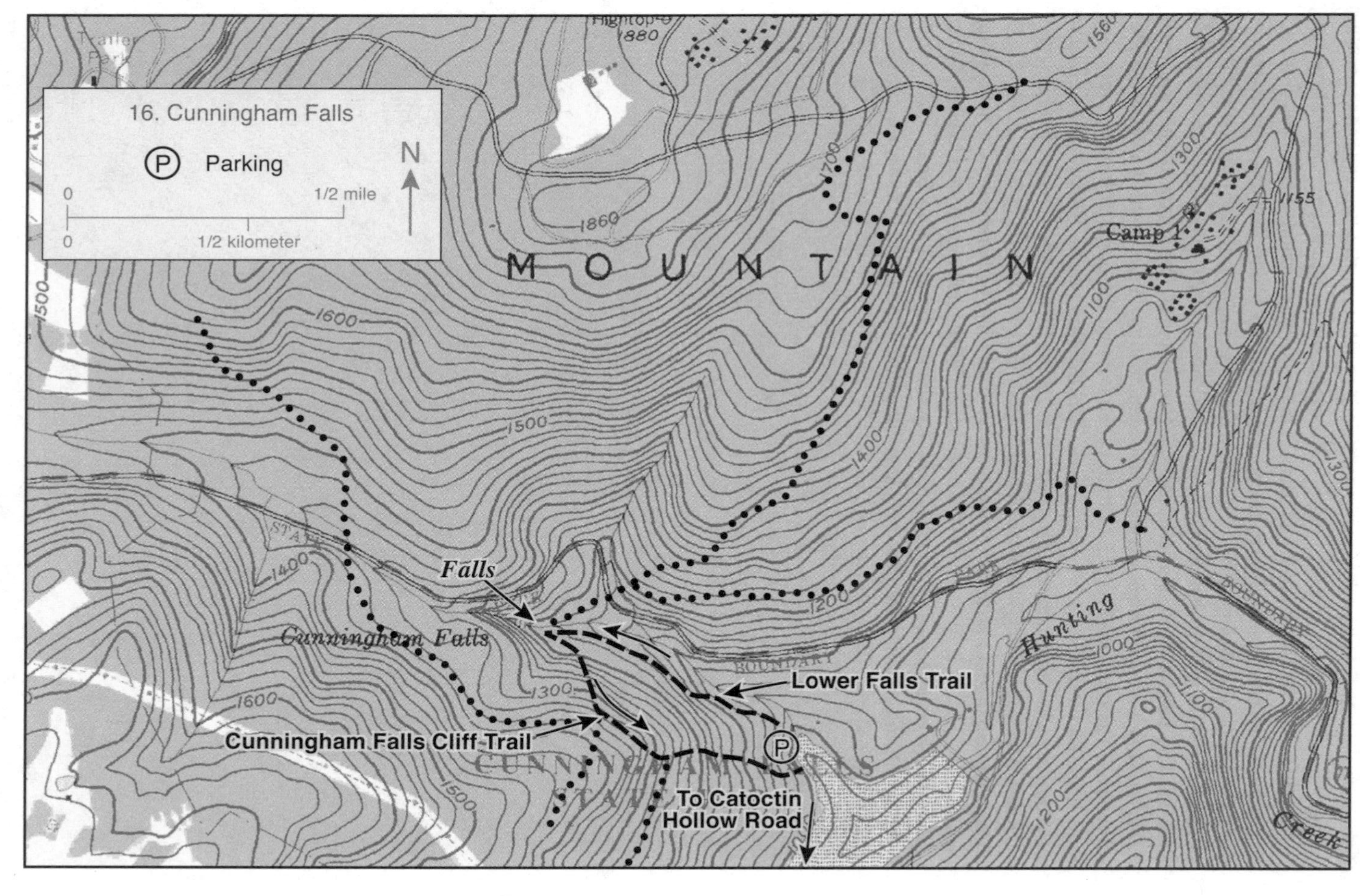

16. Cunningham Falls
P Parking
0
1/2 mile
0
1/2 kilometer
N
MOUNTAIN
Camp 1
Falls
Cunningham Falls
Lower Falls Trail
Cunningham Falls Cliff Trail
To Catoctin Hollow Road
Hunting Creek

16

Cunningham Falls

Total distance (circuit): 1.2 miles

Hiking time: 30 minutes

Vertical rise: 300 feet

Maps: USGS 7½' Blue Ridge Summit (MD/PA)

There always seems to be some confusion and misinformation when it comes to the height of a waterfall. An official brochure from Maryland's Department of Natural Resources describes Cunningham Falls as a "78-foot cascading waterfall." Yet, other brochures from the department proclaim the "sparkling water tumbling from a 51-foot ledge" of Muddy Creek Falls in Swallow Falls State Park to be "Maryland's highest waterfall." Disputing this proclamation, and appearing to be correct based on the aforementioned figures, the DeLorme Maryland Delaware Atlas & Gazetteer says Cunningham Falls is the "highest in Maryland."

For the most part, these incongruities don't really matter to those of us who enjoy waterfalls. Either falls can be appreciated for its own beauty, and, luckily, both may be reached by short, fairly easy walks. Be sure to see Hike 2 for more information on Muddy Creek Falls.

Cunningham Falls is located in the northwestern corner of Cunningham Falls State Park's 5,000 acres. Within the park are picnic areas, two campgrounds with hot showers, a camp store, a playground constructed with 3,000 recycled tires, and 44-acre Hunting Creek Lake, with swimming and boating permitted. A ramp is available for those with their own boats, while canoes, paddleboats, and rowboats may be rented during the summer. Fishing along the park's edges in Big Hunting and Little Hunting Creeks is permitted with artificial flies and a catch-and-return trout policy. Anglers can also fish for bass, sunfish, catfish, crappie, and bluegill in the lake. If you venture onto some of the park's trails that do not go to the falls, you need to be aware that hunting is permitted on 3,500 acres of undeveloped wildlands.

You can drive to Cunningham Falls State Park by following US 15 north from Frederick. (If you want to take a worthwhile side trip on the drive northward, watch for signs directing you to Catoctin Furnace on MD 806, just off US 15. In an area that was once a booming industrial site, the Catoctin Iron Furnace operated from 1776 to 1903.) Near Thurmont, approximately 15 miles north of Frederick, take MD 77 west for 4 miles and turn left (shortly after the Catoctin Mountain Park Visitor Center) onto Catoctin Hollow Road. Make a right turn into the William Houck Area of Cunningham Falls State Park 1.2 miles later. Pass by the campground road in an additional 0.1 mile, and continue 0.5 mile more to the falls trailhead parking.

The walk begins by taking the red-blazed Lower Falls Trail (the one to the right) and rising into a magnificently dark and mature forest of giant sugar maple and hemlock trees. Native Americans taught early settlers how to tap sugar maple trees in the springtime to harvest the rising sap. An average-sized tree yields approximately 20 to 25 gallons of sap; it takes about 40 gallons of the liquid to make just 1 gallon of maple syrup. The park presents a maple-syrup demonstration during the first two weekends of March every year.

Sadly, the towering hemlock trees in this forest—some at least 200 years old—are succumbing to an insect known as the hemlock woolly adelgid. First appearing on the West Coast in the 1920s, these insects had only a minimal effect on western hemlocks, but by the 1950s, eastern hemlock trees began to show the effects of infestation. Apparently having no resistance to the bugs, which suck the sap from the base of the trees' needles, eastern hemlocks have been dying at an alarming rate, and some botanists predict a virtual elimination of the species in the not-too-distant future.

The sound of rushing, tumbling water becomes audible at 0.4 mile as you begin to descend toward the falls. Coming to an intersection at 0.5 mile, bear right and take the wooden walkway to the base of Cunningham Falls.

This surely has to be one of the most eye-pleasing places in all of Maryland. With rays of sunlight—which have filtered through the forest canopy—shining upon and making individual droplets of water sparkle, Big Hunting Creek splashes, gurgles, and plunges 78 feet down a sloping rock facing. The hemlock trees and mosses growing on the rocks keep this area green year-round, while the pool at the base of the falls is custom-made for dangling feet on hot summer days.

Spend 15 minutes, an hour, or a full afternoon here, but when you are finally ready to leave, retrace your steps (the trail that continues on from the falls is a barrier-free pathway leading to MD 77) back to the intersection. So as to cover a bit of different ground on the way back to your car, turn right on the yellow-blazed Cunningham Falls Cliff Trail and ascend among large rocks and boulders, steeply at times.

About 600 million years ago, huge flows of lava spread across the landscape from southern Pennsylvania, into Maryland, and all the way to southern Virginia. These extensive, deep flows hardened into a black basalt rock peppered by numerous gas-bubble holes. Over the course of time, heat, pressure, and waterborne minerals changed the black basalt into the fine-grained Catoctin greenstone rocks you are walking by today.

Typical of the way greenstone breaks along joints, a craggy rock facing is at 0.6 mile. Almost hidden from view, jack-in-the-pulpit grows within the narrow crevices. The blue-blazed Catoctin Trail (see Hike 14) comes in from the right to join up with the pathway you have been following; keep left and descend. The orange-blazed Campground Trail comes in from the right at 0.9 mile, while the Catoctin Trail veers right 200 feet later; keep left at both intersections. Songbirds are especially active in this part of the forest in early morning, while the drill of woodpeckers is often heard throughout the day. These birds have special air pockets in their heads to soften and absorb the shock of hammering their beaks into tree trunks.

Return to your car at 1.2 miles and head out to sample some of the other hikes available within a short drive of Cunningham Falls State Park. (See Hikes 14, 15, 17, and 18.)

17

Catoctin Mountain Park

Total distance (circuit): 8.1 miles

Hiking time: 4 hours, 40 minutes

Vertical rise: 1,110 feet

Maps: USGS 7½' Blue Ridge Summit (MD/PA); park map

Just as it had done with land obtained for Shenandoah National Park in Virginia, the federal government purchased land for Catoctin Mountain Park to demonstrate how national parks for recreation and conservation could be created from worn-out lands. For nearly 200 years, earlier owners and settlers of the land had clear-cut many acres of forest to make charcoal for the nearby Catoctin Iron Furnace, stripped oak trees of their bark for tanning, and employed farming practices unsuited to the region's terrain and soil.

From the late 1930s to the early 1940s, groups from the Civilian Conservation Corps and the Works Progress Administration built roads, trails, cabins, and other structures on the park lands. In 1954, the federal government deeded close to 5,000 acres south of MD 77 to Maryland to be developed into Cunningham Falls State Park while retaining 5,770 acres north of the highway as Catoctin Mountain Park.

Located just a few miles south of the Maryland/Pennsylvania border, these lands have been permitted to grow back to an eastern climax forest, much as it was in the 1700s. Today, the woods' leaves, branches, and undergrowth help support barred owls, pileated woodpeckers, wild turkeys, scarlet tanagers, red-tailed hawks, and more than 130 other species of birds that live here or pass through at some time of the year or another. From early spring to late fall, close to 100 species of wildflowers, such as skunk cabbage, bloodroot, spring beauty, Dutchman's breeches, nodding trillium, pussytoes,

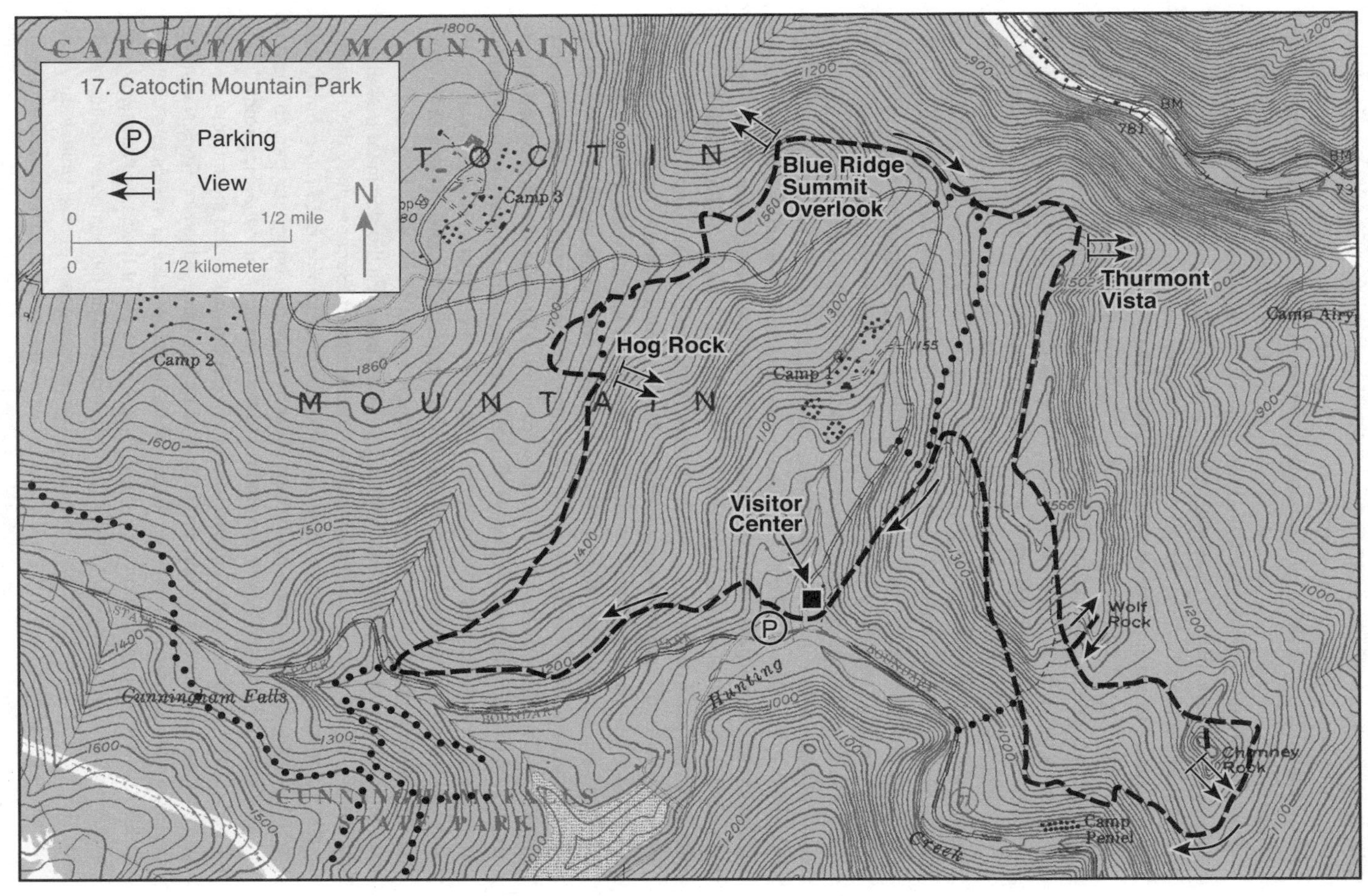

17. Catoctin Mountain Park
Parking
View
0
1/2 mile
0
1/2 kilometer
N
CATOCTIN MOUNTAIN
Blue Ridge Summit Overlook
Thurmont Vista
Hog Rock
Camp 1
Camp 2
Camp 3
Camp Airy
Visitor Center
Wolf Rock
Chimney Rock
Camp Peniel
Hunting Creek
Cunningham Falls
CUNNINGHAM FALLS STATE PARK

beardtongue, fleabane, wild bergamot, and Queen Anne's lace rise from the soils of the forests, clearings, roadsides, and streambanks.

Catoctin Mountain Park has a visitors center, picnic areas, campground with hot showers, rustic rental cabins, camp complexes available to organized groups, a couple of backcountry Adirondack shelters, and a scenic drive. Interpretive seasonal activities, including cross-country skiing seminars, wildflower walks, and evening programs, are run by volunteers and park personnel. Well hidden from view and not open to the public, the US presidential retreat, Camp David, is located within the park. Running along MD 77 is Big Hunting Creek, known to anglers for the quality of its trout fishing. Approximately 26 miles of trail, including the northern portion of the Catoctin Trail (see Hike 14), reach nearly every corner of the park. The hike described here takes in the many natural vistas it has to offer.

You can drive to Catoctin Mountain Park by following US 15 north from Frederick. Near Thurmont, approximately 15 miles north of Frederick, take MD 77 west for almost 4 miles to the Catoctin Mountain Park Visitor Center on the right. Take a few moments to examine the center's exhibits to learn more about the human and natural history of the area. You should obtain a map of the park and the brochure for the Hog Rock Nature Trail before moving your car across Park Central Road to the trailhead lot.

Walk into the woods by following the sign for Cunningham Falls, and follow the small ups and downs of a landscape littered with rocks and boulders. Begin to descend at 1 mile, toward the automobiles traveling along MD 77. Arrive at an intersection just a few steps before you would walk onto the highway. The trail to the left heads to Cunningham Falls (see Hike 16); bear right and begin the long ascent on a rocky pathway toward Hog Rock. Many of the ankle-turning rocks and stones along this route are Catoctin greenstone, which had it origins hundreds of millions of years ago when Maryland was covered by deep, wide lava flows. (Catoctin greenstone is discussed at greater length in Hike 16.)

Level out for a short distance at 1.3 miles before continuing in a general upward direction (although there are several ups and downs). Cross a small water run–which may dry out late in summer–at 2 miles and come to Hog Rock Overlook at 2.1 miles. Looking southward over the Monocacy River Valley, this vista is most impressive in the fall, when the valley and slopes that are spread out before you are bejeweled with the yellow, orange, and rich red leaves of the sugar maple trees. As it heads south to meet the Potomac River, the Monocacy River drains a number of counties in southern Pennsylvania, in addition to portions of Carroll, Frederick, and Montgomery Counties. You may not be able to actually see its water flowing from your vantage point in the mountains, but you can easily trace its route during the warmer months. A long, narrow band of dark green–the leaves of large, mature trees growing along the river's bank–twists its way through the lighter greens and browns of the farmlands.

Oak trees are the dominant tree around the viewpoint. Because they drop massive numbers of acorns onto the ground, local farmers used to bring their pigs to this area to feed, giving it the name Hog Rock.

Take the pathway to the left from the viewpoint. You can use the Hog Rock Nature Trail brochure (available at the visitors center) to learn more about the natural history of trees by matching up the numbered posts with the brochure's descriptions. Unless they have been changed by the time you hike here, you

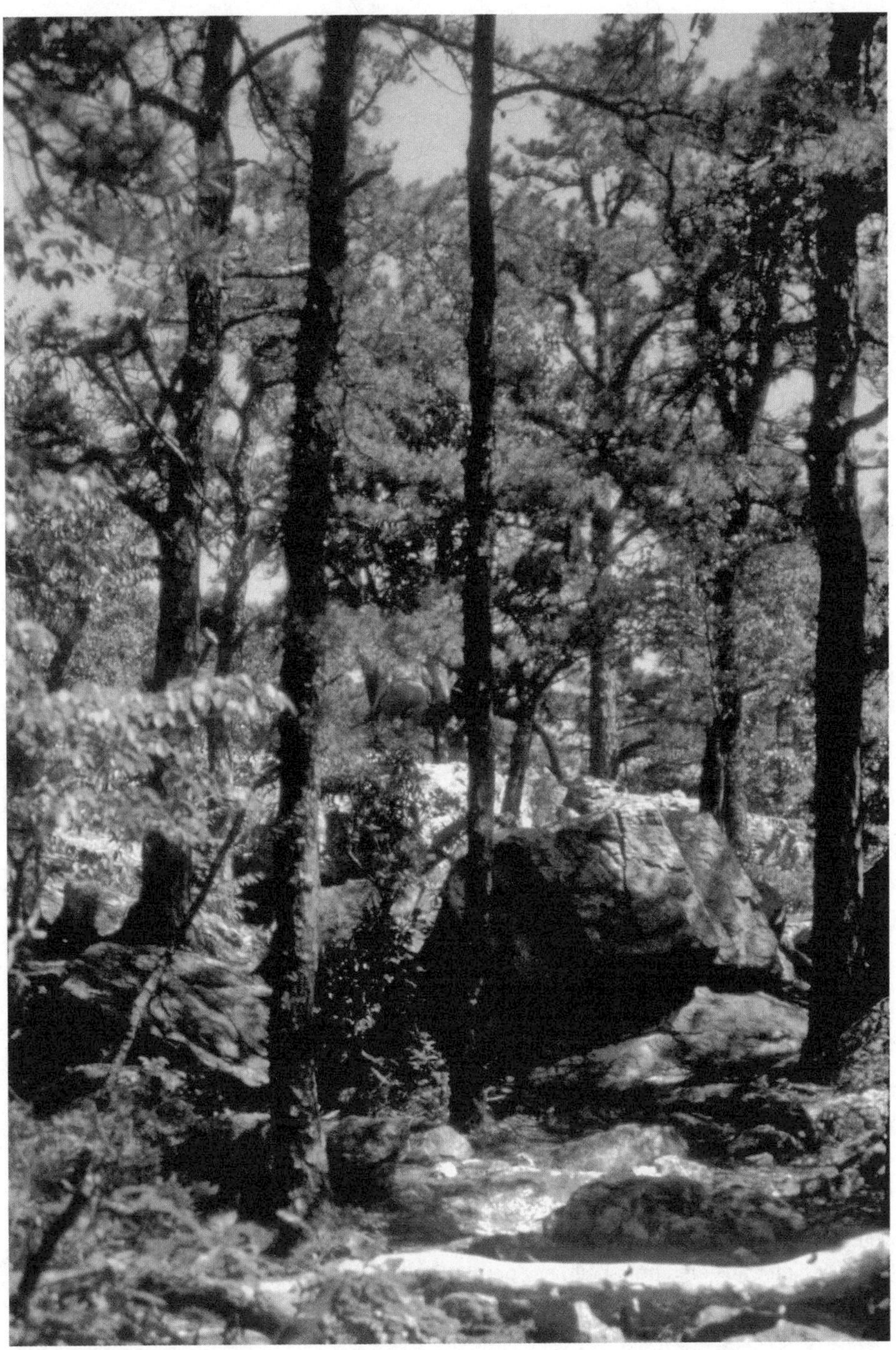

Quartzite rocks at Wolf Rock

may pass by a couple of confusing directional signs. Be sure to stay on the nature trail's main route.

After hiking 2.5 miles from the visitors center, come to an intersection and turn left toward the Hog Rock parking area. Cross the paved Park Central Road at 2.8 miles, pass through the parking area (and by a couple of outhouses), and descend into a woods dominated by tall oaks and maples.

Swing right at 3 miles, ascend, and take the short trail to the left at 3.1 miles to the Blue Ridge Summit Overlook, so named because its view is northward over Catoctin Mountain to the Blue Ridge Summit region of Pennsylvania. Return to the main trail, turn left, and descend steeply.

You may notice the rows of circular holes that yellow-bellied sapsuckers have drilled into the inner bark of tree trunks as you begin to rise at 3.7 miles. In addition to gaining nourishment from the sap, these woodpeckers are adept at catching insects while on the wing. You will most likely see them during the colder months of late winter and early spring, as they migrate farther north–some almost to the Hudson Bay in Canada–to spend the summer.

Come to a four-way intersection at 3.9 miles. If you have become tired or run out of time, the visitors center is only 1 mile straight ahead. The Charcoal Trail parking area on Park Central Road is a few hundred feet to the right. To continue on this hike, bear left onto the trail marked for the Thurmont Vista.

The pathway to the left at 4.1 miles heads to Camp Airy; keep right and arrive at Thurmont Vista, overlooking the town of Thurmont, at 4.3 miles. From this vantage point, you can see how the settlement came by its name, which translates from Latin as "gateway to the mountains." Be sure to make it a stop on your drive home if you are here during the middle two weekends of March. A maple-syrup festival combines interpretive talks with hayrides and lots of good eating.

Continue along the trail from the vista, following the undulations of a ridgeline whose understory is dominated by mountain laurel. Begin to descend at 4.9 miles, bypassing the trail to the right at 5 miles, which runs about 0.5 mile to Park Central Road.

You will first encounter Wolf Rock at about 5.3 miles, but continue on to the second Wolf Rock sign before bearing left onto the rock. You might try to use your imagination–the same imagination that is supposed to enable you to picture a bear in the Big Dipper–to see if you can make out the shape of a wolf's head as you ascend this sloping formation. There is no imagination needed to know that Wolf Rock is composed mostly of quartzite, a hard, metamorphic rock so resistant to erosion that it makes up many of the ridgelines found in today's Appalachian Mountains. Metamorphic rocks form when heat, pressure, water solutions, and stress cause a change in the minerals and texture of the rock.

Return to the main route and bear left, watching for when the trail makes an abrupt switchback to the left at 5.7 miles. Be alert 200 feet later and stay to the right when the trail marked for Crows Nest Campground (a private camp) heads off to the left. Just a few steps beyond this, bear right onto the boulders of Chimney Rock. This is a favorite viewpoint with the locals of Thurmont and northern Frederick County. It is also the best place you have come to so far to enjoy a vista and take a rest break.

The buildings and outskirts of Thurmont are visible on the rolling piedmont to the east, while directly in front of you is the deep laceration Big Hunting Creek has made into the ridgeline of Catoctin Mountain. The outcrop you see to the south is Cat Rock in Cunningham Falls State Park. (See the following on how to reach it as a side trip during this hike.)

After enjoying the cool breeze gliding across this aerie, munching on a few handfuls of gorp, and taking a couple of gulps of water, return to the previous intersection on the main trail. This time, bear right toward the Crows Nest Campground. However, you need to avoid the route that goes left to the campground at 6.4 miles by keeping right to descend toward MD 77. There are so many mountain laurel bushes here that it would be a shame not to be taking this hike in early June, when thousands of white and pink blossoms line the trail. The vegetation continues to become more lush as you lose elevation.

Arrive at an intersection at 6.9 miles. The trail to the left heads to Crows Nest Campground, while you want to take the pathway that descends to MD 77, near the Catoctin Mountain Park Headquarters. Stay on the same route as you come close to the headquarters and parallel MD 77 all of the way back to the visitors center and the end of the hike at 8.1 miles.

18

Deerfield Nature Trail and Owens Creek

Total distance (circuit): 3.0 miles

Hiking time: 1 hour, 25 minutes

Vertical rise: 600 feet

Maps: USGS 7½' Blue Ridge Summit (MD/PA); park map

Located below a 1,600-foot knob in the northwestern corner of Catoctin Mountain Park, Owens Creek Campground sits next to the softly flowing headwaters of its namesake stream. Because the campground is within a short driving distance of the populations of Frederick, Hagerstown, and even the Baltimore/Washington, D.C., metropolitan area, its 50 sites (operated on a first-come, first-served basis) can fill up quickly on nice spring or fall weekends, and it is not unusual for it to be at capacity throughout the summer.

You may be pitching your tent in the woods when you come here, but with kids riding bicycles from one site to another, cars pulling in and out, happy campers having loud conversations, and an occasional generator or boom box cranking out reminders of the modern world, it might become a bit hectic and noisy.

Luckily, this fairly easy and pleasant stroll, which the whole family should be able to enjoy, begins in the campground. The first portion of the hike makes use of the Deerfield Nature Trail as it parallels one of the uppermost tributaries of Owens Creek. The central portion is along the park's bridle path through a predominantly oak and hickory forest, while the last part of the hike follows an unmarked but obvious route that can help you hone your route-finding skills.

The trailhead may be reached by driving northward from Frederick on US 15 for close to 20 miles, to turn westward on MD 77 near Thurmont. A little more than 3 miles later, turn

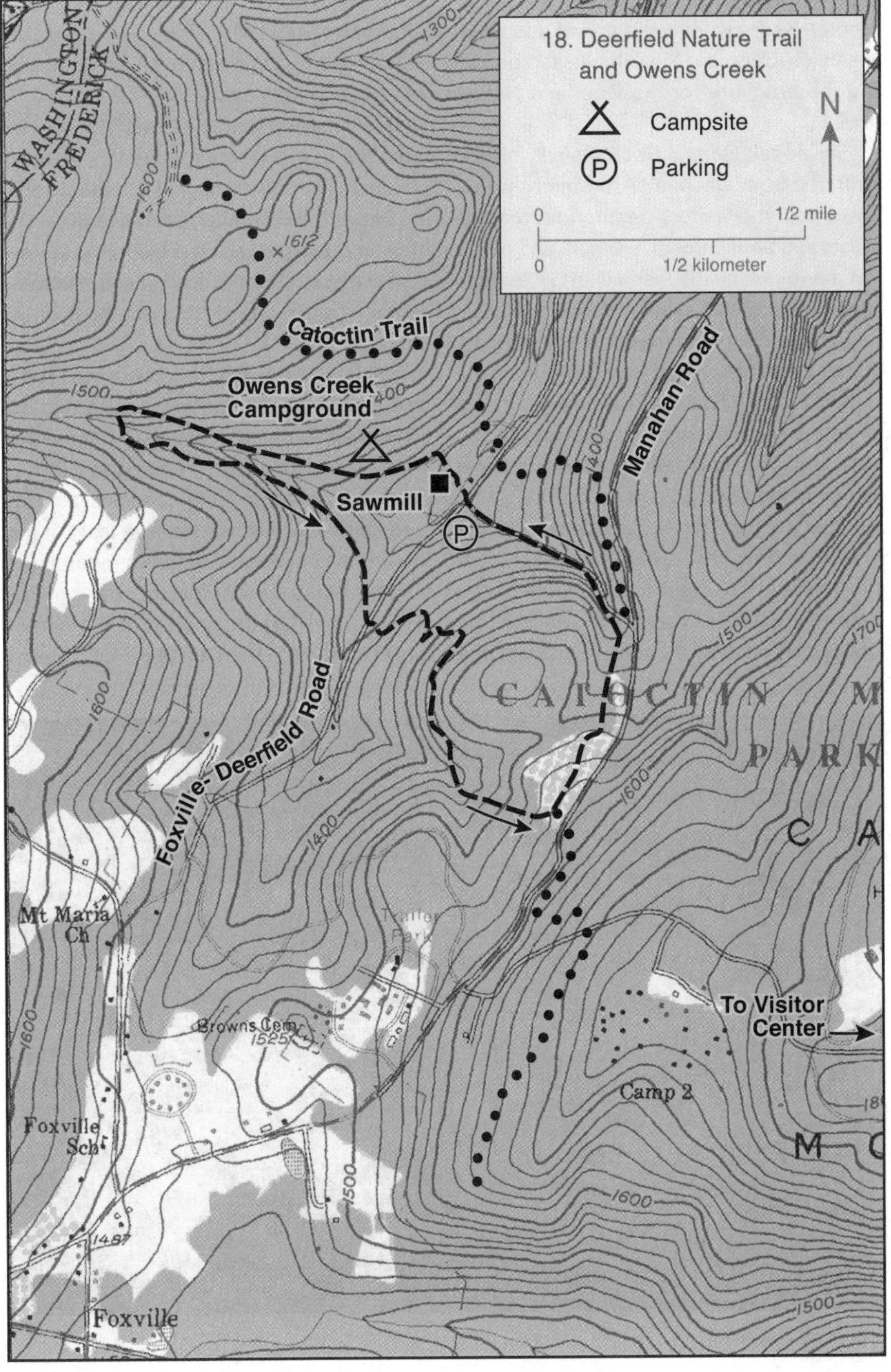
18. Deerfield Nature Trail
and Owens Creek
Campsite
Parking
N
0
1/2 mile
0
1/2 kilometer
Catoctin Trail
Owens Creek
Campground
Sawmill
Manahan Road
Foxville- Deerfield Road
CATOCTIN
PARK
To Visitor
Center
Camp 2
Mt Maria
Ch
Browns Cem
Foxville
Sch
Foxville
WASHINGTON
FREDERICK

right at the Catoctin Mountain Park Visitor Center, where you should spend a few moments checking out the exhibits and obtaining the brochure for the Deerfield Nature Trail.

Drive Park Central Road (usually closed to traffic from December to March) northward from the visitors center, following its twists and turns through the park and past a number of trailheads (see Hike 17). Several miles later, cross Manahan Road, soon making a right turn onto Foxville-Deerfield Road. About a mile later, leave your car in the parking area for the Sawmill Trail on the left side of the road. (Those of you staying in the campground should continue just a few feet farther to the campground entrance.)

Take the barrier-free boardwalk into the woods, cross the creek with its moist-environment vegetation, and come to the sawmill at 0.1 mile. Bear right to encircle the display, which is built on the actual site of a direct-drive undershot sawmill of the 1800s. Undershot sawmills were powered by the water passing underneath the wheel instead of dropping from above.

Continue uphill on the boardwalk, turn left onto the paved campground road, and stay on the main route through the campground.

Leave the road near Campsite 30 at 0.4 mile and merge onto the Deerfield Nature Trail. Keep to the left a few hundred feet later, when a trail heads to the right, back to the campground.

With the large number of deer seen today in Catoctin Mountain Park, it is hard to believe that at one time they had been eradicated from the region. Hunting and loss of habitat from the building of homes, farming, and timbering was so extensive that not one deer remained on the land the federal government purchased for the park in the 1930s. In an effort to restore the natural order of things, the National Park Service

Along the Sawmill Trail

brought a few white-tailed deer that had been captured elsewhere and placed them inside park boundaries in the 1940s. With the absence of natural predators (wolves and mountain lions having been extirpated from the Appalachian Mountains years before), the deer prospered. The whitetails' increased numbers, not just in the park but throughout the eastern United States, have been used by some people to argue that hunting regulations should be eased so as to keep deer from browsing on suburban dwellers' backyard gardens. Perhaps a more appropriate way of looking at this problem would be to realize that it is humans who are eating away at the traditional territory of the deer.

Although they can be seen grazing at all hours of the day and night, deer are most active in the early evening and early morning, the best times of day in many hikers' opinions to take this walk.

Pass by an old stone wall at 0.6 mile. Structures such as this were used to mark the boundaries of homesteads and farms. Some were in open fields where cattle grazed, while others snaked around the trees of a forest to keep swine from wandering too far in their search for nuts, grubs, and other delicacies of the woods. For this reason, the stone fences soon came to be known as hogwalls.

The route to the right at 0.8 mile connects with the Catoctin Trail (see Hike 14); you need to bear left and cross the creek. The depression beside the trail at 1 mile is the remnant of a flat hearth, where timber cut from the surrounding forest was reduced to charcoal to be used as a fuel in the numerous iron furnaces of the region.

Avoid the trail at 1.2 miles that heads left to the campground. Keep right and pass through an area of thick vegetation where jack-in-the-pulpit grows well. These plants are perennials that grow from corms, underground food storage organs to which the roots are attached. From year to year the corm determines which sex the flower will be. In times of abundant nutrients, the corm will produce a female whose flower looks like small green berries surrounding the base of the column. If food is less bountiful, a male flower, which resembles pollen-covered threads, will result. Every once in a while, there will be a bisexual flower, with the male components above the female parts. A jack-in-the-pulpit with only one leaf and no flower means the corm was basically starved for food during the previous year.

At 1.4 miles, cross a tributary of the creek you stepped over earlier. Go across Foxville-Deerfield Road just a few hundred yards later and continue along the horse trail. However, be alert, as the route makes a sudden left uphill and soon ascends steeply.

Upon reaching the top of the ridge at 1.8 miles, descend and walk all the way across a field, which is part of the Youth Camping Area. Reenter the woods on a dirt road and ascend. Just a few steps before you would walk onto the dirt and gravel Manahan Road, make an abrupt left at 2.1 miles to begin to follow a pathway that is now both the horse trail and the Catoctin Trail.

Bear right onto a woods road at 2.3 miles, but make an almost immediate left to continue along the blue-blazed pathway. Cross a stream at 2.5 miles and avoid the road to the right by keeping to the left on the blue-blazed trail.

Be alert at 2.6 miles, for this is where you are going to leave the blue-blazed pathway going off to the right, and turn left to descend along the unmarked dirt and gravel road. (If you are hesitant about taking an unmarked trail, you can continue along the blue-blazed pathway, which will return you to the campground entrance road.)

The unmarked road becomes paved for a short distance, but when the pavement comes to an end, you need to keep to the left and descend the grassy roadway. The hike is coming to an end, so why not slow down to enjoy the quiet of this little valley that was created by the small mountain creek that tumbles down the sloping forestland? Another tributary of Owens Creek, the stream nourishes a more luxuriant growth of vegetation than that next to the old roadbed upon which you are walking.

Pass through a park service gate, cross Foxville-Deerfield Road, and return to your car at 3 miles.

There are a number of other family-friendly interpretive trails in the park that you should consider walking in order to learn more about the human and natural history of this area. The 0.4-mile round-trip Brown's Farm Trail provides a glimpse of how nature is restoring a former farmsite, the 0.5-mile round-trip Charcoal Trail describes the process of making charcoal in the 19th century, and the 0.2-mile round-trip Spicebush Trail is a barrier-free pathway that teaches the ecology of the forest. The 2.8-mile round-trip Cunningham Falls Trail will take you from the visitors center to the falls while furnishing an introduction to your surroundings. How and why moonshine was made is explained along the 0.6-mile round-trip Blue Blazes Whiskey Still Trail. All of these routes either have trailside interpretive signs or printed guides that are available from the visitors center.

19

Sugarloaf Mountain

Total distance (circuit): 7.5 miles

Hiking time: 4 hours, 20 minutes

Vertical rise: 1,470 feet

Maps: USGS 7½' Buckeystown (MD/WV)

Sugarloaf Mountain is such a significant feature on the gently rolling lands of Maryland's piedmont that it is easily visible for miles around it. A monadnock–a residual hill or mountain that stands alone above a surrounding peneplain–Sugarloaf rises more than 800 feet above the farmland below. Its upper layer is composed primarily of quartzite, an extremely erosion-resistant material that was formed by compression about 500 million years ago. In contrast, the piedmont around it is believed to be mostly metamorphic rock, much more susceptible to the erosive effects of wind and water.

Whereas the lands of nearby Gambrill State Park remain in their natural state because of a group of concerned conservationists (see Hike 15), the preservation of Sugarloaf is the result of a concerted effort on the part of only two people, Gordon and Louise Strong. Seeing the mountain for the first time in 1902, Gordon recognized its significance, and he spent the next few decades purchasing as much of it as possible. In 1946 he created a private, nonprofit organization, Stronghold, Incorporated, to ensure the mountain would continue to serve for the public's "enjoyment and education in an appreciation of natural beauty." The corporation held more than 2,300 acres when Gordon passed away in 1954 and has acquired approximately 1,000 additional acres since then. Continuing in the tradition established by the Strongs, no entrance fee is charged.

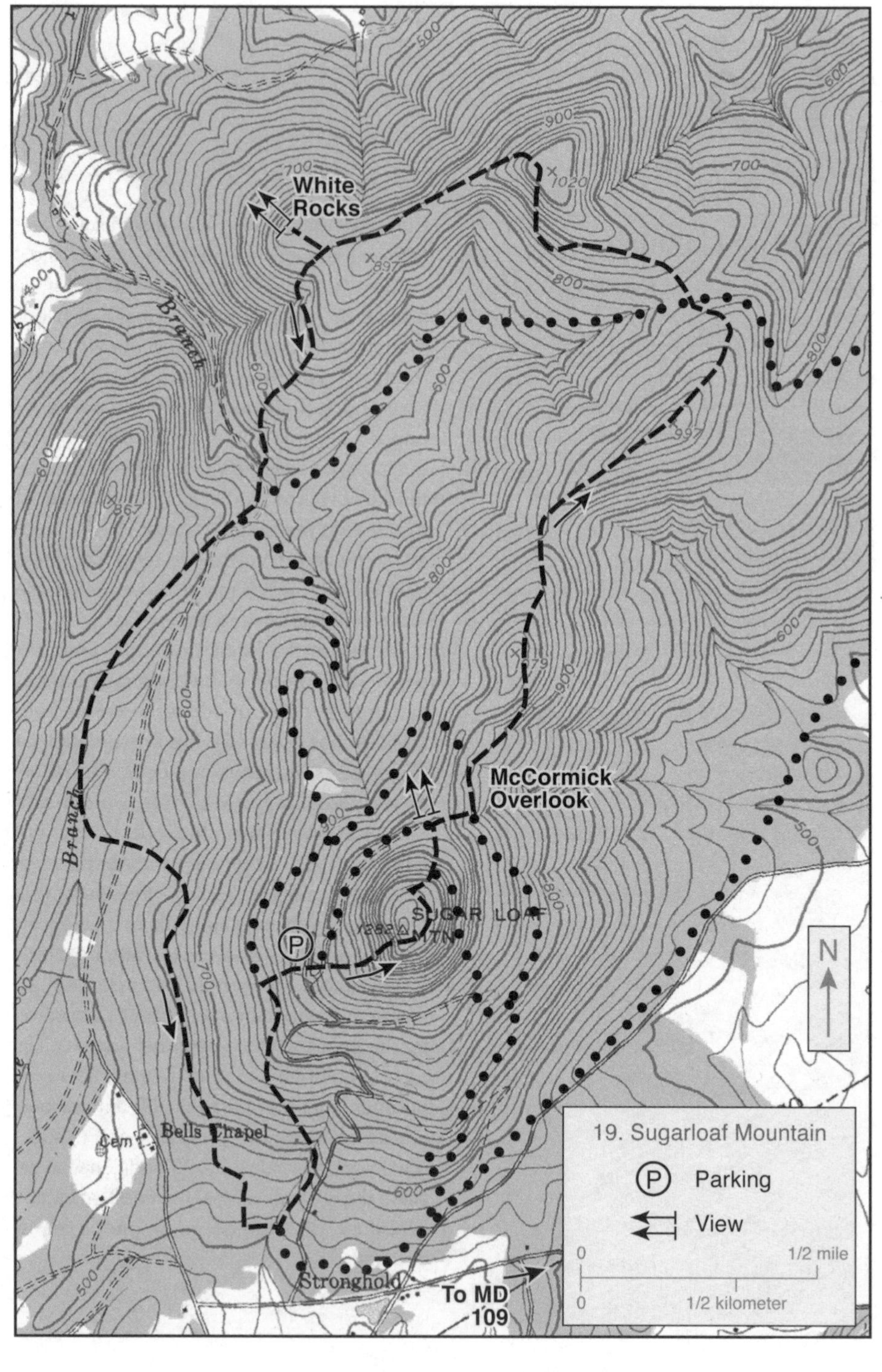
White Rocks
McCormick Overlook
SUGAR LOAF MTN
Branch
Branch
Bells Chapel
Cem
Stronghold
To MD 109
N
19. Sugarloaf Mountain
P Parking
View
0
1/2 mile
0
1/2 kilometer

Funds for maintenance and improvement do not come from any governmental sources, only from a modest trust fund, membership dues from those who wish to support the corporation, and gifts and bequests from people interested in protecting the mountain.

A network of more than 15 miles of trails (of which this hike takes in more than half) enables visitors to see for themselves what the Strongs found so intriguing and attractive about the mountain, and why it was named a National Natural Landmark in 1969. While the trails are open from sunrise to sunset, you should be aware that the road to the top of the mountain does not open until 8 AM. It closes at varying times (posted at the entrance gate) based upon the time of sunset throughout the year. All of the trails are open to hikers, one is for equestrians, and–in recent years–some have been opened to mountain bikers on certain days.

The corporation encourages nature study and picnicking and allows pets on the trails as long as they remain on a leash. Fires and overnight camping are prohibited. It should go without saying, but remember–all natural resources are protected, so do not pick plants, disturb wildlife, or remove rocks.

Sugarloaf Mountain may be reached by driving I-270 between Gaithersburg and Frederick to take exit 22 onto MD 109. Now headed in a southwestern direction, follow this roadway for 3 miles and make a right turn onto MD 95 (Comus Road). An additional 2.4 miles of driving brings you to a wide area in the road, where the entrance to Sugarloaf Mountain is on the right. Follow the mountain road all the way to its end, just below the summit.

Walk from the parking lot past the snack bar, pick up a map from the receptacle, read the information on the bulletin board, and begin to climb along the green-blazed A. M. Thomas Trail. This amazing set of stone steps you are quickly ascending was constructed by Mr. Thomas, the first superintendent of Stronghold, Incorporated.

The huge quartzite boulders beside the route are covered in an array of lichens and mosses. Spreading across the surface of a rock, lichen anchors itself by way of minute rootlike holdfasts that pry loose small bits of the rock. In addition, a weak acid emitted by the plant chemically dissolves minerals in the rock, hastening additional wear.

Upon reaching the summit (1,282 feet) at 0.25 mile, continue across it to some rocks on the left, which provide a view of the flatter lands to the south and west of the mountain. From this vantage point it is easy to understand why both Union and Confederate troops used Sugarloaf as a signal station and lookout during the Civil War. (A log cabin that served as a hospital during the conflict still stands at the base of the mountain.)

Retrace your steps for a few feet and begin to follow the red-blazed Monadnock Trail past growths of poison ivy, black cohosh, and mountain laurel. Keep to the left at 0.4 mile, where the orange-blazed Sunrise Trail comes in from the right. Descend steadily. At one time, American chestnuts were the dominant tree along the ridgeline, but all of them were killed by the blight of the 1930s. (Stronghold, Incorporated, commits much of its resources to helping researchers develop a blight-resistant tree.) Sadly, oak trees, which became the primary trees of the forest when the chestnuts died, are now in a decline of their own, in large part due to another foreign introduction, the gypsy moth.

Intersect the blue-blazed Northern Peaks Trail at 0.6 mile, but continue straight for a few feet to enjoy the vista from the McCormack Overlook. Looking northward, you should be able to delineate the route you will be following along the main part of Sugarloaf Mountain and the adjoining White Rocks ridgeline.

Retrace those few steps and turn left, following the blue blazes downhill. The white-blazed Mountain Loop Trail comes in from the right at 0.75 mile; turn left and continue along the combined pathways through a forest of towering oaks and maples. Watch for the green "pulpits" of jack-in-the-pulpits in the spring, or the plants' red berries in late summer, along the side of the trail.

Keep to the right along the blue blazes at 0.9 mile, when the white-blazed route continues to the left. You will soon ascend, and descend, the first of the Northern Peaks (1,079 feet) before dropping into a saddle where mountain laurel and other undergrowth become more common. Rising to the second peak (997 feet) at 1.6 miles, there are some limited views from the rocks to the left.

Mountain laurel again becomes quite profuse as you begin to descend. Cross the yellow-blazed Saddleback Horse Trail at 2.25 miles and ascend, continuing along the blue-blazed route. The treadway becomes rougher and steeper at 2.6 miles as you work your way to the third peak (1,020 feet) at 2.75 miles. Descend.

Soon after you pass just below the fourth peak (897 feet), take the trail to the right at 3.5 miles to revel in the vistas from White Rocks. This is the lowest you have been at any of the overlooks, so it is now possible to make out in greater detail the buildings, houses, and farmlands of the Monocacy Valley. The view of the southern landscape looks back toward the summit of Sugarloaf, while the four lanes of I-270 and the lands of the Monocacy National Battlefield are visible from the northward-facing rocks.

Return to the main route, turn right, and descend toward Mount Ephraim Road. Bear left onto a gravel road at 4.4 miles, with the yellow-blazed trail coming in from the left a very short distance later. Swing to the right and follow the now combined yellow and blue routes.

A few hundred feet later, the blue-blazed trail heads off to the left. (If you are running out of time or have become tired, you could bypass almost 1.5 miles of walking by following the blue blazes up the mountain, turning right at an intersection with the white-blazed pathway, and rejoining this description at the 7.4-mile point.) To continue with this hike, stay to the right along the yellow-blazed route. Pay attention, though, for just a few hundred feet later you need to follow the yellow blazes as they lead to the right off the roadway and then make another right onto a gated gravel road.

As you pass through the Demonstration Forest, you might notice a pleasing fragrance rising up from the grassy strip in the middle of the road. Members of the mint family are such interesting plants that it warrants getting down on your hands and knees to observe them. It may be hard for anyone other than a dedicated wildflower enthusiast to be able to name or differentiate the scores of mint species; however, you can usually identify a mint by its aroma, tiny flower petals, and by the fact that almost all mints have square stems, a rare trait in the plant world. Among the species that may be found in Maryland are henbit, motherwort, wild mint, peppermint, catnip, and wild basil.

Coming to a Y intersection at 5.1 miles, bear left and drop into a stand of American

The step trail to the third peak

beech trees. Cross Mount Ephraim Road at 5.4 miles and begin the ascent back toward Sugarloaf's summit. You must be alert less than 500 feet later, when the yellow-blazed route you need to continue upon makes a sudden right turn off the gravel road.

Eastern cottontail rabbits inhabit Sugarloaf, and while you may see them anywhere, it is in an area like this, where there is a transition from openness to denser forest, that you are most likely to spot one. Fairly large, they have ears that are more than 2 inches long, a head and body that measure approximately 15 inches in length, and a fluffy tail about 2 inches long. Each female is able to produce several litters of three to nine young each year. Within hours of giving birth, the female is able to mate and conceive again. In addition, a female born in early spring is ready to mate by late summer. One male and one female, together with offspring, could produce 350,000 rabbits in only five years. Yet, being preyed upon by nearly every omnivore and carnivore of the forest or sky, rabbits' lives are quite precarious, and most never make it past their first birthday.

Rising and descending across a low spur ridge in a attractive forest, you'll come to an intersection at 6.6 miles where the yellow-blazed Saddleback Horse Trail goes both left and right (a short distance to Mount Ephraim Road). You need to bear left, coming to an intersection with the white-blazed Mountain Loop Trail at 6.75 miles. Turn left to follow the blazes of the combined trails and begin a moderately steep and steady climb.

The pathway to the right at 7.3 miles heads to the Potomac Overlook (which you will pass when you drive down the mountain). The white and blue blazes veer to the left at 7.4 miles; keep right and make the final ascent along the blue-blazed trail. Return to the summit parking area at 7.5 miles, hopefully now better able to understand what Gordon Strong meant when he stated, "Those who appreciate natural beauty will be better people, people who will treat each other better."

20

Edwards Ferry to the Monocacy River Aqueduct

Total distance (one-way): 11.7 miles

Hiking time: 5 hours, 30 minutes

Vertical rise: 35 feet

Maps: USGS 7½' Sterling (MD/VA); USGS 7½' Leesburg (MD/VA); USGS 7½' Waterford (MD/VA); USGS 7½' Poolesville (MD/VA)

Sunny weather on the weekends often entices so many people outdoors that the C&O Canal and the trails around Great Falls (see Hikes 24, 25, and 26) can almost become clogged highways of walking, running, and bicycling human beings. Yet, a drive of a just a few miles to the west will enable you to enjoy the flat terrain and natural beauty of the towpath without feeling like part of an invading horde.

In addition to the flora, fauna, and scenery to be appreciated between Edwards Ferry and the Monocacy River Aqueduct, you will come across a number of historic sites and architectural structures worth spending a few minutes to study. There is also the festive option of taking the only remaining ferry across the Potomac, which provides you with a chance to look at the river and the towpath from a different perspective.

This is a one-way hike, so unless you want to do some backtracking, a car shuttle is necessary. The drop-off point for the first car may be reached by driving I-270 between Gaithersburg and Frederick to take exit 22 onto MD 109. Now headed in a southwestern direction, follow this roadway for 3 miles and make a right turn onto MD 95 (Comus Road). An additional 2.4 miles of driving brings you to a wide area in the road, where the entrance to Sugarloaf Mountain is on the right (see Hike 19). Turn left onto Mount Ephraim Road and follow it for more than 2 miles to make a right onto Mouth of Monocacy Road. Continue on this route, and once you cross MD 28, proceed 1.3 miles farther to bear left into the canal parking area.

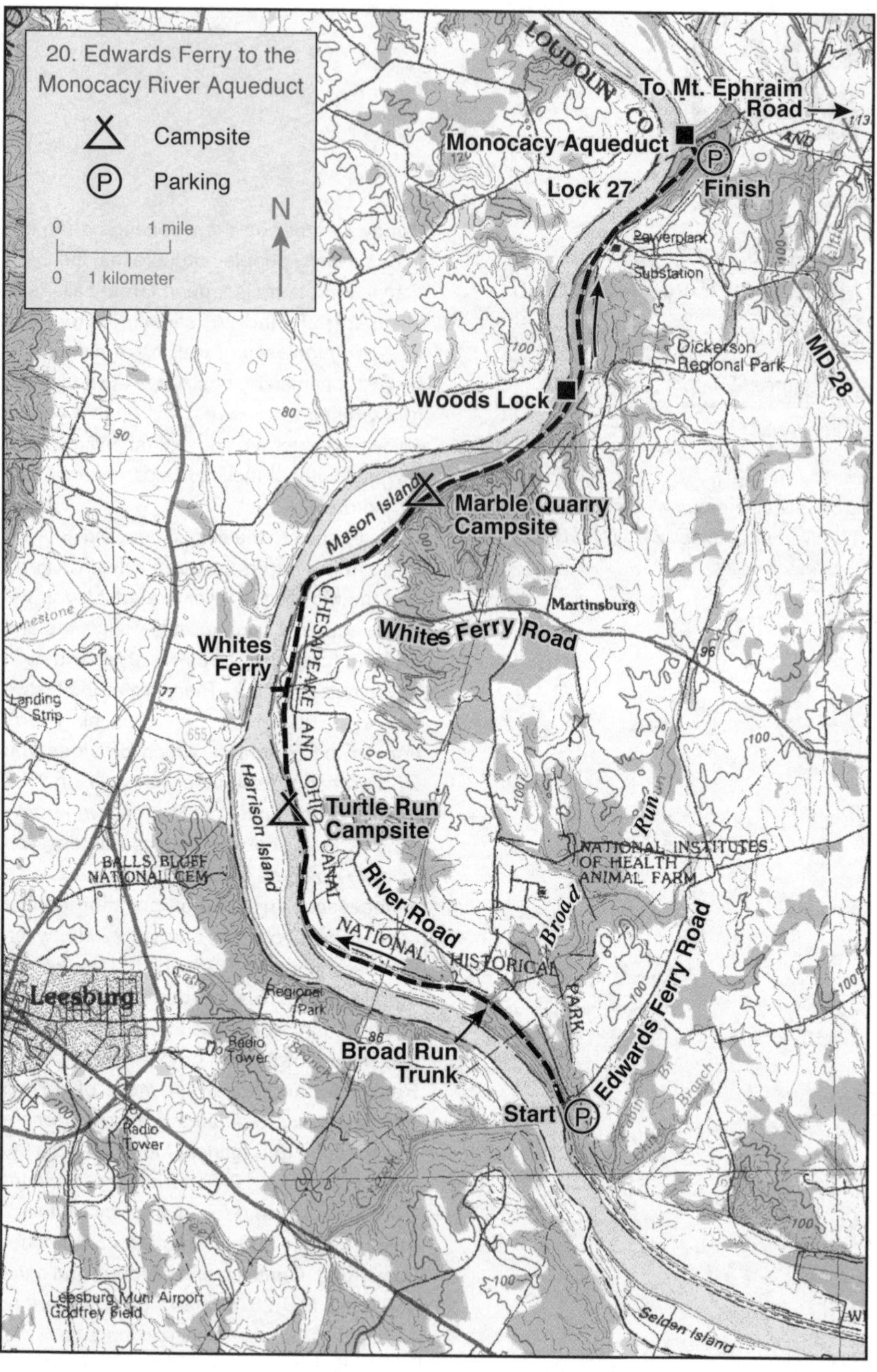

20. Edwards Ferry to the Monocacy River Aqueduct
Campsite
Parking
0
1 mile
0
1 kilometer
N
To Mt. Ephraim Road
Monocacy Aqueduct
Finish
Lock 27
Woods Lock
Marble Quarry Campsite
Mason Island
Whites Ferry Road
Whites Ferry
Turtle Run Campsite
Harrison Island
River Road
Broad Run Trunk
Start
Edwards Ferry Road
Leesburg
MD 28

Drive the second car back to MD 28 and turn right, following it through twists and turns to bear right onto MD 109 in Beallsville. Less than 3 miles beyond this small settlement, turn right onto MD 107, watching for the left turn 2 miles later onto Edwards Ferry Road, which is followed to its end, at the canal parking area.

Begin the hike by walking westward along the towpath and looking for the brick remains of Jarboe's Store, which once sold provisions to the travelers and workers on the canal. The boat ramp into the Potomac marks the site of Edwards Ferry, where Union troops crossed the river during the battle of Balls Bluff in 1861.

The remains of Broad Run Trunk are passed 1.1 miles into the hike. Unlike most of the other aqueducts along the canal, which were supported by masonry arches, this one was constructed with wood.

Because of its low elevation and resulting warmer temperatures, the soil along the towpath is some of the first in Maryland to burst forth with the colorful blossoms of springtime. Arriving in March are the white petals of the bloodroot, followed closely by the pinkish, miniature hearts of squirrel corn. Also be on the lookout for columbines, shooting stars, violets, bluets, and a mint, named gill-over-the-ground.

As you walk along enjoying this beauty, you might want to utter a small word of thanks to Supreme Court Justice William O. Douglas. When *The Washington Post* endorsed a plan to turn canal lands into a highway in 1954, Justice Douglas wrote a letter of protest to the newspaper's editors and invited them to join him on a walking tour of the entire towpath. The walk and its resulting publicity helped showcase what a national treasure the canal was, and, even though alternate plans were continually proposed, the C&O Canal was finally protected as a component of the National Park Service in January 1971.

In addition to providing an accounting of his many outdoor travels throughout the United States, Douglas evocatively describes the wonders of the natural aspects along the canal in his book, *My Wilderness: East to Katahdin, Adventures in the American Wilderness from Arizona to Maine.* He was also an ardent supporter of a national system of trails and is the only person ever appointed to the Supreme Court to have hiked the full length of the Appalachian Trail.

The Turtle Run Campsite at 3.5 miles (which has chemical toilets and water in season) overlooks Harrison Island in the middle of the river. The island is now uninhabited, but it is believed to have been home to a band of Piscataway Indians in the late 1600s.

The structure at 4.7 miles is all that remains of a bridge built in 1876 so that road traffic had access over the canal to make use of Whites Ferry across the Potomac. The crumbling brick building across the towpath once served as a warehouse.

It is recommended at this point that you take the diversion mentioned earlier, and turn left along Whites Ferry Road to do as the folks in the 1800s did. Although this is a utilitarian boat, the round-trip ride across the river can be a scenic and enjoyable one as you watch waterfowl and other birds wing their way above the river. The trip costs just about as much a can of soda, so what excuse can you use not to go?

However, even if you don't want to take the ride, you should at least walk over to the store for a freshly made sandwich, some ice cream, or a cold drink. All of this and restrooms are available in season. The store (301-349-5200) also rents canoes and provides shuttles, so if you call before you begin this hike, it is possible that employees will help you with the car shuttle and you will only need to bring one car from home.

Resume the hike by continuing westward along the towpath. Mason Island comes into view just as the canal mimics the Potomac River by swinging slightly to the right at 5.9 miles. A short time later, you may believe you have been walking faster than you really are; milepost 38 is misplaced and is only 0.7 mile from milepost 37.

The Marble Quarry Campsite at 7.5 miles (which has water and chemical toilets in season) overlooks the narrower, upstream end of Harrison Island. Marble taken from a quarry near here–long before the canal was built–was used in the construction of Statuary Hall in Washington, D.C.

Close to 8 miles into the hike is the approximate site of Whites Ford, named for the same person who operated the ferry downstream. Confederate Lieutenant colonel E. V. White owned land on the Virginia side of the river and informed Southern military leaders about the ford, deemed to be the best place below Harpers Ferry to bring heavy equipment across the river.

Come into an open area at 8.9 miles, where the increased sunlight allows daisies and asters to grow. Oxeye daisy did not exist in North America until the early settlers began arriving from Europe. Its seeds were probably imported when they were inadvertently mixed with shipments of crop seeds or in the fodder used to feed livestock on the long ocean voyages from the Old World. Once here, it did not take the plant long to spread across the land, often overtaking open fields and garden lands. It is now found throughout most of the United States and Canada.

The aqueduct near Whites Ferry

This small clearing is the site of Woods Lock (Lock 26), built of red sandstone. The ruins of the lock house are surrounded by the canal and a stone bypass flume.

The canal loses much of its natural feeling once you pass the access route to the Dickerson Conservation Park at 10.2 miles, as you will soon be walking by the Dickerson Power Plant, built in the 1950s.

The towpath becomes a bit more peaceful by time you reach Lock 27 at 10.9 miles, damaged by Confederate troops in 1862. This was also the site of Spinks Ferry, out of operation for decades now.

At 11.4 miles, milepost 42 (placed only about 0.8 mile from milepost 41) marks the canal's entrance into Montgomery County. The Monocacy River Aqueduct, with its seven arches constructed of quartzite taken from Sugarloaf Mountain (see Hike 19), is at 11.6 miles. Come to the end of the hike a few hundred feet later, when you return to your shuttled car in the parking area.

21

Schaeffer Farm

Total distance (circuit): 9.8 miles

Hiking time: 5 hours

Vertical rise: 700 feet

Maps: USGS 7½' Germantown; park map

At one time, it was almost a universal experience for the residents of Maryland to wander through the fields and woodlots of cultivated farmlands. If they did not live on a farm themselves, they at least knew and visited someone who did. As we have become increasingly urbanized, however, fewer and fewer of us have maintained ties with those in the country, and rural landowners are more reluctant than ever to allow people on their lands.

Thankfully, in an out-of-the-way section of Seneca Creek State Park, local citizens have cooperated with authorities and put in many volunteer hours constructing and maintaining a 10-mile network of trails. Hikers, bikers, and horseback riders can now freely visit such a landscape over and over again, watching the crops advance from tiny seed sprouts to tall mature plants. The variation from open land to wooded tracts ensures a wide variety of wildlife such as white-tailed deer, gray and red foxes, wild turkeys, squirrels, chipmunks, beavers, and groundhogs. Warblers, vireos, meadowlarks, woodpeckers, vultures, and owls have all been seen visiting or living here.

The trailhead may be reached by taking I-270 exit 10 in Gaithersburg and following MD 117 (Clopper Road) westward. In 2 miles you will pass the entrance to the main part of the state park, but continue along MD 117, going through the intersection with MD 118 (Germantown Road). After making a left onto Schaeffer Road at the next intersection, continue an additional 2.5 miles to turn left onto what looks like a private driveway at

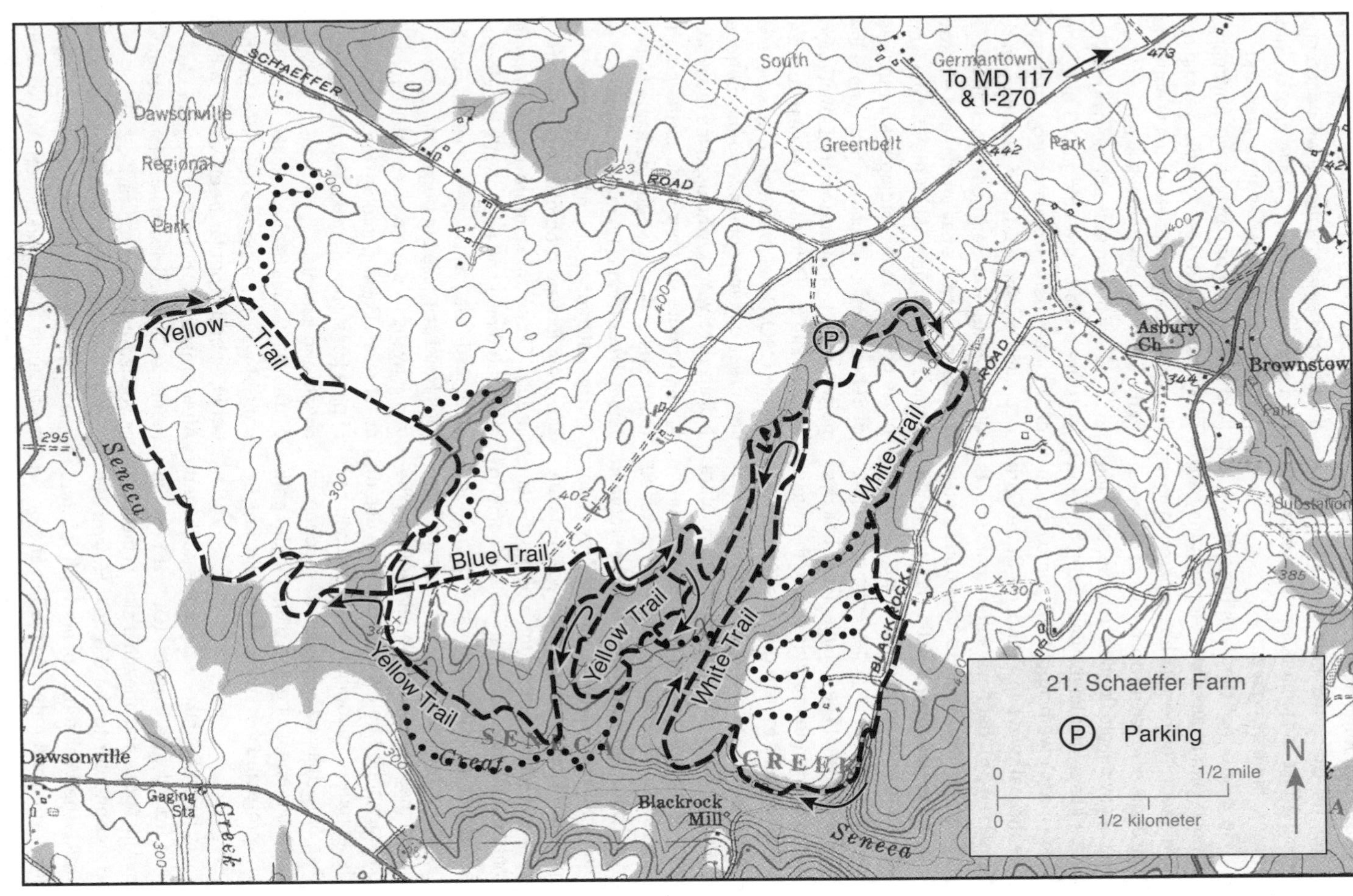

21. Schaeffer Farm
Parking
0
1/2 mile
0
1/2 kilometer
N
To MD 117 & I-270
South Germantown
Greenbelt
Park
Dawsonville Regional Park
SCHAEFFER ROAD
BLACK ROCK ROAD
Asbury Ch.
Yellow Trail
Blue Trail
Yellow Trail
Yellow Trail
White Trail
White Trail
SENECA CREEK
Great
Seneca
Seneca
Blackrock Mill
Dawsonville
Gaging Sta
Creek

14938 Schaeffer Road. (There are also signs for Schaeffer Farm and Grey Rock Ranch.) Take the left fork in the driveway and arrive at the parking area.

Be aware that the trails here are more popular with mountain bikers than they are with hikers. You need to be prepared to have one come screeching up in front of or behind you at any minute. In their defense, all of the riders I have met have been courteous and given me fair warning of their approach. Unlike the pathways in Patapsco State Park (see Hike 35) that have suffered the effects of bicyclists who seem to have trouble staying on the designated pathways, the Schaeffer Farm trails are in good shape, proof that the riders here are a conscientious group.

Please Note: The Schaffer Farm Trail System is one of the few in the state that has a winter closure to help give the trails a rest, generally preventing use during freezing and thawing cycles. The closure usually occurs from around mid-December to mid-March. Also, the entire Schaffer Farm area is closed to the public for a managed hunting program that most often occurs from late November into early December and then again in early January. Call the park for the most up-to-date information. Also note that you will come to a number of intersections with orange-, green-, or red-blazed trails. I have not mentioned these because at no time during the hike described below will you make use of those routes. In addition, please remember that, other than edibles such as raspberries and mulberries, all of the plants in the park are protected by law and should not be picked.

To begin the hike, walk to the cultivated field from the parking lot. (Do not take the trail that goes from the other side of the lot; it is a connector to the 6.3-mile Hoyles Mill Trail.) The White Trail bears both left and right; you want to turn to the left and enter the woods soon afterward. As you hike through Schaeffer Farm, you will notice one field is planted in corn, while another has soybeans. Come back another year, and the field that had corn may have soybeans. These crops are rotated to avoid wearing out the soil; the soybeans return many nutrients to the earth that the corn takes out.

If you are here in the early morning as you skirt the edge of the field at 0.3 mile, the crow of a rooster from a nearby farm may add another element to the bucolic nature of this hike. The trail goes back into the woods to cross a small stream and emerge beside another field. All of the streams you cross or pass on this outing are tributaries of Seneca Creek, which has its origins in the northern part of Montgomery County and empties into the Potomac River near Lock 24 on the C&O Canal. Some historians believe the creek's name comes from the Seneca Indians of New York, who used the creek valley as a route on their raids to the south. Other authorities point out the name means "stony creek" and is merely descriptive.

The patch of raspberries at 0.5 mile may slow your forward progress when they ripen in July. Cross three more small streams around 0.6 mile and rise to walk beside another field. The trail is located next to Blackrock Road at 1 mile but begins to veer away from it by the time you cross a small dirt road at 1.1 miles. Passing through the dark shade of pine trees, you will make several short descents and ascents.

The White Trail begins to make use of the right-of-way for a transcontinental phone cable, lined by poplar trees, at 2.1 miles. After crossing a couple of Seneca Creek tributaries, you will rise steeply for a distance as you leave the right-of-way.

You will come to a T intersection at 3 miles where the White Trail continues right (and returns to the parking lot). You want to

The open fields of Schaeffer Farm

bear left onto the Yellow Trail and walk beside a fence line for a few feet at 3.2 miles before entering the woods and beginning a downward trend.

Emerge onto, and walk beside, the edge of a cultivated field at 3.7 miles and come to an intersection once you return to the woods at 3.9 miles. The Blue Trail heads off to the right, but you want to continue left along the Yellow Trail, winding in and out and up and down a number of small gullies.

This is one of the prettiest parts of the hike, and chipmunks are often seen darting along the ground, weaving around small patches of squawroot and Indian pipe. The latter's ghostly color, its tendency to feel cold and turn black when touched, and the viscous fluid it oozes when its flesh has been broken have given rise to a number of other common names such as ghost flower, corpse-plant, ice plant, and fairy smoke.

Coming close to the edge of a field at 4.7 miles, the Blue Trail heads to the right, but you want to keep to the left. Just a few feet later, another section of the Blue Trail comes in from the right; again you need to keep to the left on the Yellow Trail.

Return to the field at 4.8 miles, where a grand old oak tree has spread its limbs for many yards in all directions. Indian pipe and jack-in-the-pulpit grow in the understory of the forest as you descend to cross a couple of water runs and rise back to the field at 5.5 miles.

Arrive at a four-way intersection at 5.6 miles. The Blue Trail goes to the right along a dirt road, while the Yellow Trail splits and continues both straight and to the left. You want to bear left and descend along a dirt road. There's a lot to see at this particular spot. The open spaces of the meadows urge your eyes upward to take in the vista of the surrounding low ridges, while tiny Deptford pink flowers may cause a downward glance—where you might also spy a rabbit jumping quickly into a brier patch in the hope of not having been seen.

Blackberries can add an additional taste to the hike as you cross a creek at 5.9 miles. There are even more of them where you diagonally cross a gravel road at 6.2 miles and descend along the edge of a field. Ironwood and juniper trees obviously enjoy the moisture that Little Seneca Creek provides to the surrounding soil at 6.4 miles. Ironwood is also known as eastern hop hornbeam, a name that came about because its clusters of fruits reminded people of hops, a major ingredient in beer.

The Red Trail comes in from the left at 7.1 miles. Keep to the right along the Yellow Trail amid the vegetation of a cultivated field. There have been so many soybeans along this journey that my notes from scouting this hike read, "At times, I feel like I'm afloat in a sea of soybeans!"

From midsummer to late in the fall, chicory lines many of the fields you have been walking beside. The early colonists imported it from the Old World, where it had been cultivated for centuries. Egyptians harvested the plant from gardens along the Nile River more than 5,000 years ago, and the Greeks who were contemporaries of Christ used it for medicinal purposes. Recent scientific investigations have found that the plant has antibacterial properties and that a substance in its roots can lower heart rates.

Continuing along the Yellow Trail, you will soon cross a stream lined by jewelweed. At 7.9 miles, bear left, now following the route of the Blue Trail.

At 8.1 miles, you will have returned to the same four-way intersection you were at 5.6 miles into the hike. Avoid all of the other routes and turn to the left, following the Blue Trail along a dirt road with the wide-open sky above you. Be alert at 8.5 miles. The dirt road swings to the left, but you need to leave it and bear right to continue along the Blue Trail.

Pay close attention when you come to the T intersection at 8.6 miles. The Yellow Trail runs both left and right. You need to take the left track for just a few feet so that you can make another left onto the Blue Trail where the Yellow Trail swings to the right.

The Blue Trail comes to an end at the T intersection with the Yellow Trail at 8.8 miles. Bear left and make another left when the Yellow Trail comes to an end at its intersection with the White Trail at 9.6 miles.

Walking through the same field in which you began the hike, return to your car at 9.8 miles.

If you have not had enough walking for one day or are looking for a new place to go some other time, give the trails in the nearby main part of Seneca Creek State Park a try. The 3.7-mile Lake Shore Trail encircles Clopper Lake, passing through fields of wildflowers. Long Draught Trail is 2.5 miles long and follows a stream to a wetland area and onto a laurel-covered hillside. The Great Seneca and Mink Hollow Trails are each 1.25 miles in length and traverse forested slopes and marshlands. The Old Pond Trail, only 0.33 mile long, passes by a pond in its last stages of succession. All of these pathways interconnect in some way or another.

22

Little Bennett Regional Park

Total distance (circuit): 9.6 miles

Hiking time: 4 hours, 50 minutes

Vertical rise: 900 feet

Maps: USGS 7½' Urbana; park map

Unlike many other parks located close to large population centers, Little Bennett Regional Park is not overdeveloped with swimming pools, amusement centers, skating rinks, basketball courts, and the like. It does offer a 91-site campground with hot showers and a camp store, horseshoe and volleyball areas, and an activities center; yet, these facilities are concentrated on just a few acres of its southern edge off MD 355 (and are only available to campers). Thankfully, the rest of the park has been–more or less–left in its natural state, and 20 miles of trails are available to lead visitors onto 3,700 acres of dense forests, open meadows, narrow hollows, low-rising ridgelines, and small stream valleys lush with vegetation. Humans did make use of these acres in the past, and several reminders of their way of life remain in the park.

The trailhead may be reached by driving I-270 between Gaithersburg and Frederick to take exit 18 onto Clarksburg Road. Heading northward, stay on Clarksburg Road for 2.6 miles to the parking area on the right (Hyattstown Mill Road is on the left).

Please note: Severe storms just before this book went to press have washed out bridges, and some trails may be rerouted due to environmental concerns. Be sure to check with authorities for current information. Also, due to a trail closure, it will now be necessary to walk along busy Clarksburg Road for almost a half mile if you wish to experience everything this write-up describes. However, if you don't want to face this exposure to (possibly heavy) traffic, you can start

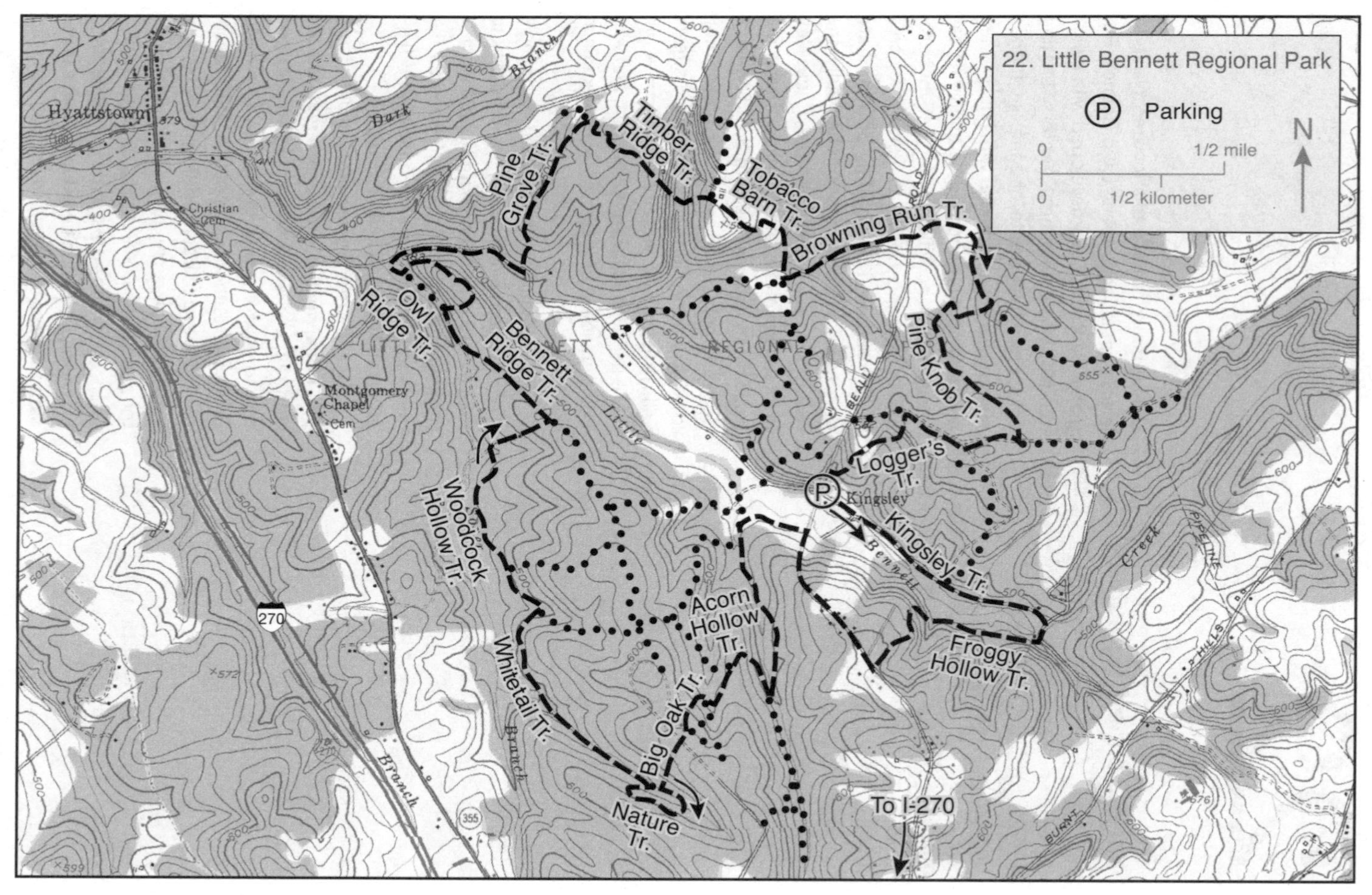
22. Little Bennett Regional Park
P Parking
0
1/2 mile
0
1/2 kilometer
N
Timber Ridge Tr.
Tobacco Barn Tr.
Pine Grove Tr.
Browning Run Tr.
Owl Ridge Tr.
Bennett Ridge Tr.
Pine Knob Tr.
Logger's Tr.
Kingsley Tr.
Froggy Hollow Tr.
Woodcock Hollow Tr.
Acorn Hollow Tr.
Whitetail Tr.
Big Oak Tr.
Nature Tr.
To I-270
Hyattstown
Christian Cem
Montgomery Chapel
Cem
Kingsley
Dark
Branch
Little
Bennett
Creek
PIPELINE
270
355

this hike by crossing the road (use caution) from the parking area, following that route for 0.1 mile, and turning left onto Stoney Brook Trail for 0.2 mile to join up with the hike description below at its 1.9 milepoint.

To do the complete hike, do not cross the busy roadway; rather, take the gravel road from the parking lot (Kingsley Trail), and walk by a few juniper trees and a number of black locust trees. By mid- to late summer, many of the locust leaves will be turning brown, the work of a beetle, the locust leaf miner. Overwintering in bark crevices, the adult leaf miners feed upon and skeletonize the lower surfaces of newly emerged spring leaves. Soon they deposit eggs from which larvae emerge to bore into the leaves and feed. By midsummer they begin the season's second generation, which results in the early browning and dropping of leaves.

The Hard Cider Trail comes in from the left at 0.4 mile; stay to the right on the road where grapevines drape over tree limbs. The road swings to the left at 0.7 mile, but you want to bear right and take the swinging bridge across Little Bennett Creek to the Kingsley School House (known to locals as Froggy Hollow). Built in 1893, the school served the community until 1935, when the Great Depression caused residents to vacate the area in search of work elsewhere. There are a number of one-room schoolhouses that still exist in Montgomery County, but this is the only one to remain in an unaltered state.

To continue the hike, take the Froggy Hollow Trail to the right of the building, passing through a pine plantation at 0.9 mile and rising to cross under a utility line.

When the previous editions of this book were printed, the Froggy Hollow Trail crossed the busy highway at 1.3 miles and continued. That section of trail has been closed, so you will now need to turn right to walk along the road (use extreme caution!), turn left onto the Wilson Mill Trail at 1.7 miles, cross the stream a 1.9 miles, and turn left to follow the Stoney Brook Trail. Jack-in-the-pulpit grows profusely on the forest floor, while poison ivy vines creep over tree trunks and branches. Bear right at 2.4 miles and ascend along the Acorn Hollow Trail. Less than 500 feet later, leave that pathway and turn left onto the Big Oak Trail, lined by running cedar.

The Little Oak Trail comes in from the left at 2.7 miles. Stay on the Big Oak Trail, which brings you to the campground amphitheater, where you bear right to the Hawk's Reach Activity Center, with displays, restrooms, and a soda machine. (If the center is closed, restrooms are just a short distance away along the campground road.) This is a good place for a rest break, so take a few minutes to leisurely stroll the Wild Wings Garden, which has flowers planted specifically to attract butterflies. More than 60 species have been observed here or at other sites throughout the park.

Because it has a flight period lasting from May through August, the black swallowtail is possibly seen by more park visitors than any other butterfly. Although the male and female differ slightly in size and coloring, both have velvety black wings marked by rows of yellow spots and splashes of lustrous blue. They feed on a number of plants, but a favored one seems to be milkweed. Interestingly, in the caterpillar stage, they have small orange horns from which they emit a nauseating odor to fend off predators.

To continue the hike, cross the campground road, pass through a small wooded area on a pathway, cross another section of the campground road, and reenter the woods on the Nature Trail.

Have you ever wondered what red oak, chestnut oak, tulip poplar, red maple, or

Open fields intersperse with woods during the hike

black oak look like? Turn left onto a different section of the Nature Trail at 3.1 miles to find out (the Whitetail Trail continues to the right). These trees, and others, are labeled, permitting you to make close-up observations of the texture of their barks, shapes of leaves, kind of seeds or flowers, and other identifiable characteristics.

Pass by trails bearing left to the campground at 3.2 miles, coming into an area where both Virginia creeper and poison ivy snake their way up tree trunks. The poison ivy has three leaflets, while the creeper's leafstalk bears five.

The pathway to the right at 3.3 miles returns to the campground; turn left and follow the Whitetail Trail, soon crossing a small water run and rising along carpets of crow's foot. Descend and intersect the Antler Ridge Trail coming in from the right; keep left, cross a tributary of Soper's Branch at 4.1 miles, and ascend through an evergreen forest.

The Whitetail Trail comes to an end at 4.5 miles, where the Woodcock Hollow Trail goes both left and right; turn left and descend. Crossing another Soper's Branch tributary at 4.7 miles, pass through open meadows highlighted by the white blossoms of daisies, the golden petals of black-eyed Susans, and the fluttering of scores of butterfly wings.

The Woodcock Hollow Trail terminates upon reaching the Bennett Ridge Trail, which heads both left and right. Bear left along this grassy roadway, which was built to facilitate the construction of a sewer line. The large piles of loose dirt you are wondering about beside the route are the work of Allegheny mound-builder ants. Scientists speculate that the mounds help protect the colony from heat and loss of moisture.

To avoid some wet areas along the Bennett Ridge Trail, turn right along the Owl Ridge Loop Trail at 5.4 miles. Both of these trails come back together when they meet up with Hyattstown Mill Road at 5.8 miles, an area in which David Zeigler operated a couple of mills from the early to mid-1800s. The first mill crushed the stems and berries of sumac for tanning leather, while a later mill cut wood for lumber and crushed animal bones to be used by farmers as fertilizer.

The remains of the millrace are visible as you turn right on Hyattstown Mill Road. Jack-in-the-pulpit evidently loves the moist soil here, for it attains some of the largest sizes ever seen by many hikers. Ford Little Bennett Creek at 6 miles, noticing that the sound of the running water and the wind passing through the trees have drowned out the traffic noise of MD 355 and I-270.

Just a few steps before you would cross a road barrier, make a left and ascend along the Pine Grove Trail, aptly named as you soon pass through a pine plantation. The churned ground of the pathway and the copious amounts of horse droppings quickly inform you that this is an equestrian route.

Be alert at 6.7 miles, or you will miss the sudden turn to the right you need to make onto the Timber Ridge Trail. Pass through a couple of overgrown clearings, use a wooden bridge to negotiate a wet area at 7.2 miles, and come to the end of the Timber Ridge Trail in an open meadow at 7.4 miles.

Turn to the right onto the Tobacco Barn Trail (which also goes left), passing by the foundation that is all that is left of the old barn that had been constructed with mud-and-stone chinking. Another rest break may be in order now. There are no Olympian views like those found in the mountains to the west, yet this spot provides you with the most expansive vista of the hike. For 360 degrees you can look across the forest to the surrounding ridgelines. In addition, why not take the time to become a child again? Assume a horizontal position on the grass, stare up at the sky, and try to make out the shapes of dragons, castles, and chivalrous knights in the clouds as they float by.

Resume the hike by descending into the woods at 7.6 miles, fording Browning Run and coming to a four-way intersection. The Tobacco Barn Trail continues straight ahead, while the Browning Run Trail runs both left and right. Turn left into the woods and cross a tributary of Browning Run at 7.8 miles.

Avoid the unauthorized trail to the left less than 500 feet later, coming into an open area populated by sundrops. If you had the time to spend an entire day next to these yellow blossoms, you could bear witness to one of the natural world's small dances. At about the same time the early-morning light begins to spread across the horizon, the sundrop's tightly wound, reddish-orange, tapering buds will begin to spread outward, eventually opening up to become deep golden blossoms whose pigment mimics that of the solar orb rising higher into the sky. As the shadows from the surrounding vegetation begin to lengthen in the evening, you would notice that the flowers are folding up, as if retiring for the day and preparing for the cooler night

Poison ivy has three leaflets; Virginia creeper's leafstalk bears five

air. The next morning, the blooms you watched the day before will probably have withered away, and it will be new ones that will help you greet the promise of a fresh dawn.

Use caution once again when you cross Clarksburg Road at 8.1 miles. The Browning Run Trail continues to the left at 8.4 miles, but you want to bear right onto the Pine Knob Trail, passing first through a stand of pine and then of beech trees. Intersect and turn right onto the Logger's Trail at 8.9 miles, keeping right again along this same pathway when the Hard Cider Trail comes in from the left at 9.1 miles. Be alert along the descent at 9.3 miles. The Logger's Trail, which you want to continue upon, makes a sudden left off the old roadway you have been following. A few hundred feet later, it makes a hard right, but you need to descend the connector trail to return to your car and bring this outing to an end at 9.6 miles.

23

Rock Creek Regional Park and Lake Frank

Total distance (circuit): 4.3 miles

Hiking time: 2 hours, 30 minutes

Vertical rise: 800 feet

Maps: USGS 7½' Kensington; park map

Within the Maryland–National Capital Park and Planning Commission, the Montgomery County Department of Park and Planning operates more than 300 sites throughout the county. Many are smaller than 10 acres in size and only contain playgrounds, picnic areas, and ball fields and courts. Others, such as Little Bennett (see Hike 22), Black Hill, and Rock Creek Regional Parks encompass thousands of acres.

Located close to the center of the county, Rock Creek Regional Park has two distinct sections. The portion around Lake Needwood is quite developed, with an 18-hole golf course and the usual amenities that go along with such a facility: an archery range, numerous picnic areas and shelters, a playground, a snack bar, and a boat shop that rents canoes, rowboats, and paddleboats in season. There is even an outboard motor-powered pontoon boat that carries 25 people onto the lake for 20-minute cruises on weekends and holidays throughout the summer season.

In contrast, the section of the park near Lake Frank has been left in a more natural state. Other than an outdoor education facility on the outer edge of the park, the modest-sized Meadowside Nature Center, a farmstead, and a small aviary for permanently injured raptors, the only other development is a well-designed network of trails that traverses a wide variety of habitats and environments.

The moderately easy hike described here has only a few short ups and downs and makes use of most of the pathways as it goes beside a small pond, comes into contact with several streams and open areas, and swings around the lake. Tulip poplar, sycamore, birch, maple, and oak are just some of the trees you will be walking under, while azalea, mountain laurel, and dogwood grow at about eye level. If you walk quietly and are lucky, you may be privileged to watch some of the park's inhabitants–such as squirrels, rabbits, white-tailed deer, snakes, frogs, salamanders, raccoons, weasels, foxes, and beavers–go about their daily lives.

Please note: Severe storms just before this book went to press have damaged some trails. Be sure to check with authorities for current information.

There are obviously a number of ways to drive to the beginning of this hike, but to take advantage of one of the most direct routes with the least amount of traffic, leave I-270 at exit 8 in Gaithersburg and travel along I-370 East. Continue for 2.2 miles and merge onto Shady Grove Road East, which you follow for 1.5 miles to make a right turn onto Muncaster Mill Road (MD 115). Turn right into the park 3.3 miles later and continue an additional 0.4 mile to the Meadowside Nature Center parking lot. The trails are open from sunrise to sunset; the nature center is open from 9 AM to 5 PM, Tuesday through Saturday. Pets are permitted but must be kept on a leash.

The displays and exhibits in the nature center are better and more comprehensive than those found in the nature or visitors centers of many state parks, so take a few minutes to learn about the natural and human history of the area you are about to visit. Also, be sure to pick up a brochure that details the wide range of outstanding interpretive programs offered to both children and adults at numerous park sites in the county.

When you emerge from the nature center, bear slightly to the left and ascend to the sign for the Meadow and Pioneer Trails. Deptford pink dots the ground where, at the top of the little knoll, you want to bear right onto the blue-blazed Pioneer Trail and descend. Swing to the left along the boardwalk around Pioneer Pond at 0.15 mile. This is an especially pretty place to be around sunrise, as the first light of day spreads across the pond, illuminating the polished green surfaces of the water lily leaves. In a wonderful example of adaptation and evolution, the pores of the water lily are located on the upper surface of its leaves, unlike most other plants, whose pores are on the underside.

About halfway around the pond, bypass the first trail to the left, taking the second one left into the woods and watching for the work of resident beavers. About 200 feet later, bear right for just a few feet before making a left onto the Pioneer Trail. Avoiding trails to the left and the right, cross a stream on a covered bridge built by the Montgomery County Students Construction Trades Foundation in 1976 in memory of Rockville teacher Joan Valieant.

This stream and the moist woodlands around it are good places to find salamanders, of which at least 10 species have been found in the park. One of the most common, the eastern newt, can grow to be more than 5 inches long. Young eastern newts, known as efts, have rows of bright red spots across their backs and spend most of their time on land. As they age, the red spots fade away, and the newt returns to the water to feed upon crustaceans, larvae, and amphibian and fish eggs.

Immediately after the bridge, bear left onto the Springs Trail, soon staying to the left and joining up with the Muncaster Mill Trail. Bear left at the next intersection and cross over a bridge, making an immediate right afterward onto the Meadow Trail. Rise at a steady rate.

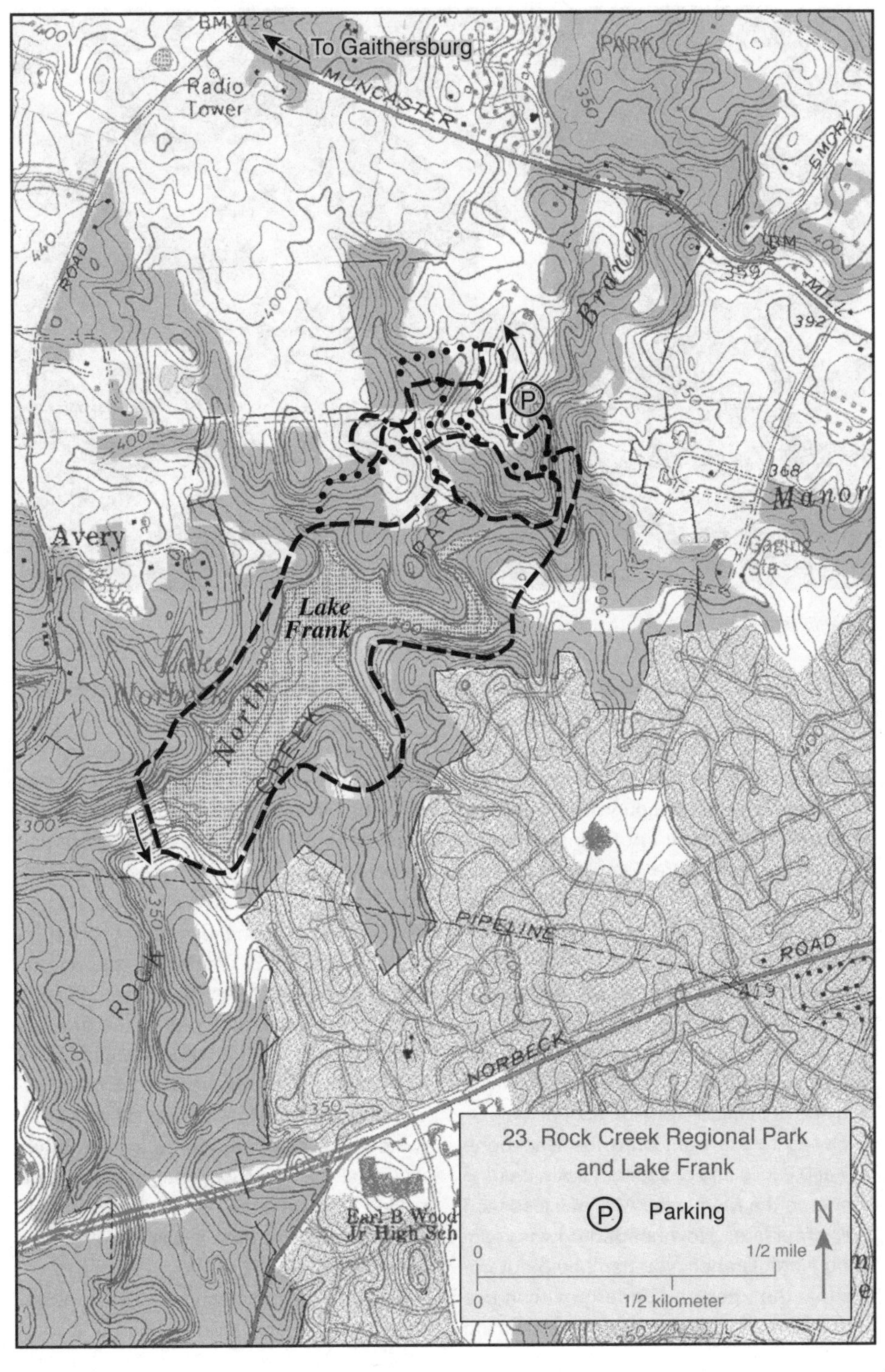
To Gaithersburg
BM 426
Radio Tower
MUNCASTER
PARK
EMORY
MILL
BM
359
392
368
Branch
Manor
Gaging Sta
Avery
Lake Frank
North
CREEK
PIPELINE
ROAD
NORBECK
ROCK
Earl B Wood Jr High Sch
23. Rock Creek Regional Park and Lake Frank
Parking
N
0
1/2 mile
0
1/2 kilometer

Water lilies

With the nature center in sight, make a hard right onto the Rocky Ridge Trail at 0.8 mile. The cries of owls have often been heard in these woods in the early-morning and early-evening hours. Although barn and saw-whet owls have been spotted in the park, they are quite rare here. One of the largest, the great horned owl, and one of the smallest, the eastern screech owl, are probably the two owls with which most people are familiar, due to their ability to adapt to suburban areas. Incidentally, all owls cough up those pellets of undigested fur, feathers, and bones that you broke apart as a student in biology class in middle or high school.

Swing to the right onto the Backbone Trail at 0.9 mile and descend quickly, bearing right onto the Muncaster Mill Trail less than 1,000 feet later. Now headed downstream along North Branch, you can't help but notice that the trees and undergrowth in this bottomland are different from the vegetation you were walking through just a few minutes ago.

Cross a tributary of North Branch at 1.2 miles and be alert. Do not go left, but keep to the right. However, less than 300 feet later, bear left onto the Big Pines Trail, staying on this route until the intersection with the Lakeside Trail at 1.4 miles. With views of Lake Frank visible through the vegetation, keep to the left along the Lakeside Trail, passing by large maple trees towering above and jack-in-the-pulpit growing close to the ground. Again, stay to the left when the Old Nasty Trail comes in from the right at 1.5 miles.

Not long after crossing a small water run, come to what appears to be a major intersection at 2.2 miles. Continue straight, soon making a left onto the paved hiker/biker trail and crossing the dam at the lower end of Lake Frank.

The lake was created in the 1960s by the Soil Conservation Service as part of a flood reduction and recreation plan for the Rock Creek drainage area.

This is the best view you are going to have of the reservoir, so take a rest break and enjoy the warmth of the sun. Red-shouldered and red-tailed hawks may soar overhead, while the slap of a beaver tail may bring your attention back to the lake. Small ripples moving across the water in a zigzag fashion may indicate a snake gliding to the opposite shore. The odds are good that it is a water snake out in search of a meal of fish, toads, frogs, or slugs.

Resume walking along the paved route around the lake, soon swinging away from the water and passing through an old parking lot at 2.8 miles. Continue on the same route as it passes an entrance road coming in from the right at 3.2 miles. It can feel strange to walk on this road with no traffic and pass through abandoned parking lots, almost as if you are the lone survivor in a science fiction movie about the aftermath of an atomic war.

Take the footpath (the Lakeside Trail) and reenter the shade of the woods when you come to the far end of the second parking lot at 3.4 miles. Be sure to avoid the two trails coming in from the left as the trail becomes a bit narrower at 3.7 miles.

You may not have been paying attention, but the cry and rat-a-tat-tat of woodpeckers have probably accompanied you throughout much of this journey. The downy, hairy, red-bellied, and pileated woodpeckers are year-round residents in the park, and they all favor a woodland environment. Because they share many of the same identifying marks–white back, white underparts, white-spotted black wings, and black-and-white streaked heads–the downy woodpecker may be hard to distinguish from the larger hairy woodpecker. Besides overall body size, the best way to tell them apart is that the downy's bill is about half the size of its head while the hairy's bill is almost as long as its head.

Cross a tributary of North Branch at 3.9 miles that is large enough that you will need to use stepping-stones to keep from getting wet feet. Immediately afterward, the Sunfish Trail comes in from the right; keep to the left. Be alert at 4 miles. You want to make a sudden turn to the left off the pathway you have been following and cross the wide North Branch on large, strategically placed stones. Once on the far side, turn right along the Muncaster Mill Trail.

With steps rising up from the stream at 4.1 miles, make a switchback to the left and ascend. (The trail to the right would take you to the ruins of the Muncaster lumber and gristmill in a little more than 0.5 mile.) Emerge out of the woods and arrive at the parking lot, where your car awaits for you to finish the hike, at 4.3 miles.

24

Potomac River at Carderock

Total distance (circuit): 5.8 miles

Hiking time: 2 hours, 45 minutes

Vertical rise: 200 feet

Maps: USGS 7½' Falls Church

Forming the boundary with West Virginia and Virginia, the Potomac River is, without a doubt, Maryland's mightiest stream. Rising from a small spring in West Virginia, the river has been flowing eastward for millions of years, mingling with the waters of the Chesapeake Bay (when it began to form about 10,000 years ago) near Point Lookout.

During the course of time, it has cut a 287-mile route through the Allegheny Plateau, the Blue Ridge Mountains, and the Piedmont and the Tidewater. Around Great Falls (see Hikes 25 and 26) it tumbles through a narrow gorge, creating some of the most dramatic and engaging scenery in Maryland. In the Carderock area, which is just southeast of the falls and is the section of the river explored in this hike, the streambed becomes just a bit wider and is split into several channels by a number of small islands. With only a few very minor ups and downs and a couple of traverses of short rocky areas, this circuit hike enables you to experience the landscape without having to expend a great deal of effort or energy. It consists of two loops, with your parked car being in the middle, so you could decide to do the loops on two separate occasions if you don't have the time or inclination to do the entire outing all at once.

To reach the trailhead, leave I-495 (Capital Beltway) northwest of Washington, D.C., at exit 41 (the last exit just before the Beltway crosses the Potomac River). Drive westward along the Clara Barton Parkway for 1 mile to take the overpass at the Naval Surface Warfare Center. Entering the Carderock

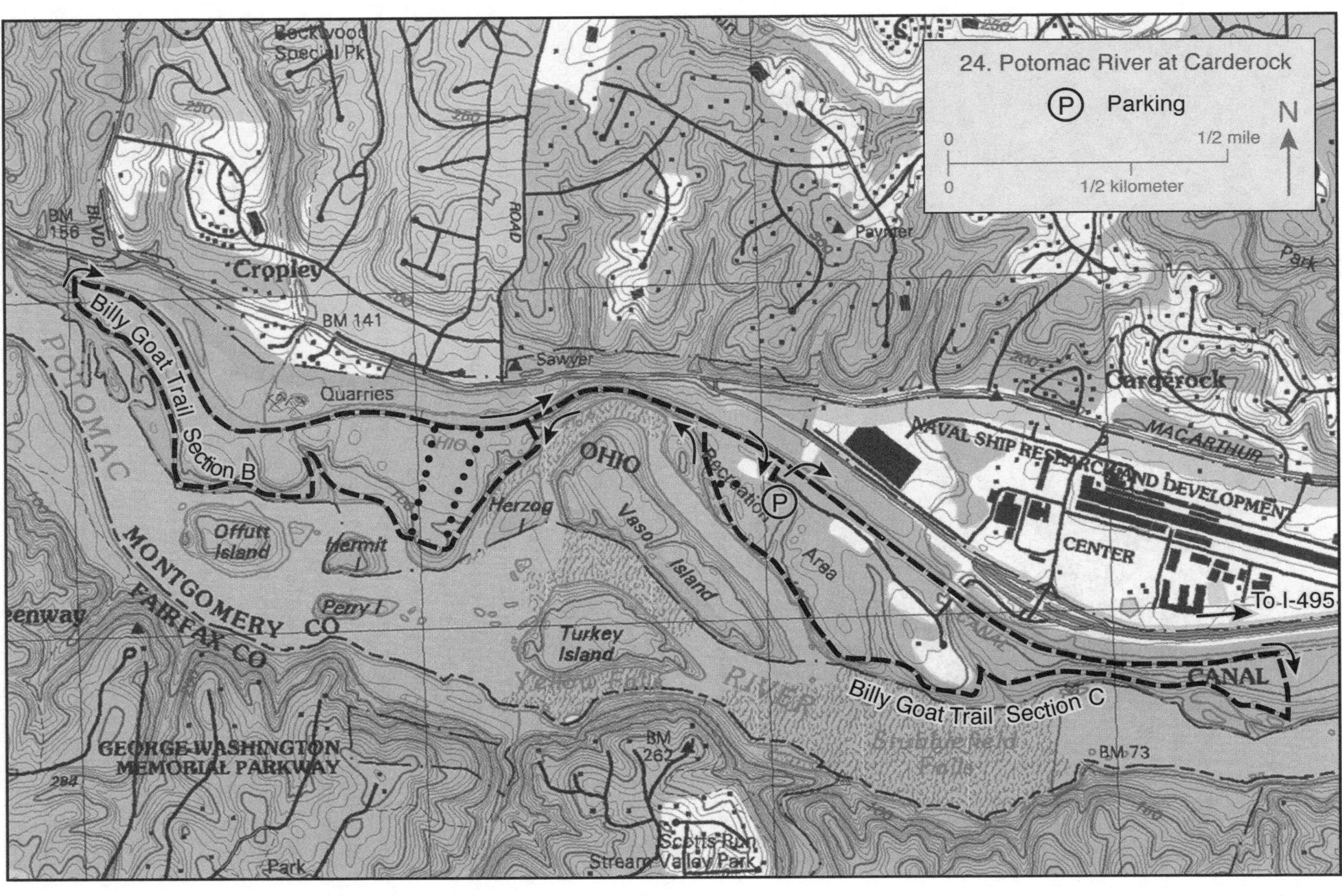
24. Potomac River at Carderock
Parking
N
0
1/2 mile
0
1/2 kilometer
Special Pk
BM 156
BLVD
Cropley
BM 141
ROAD
Sawyer
Paynter
Park
Carderock
Quarries
Billy Goat Trail Section B
OHIO
Herzog
Vaso Island
Recreation Area
NAVAL SHIP RESEARCH AND DEVELOPMENT CENTER
MACARTHUR
To I-495
Offutt Island
Hermit I
Perry I
Turkey Island
MONTGOMERY CO
FAIRFAX CO
POTOMAC
RIVER
CANAL
Billy Goat Trail Section C
BM 73
BM 262
GEORGE WASHINGTON MEMORIAL PARKWAY
Scotts Run Stream Valley Park
Park
284

The Potomac River as seen from the towpath

Recreation Area, turn right and continue 0.4 mile to leave your car in the far parking lot.

Walk the short pathway from the parking lot and turn right onto the towpath. For the most part, the canal has been restored for its first 23 miles, and it is rather common to see a variety of wildlife in, on, and near the water. The painted turtle, with red markings on its shell and red and yellow stripes on its head, legs, and tail, is fond of basking in the sun, and a dozen or more are often seen on a single floating log. Having no teeth, they use sharp gums and claws to tear fish, tadpoles, worms, and aquatic plants into pieces small enough to eat.

Cross over the road on which you drove in at 0.5 mile, looking along the canal for the speckled blossoms of jewelweed. Come to the remains of a pivot bridge at 1 mile, which was built after the canal company ceased operation and was used by members of the Civilian Conservation Corps camped nearby.

Directly across from the remains, turn right and descend along section C of the Billy Goat Trail. Trumpet creeper and morning glory vines intertwine along the ground as you come to the river and swing to the right. Ducks and geese often float close to the water's edge.

If you are the first person of the day to be walking here, you may find yourself flailing your arms wildly at the hundreds of spiderwebs stretched across the trail. Cross a water run with small cascades at 1.3 miles, and use the wooden footbridge to step over another stream at 1.6 miles. You need to avoid the trails to the right and swing left to continue to follow the blue blazes and return to the river's edge.

Cross a gully at 2 miles and another at 2.3 miles, rising to a view of Vaso Island. Soon afterward, be alert and do not take the trail to the right, but keep to the left along the top of the cliffs. The vertical walls below are a popular destination for rock climbers of the area, who have drolly given the cliffs names like the Guillotine and Matt's Splat.

The trail to the right at 2.5 miles leads back to the comfort stations and your car. Keep to the left, watching closely for the blue blazes; many unauthorized trails wander off through the bits of mountain laurel.

Turn to the left onto the towpath at 2.6 miles, at a point where small cliffs rise above an unusually wide section of the canal. Duckweed floats free along the surface of the water, while a few species of arrowhead have roots and rhizomes attached firmly in the mud.

Turn left onto section B of the Billy Goat Trail at 3 miles, entering a forest populated by a number of hickory trees. Living trees produce oxygen, provide homes for wildlife, and help stabilize soil. When they die, they take on a new role as homes for insects, bacteria, and fungi. As the wood decomposes it turns into a rich compost, adding nutrients back to the soil. In fact, if you take a few moments to look at the downed trunks around the trail that have become "host trees," you will notice that young plants and new trees have begun to sprout from them even before they have completely deteriorated.

The hike becomes more rugged and difficult for the next 2 miles as the pathway becomes narrower and traverses several sections of rocky terrain. Make sure to stay on the route marked by blue blazes. The high walls you walk along at 3.4 miles are crystalline metamorphic rocks of the Precambrian Age, which have been exposed by the river's erosive action. This spot also overlooks Hermit Island, and black ducks and great blue herons are often seen in the small channel that separates it from the mainland.

Soon after turning right to parallel a stream, be alert at 3.7 miles. The trail to the right leads to the towpath, but you want to bear left and cross the creek, coming to another short rocky stretch at 3.8 miles where you may again need to pay close attention to the blue blazes. A few small cedar trees growing among the boulders that overlook Offutt Island at 4.1 miles give the impression that this is a younger portion of the forest.

Be alert at 4.4 miles. The blue-blazed trail you want to follow bears right (it would be easy to mistakenly continue along a pathway beside the river) and returns to the towpath 250 feet later. Turn right, walking beside the canal, where your spirits will be brightened by the darting antics of dozens of dragonflies.

With the acrobatic contortions they have to go through to mate, it is a miracle there ever get to be so many dragonflies. The male flies slightly behind the female, and if she is amenable, he fastens a clasping organ located at the end of his tail into a slot in the back of her neck. This, however, places his sex organs far from the female's, which are located at the end of her tail. In order to complete the ritual, he must twist his sex organs into a pocket in his abdomen and fill it with sperm. She then swings her abdomen up and puts the end of her tail into his pocket, thereby fertilizing her eggs. Some species of dragonflies do all of this while continuing to fly!

On hot summer days you will be happy to know that just after passing the entrance to the Marsden Tract Day Use Area at 5.1 miles, there is a water fountain at the far end of the footbridge to the left. At 5.3 miles, pass by the entrance to section B of the Billy Goat Trail you turned onto an hour or so ago.

Section C of the Billy Goat Trail comes in from the right at 5.6 miles, but you want to continue along the towpath for 500 more feet and turn right onto the short connector pathway to the parking lot, coming to your car and the end of the hike at 5.8 miles.

25

Great Falls Recreation Area

Total distance (circuit): 5.8 miles

Hiking time: 3 hours

Vertical rise: 520 feet

Maps: USGS 7½' Falls Church (MD/VA); USGS 7½' Vienna (MD/VA); USGS 7½' Rockville (MD/VA)

Of its many natural and historical features, the C&O Canal's visitors most often cite Great Falls as their favorite destination. Families enjoy the kid-friendly activities centered on Great Falls Tavern, bicyclists welcome the miles of flat riding along the towpath, extreme kayakers test their mettle by trying to negotiate the falls, and canoeists paddle the slightly more sedate waters downstream. Naturalists come knowing that this section of the canal is popularly regarded as having the greatest number of rare plants and animals in Maryland; the abundant bird life is an added bonus. Everybody comes to take in the dramatic scenery of the falls as the Potomac rushes and churns over a series of drops within the narrow confines of the gorge it has etched out of the landscape.

Luckily for you, the outing you will be taking will bring you onto pathways that most people ignore, so you don't have to worry about feeling crowded in the woods. With only a few short ups and downs, the moderate hike takes you through a serenely deep forest typical of the Potomac River Basin, past reminders of gold-mining days, and enlightens you as to just how much wildlife can exist in proximity to large population centers.

To reach the trailhead, leave I-495 (Capital Beltway) northwest of Washington, D.C., at exit 41 (the last exit just before the Beltway crosses the Potomac River). Drive westward along the Clara Barton Parkway for 1.5 miles to where it ends at MacArthur Boulevard. Turn left onto that highway, continue for another mile, and turn left into the trailhead

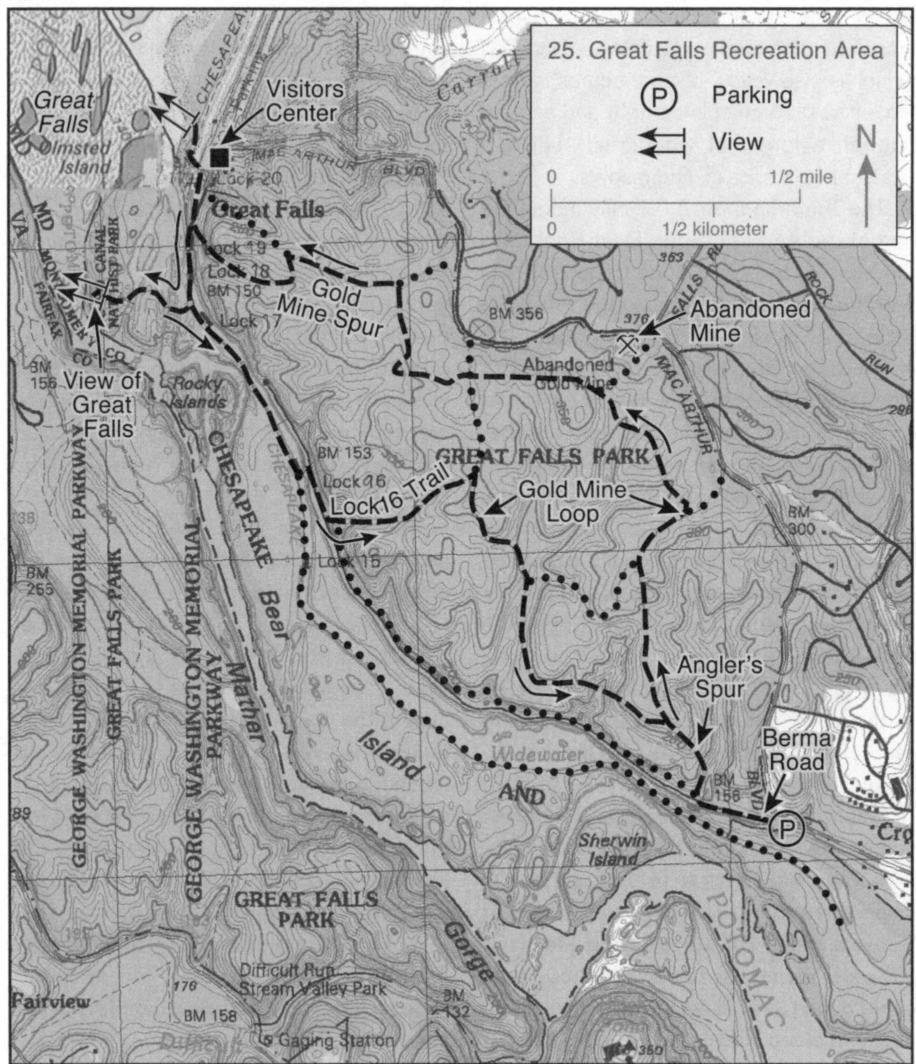

parking area across the road from the Old Angler's Inn.

Be forewarned. Because this parking lot is also the starting point for the popular Billy Goat Trail (see Hike 26) and a scenic walk along the canal towpath to Great Falls, it can fill up early in the morning on a nice Saturday or Sunday. You might want to think about doing this outing in the middle of the week to avoid the parking hassle. (You could also start this hike from the parking lot for the Great Falls Tavern, but it occasionally becomes even more crowded–and an entrance fee is charged.)

Walk onto Berma Road (the upper route) from the parking lot and come to a fence around a water supply apparatus at 0.15 mile. Turn right onto the yellow-blazed

Angler's Spur, avoiding the Valley Trail, which branches off to the right. The Woodland Trail (which is also yellow-blazed) comes in from the left at 0.25 mile; keep right and ascend through a forest of wonderfully tall and straight poplars, oaks, and maples.

The T intersection at 0.7 mile marks the end of the Angler's Spur. Bear right onto the blue-blazed Gold Mine Loop (you will be returning via the route to the left). The Valley Trail comes in from the right at 0.8 mile; keep left here and 200 feet later when the Rockwood Trail heads off to the right. The trenches and depressions beside the trail–in which jack-in-the-pulpit grows profusely–were dug to facilitate the mining of gold.

Following the Civil War, during which soldiers found flakes of gold in the sand near Great Falls, a sort of gold fever gripped the area. By 1901, there were at least six working mines close to the Potomac River. Operations were sporadic in the succeeding years, finally coming to an end around the 1940s.

Begin a gradual descent at 1.1 miles, soon passing a spring that may be dry late in the season. The trail to the right at 1.2 miles goes about 0.2 mile to MacArthur Boulevard and the ruins of the Maryland Mine, which processed close to 6,000 tons of ore during its lifetime. Keep to the left and descend along the remains of a trench that was probably dug in the early 1900s, when there was extensive prospecting for the gold-bearing quartz veins.

There is a major intersection just as the trench comes to an end at 1.5 miles. The trail that angles to the right leads to MacArthur Boulevard. You need to turn left for just a few steps before you bear right onto the trail marked as leading to the tavern. (If you turned left, you would loop back around to the beginning of the hike.)

Continue to descend and avoid the unmarked trail that comes in from the left at 1.7 miles. The chattering and antics of squirrels jumping from limb to limb or hopping upon the ground can't be beat for entertainment. Flying squirrels make their home in this forest, but since they are nocturnal, it is probably gray squirrels that are amusing you. In late summer and early fall, they are actively eating and gathering the nuts of hickory, beech, walnut, and oak trees, which they drop to the ground to retrieve and store for winter. At times, hikers must be wary, for several squirrels dropping nuts along the same portion of trail can make for quite an aerial bombardment.

Turn left when you come to a T intersection at 1.9 miles (the unmarked trail on the right leads to the boulevard). This wide pathway you are walking upon is the roadbed of the defunct Washington and Great Falls Railway, which once ran trolleys to the falls and tavern. The roadbed splits in two at 2.1 miles to form the circle on which the trolley turned around. Soon after this split, bear right, drop off the elevated right-of-way, and make a left turn onto the trail marked as leading to the towpath.

Cross a small gully at 2.2 miles, keeping to the right and continuing to descend. Again, keep to the right 500 feet later, descend to Lock 19, and follow the trail and dirt road to the visitors center.

There is much to see and do here. The visitors center is housed in the former Great Falls Tavern (constructed in the early 1800s), which served as a lock house and hotel for canal travelers and visitors to the falls. Restrooms and water are available, as are brochures, maps, books, exhibits, and audiovisual programs about the canal. Next to the tavern, if you are lucky, you may get to see Lock 20 in action, as a mule-drawn boat, operated by a crew in period clothing, prepares to take a load of visitors upstream on a 60-minute, round-trip ride in the waters of the canal.

Before leaving this area, cross the canal on the bridge and turn right along the towpath to ascend the concrete platform above the Washington Aqueduct intake for an impressive view over the Potomac to the Virginia shore. The dam you see stretching into the river diverts water into the underground aqueduct to be treated and consumed by the residents of the District of Columbia and parts of northern Virginia.

When ready to resume the hike, step off the concrete overlook platform, turn right along the towpath, and head downstream. You will have been walking for 3.1 miles since you left your car when you bear right to cross a footbridge onto Olmsted Island (named for Frederick Law Olmsted, a noted landscape architect) for a view of Great Falls. The island contains what is known as a bedrock river terrace forest, which occurs only along large rivers near the Atlantic coast. Within the forest are a number of rare, threatened, or endangered plants, such as hairy wild petunia, wild false indigo, and Canada milkvetch. As you make your way across the island, you can easily see the routes the Potomac takes when it is in flood stage.

At 3.3 miles, come to the overlook of Great Falls, the point where the Potomac River drops the greatest distance as it flows from the piedmont to the coastal plain. The river–having gathered strength and force from its humble beginnings in the mountains of West Virginia–rushes and roars over the rough, jagged rocks of narrow Mather Gorge (named for the first director of the National Park Service). This display can be both beautiful and breathtaking. In recent years, the falls have become a favorite of expert, almost daredevil, paddlers.

Great Falls Tavern Visitor Center

Return to the towpath and resume the hike downstream. An entrance to section A of the Billy Goat Trail (see Hike 26) comes in from the right at 3.9 miles. Use the stop lock and pedestrian bridge to cross the canal and turn right along Berma Road, which sits directly above the route of the Washington Aqueduct.

Pass by Lock 16 and its lock house at 4.1 miles; be alert just 600 feet later and turn left onto the yellow-blazed Lock 16 Spur. (If you wish to avoid the ups and downs of the rest of this hike, you could continue along Berma Road and return to your car in approximately 1.3 miles.) Ascend along a narrow and attractive stream valley whose forest contains a large number of beech trees.

The Lock 16 Spur comes to an end at 4.5 miles. Turn right onto the blue-blazed Gold Mine Loop (a left would take you back to the tavern). Just as you come to a small wetlands area at 4.8 miles, turn right onto the yellow-blazed Woodland Trail and descend beside a small stream. Be sure to look for small animal tracks in the mud along the creek when you cross it a few steps later. Here are a couple to look for:

The triangular-shaped hind paw print of a chipmunk is almost 2 inches in length, and it has five toes and claws. Its forepaw print is round with four toes and claws.

The track of the 2-inch-wide hind paw of an opossum shows a first toe that has no claw. The three middle toes are close together, with a fifth one pointing outward. The opossum's front paw is a bit smaller, with the five toes spreading outward like the fingers on an open human hand.

Swing away from the stream at 5 miles and gradually ascend to begin a series of ups and downs across several low ridges and small water runs. The Woodland Trail reaches its terminus at 5.5 miles; turn right and descend along Angler's Spur, making a left onto Berma Road about 500 feet later. Return to the parking lot and your car 5.8 miles after leaving them.

26

Billy Goat Trail

Total distance (circuit): 3.8 miles
Hiking time: 2 hours, 15 minutes
Vertical rise: 130 feet
Maps: USGS 7½' Falls Church

Section A of the Billy Goat Trail in the Great Falls section of the C&O Canal National Historical Park may hold the distinction of having the most awkward and exhausting 1-mile portion of trail in all of Maryland. Yet, approached with the right attitude, this could also be one of the most fun and scenic outings you will ever undertake.

In order to complete the hike, you are going to use your hands, feet, legs, and knees in order to scramble over giant boulders, slide down bare rocks, and negotiate jagged cliffs. If you are mentally prepared for these stone formations, you will feel like a kid again, bouncing around on a giant playground. If you view them as obstacles, you will probably have a miserable time. As a bit of compensation, there are remarkable views of the Potomac River rushing through narrow Mather Gorge—and the return route along the C&O Canal is easy, level, and one of the most scenic along the towpath.

This is such an extremely popular hike, and already receives such heavy use, that I hesitated to include it in this book. However, it is such a wonderful experience that excluding it would be a disservice to you. To avoid the largest crowds, do the hike during the middle of the week. To reach the trailhead, leave I-495 (Capital Beltway) northwest of Washington, D.C., at exit 41 (the last exit just before the Beltway crosses the Potomac River). Drive westward along the Clara Barton Parkway for 1.5 miles to where it ends at MacArthur Boulevard. Turn left onto that highway, continue for another mile,

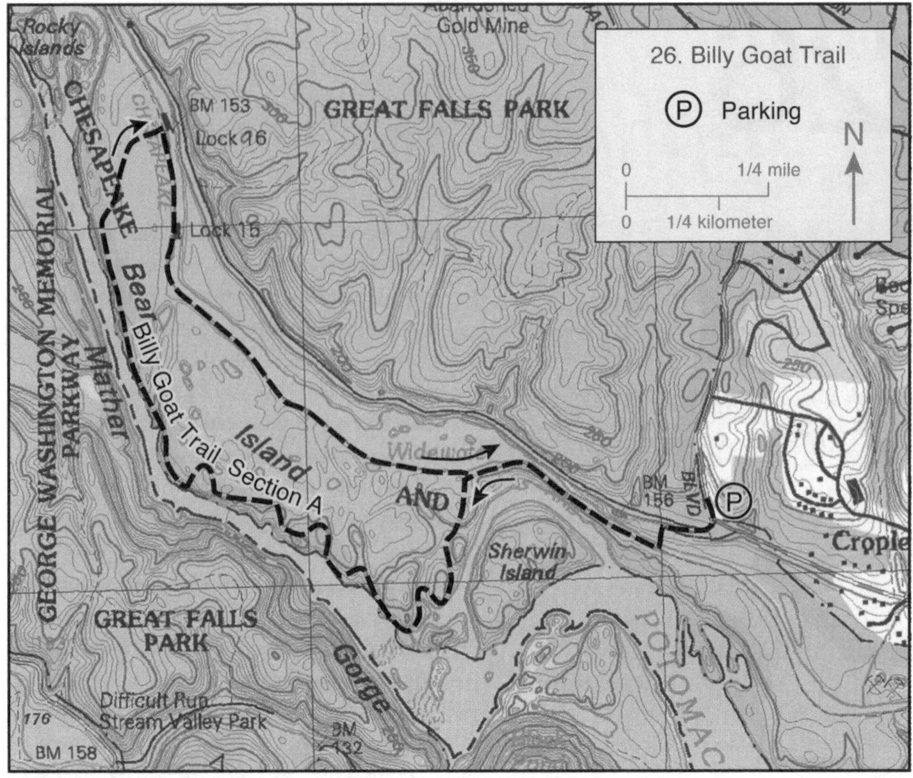

and turn left into the trailhead parking area across the road from the Old Angler's Inn.

Walk onto the lower road (the upper road is the beginning of Hike 25), follow a short trail, and turn right onto the towpath. The songs of various warblers resound through the oak forest around the canal; yellow, chestnut-sided, mourning, and yellowthroat warblers spend their days searching for insects and nesting in the crotches of small trees.

The rocks to the left at 0.25 mile provide a limited view of Sherwin Island, separated from the mainland by a small river channel. Widewater, a broad area of the canal, begins at 0.5 mile. A channel that the Potomac River abandoned centuries ago, this natural feature was incorporated into the route of the canal. It is here that you want to turn left onto section A of the Billy Goat Trail, skirt the edge of a wetlands, and descend along the blue-blazed pathway.

Wildflowers, such as Virginia bluebell, golden ragwort, hepatica, trillium, bloodroot, and spring beauty, abound in the rich soil of this floodplain. True to its name, the spring beauty is one of the first to emerge as the weather gets just a bit warmer. Lining the trail with flowers of pinkish white, it is genetically quite interesting. We humans all have a stable number of chromosomes, 46. But the number in the spring beauty varies from plant to plant, with botanists having discovered more than 50 chromosomal combinations.

Your gentle stroll is over when you swing right at 0.6 mile to parallel the river upstream and come to the first set of rocks. Pay close attention to the blue blazes from this point on, as many times the correct route will not be obvious. It is only the paint marks that may keep you from having to turn around and slide back down a large boulder you didn't have to go over in the first place. As you continue along, remember to think of the huge rocks you are going to have to use all of your limbs to climb over, under, and around as nature's own "jungle gym." Doing this may keep you from becoming frustrated about how slowly you are progressing. After crossing through a gully at 0.7 mile, rise over another set of rocks before descending again.

The rocks at 0.8 mile provide a view of a wider stretch of the river as it winds around a couple of small islands. The forested slope on the Virginia side rises steeply to the large auditorium of the Madeira School–seemingly perched on the edge of the precipice. Trumpet vine, also known as cow itch because it can cause contact dermatitis, grows out of the cracks and crevices in the rocks and usually begins to bloom sometime in July.

Step over a pond outlet at 1 mile, rising to the first of several rocky high points at 1.2 miles. Potholes indicate that the land here was once the riverbed. These circular indentations are the result of stones and pebbles being caught and swirled around and around over the same place by underwater eddies. As the river eroded an ever-deeper channel for itself, the potholes and the rock you are walking upon were exposed.

A grove of pine trees provides a short respite from the rocks at 1.4 miles before you come to an open area with the trail on a cliff of jagged and tilted rocks above Mather Gorge. The river is so narrow here that the Virginia bank is not much more than 200 feet away.

Along the Billy Goat Trail

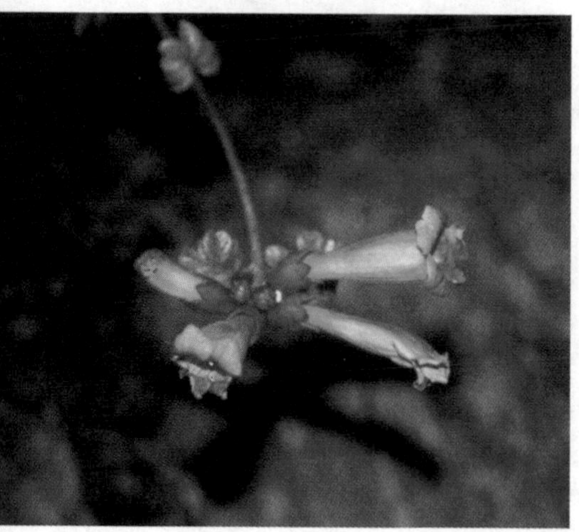

Trumpet vine

Dropping off the rocks at 1.8 miles, you may find it hard to adjust to walking like a normal person again–no slanted rock slabs threatening to pitch you sideways or large, loose boulders to twist your ankles.

Stop for a few moments to enjoy the final view of the river as the trail swings away from it at 2.25 miles. Upstream, the water is split into three channels by two large islands, the Rocky Islands. Visible behind them is Olmsted Island, which, unseen to you from this vantage point, forms the Maryland side of Great Falls.

Continuing to follow the blue blazes, keep your eyes open, as more white-tailed deer are seen along this section of trail than on any other of the hike. The Billy Goat Trail comes to an end at 2.35 miles; turn right onto the towpath and stay on it when a footbridge crosses over the canal to connect with Berma Road (see Hike 25).

You will come to the upper end of Widewater at 2.6 miles, which, with its rocky shoreline and small cliffs dotted with pine trees, looks more like the lakes and ponds in New York than the typical Potomac River Basin scenery. This is such a pretty spot that local colleges bring in vanloads of art students, who set up easels and try to capture the beauty on canvas. A boardwalk enables you to stay dry as you walk across a portion of the towpath that has been prone to flooding.

The entrance to the Billy Goat Trail, onto which you turned just a short time ago, is on the right at 3.3 miles. From here it is simply a matter of retracing your steps back to the parking lot and your car at 3.8 miles.

27

Greenbelt Park

Total distance (circuit): 7.0 miles

Hiking time: 3 hours, 20 minutes

Vertical rise: 440 feet

Maps: USGS 7½' Washington East (MD/DC); park map

Just as the land in Shenandoah National Park in Virginia was worn out by unsound farming practices by the time it was purchased to establish the park, so too was the soil in Greenbelt Park. The Algonquian Indians and other smaller tribes who used the area for hunting had little impact on the land; it was the colonists who cut down the trees, turning the forests into farmland and planting crops such as corn and tobacco. The latter is especially hard on the soil, taking out many nutrients and giving little in return.

By 1875 the trees were all gone (denuded, in more technical terms), and the farmers' yield became less and less each year. Agriculture ceased near the end of the 19th century, but due to the lack of ground cover, erosion washed away much of the topsoil and changed the lay of the land. At about the same time, the urban areas around Washington, D.C., began to spread quickly, eating away at whatever undeveloped tracts were in their way.

Strangely, it was a bureaucratic housing project that ended up saving the natural environment of Greenbelt Park. The land was acquired in the 1930s by the federal government to be part of Greenbelt, Maryland, one of a number of model towns within a belt of open space to be developed around the District of Columbia. Although some housing was constructed, the project never progressed as its planners had hoped, and the government sold the buildings to a local cooperative. Most of the remaining land became a part of the National Agricultural Research Center, while, in 1950, the National Park Service took over the tract that became Greenbelt Park.

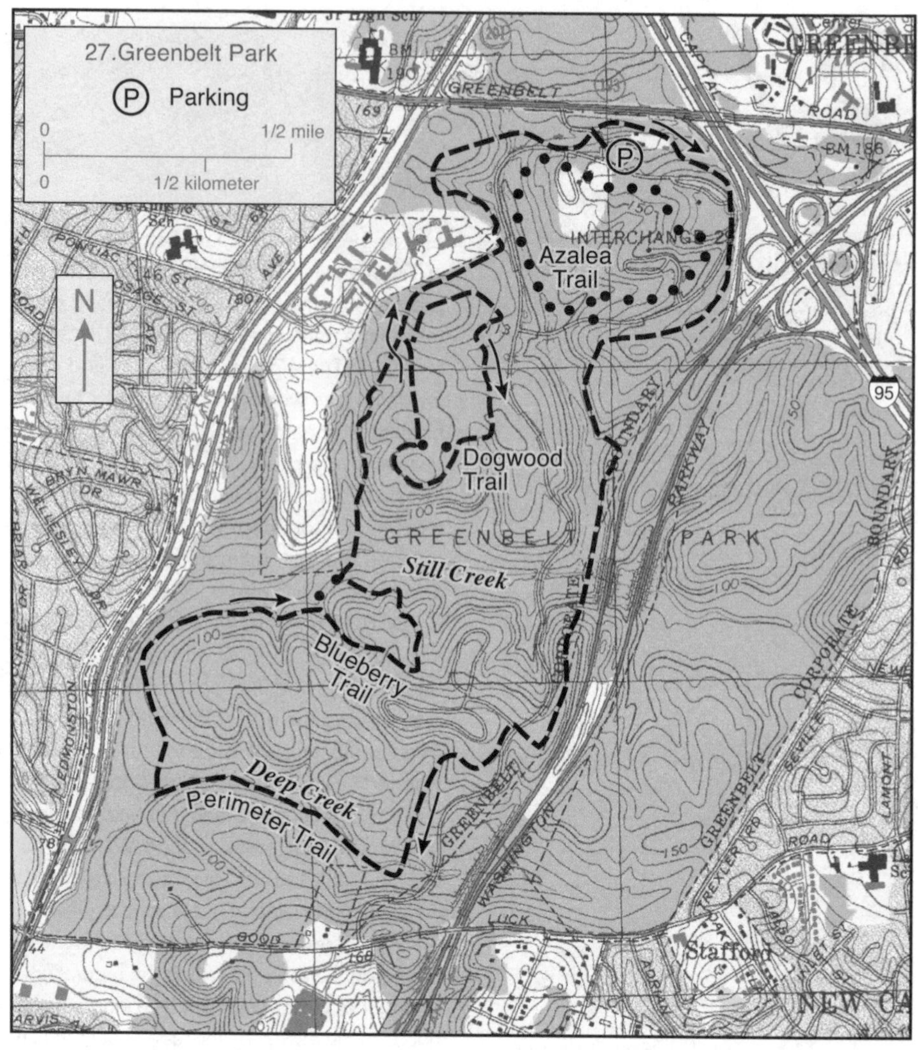

During the century that has passed since farming ceased, nature has been slowly reclaiming the land. First came shrubs and pines; now the largest percentage of the park is nearing a climax forest of oak, hickory, yellow poplar, and other deciduous trees. Being surrounded by high-speed highways, strip malls, and multistory apartment buildings, it is certainly not a wilderness area. Yet, the park allows you to make a quick escape from all of these things and enjoy the dogwood, mountain laurel, azalea, fern, beech, club moss, white-tailed deer, red fox, raccoon, woodpeckers, and more that have returned to make their home barely more than 10 miles from the Washington Monument.

The hike described here makes use of the Perimeter Trail (also open to equestrians) and two side routes, passing through a wide variety of environments. In addition to the trail system, the 1,078-acre park has a 174-site campground open all year, three picnic areas, and a year-round interpretive schedule that includes guided walks, talks, and evening programs. The park is open from sunrise to dark; pets are permitted but must be on a leash.

The easiest access to Greenbelt Park may be obtained by taking I-495 (Capital Beltway) exit 23 northeast of Washington, D.C., onto MD 201 South (Kenilworth Avenue). Almost immediately, exit onto MD 193 East (Greenbelt Road). Less than 0.5 mile later, turn right at the traffic light into the park and proceed to the parking lot across from park headquarters.

Start the hike by walking the road back toward the park entrance and making a right onto the yellow-blazed Perimeter Trail at 0.1 mile. Sweetgum, a tree not found in the elevated topography of Western Maryland, lines the trail and is often confused with the red maple. The sweetgum's leaves are deeply notched and more closely resemble a star when compared to the red maple's leaves. Also, the leaves on a maple are directly opposite each other along the stem, while the sweetgum's alternate (or stagger) along the two sides of the stem. Both trees, however, put on a brilliant crimson countenance in the fall.

Swing around the park work center at 0.3 mile and gradually ascend through a pine and hardwood forest with hundreds of gumballs, the seed packets of the sweet gum trees, under your feet. As evidenced by traffic noise, you are on a narrow strip of land between the Baltimore-Washington Parkway and the park road. A number of other trails may wander off the main pathway; be sure to always follow the yellow blazes, and begin a descent toward North Branch Still Creek at 0.8 mile.

Be alert when you come to a four-way intersection at 1 mile. Your route makes an abrupt turn to the left and descends quickly for a short distance. Running cedar and

Footbridges appear throughout the hike

Running cedar

other undergrowth become more lush as you lose elevation.

Cross a small tributary of North Branch Still Creek at 1.2 miles and continue to follow the minor ups and downs of the terrain. Step across Still Creek on a footbridge over a culvert at 1.5 miles, and you'll soon traverse a knoll whose understory is primarily mountain laurel. Come to a T intersection at 1.9 miles, turn right, and cross Park Central Road. Bear left at the very next trail intersection and swing around the campground, descending toward Deep Creek.

The vegetation changes a bit where you cross a wetlands on a boardwalk at 2.4 miles. Thriving in the moist soil are ironwood trees and an abundance of jack-in-the-pulpit. Ironwood has also been commonly called musclewood tree, a reference to the sinewy, muscled look of its trunk and bark.

Turn right when you come to a T intersection at 2.5 miles, avoiding the trail that heads to a private home on the left a few moments later. This bottomland forest beside Deep Creek is just about the quietest spot you have come to so far and has the most lush vegetation of the hike. Tall, straight tulip poplar trees rise high above a thick undergrowth of sassafras, running cedar, crow's foot, jack-in-the-pulpit, and a variety of ferns. Attaining heights of 80 feet to more than 100 feet, the nearly smooth, ashy-gray bark of a young tulip poplar becomes thicker and develops interlacing deep furrows as the tree ages. Its shiny, hairless, dark green leaves emerge folded, but open up to an unmistakable square shape that measures 3 to 6 inches long and wide.

Turn right when you come to a T intersection at 3.1 miles, but be sure to make an almost immediate left to continue to follow the yellow blazes. Reminding you that you are walking in a park that is surrounded by urban sprawl, Kenilworth Avenue is visible through the vegetation to the left. With Still Creek also to your left, cross a woods road at 3.7 miles.

For a change of pace from the Perimeter Trail, turn right at 3.8 miles and ascend along the blue-blazed Blueberry Trail, which is the only trail in the park where the eastern white pine tree grows. Its presence, in turn, helps the blueberry bushes thrive, as they enjoy the acidic soil created by the pines' dropped needles. The berries make an appearance in late June or early July. Go ahead an enjoy a berry or two, but remember that many of the woodland creatures depend on the berries for food.

The forest is composed of beech and holly trees, running cedar, crow's foot, and greenbrier when you come to a T intersection at 4.1 miles. Keep to the left (the trail to the right heads to the campground, where restrooms and water are available). The small downy woodpecker, about the size of a sparrow, is a permanent resident in Maryland and often visits this part of the park. You may not see one, but drill holes in the trees are proof of their presence. Return to the Perimeter

Trail at 4.5 miles and turn right, crossing a footbridge over Still Creek at 4.6 miles.

Be alert at 5.1 miles. For another side trip, take the short unmarked trail to the right, walking toward some benches and meeting up with the red-blazed Dogwood Trail, onto which you want to bear left. (If you don't wish to take this pathway, skip down to the 6.3-mile point of the route description below.) American holly, sweetbay magnolia, fern, and moss flourish in the small wetlands you use a footbridge to walk over at 5.4 miles. A plant native to America that enjoys the wet soils of the coastal plain, sweetbay magnolia is such an attractive ornamental that it was introduced and planted in European gardens in the 17th century. You can easily identify it in late spring by its white, cup-shaped flowers and in the early fall months by its deep red, 2-inch, pineconelike fruits.

The trail to the left at 5.5 miles leads to the Dogwood Trail parking lot; keep to the right. A shortcut comes in from the right at 5.7 miles, but since you want to enjoy this walk as long as possible, keep left. The other terminus of the shortcut trail intersects your route at 6 miles; keep left, come back to where you first encountered the Dogwood Trail, and return to, and bear right onto, the yellow-blazed Perimeter Trail at 6.3 miles.

Pay close attention at 6.4 miles when the trail comes close to an apartment complex. You need to keep to the left for just a few feet before making a right to avoid the complex's parking lot. Swinging around the headwaters of North Branch Still Creek, walk by the park police office building at 6.8 miles and turn right onto the park entrance road. The hike comes to an end as you bear left and return to your car at 7 miles.

If you still feel the need to stretch your legs, the park's 1.2-mile, white-blazed Azalea Trail connects the three picnic areas and passes through plant communities that grow along the streams, floodplain, and hillsides. Covered with soft wood chips, the route is a favorite of exercise walkers and joggers. The soft cooing of mourning doves or the raucous cries of blue jays are often heard along the trail.

28

Patuxent Research Refuge

Total distance (circuit): 3.1 miles

Hiking time: 1 hour, 30 minutes

Vertical rise: 90 feet

Maps: USGS 7½' Laurel; refuge map

Theodore Roosevelt, the US president who helped instigate a worldwide movement of protecting lands and wildlife through the establishment of national parks, created another mechanism for reaching the same goal by pronouncing Florida's Pelican Island the country's first national wildlife refuge in 1903. Administered by the Department of the Interior's US Fish and Wildlife Service, there are now more than 500 refuges throughout America.

By executive order, President Franklin D. Roosevelt established the Patuxent Research Refuge in 1936. Located between Washington, D.C., and Baltimore, the refuge's size has grown from an original 2,670 acres to nearly 13,000 acres. It supports a diversity of wildlife by the management of its typical Maryland landscape of meadow, wetland, and forest habitats for the protection and benefit of native and migratory species. Although the more than 200 species of birds that are known to be in the refuge at one time or another receive the greatest share of visitors' attention, deer, beavers, squirrels, muskrats, snakes, lizards, turtles, frogs, salamanders, raccoons, rabbits, and mice are also part of the environment.

The refuge is divided into three areas. Its North Tract offers more than 20 miles of roads and trails that are open to hikers, bikers, and horseback riders. The Central Tract contains offices and study sites and is closed to the public. The South Tract is probably the most visited portion of the refuge, with a network of scenic trails (open only to foot travel),

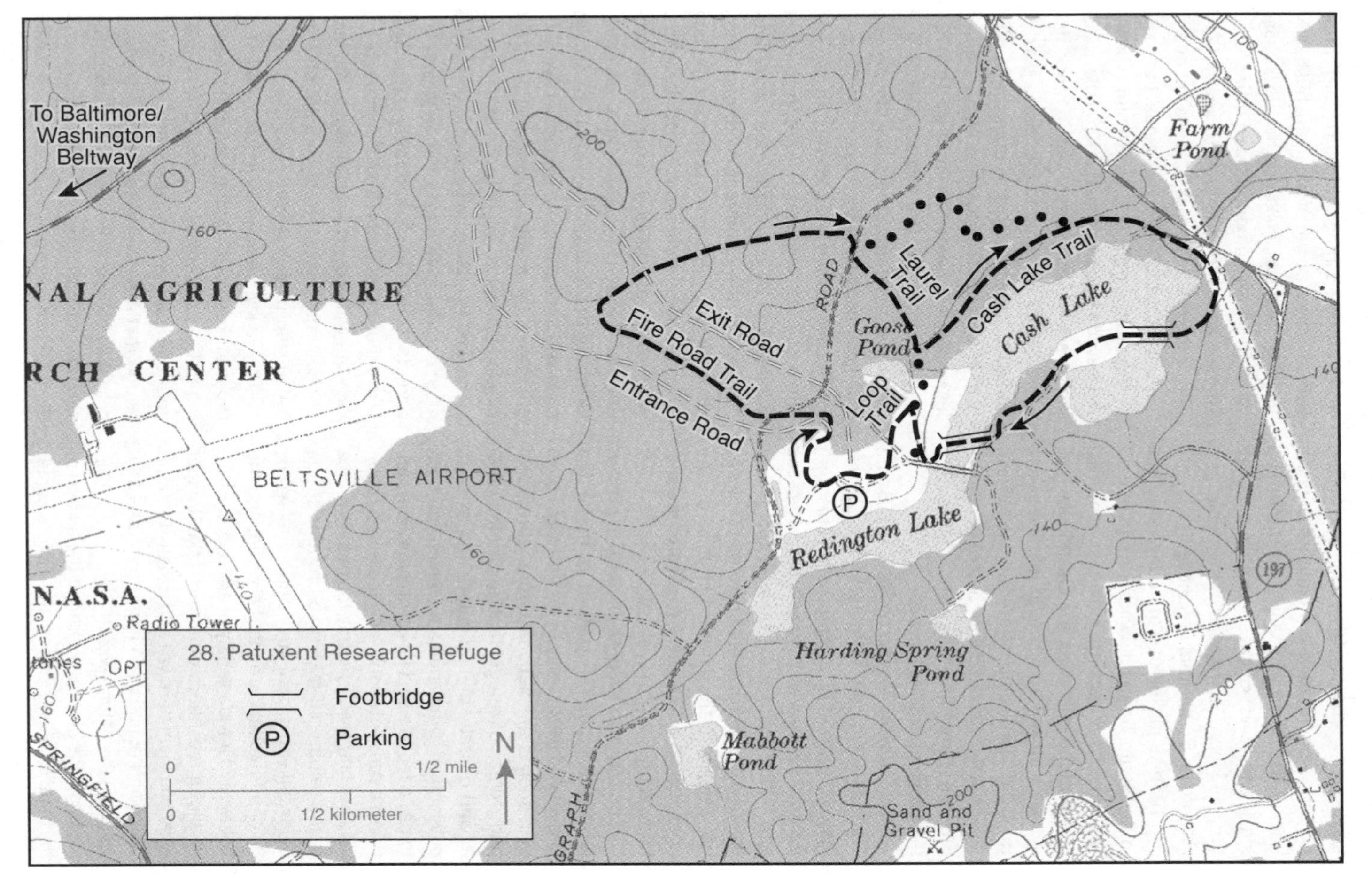
To Baltimore/
Washington
Beltway
NAL AGRICULTURE
RCH CENTER
BELTSVILLE AIRPORT
N.A.S.A.
Radio Tower
SPRINGFIELD
Exit Road
Fire Road Trail
Entrance Road
ROAD
Laurel
Trail
Cash Lake Trail
Cash Lake
Goose
Pond
Loop
Trail
Redington Lake
Farm
Pond
Harding Spring
Pond
Mabbott
Pond
Sand and
Gravel Pit
GRAPH
197
28. Patuxent Research Refuge
Footbridge
Parking
0
1/2 mile
0
1/2 kilometer
N

two large lakes, and a visitors center. Pets are permitted on the trails but must be leashed. Luckily, for those who enjoy early-morning strolls when wildlife it at some of its most active, the North Tract opens to the public at 8 AM and the South Tract at sunrise.

This hike makes use of nearly every trail in the South Tract, following a route that involves no backtracking. However, a portion of one of the pathways, the Cash Lake Trail, is usually closed from late fall into the spring to avoid disturbing wintering waterfowl. Check at the visitors center before beginning the hike; directions follow on what to do if the section of trail is closed.

The Patuxent Research Refuge's South Tract and National Wildlife Visitor Center may be reached by driving the Washington-Baltimore Parkway between the two cities and taking the exit for Powder Mill Road. Headed eastward, continue on that highway for 2 miles to the refuge entrance on the right. It is an additional 1.4 miles to the visitors center.

The National Wildlife Visitor Center can be a destination in itself. It is by far the largest and best facility of its kind that I have ever seen in any national, state, or regional park, forest, or refuge. Its size and the quality and quantity of its displays and exhibits outshine many museums for which you have to pay a fee to visit. Hands-on activities, multimedia presentations, and life-sized dioramas not only vividly portray the natural drama of the refuge but take on a broader scope by examining global environmental issues, different habitats around the world, and the behavior of a wide variety of animals. Be sure to allot a few hours of time to take it all in; what you learn here will add greatly to future walks and outings you happen to take anywhere in the natural world.

Begin the hike by walking to the far end of the middle parking lot from the visitors center and entering a pine and hardwood forest with an undergrowth of blueberry bushes on the Fire Road Trail. Following the old fire road through an experimental tree-cutting area, you are almost guaranteed to see at least one of the refuge's many white-tailed deer.

Amid a stand of Virginia pines, the route swings to the right at 0.4 mile and crosses the paved refuge exit road at 0.5 mile, passing by several holly trees. With a range that stretches from Texas to Florida to Massachusetts, this is the tree all of us are familiar with at Christmastime, when its dark green leaves and red berries are fashioned into holiday wreaths. What you may not know is that its lumber resembles the color of ivory and was once used for piano keys.

The Fire Road Trail comes to an end when you cross gravel Telegraph Road at 0.9 mile and begin to follow the Laurel Trail. Named for the abundant mountain laurel along its route, this pathway passes through a successional forest that is popular with a wide variety of songbirds, such as flycatchers, chickadees, thrushes, and warblers. Contrary to the large majority of birds, the male and female of most species of flycatchers have the same plumage. The great crested flycatcher, the only one of the genus in the East to nest in holes, is also one of the most colorful, with a gray throat, yellow underside, brown back, and rusty red wings. Like other flycatchers, it snares insects on the wing with a quick snap of its bill. You may not see one, but listen for its loud, distinctive *wheep-wheep-wheep* call.

The Valley Trail comes in from the left at 0.9 mile; keep right on the Laurel Trail, coming to Goose Pond at 1.2 miles. This small impoundment is one of a number in the refuge that is a controlled wetland, periodically drained during the growing season. The variation in moisture permits an array of plants, such as red-rooted sedge and wild millet, to grow. The pond is reflooded with 8 to 10 inches of water when these plants mature, and their seeds provide a source of food for birds migrating south for the winter.

If you need to cut this hike short, the visitors center is approximately 0.3 mile straight ahead. Otherwise, turn left onto the Cash Lake Trail as you begin to encircle the pathway's namesake body of water. Take the side trail at 1.3 miles for a view across the lake and a chance to observe the refuge's varied waterfowl in their favored habitat. Found throughout the year are Canada goose, American black duck, mallard, and great blue heron. Of course, the fall migration season brings the largest numbers to the lake and its environs. It is possible that on any given day you might see more than 30 species, ranging from the pie-billed grebes to wood ducks to occasional tundra swans. Among those that only appear in winter are buffleheads, hooded, common, and red-breasted mergansers, and ruddy and ring-necked ducks.

Return to the main route and turn right, coming to a break in the forest that permits an open view of the lake at 1.6 miles. Keep to the right a few hundred feet later when the Valley Trail comes in from the left. The hundreds of gumballs dropped onto the trail by the sweetgum trees may twist and turn your feet and ankles in unfamiliar angles.

Emerging into an open area, you will pass by the barrier-free fishing pier (information and permits are available from the visitors center) at 1.9 miles. Beyond this point is the section of the Cash Lake Trail that is seasonally closed. If you find it so, retrace your steps back to Goose Pond, returning to the visitors center via the Loop Trail and completing a hike of about 2.9 miles in length.

If the trail is open, continue beyond the pier, reenter the woods, and swing around the northeastern edge of the lake. The floating pontoon bridge you walk across at 2.1 miles may wobble a bit, but it will bring you safely across an arm of the lake, where a bit of a meadow provides one of the nicest vistas of the hike. The blue of the sky, the white of the floating clouds, and the green of the lakeside vegetation are mirrored by the surface of the water enfolding the narrow point of land you are walking upon.

Crow's foot lines a part of the trail when you reenter the woods a few hundred feet later. Be alert at 2.3 miles. The trail makes an abrupt right off the road you have been following and swings left to come to the northern end of Lake Reddington. The numerous high-pitched, birdlike peeps coming from a multitude of tiny spring peeper frogs can become almost deafening when experienced at close quarters, which you will be when you turn right to cross a second pontoon bridge. Although they have been heard into late October, peepers are most vocal in early spring; later in the summer, they migrate 50 to 60 feet up in the trees.

Turn right on the barrier-free, paved Conservation Heritage Loop Trail at 2.7 miles, reading the interpretive signs as you walk along to learn more about habitat manipulation and management. Keep to the left when the Goose Pond Trail comes in from the right at 2.8 miles. Cross the tram road, stay on the Loop Trail, and bear right to the visitors center.

The easiest way back to the parking lot is to walk through the building, returning to your car at 3.1 miles.

III Southern Maryland

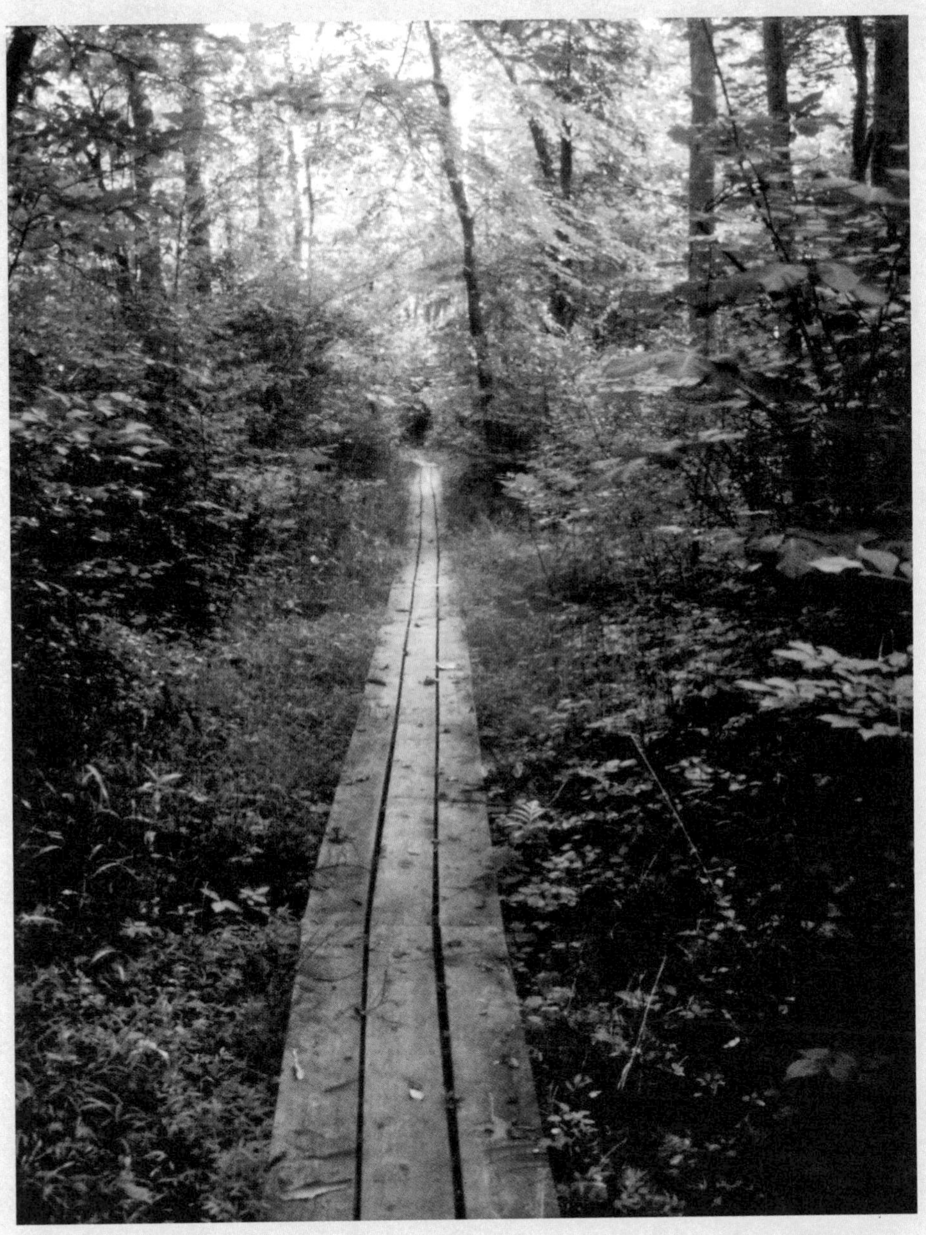

29

Merkle Wildlife Sanctuary

Total distance (round-trip): 3.5 miles

Hiking time: 1 hour, 30 minutes

Vertical rise: 80 feet

Maps: USGS 7½' Lower Marlboro

The Merkle Wildlife Sanctuary exists because of one man's vision and many people's hard work. Edgar Merkle, founder of the Merkle Press in Washington, D.C., originated a breeding plan to reintroduce Canada geese to the western shore of Maryland. Starting in 1932 with only a few breeding pairs and a habitat improvement plan, he was eventually able to attract thousands of geese to his 400-acre farm, with some staying year-round to nest and raise their young.

The Maryland Department of Natural Resources obtained the farm from the Merkles in the 1980s (some tracts purchased, some donated) with the agreement that it would continue to be managed for Canada geese. Additional purchases of adjacent land by the state have brought the sanctuary to its present size of more than 1,600 acres.

Ponds, wetlands, upland and bottomland forest, cultivated fields, and creeks provide a variety of scenery restful to the eyes and habitats for plants and animals. It takes six pages of a pamphlet to catalog all of the birds observed in the sanctuary, while raccoons, rabbits, squirrels, skunks, foxes, and white-tailed deer have been spotted making quick dashes from field to forest. A list of flowers blooming in just one month, July, contains nearly 100 species.

The sanctuary may be reached by driving along I-95/495 (Capital Beltway) east of Washington, D.C., taking exit 11 onto MD 4 (Pennsylvania Avenue), and continuing for almost 8 miles to turn south onto US 301. Less than 3 miles later, turn left onto Croom Station Road, following it for another 1.8

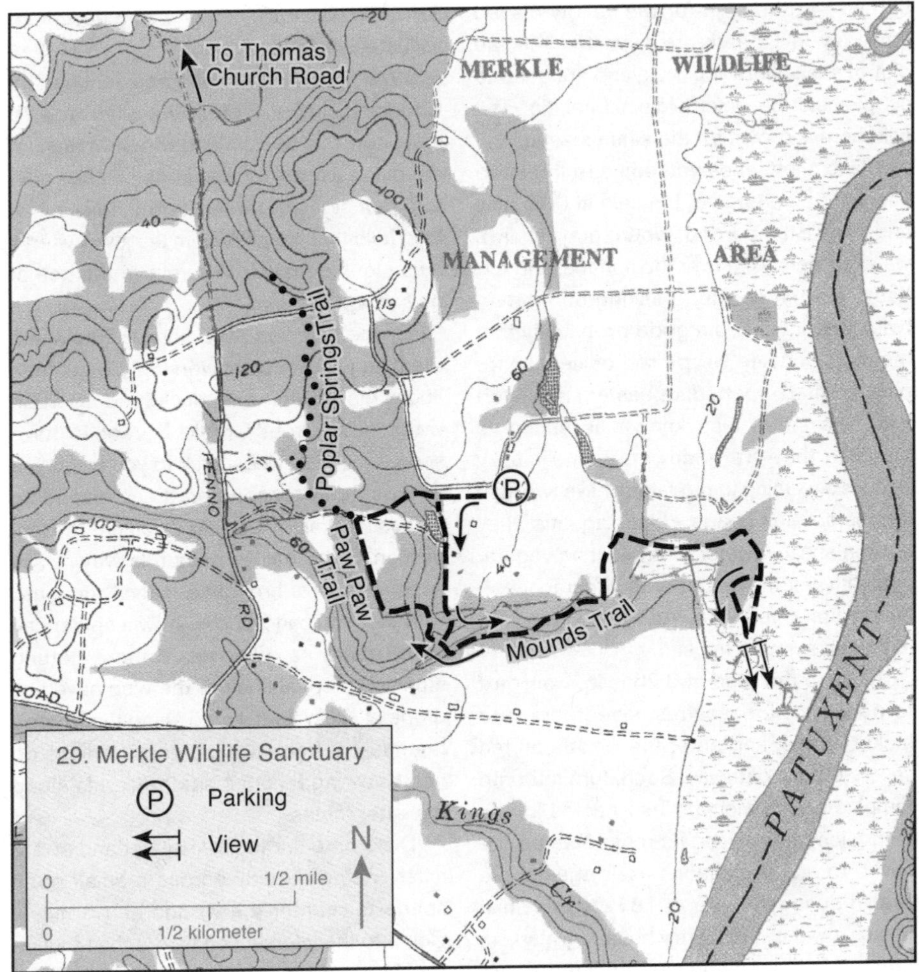

miles to bear left onto MD 382 (Croom Road). Stay on this route for 2.6 miles (passing by Croom Airport Road to the left, which leads to Patuxent River Park Jug Bay Natural Area) and make a left onto Saint Thomas Church Road (which soon becomes Fenno Road). Drive for another 3 miles to make a left into the sanctuary and park at the visitors center.

Exhibits, including live animal displays, in the center focus on the life history of the Canada goose, management techniques, and local human history. An observation deck with telescopes overlooks Merkle Pond, and an extensive schedule of interpretive programs is offered throughout the year. The center opens at 10 AM daily; trails are open from 7 AM to sunset. Rover and Fido must be left at home.

Walk from the visitors center back along the road on which you drove in and turn left within a few hundred feet onto the mowed pathway at the sign for the yellow-blazed Paw Paw Trail. Seeds are harvested from the plot of sunflowers you pass and are used to supplement the waterfowl's natural diet. The field corn is grown for the same reason.

Make a left when you come to the intersection on the edge of the field at 0.15 mile and pass Stump Pond, where crayfish live, water striders skim over the surface, and turtles are often spotted basking on floating twigs and logs. It is a good probability that the ones you see will be red bellied, snapping, painted, spotted, or eastern musk turtles. The latter, also known as stinkpots because they are endowed with a musky odor as a warning to predators, have two light stripes on their heads. Highly aquatic, they bask in shallow water or on floating vegetation with just the center of their carapaces–which are often covered with algae and moss–showing to the sun.

Cross a dirt road at 0.25 mile; walk next to poplar, oak, sassafras, sweetgum, and hickory trees, and enter the woods on the yellow-blazed pathway. Soon, turn left onto the blue-blazed Mounds Trail, named for the long piles of dirt along its route that are believed to be fortifications used against the British during the War of 1812. (Some historians say they are merely boundary markers created by past landowners.) The makeup of the forest changes a bit after you cross a tributary of Lookout Creek a few minutes later. The large poplars remain, but they have been joined by beech, holly, and mountain laurel. Songbirds are especially active in the early morning along this portion of the hike.

At least a dozen species of warblers have been known to nest in the sanctuary, with northern parula and the yellowthroat being two of the most common. Making its home close to the ground near water, the yellowthroat's call is a distinctive *witchy-witchy-witchy-witch.* The northern parula's call is bit harder to distinguish, often being described as just a single *bzzzzp* note.

With the chirping of frogs joining the woodland chorus, recross the creek at 0.75 mile, now in a bottomland forest of jack-in-the-pulpit, poison ivy, and large patches of 4- to 5-foot-high jewelweed. Folk medicine has long held that the juice from the jewelweed's succulent stem will help relieve the itch of poison ivy.

By the time you have gone 0.9 mile into the hike you will be traversing a bank high above the slow-moving, duckweed-crowded water of Lookout Creek. Expect to have scores of spiderwebs stick to you when you unexpectedly encounter them extending across the trail–especially if you are the first person of the day to pass this way. If you happen to have brought a magnifying glass with you, you can discover how a spider can move along its own web without getting stuck. The spiral lines of the web have tiny drops of sticky fluid strung along them, while the spokes, framework, and centerlines do not. Knowing this, the spider travels along the latter routes.

Drop onto another small wetland at 1.2 miles, going directly across a small open space to reenter the woods at 1.3 miles. Come to the intersection where the Mounds Trail begins to make a loop; bear right away from the stream. By the time you have swung around to return to the stream, the aquatic growth will be even more lush in this part of Lookout Creek, which is really just a backwater area of the Patuxent River at this point.

Before continuing, stop to do some birdwatching along the creek. An osprey may drop to the water, rising a few moments later with a fish grasped in its talons; ducks often come floating close to the shore; and red-winged blackbirds may be nesting inside the tall creekside vegetation. A breeding pair of red-winged blackbirds may raise two or three

Early morning

sets of young each season, building a new nest each time. The males are the only all-black bird with bright red and yellow shoulder patches, so identification is quite easy. Females are quite different, with brown striping over their bodies.

Also watch for small cone-shaped holes made by ant lions in the sandy soil. These enterprising larvae make use of the "angle of repose" by crafting the sides of their dens at about a 30-degree angle, the steepest slant at which dry sand can sustain a slope. Unsuspecting insects stepping onto this sand steepen the slope by just a degree or two and are sent tumbling into the clutches of the lion hiding in the sand below.

Maturing after two to three years in the pit, the ant lion spins a circular cocoon of silk and sand, changing to a pupa within its protection. The adult that emerges resembles a dragonfly, with two pairs of large, veined wings.

Return to the loop trail intersection at 2 miles, and bear right to retrace your steps along the blue-blazed Mounds Trail.

When you re-cross the small wetland areas at 2.3 miles and 2.7 miles, you might be amazed to find that some of the spiderwebs you broke on the way out have already been partially reconstructed.

Return to the yellow-blazed Paw Paw Trail at 3 miles, where you could bear right to return to the visitors center along the route upon which you started the hike. However, to enjoy the outdoors as long as possible, turn onto the yellow-blazed pathway to the left. Emerge into an open field at 3.1 miles, turn right, and stay along its edge next to the woods. These mowed grassy areas between the crop fields and woodlands capture soil that is being carried away by rain runoff before it reaches a stream, thereby preserving nutrients and protecting waterways from excessive silting.

Be alert at 3.4 miles. Pass by the red-blazed Poplar Springs Trail and swing right around two corners along the field. Watch for your yellow-blazed pathway to make a left (which may be partially obscured by growth) into the woods.

Turn right onto the park road and proceed back to the visitors center along either the road or the mowed strip of grass next to it. The outing comes to an end when you return to your car in the parking lot overlooking peaceful Merkle Pond at 3.5 miles.

Patuxent River Park Jug Bay Natural Area has 2,000 acres that adjoin the sanctuary and offers more than 8 miles of trails to explore while you are in this area. The aforementioned directions can guide you to the park.

30

Zekiah Swamp Run and Wolf Den Branch

Total distance (circuit): 5.6 miles

Hiking time: 2 hours, 40 minutes

Vertical rise: 260 feet

Maps: USGS 7½' Brandywine; USGS 7½' Hughesville

Harboring some of Maryland's rare and endangered species, such as the bald eagle, red-bellied woodpecker, and diamondbacked terrapin, Zekiah Swamp is the state's largest freshwater swamp. Stretching to the southwest for approximately 20 miles from Cedarville State Forest to the Wicomico River, it is almost a mile wide in some places.

Within the boundary of the state forest are two of the swamp's principal tributaries, Wolf Den Branch and Zekiah Swamp Run. Although the drier soil in the uplands is dominated by oaks, this hike crosses and parallels these two headwater streams a number of times, where the extra moisture enables the vegetation to become more lush and thick. This provides a wonderful feeling of walking along a swamplike environment, but without having your boots become mired in several inches of mud and ooze. In addition, the deep forest filters out much of the noise from the outside world, creating a quiet sense of isolation.

The Maryland Department of Natural Resources purchased the land in 1930 for the purpose of demonstrating forestry techniques. While timber is still harvested from the nearly 4,000 acres, the activity is, for the most part, not intrusive on the quality of the hike. While it is possible that you might happen across plots that were freshly cut, most likely the only reminders of timbering you will see are plantations of loblolly trees or 20- to 30-year-old woods that are naturally regenerating themselves.

Some of the trails you follow on this hike are extremely popular with mountain bikers,

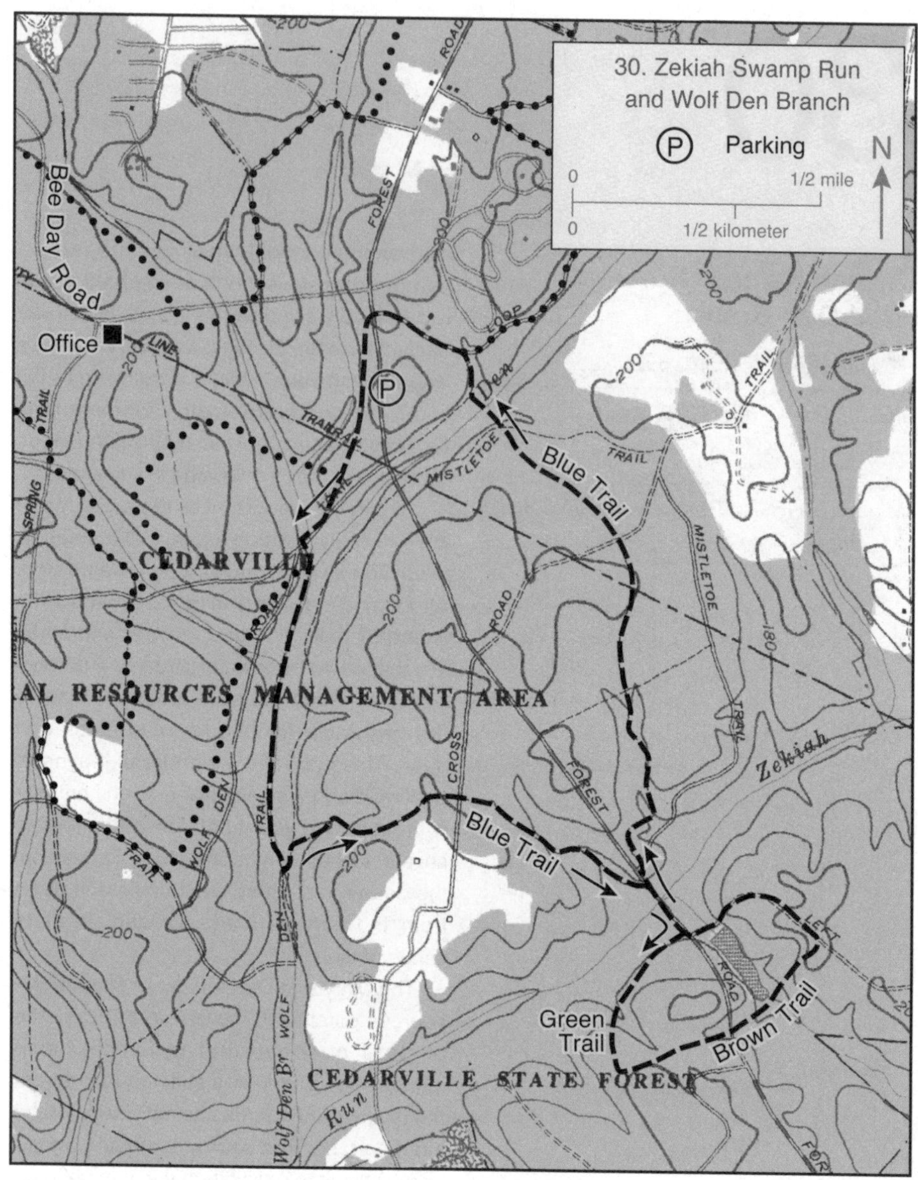

so be prepared to be startled at a moment's notice. Other trails do not seem to appeal to the wheeled set and are, in fact, so little used that you may think you are the first person to come to that particular part of the forest for quite some time. Equestrians are also permitted to use the trails but seem to have little impact on them. Although the routes you want to follow are blazed, there are a number of intersecting trails that are also blazed and may cause some confusion; you may need to refer to the following directions often. Be aware that hunting is permitted in season, and that pets must be kept on a leash.

Cedarville State Forest may be reached by driving along I-95/495 (Capital Beltway) southeast of Washington, D.C., taking exit 7 onto MD 5 (Branch Avenue), and continuing for approximately 11 miles to turn eastward onto Cedarville Road. (Be watching for this turn about 2 miles after MD 5 and US 301 join together.) Continue for another 2.4 miles and turn right onto Bee Oak Road and into the state forest. Turn right onto Forest Road after an additional 1.7 miles. Less than 0.5 mile later, turn right and leave your car in the small parking area next to the last remaining charcoal kiln.

Your exploration of this land, which was once used by the Piscataway Indians as a winter camping ground, begins by walking the short pathway into the woods from the parking area. Turn left onto the Blue Trail in 100 feet. The Orange Trail comes in from the right about 300 feet later; keep to the left in a bottomland forest whose floor is lush with ferns and running cedar.

Bear right onto a woods road at 0.25 mile, turning off it to the left in just a few feet and crossing two tributaries of Wolf Den Branch in quick succession. Be alert when you come to the confusing intersection at 0.5 mile. A green-blazed pathway comes in from the left, but you need to keep swinging to the right along the Blue Trail. The mushrooms and other abundant fungi growing on the downed trees aid in the wood's decay and the return of nutrients to the soil.

A white-blazed pathway comes in from the right at 0.8 mile; continue left along the Blue Trail, making a gradual rise beside holly and loblolly trees. Enter a stand of even-aged loblollies at 1.1 miles. In addition to constructing some of the roads and other facilities in the state forest, the Civilian Conservation Corps planted a number of these pine plantations during the 1930s.

Step over the dirt Cross Road at 1.2 miles and go through a target practice area, hopefully at a time when no one is practicing. Be alert at 1.4 miles. There are trails going straight and to the right; be sure to bear left in a forest of sweetgum and river birch. With its peeling bark, the latter is more reminiscent of New England than Southern Maryland. It is, however, the southernmost-occurring birch in the United States and has a range that reaches to northern Florida and eastern Texas. Most often found in environs such as the one you are in now, its roots help prevent the erosion of the moist soil.

Turn right onto Forest Road at 1.6 miles, make another right onto the Green Trail in about 300 feet, and parallel Zekiah Swamp Run. Because they grow side by side, this is a great place to learn how to identify two similar-looking club mosses. Crow's foot has dark green needle leaves that are so tiny that it is hard to distinguish one from the other. Conversely, it is easy to make out the individual, lighter green needle leaves of the running cedar. Looking like tiny hemlock or pine trees, both of these plants can trace back their beginnings more than 300 million years, to when their ancestors grew to be more than 100 feet tall.

The loblolly trees you walk by at 2.1 miles are older than those you passed earlier, but you will soon merge onto a woods road lined with ones that are younger.

With a woods road on the left at 2.3 miles, keep right and come to an intersection 500 feet later. The Green Trail continues to the left, but you want to bear right to begin traversing the Brown Trail. Private homes visible through the vegetation to the right at 2.75 miles are a sure sign that you are near the boundary of the state forest. Cross over

Cedarville Pond

a woods road, making sure to continue to follow the brown-blazed route.

In fact, you need to be alert for the next several minutes. Cross the wetland area of the Cedarville Pond inlet at 3.1 miles, keeping to the right along the brown-blazed pathway. Coming to a T intersection at 3.3 miles, turn left (a right goes out of the forest boundary), only to make another left a few feet later when an unmarked trail comes in from the right.

Come to the road and parking area for Cedarville Pond at 3.8 miles and climb onto the dam to take a break and enjoy the surrounding scenery being reflected on the surface of the placid water.

When ready to continue, walk Forest Road away from the pond, and almost immediately after crossing Zekiah Swamp Run, turn right into the woods on the Blue Trail. Cross Mistletoe Trail at 4 miles and a woods road (Cross Road) at 4.5 miles. You will step over an older woods road that has deteriorated into not much more than a pathway at 4.8 miles.

Looking around you, it can seem that the forest goes on forever, and, indeed, the 4,000 acres of the state forest is an extensive tract of unbroken woodland to exist just a few miles south of Washington, D.C. Yet, when explorers from Europe first arrived in North America, an expansive forest spread out along the coastal area from Florida to Canada, went inland over the piedmont to cover the ridges and valleys of the Appalachian Mountains, and stretched as far as the banks of the Mississippi River and a bit beyond.

Some botanists theorize that, farther back in time, this great forest covered even more land. About 200 million years ago, when the Appalachian Mountains were experiencing their final upward thrust, all of the continents of the world had joined together into one supercontinent, Pangea. About the mid-Mesozoic Age, Pangea split into two, with North America and Eurasia united as the northernmost of the two resulting masses. Eventually, those two large continents began to drift apart, but North America continued to be joined to Asia by a land bridge between Alaska and Siberia. With earth experiencing a rather mild climate, even up into the arctic regions, a vast deciduous forest covered much of both of the continents.

Cross Wolf Den Branch at 4.9 miles and come to an intersection. The Orange Trail comes in from the left; you need to swing right and follow the blue/orange-blazed route.

There is another intersection at 5.1 miles. The Orange Trail comes in from the right; make a hard left to continue to follow the route of the Blue Trail, which merges onto a gravel road.

Cross Forest Road at 5.3 miles, reenter the woods on the Blue Trail, and watch for the short connector trail to the left that will return you to your car at 5.6 miles.

31

Myrtle Grove Wildlife Management Area

Total distance (circuit): 4.0 miles

Hiking time: 1 hour, 45 minutes

Vertical rise: 160 feet

Maps: USGS 7½' Port Tobacco; management area map

While state parks were primarily established to provide outdoor recreation and state forests founded for silviculture, wildlife management areas were created with the emphasis on protecting and harvesting game animals. Habitats for waterfowl, white-tailed deer, ruffed grouse, fish, rabbit, squirrel, and others are created and maintained using funds from excise taxes on hunting and fishing equipment and sporting licenses.

Within the last few decades, the public has also come to see these areas as places of conservation for nongame species and recreation for the general public. Thousands of Marylanders have donated to the Chesapeake Bay and Endangered Species Fund, helping to protect eagles, falcons, pelicans, reptiles, amphibians, and more.

Yet, with close to 40 of them spread throughout the state, wildlife management areas, administered by the Department of Natural Resources Wildlife Division, remain the state's most-often overlooked parcels of public lands. In many ways, they can't be beat if you are looking for an uncrowded and primitive experience. Amenities such as picnic areas, restrooms, and the like are usually nonexistent, and trails are most often informal, unmarked pathways created by the footsteps of occasional hunters. Except during hunting season (usually mid-September through January and mid-April to mid-May), when it may be best to avoid them, many of the areas can go for days on end without anyone visiting their inner reaches. Sadly, while most other states permit backcountry camping in the majority of their wildlife

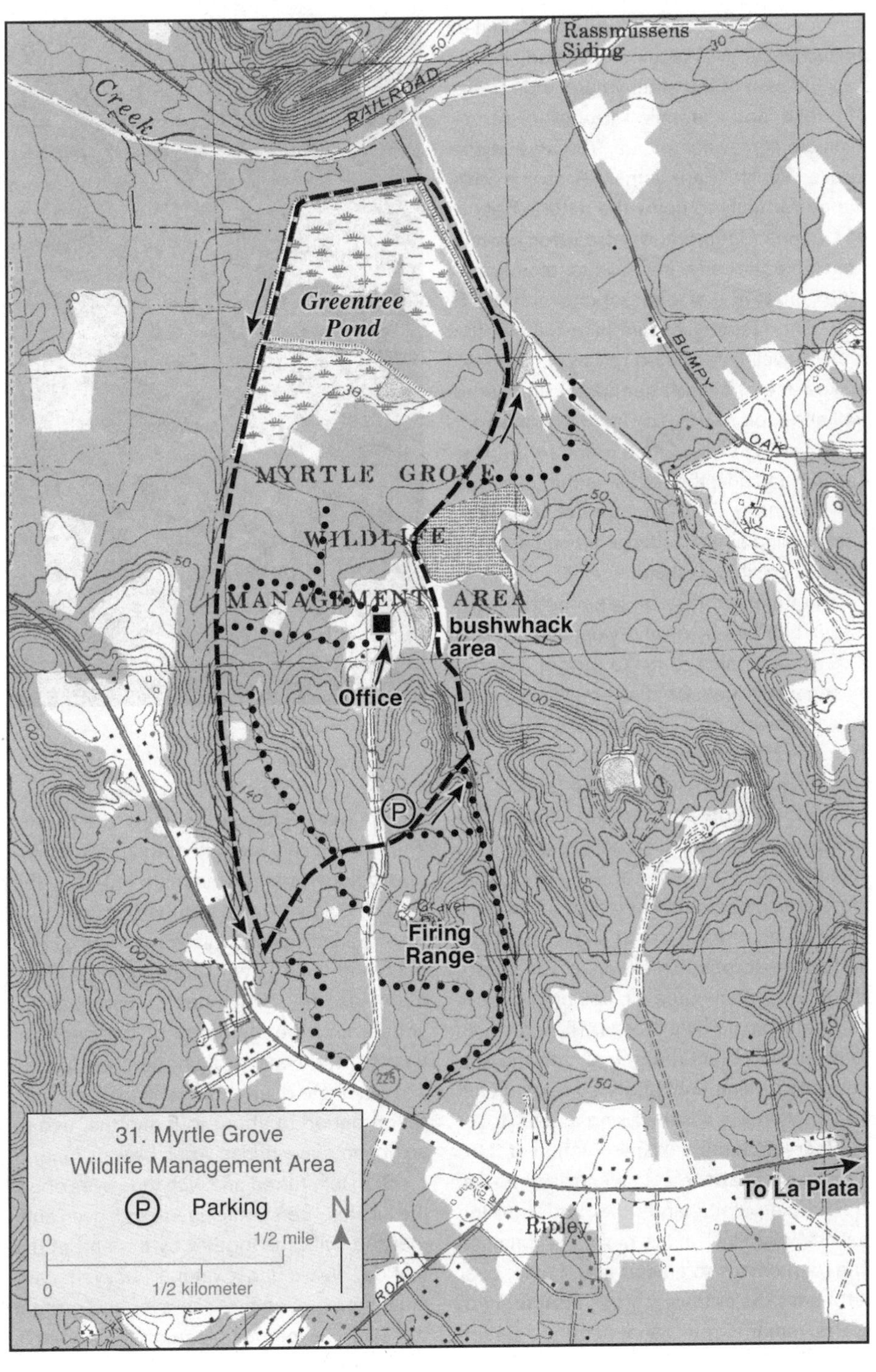
Rassmussens Siding
Creek
RAILROAD
Greentree Pond
BUMPY
OAK
MYRTLE GROVE
WILDLIFE
MANAGEMENT AREA
bushwhack area
Office
Gravel Pit
Firing Range
To La Plata
Ripley
ROAD
31. Myrtle Grove
Wildlife Management Area
Parking
N
0
1/2 mile
0
1/2 kilometer

management areas, Maryland prohibits it in almost all the WMAs under its jurisdiction.

In an area of the state where large tracts of public land available for outdoor recreation are somewhat sparse, 900-acre Myrtle Grove Wildlife Management Area provides the opportunity to enjoy the natural beauty of Charles County and retreat for a while from the traffic, strip malls, liquor stores, and other modern-day distractions along US 301. The majority of this hike follows the route of well-established roadways but also makes use of a short section of unmarked trail and a bit of a bushwhack to hone your route-finding skills. Once home to the Piscataway Indians, the terrain is that of a typical Southern Maryland landscape, with gently rolling hills of fields and forest and natural and created wetlands.

Cardinal flower

The trailhead may be reached from US 301 in La Plata by driving westward on MD 225 for 5.8 miles to make a right into the management area. Continue on the dirt road for an additional 0.5 mile and leave your car in the parking area on the right (the first one after the parking lot for the firing range).

Walk through the gate and follow the woods road, making a left onto another road less than 200 feet later. It is amazing that there are spiderwebs stretching across the entire width of the road. In order to get the first string across this expanse, the spider lifts its abdomen in the air, spinning out silk as it gets caught by a breeze. The silk sticks to whatever object it touches, and the spider pulls the line tight and then reinforces it with another line while walking across it.

Bear left at the next intersection at 0.25 mile, walking above a small stream. Ferns, jack-in-the-pulpits, and other undergrowth become more lush in this moist environment. The road comes to an end at 0.4 mile; bear right onto the pathway, cross a tributary of Mattawoman Creek, and continue downstream beside beaver-gnawed tree trunks. These mammals are one of the most family- and colony-oriented animals found in the wild. A colony, which can be composed of up to 12 individuals, will usually consist of a male and female (which biologists believe mate for life), a number of two-year-old young, and the members of the previous year's litter. Having only one litter a year, beavers mate during the winter. After a gestation period of about four months, two to six young arrive during April, May, or June.

Born fully furred and with their eyes open, the kits may be swimming around, even submerged, with the mother by the end of the first day. While underwater, all beavers have clear membranes that slip over and protect the eyes, valves that close off their nostrils and ears, and bits of skin that cover the mouth but leave incisors exposed so that branches and food can still be carried. Parents spend great amounts of time educating their young, swimming and diving with them, leading them to food, showing them the intricacies of getting in and out of lodges, and warning them of danger.

Be alert at 0.5 mile. The trail you have been following swings to the right, ascends, and soon enters private property. This is the place where you will have to determine your own route through the woods. You need to turn left, ford the stream, and bushwhack uphill for 300 feet toward the field. Once you are out of the woods, turn right along the edge of a pond that appears to be nearing the end of its life cycle and that may be dry by the time you hike here.

Come to Myrtle Grove Lake at 0.7 mile and swing around its left side to follow the dirt road toward the far end of the water. No matter what time of day or year, it seems as if there is almost always at least one angler trying his or her luck for bluegill, pickerel, catfish, and largemouth bass.

Take your leave of the lake by bearing left onto the next road at 0.9 mile. The vegetation along its edges is a veritable cornucopia of plants you want to avoid. Long, thorny strands of greenbrier creep over downed limbs and stretch toward the road, poison ivy climbs onto tree trunks, and stinging nettle makes up a large proportion of the undergrowth.

Keep to the right when a road comes in from the left at 1.1 miles, while you want to keep left when the next road comes in from the right 700 feet later.

The long, narrow, artificially created ponds you begin walking beside at 1.5 miles are called greentree reservoirs and are deliberately flooded in the fall and winter while trees are dormant. The nuts and seeds dropped by the trees are then used by migrating and wintering waterfowl.

In a perfect example of how changing one element of an environment affects another, cardinal flower–which would not be here without the existence of the moist soil it needs to establish itself–lines the perimeter of the greentree reservoirs. Once described by Roger Tory Peterson as America's favorite, the plant is named not for the state bird of Virginia and West Virginia but rather for the color of vestments worn by cardinals of the Roman Catholic Church.

Swing left to continue following the road around the reservoir at 1.6 miles. Great blue herons, which can be full-time residents in this part of Maryland, often troll the shallow water of the reservoir in search of fish or frogs. These temporary pools are also the preferred breeding areas of the endangered tiger salamander in late winter and early spring. With large heads and small eyes, these are the world's largest land-dwelling salamanders, some growing to be a foot long.

A connector road comes in from the left at 2.2 miles; keep right and reenter the deep shade of the woods at 2.5 miles. On hot, humid days, the large leaves of pawpaw trees, thick draping vines, luxuriant folds of ferns, and the buzz of insects and calls of dozens of songbirds may make you think you have walked into a tropical rain forest.

Continue straight at the four-way intersection at 2.7 miles, keeping right onto a lesser-used route at the next intersection 700 feet later. Several private homes along MD 225 become visible as you negotiate a series of short, gradual ups and downs.

Be alert at 3.5 miles. Immediately after passing by a deteriorating building on the right that is partially hidden by vegetation, turn left and follow a wide, grassy roadway through the forest. Because they expose individual trees along their edges, road cuts such as this enable you to identify the different species of oak, sweetgum, poplar, and dogwood. Along the border of the road are a number of black locust trees, a succession plant that would transform this clearing into a full-fledged forest if not kept cut back. A bacterium in its roots allows it to "capture" nitrogen from the air and use it for its own purposes. Once the tree decays, it releases this nitrogen into the ground, adding a nutrient to the soil that was previously absent or apparent in lower concentrations. Other trees needing a more nitrogen-rich soil can then establish themselves and, probably, crowd out most of the black locusts.

Continue straight when you come to the four-way intersection at 3.9 miles, walk around the gate, and return to your car at 4 miles.

Also worth some of your foot-travel time in the western part of Charles County are Chicamuxen Wildlife Management Area (south of Mason Springs) and Doncaster Demonstration Forest (along MD 6). The first has a woods road that can be walked to marshland along Chicamuxen Creek, while the latter contains a network of interconnecting pathways.

32

Calvert Cliffs

Total distance (circuit): 5.2 miles

Hiking time: 2 hours, 30 minutes

Vertical rise: 510 feet

Maps: USGS 7½' Cove Point; park map

Impressively rising to heights of more than 100 feet above the water, Calvert Cliffs were formed between 10 million and 20 million years ago when Southern Maryland was under a shallow sea. Through the centuries, more than 600 species of sea creatures, such as whales, sea cows, porpoises, rays, sharks, seabirds (the size of small airplanes!), crocodiles, mollusks, and reptiles swam and lived on or in the warm waters.

When the geological Middle Miocene Epoch drew to a close, Earth's climate began to cool, and the polar ice caps grew and the ocean receded. Once the cliffs were exposed to the erosive effects of wind and precipitation, they began to crumble, revealing skeletal remains that had become entombed within the 24 distinct layers of sand, silt, and clay.

As far back the 1600s, people have been coming to the base of the cliffs to see what new fossils they would yield. Whale ear bones and skulls, sea cow ribs, crocodile snouts (and fossilized dung), and even peccary scapulas and fossilized pinecones have been uncovered. But it is the thousands and thousands of fossilized sharks' teeth, some from the extinct great white shark, that have made the cliffs famous and drawn generations of schoolchildren and other visitors to the area.

Today most of the cliffs' 30 miles are privately owned, so we are lucky that the state has set aside a short stretch of the shoreline as Calvert Cliffs State Park. Here, on public land, we can walk to the water's edge, study the bay's ecology, search for

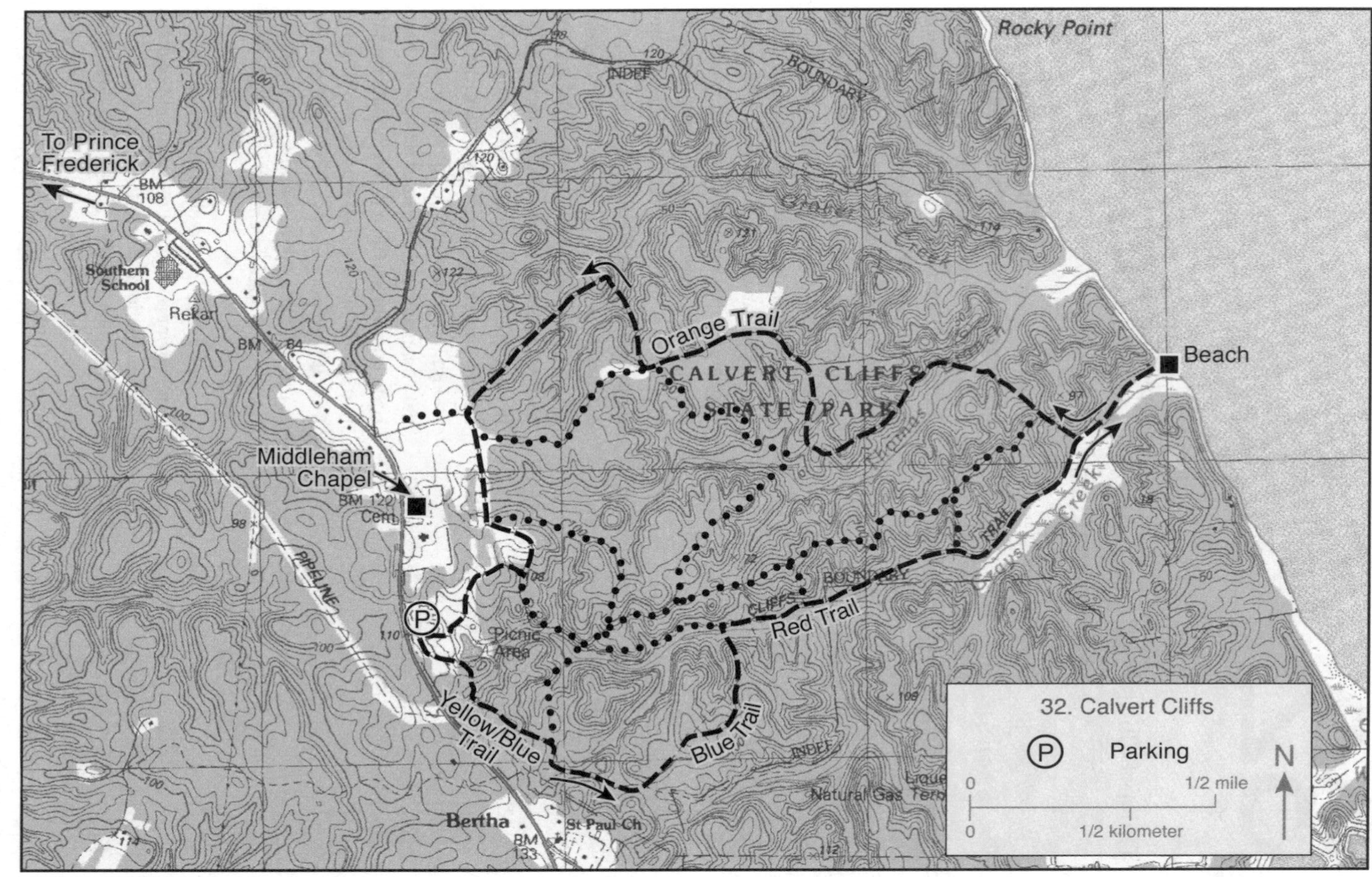

Rocky Point
To Prince Frederick
BM 108
Southern School
Rekar
BM 84
Orange Trail
CALVERT CLIFFS STATE PARK
Beach
Middleham Chapel
BM 122
Cem
PIPELINE
Picnic Area
Red Trail
Yellow/Blue Trail
Blue Trail
Bertha
BM 133
St Paul Ch
Natural Gas
32. Calvert Cliffs
Parking
N
0
1/2 mile
0
1/2 kilometer

small paleontological treasures hidden in the sand, or just sit peacefully on the beach. (For your own safety, walking on or below the crumbling cliffs is prohibited, and to keep them from deteriorating any faster, visitors are not permitted to dig for fossils on them.)

Calvert Cliffs is one of the least-developed state parks in Maryland. Occupying less than 5 acres of the park's 1,300 acres are a picnic and playground area, restrooms, a large parking lot, and a small fishing pond. This leaves a vast tract on which you can wander, using the network of marked trails through a landscape that has been left in a more or less natural state. This hike takes you into upland forests, through freshwater and tidal marshlands, onto the beach, and beside slowly flowing creeks.

The state park is located in eastern Calvert County, about 50 miles from Washington, D.C. Driving along I-95/495 (Capital Beltway) east of Washington, D.C., take exit 11 onto MD 4 South (Pennsylvania Avenue). Continue by Upper Marlboro and Prince Frederick. About 14 miles beyond the latter will be a sign directing you to make a left turn to the state park. The entrance is just a few hundred yards beyond the intersection with MD 765.

On weekends during the season, rangers conduct guided nature walks, fossil discussions, and other activities. Bicyclists are permitted only on the service road, while horseback riders may use all routes but the Red Trail. Be aware that dogs are prohibited, and that hunting is permitted in a large part of the park. It seems that the regulation allowing or denying swimming at the beach changes from time to time; the best advice is to check with park personnel or read the bulletin boards before taking a dip.

Begin the hike from the parking lot by taking the yellow-blazed Nature Trail, which is to the right and uphill from the main route in the park, the Red Trail. Passing through a loblolly pine plantation, turn left at 0.15 mile onto a pipeline right-of-way, bordered by a characteristic Southern Maryland forest of sweetgum, maple, hickory, sassafras, oak, and black locust.

Be alert at 0.3 mile. The trail suddenly veers to the left off the right-of-way and reenters the woods. The Yellow Trail heads off to the left at 0.4 mile, but you want to stay to the right, now following the Blue Trail in a forest of mountain laurel, loblolly, and holly. Keep left 1,000 feet later when another route heads off to the right.

The Blue Trail reaches its terminus as you turn right onto the Red Trail along the headwaters of Grays Creek at 1.1 miles. Stay to the right and cross the boardwalk when the White Trail comes in from the left at 1.2 miles. Spiderwebs may stick to your face, while the calls and twangs of bullfrogs and green frogs resonate through this swampy area.

The cannibalistic bullfrog, the largest frog inhabiting the United States, may attain a length of up to 8 inches. With powerful hind legs, it has been seen jumping 8 to 9 feet in one leap. Heard throughout the summer, its familiar, low, deep call of *jug-o-rum* carries for more than 0.25 mile.

About half the size of the bullfrog, the green frog's call is a low, explosive, twangy-like *c'tung,* but they often let out a high-pitched *squeenk* when startled and jumping for safety.

Soon after the creek widens into a backwater type of area at 1.7 miles, take the observation platform to the right for a close-up look at the intricacies of the swamp. This is a great place to be early in the morning as a plethora of birds greets the day with exuberant songs. The ripples of beaver moving across the vegetation-obscured water are identified by the sparkle of sunlight just

Beaver lodge in the swamp

beginning to spread across the narrow valley. Spatterock, arrow arum, broad-leaved arrowhead, tickseed sunflower, and other arrowhead-shaped aquatic plants rise up from the shallow water and along its borders. Sweet pepperbush also likes this moist environment. Return to the main road and continue to walk downstream and join up with the service road at 2.1 miles.

Arrive at the 100-yard-long beach at 2.3 miles, with the cliffs stretching to the north and south of you. Unless you are here on a busy weekend, this can be a very quiet and peaceful place. The sounds of small waves lapping along the shore are bound to have a calming effect on those willing to listen. Walk the full length of the beach, maybe watching a distant sailboat move along the horizon or an osprey wing its way through the air. The best time to search for fossils is after a storm has eroded away a bit more of the cliffs. Remember that the sharks' teeth you are looking for are most often no more than 0.5 inch long; the great white shark's 5-inch teeth are a rare find.

When ready to leave, retrace your steps and return to the intersection of the Red Trail and the service road at 2.6 miles. This time, keep right and ascend along the service road. However, you need to be alert 400 feet later, because you want to leave the road and swing right onto the Orange Trail. Be sure to bear left downhill a few feet beyond this point and not go uphill to the right.

Box turtles–so named because they are the only turtles in the United S*Old Brant Mine-*tates able to "box" themselves in completely by closing their shells–are often found crawling across the sandy soil of the forest here. Turtles are the most ancient of all living reptiles and, like sharks, have changed little since their appearance on Earth millions of years ago. Yet, their unique makeup does not seem closely related to other reptiles, and their true origin continues to baffle those who study them.

Within a wetlands area at 2.9 miles that shows the work of resident beavers, the trail merges left onto a woods road, and you begin a general upward trend. (Unless this portion of the hike has been maintained lately, the paint blazes may cease for a while.) Be alert at 3.4 miles when a road comes in from the left; you want to keep to the right.

Swing to the left when you come to a T intersection at 3.5 miles; keep left again 600 feet later as faint roads come in from an open area to the right.

The White Trail comes in from the left at 3.9 miles and runs concurrently with your route for 200 feet, where it then continues to the left. You need to bear right to keep following the Orange Trail. You also need to be alert just 300 feet beyond this junction. The Orange Trail, on which you want to continue, makes a left off the roadbed and descends and rises steeply along a footpath.

Come to a T intersection at 4.2 miles, turn left, and ascend along Grover Creek, possibly one of the shortest named streams in the entire state. This is its headwaters you are walking beside, and it comes to an end as it empties into the bay, giving it a route of not much more than 1 mile in length.

Emerge into an open field at 4.6 miles and turn left. Stay to the right when the White Trail comes in from the left at 4.7 miles, and do the same when the Silver Trail heads off to the left at 4.9 miles.

The service road joins up with your route at 5 miles. You will soon pass by the picnic area and playground and return to your car at 5.2 miles.

Flag Ponds Nature Park, operated by the Calvert County Natural Resources Division, is just a 10- to 15-minute drive north of the state park on MD 4 and is worth visiting while in this area. A network of trails courses through a similar environment and can deliver you to another beach for more fossil hunting.

33

American Chestnut Land Trust

Total distance (circuit): 5.4 miles

Hiking time: 2 hours, 30 minutes

Vertical rise: 760 feet

Maps: USGS 7½' Prince Frederick; land trust map

Hidden amid the outer suburbs and few surviving farms along the Chesapeake Bay's western shore are several parcels of protected land. Concerned over the detrimental effects that Calvert County was experiencing as a result of having the fastest population growth of any county in the Washington, D.C., metropolitan area, a group of far-sighted citizens banded together to form the nonprofit American Chestnut Land Trust.

Purchasing numerous tracts of land around the Parkers Creek watershed, the trust has been able to preserve about 850 acres and has accepted the management of additional land owned by the state. Thanks to this effort, 2,700 acres of fields, forests, marshes, swamps, and streams are no longer threatened by the encroaching modern world.

Because of the land trust, resident populations of white-tailed deer, wild turkey, foxes, beaver, raccoon, waterfowl, and songbirds will continue to have a home. Migratory birds will still have a place to rest during their travels, and certain flowers and plants have been given the protection they need so that one day they may no longer be endangered or threatened.

Among the natural features is the only known community of sweet pinesap in the state. (Much more common in the South, this white, saprophytic plant is reaching its northern limit in Maryland.) Parkers Creek, a brackish tidal stream, flows through the last pristine salt marsh on the western shore of the Chesapeake Bay.

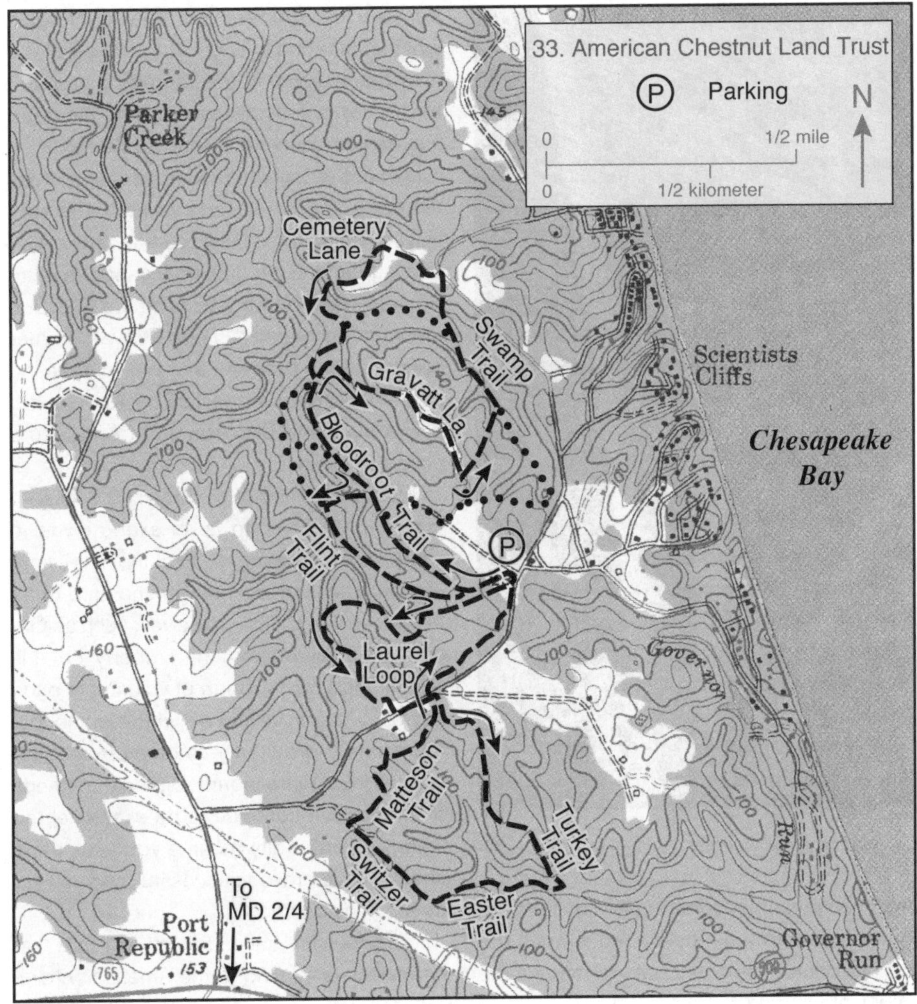

Located near the center of its holdings, the land trust has fabricated a network of pathways that the general public is welcome to use. Because they are not well known and are located off the main roadways of the county, the trails are, for the most part, blissfully underutilized.

The trailhead may be reached by driving south on MD 2/4 from its intersection with MD 231 in Prince Frederick. Approximately 4 miles later, turn left onto Parkers Creek Road, cross MD 765, and turn right onto Scientist Cliffs Road. The parking area is on the left in an additional 0.8 mile.

The trust requests that you register on the sign-in sheet and remember that the trails are open from dawn to dusk. Dogs must be leashed, and be aware that a limited amount of hunting is permitted in season. In addition, in order to protect the natural environment as

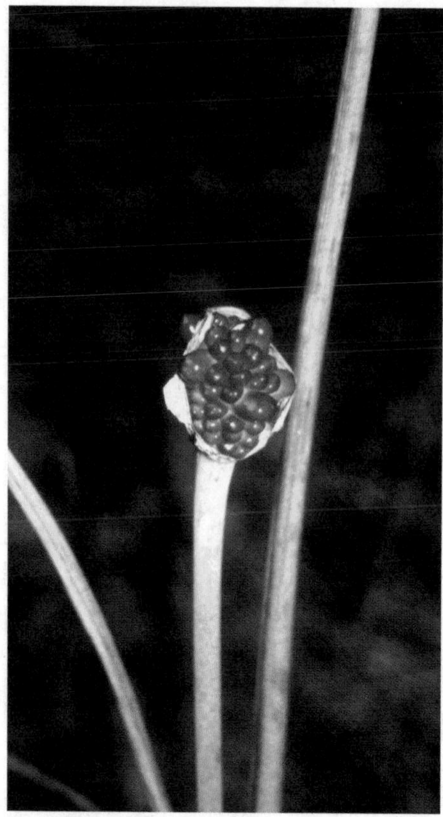

Jack-in-the-pulpit berries

much as possible, some trails may be periodically or permanently closed. Check the bulletin board or the handout trail map for the latest information.

From the parking lot, take the pathway marked as leading to the Bloodroot Trail and walk from open field to woods. Come to an intersection 300 feet later and bear right onto the route marked for the Bloodroot and Flint Trails. Keep to the right on the red-blazed Bloodroot Trail at 0.1 mile, walking through a forest of birch, holly, sassafras, sweetgum, loblolly, and oak trees.

Stay to the left when Wallace Lane comes in from the right at 0.3 mile, and keep to the right when a shortcut trail comes in from the left 300 feet later. Stay right again when another trail heads off to the left at 0.4 mile. Ferns, some of the first plants on Earth to develop a vascular system, line the pathway as you descend to Gravatt Stream.

Avoid the trails to the left after you cross the creek at 0.6 mile, and swing to the right as you rise on the red-blazed trail, now called Gravatt Lane. Both the stream and the pathway are named in honor of Annie Rathbun Gravatt and George Flippo Gravatt, former owners of the property that was purchased by the land trust in the 1980s. Mr. Gravatt was a Maryland Department of Agriculture plant pathologist.

Pass by a stand of bamboo at 0.8 mile—or maybe not. Bamboo is an exotic invasive plant that is replacing much of the native vegetation. The land trust is working hard to try to remove it and other invasives, such as Oriental bittersweet, from the property, but it is a daunting task. A group of volunteers once put in 40 hours sawing down this stand, but the bamboo grew back to be more than 20 feet tall in just one month. Different methods of eradication continue to be experimented with, and hopefully by time you walk here, one will have proved successful, and you will not see any bamboo.

Take the side trail to the left at 1 mile that is marked as leading to the American chestnut tree, whose remains you come to 500 feet later. Once one of the state's largest American chestnut trees, it succumbed to the chestnut blight, inadvertently introduced from Asia in the 1930s.

Continue past the tree's remains and intersect the yellow-blazed Swamp Trail at 1.2 miles, which runs both left and right. Turn left and bypass the pathway to the right 400 feet later, which heads to the site of Percy Howard Farm.

Be alert at 1.4 miles. In order to enjoy a different aspect of the area, turn right onto the route marked as leading to the cemetery. Turn left onto paved Scientists Cliffs Road 300 feet later (be alert for highway traffic), leaving it and turning left along Cemetery Lane in an additional 70 feet to arrive in the Hance-Chesley Cemetery.

Members of the Calvert Garden Club restored the cemetery in the 1990s, so take a few moments to wander among the headstones that date from the early to mid-1800s. The inscriptions lend insight into the lives of southern Maryland's early inhabitants. Of particular length is the one for Young D. Hance, who passed away in 1855:

> *Amid all the troubles and temptations of life / the deceased ever clung to the Cross of Christ / as the steel anchor of his hope. An affectionate / husband, an indulgent and fond father, a hospitable / and kind neighbor, may his posterity imitate his / virtues and follow him as he followed Christ.*

Resume the hike by continuing along Cemetery Lane, bordered by numerous jack-in-the-pulpits. Be alert at 1.7 miles. The road you have been following swings to the right, but you need to turn left and steeply descend to make a right onto the yellow-blazed Swamp Trail. Wood ducks, turtles, and frogs are often seen as hikers cross the boardwalk over the swamp. One of the most beautiful ducks to be found in forested areas, the male wood duck has a red and white bill, red eyes, and luminescent green, purple, and blue feathers along its head. A number of them do not migrate, so they may be found in Southern Maryland throughout the year. (Please note that this boardwalked section of the trail has in the past been flooded by beaver activity. There are plans to construct an elevated boardwalk, but if you find this section of trail closed, simply retrace your steps, and resume the hike by rejoining the description at the 2.3-mile point. This will add about a mile to the overall length of the hike.)

Turn onto and follow the red-blazed Bloodroot Trail at 2 miles. Bypass the trail to the right at 2.2 miles, but leave the red-blazed trail at 2.3 miles and make a sudden hard turn to the right on a descending shortcut pathway.

Turn left on the yellow-blazed Flint Trail at 2.4 miles, where the delicate, nodding flowers of wintergreen bloom in July. Keep to the right when the red-blazed trail comes in from the left at 2.9 miles to join the route you are following. The parking lot is almost in sight less than 400 feet later when you swing right and begin to traverse the white-blazed Laurel Loop Trail.

Although you are in Southern Maryland, the abundance of mountain laurel makes it feel like a stream valley in the mountains of the western part of the state. Take a look at this plant's individual blossoms, and you will find a most ingenious pollination mechanism. The five petals each have two small notches and are connected together to form a shallow bowl. The 10 stamens grow from the center of the petals but are curved over with tension because their anthers are tucked inside the notches. A single pistil rises to the outside of the petals. When an insect visitors (usually a bee) arrives to gather nectar, it brushes against the stamens. This moves them around enough to cause their tops to break free of the notches, spring upward, and toss pollen from the anthers onto the insect's body. Moving onto the next flower, the insect can't help but brush against its pistil, thereby depositing the pollen and ensuring fertilization.

Pass through a moist bottomland at 3.2 miles and rise to a ridgeline, staying to the left at two unmarked intersections.

Turn left onto the rugged Boundary Trail at 3.5 miles and drop quickly into a ravine. Make sure you don't grab onto the thorny trunk of a devil's walking stick when you reach for something to keep your balance.

Rising out of the ravine, turn left onto the paved road at 3.7 miles. Bypassing the first entrance to the green-blazed East Loop Trail on the right in less than 100 feet, turn right onto its second entrance across from a large oak tree. Walking along the edge of the woods, you will soon enter a forest that is obviously older than the one you had been going through.

A shortcut pathway will come in from the right at 3.8 miles, but stay left on the green-blazed route, now called the Turkey Trail. With its larger trees and less undergrowth, this just may be the most attractive forest of the hike. You will reach a T intersection 4 miles into the journey; bear right and follow the green-blazed route, now named the Steve Easter Trail. Jack-in-the pulpit and jewelweed grow along the border of Governor's Run to the left of the trail.

The shortcut trail comes in from the right at 4.2 miles. Keep left, gradually rise past the headwaters of the run, and walk along a utility line for a short distance. You might see a box turtle or two crawl across your route—now referred to as the Switzer Trail.

Be alert at 4.6 miles. The road you have been following continues to the left, but you need to turn right onto a different woods road, where the name of the route magically changes to the Matteson Trail.

Come into a stand of loblolly trees at 4.7 miles and descend, sometimes steeply for short distances. Turn right onto paved Scientists Cliffs Road at 5 miles, but almost immediately cross it and enter the woods on the white-blazed Laurel Loop Trail. (This is directly across the road from where you originally started the East Loop Trail.)

Walk through the woods as the route parallels the roadway, eventually merging onto it and turning left at 5.3 miles, returning to the parking lot at 5.4 miles.

The land trust has a smaller network of pathways, known as the North Side Trails, on its nearby 140-acre Double Oak Farm tract. It may be reached by driving back through Prince Frederick and making a right turn onto Dares Beach Road (MD 402). A little more than 2 miles later, turn right onto Double Oak Road. Continue for another mile and turn left to the designated parking on the left.

Just south of the Double Oak Farm are the 800-acre Goldstein Property and the 150-acre Ward tract; both have trails that lead to Parkers Creek. The trails are rugged but have lovely overlooks of Parkers Creek and the Chesapeake Bay. Closed during gun hunting seasons, the routes are less-traveled, but can be a rich experience for the hardy.

IV Central Maryland

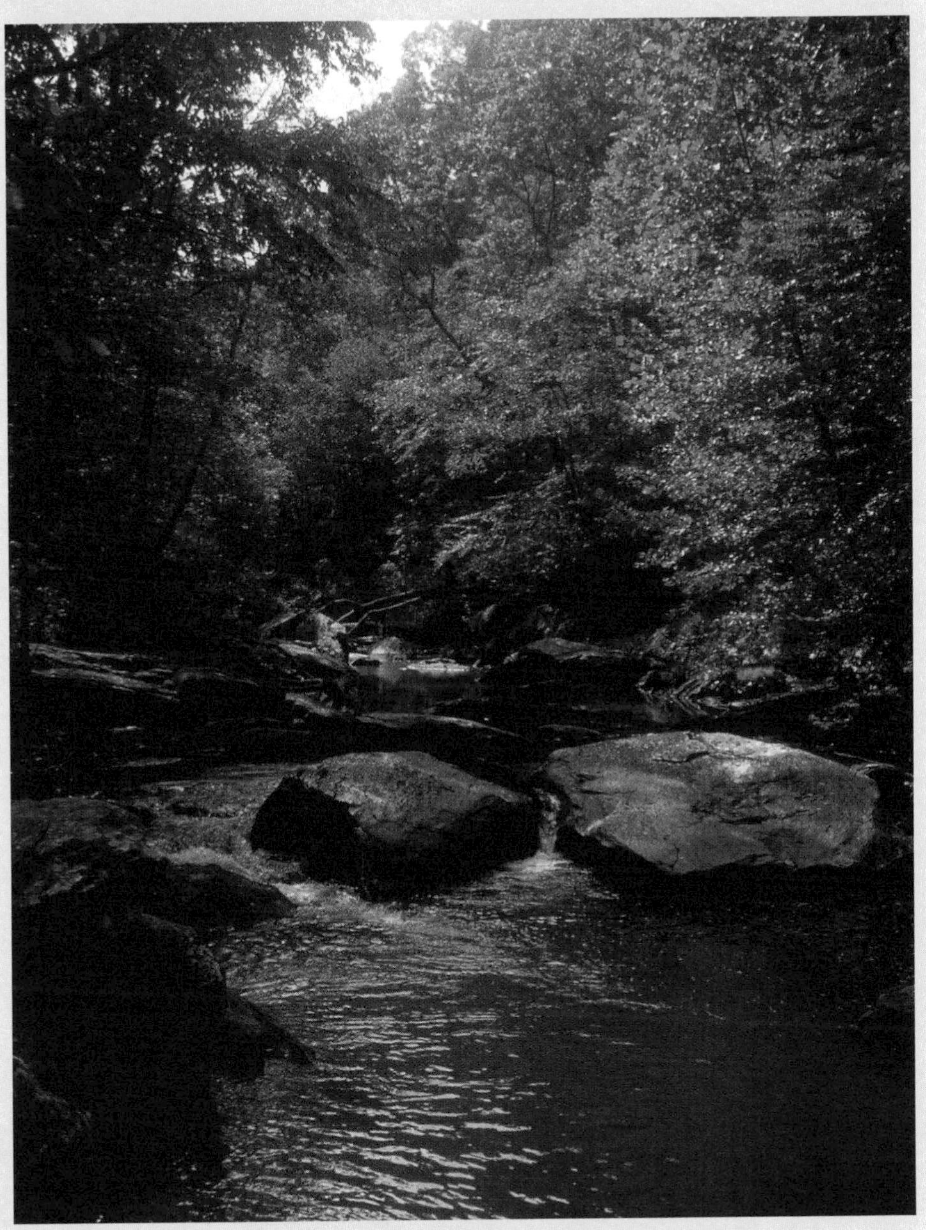

34

The Cascade and Buzzard Rock

Total distance (circuit): 5.7 miles

Hiking time: 3 hours, 30 minutes

Vertical rise: 780 feet

Maps: USGS 7½' Savage; USGS 7½' Ellicott City; USGS 7½' Relay; USGS 7½' Baltimore West

When I wrote about this hike in the first edition of 50 Hikes in Maryland, I called it "a formidable and exacting outing unlike any other in central Maryland" because it had few signs and meager trail markings. This is no longer the case. Thanks to a concerted trail maintenance program that includes a full-time trail crew, the pathways are now well marked and maintained.

The footing may be a little rough in places, and you will be traversing some rugged terrain, but this is a highly recommended excursion. Surprisingly detached from the signs of civilization surrounding the park, this exquisitely beautiful area offers a walk beside tumbling streams and along quiet hillsides. Rest breaks next to a small waterfall and a viewpoint overlooking the river valley are added rewards.

To reach the hike, take exit 13 off I-695 (Baltimore Beltway) southwest of Baltimore and drive west on MD 144 (Frederick Road). In 1.25 miles, turn left onto Rolling Road, only to keep right onto Hilton Avenue in less than 0.2 mile. Continue on Hilton Avenue for 1.5 miles to make a right turn into Patapsco State Park. Follow the one-way park road for 0.2 mile, pulling into the parking area just beyond the sign for the blue-blazed Forest Glen Trail.

Walk back to the trail sign, turn left into the woods, and begin descending. You will see squirrels scampering on the ground or jumping from limb to limb everywhere on the hike, but for some reason their numbers appear to be greater here.

Begin to switchback down the mountainside at 0.3 mile. In order to decrease erosion,

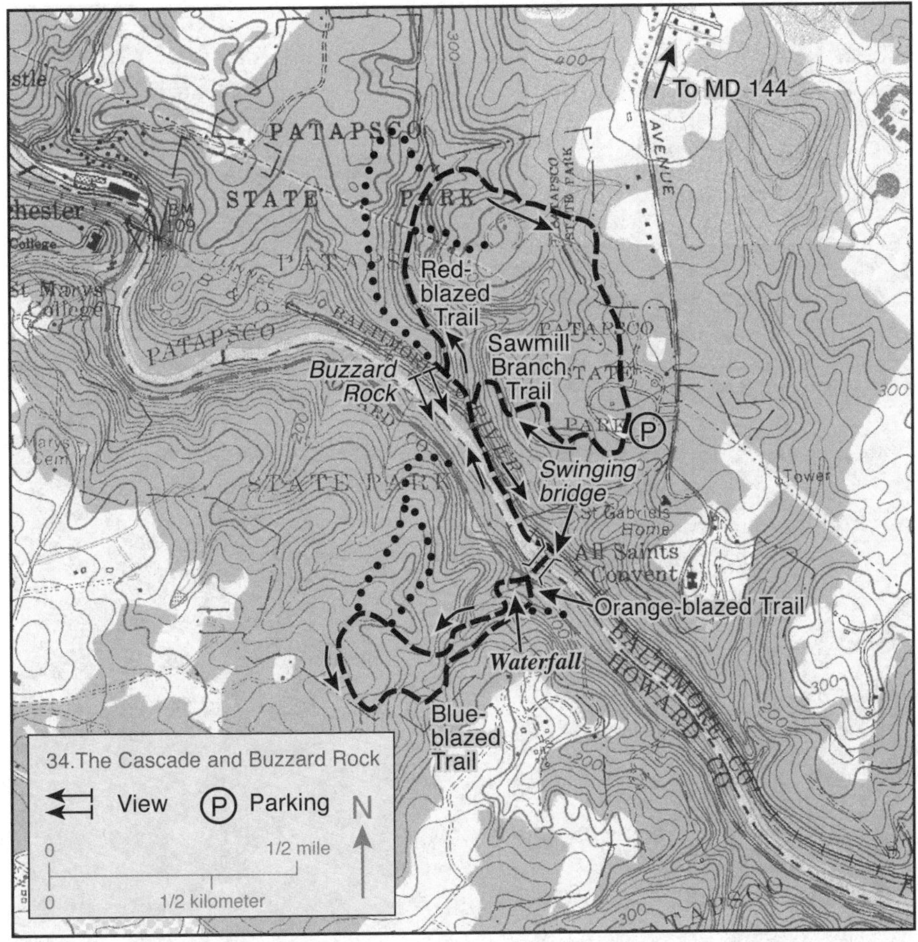

please stay on the switchbacks and do not take any shortcuts or side trails, as many people evidently have. This appears to be a problem throughout the park, so please follow this advice during the hike. Sadly, I have seen a number of people on my walks here who do not pay attention to this simple policy of how to treat the land with respect.

Begin paralleling Sawmill Branch at 0.4 mile, following it downstream. Although it almost appears that the trail crosses the stream at 0.5 mile, it does not. Stay on the same side of the water, continuing on the blazed pathway.

Walk through a culvert underneath the railroad at 0.6 mile. This can be an exciting and deafening experience if you happen to be here when a train goes rumbling overhead. Keep left once you are through the culvert, now walking downstream along the Patapsco River on the wheelchair accessible route of the gray-blazed Grist Mill Extension Trail. The soft buzz of summer insects and the hushed roll of the river make this

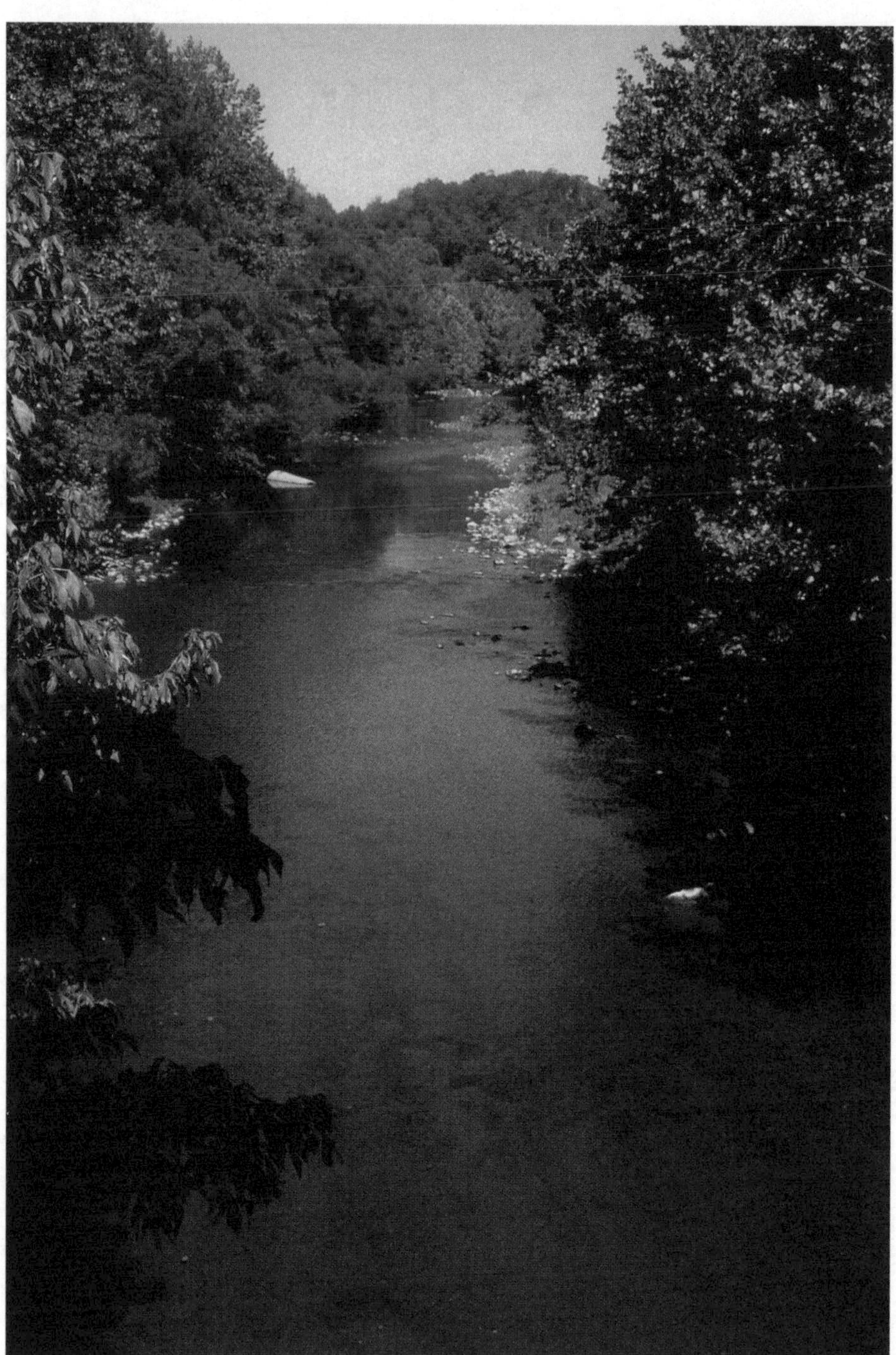

The Patapsco River

one of the most peaceful-feeling portions of the hike.

Come to the swinging bridge at 0.9 mile. If you look around a bit, you might find a foundation or other remnant of the Orange Grove Flour Mill complex, which had structures on both sides of the river. The mill operated from 1856 to when it burned down in 1905.

After crossing the swinging bridge, you will step over paved River Road and come to a large parking lot (restrooms and water are available in season). Known as Orange Grove, this was the site of a village for the mill workers who, like you, made use of a suspension bridge to get across the river.

Ascend the stone steps and begin to follow the blue-blazed Cascade Falls Trail. The pathway makes a switchback uphill and arrives at an intersection. Bear left and take a break when you come to the 15-foot waterfall dropping down various runways along the rock. Relax, sit down, and enjoy the way the sunlight filters through the leaf and hemlock needle canopy to turn the water of the pool below the falls a translucent green. On hot summer days you might want to cool your feet, making small ripples and changing the sunlight patterns in the water.

Close to the waterfall, the orange-blazed Ridge Trail comes in from the left. You want to continue on the Cascade Falls Trail, avoiding one of its spurs that goes off to the right at 1.5 miles. Pass several attractive small pools and cascades as you continue to ascend beside Cascade Branch.

Pay attention when you come to another intersection at 1.8 miles. A spur of the Cascade Falls Trail continues to the left, but you want to bear right, following a smaller tributary upstream before swinging right across the hillside to come to the intersection with the spur trail that had left the main route a short distance above the falls. Keep to the left and descend quickly to the first intersection you encountered on the Cascade Falls Trail. Again keep left, descend to River Road at 2.8 miles, and recross the Patapsco River on the swinging bridge. Once across, turn left and retrace your steps back to the railroad culvert.

At the far end of the culvert, cross Sawmill Branch and ascend switchbacks on the yellow-blazed Buzzards Rock Trail, which will lead you to Buzzards Rock at 3.7 miles. This prominent rock outcrop provides a pleasing view of the Patapsco River Valley and of the Bloede Dam upstream. Constructed in 1906 to provide hydroelectric energy for the Patapsco Electric and Manufacturing Company, Bloede Dam began to deteriorate shortly after it was abandoned in 1924. Untouched for decades, it was finally stabilized, and a fish ladder was constructed around it in the 1990s. If it were not for the dam and the railroad tracks, you would see almost no signs of human activity from your perch upon Buzzards Rock. The narrow creek valley rises steeply on both sides, the tall trees at the top blocking out anything beyond them.

From Buzzards Rock, retrace your steps back down the hillside and turn left to walk upstream beside a series of small cascades and pools along the red-blazed Sawmill Branch Trail. The trail is more rugged here than the hike has been so far. Expect lots of rocks as you ascend the quiet stream valley, with the only sounds being the gurgle of the creek and dozens of birds calling to one another.

Cross under a power line at 4.6 miles. (*Please Note:* Reroute plans for the Charcoal and Santee trails were not completed as this book went to press. Check with authorities for current information.) The orange-blazed Charcoal Trail comes in from the right. Stay to the left along the Sawmill Branch

Trail, only to leave it and bear right onto the white-blazed Santee Trail at 4.8 miles.

Cross a paved park road at 5.1 miles, and less than 500 feet later, stay to the left when the orange-blazed Charcoal Trail comes in from the right. Turn right onto a paved park road at 5.6 miles, pass through a parking area, cut through the children's playground, come to a second parking area, and return to your car at 5.7 miles.

35

Patapsco River

Total distance (circuit): 4.3 miles

Hiking time: 2 hours, 20 minutes

Vertical rise: 500 feet

Maps: USGS 7½' Sykesville; USGS 7½' Ellicott City; park map

While the topography of western Maryland is characterized by high mountain ridgelines, that of central Maryland is defined by the course of narrow river valleys. Seneca Creek, Rock Creek, Northwest Branch, the Patuxent River, Gunpowder Falls, and the Patapsco River have cut through the land, creating a piedmont and coastal plain that is not flat, but is of varying elevations. This hike will take you into one of the loveliest and most isolated of those valleys.

Although most of the land that borders its route from Sykesville to the Baltimore Harbor has been protected as a state park, the Patapsco River can certainly not be called a pristine waterway. There is no doubt it has suffered the affronts of the industrial age and the abuse of the modern world. Yet, where it flows through the McKeldin Area of Patapsco Valley State Park, it regains some of its dignity as it courses by steep hillsides rife with wildflowers and animals that still gain sustenance from it. Other than a few mountain bikers zipping past you, the dull hum of traffic noise, or the reverberation of an occasional jet making an approach to Baltimore–Washington International, there will be few reminders that you are in the 21st century.

You may drive to the beginning of the hike by leaving I-695 (Baltimore Beltway) west of Baltimore at exit 16 and heading west on I-70. Approximately 8 miles later, take exit 83 and drive northward on Marriottsville Road for 4 miles to the park entrance on the right. Leave your car in the parking lot just beyond the contact station. Pets must be leashed.

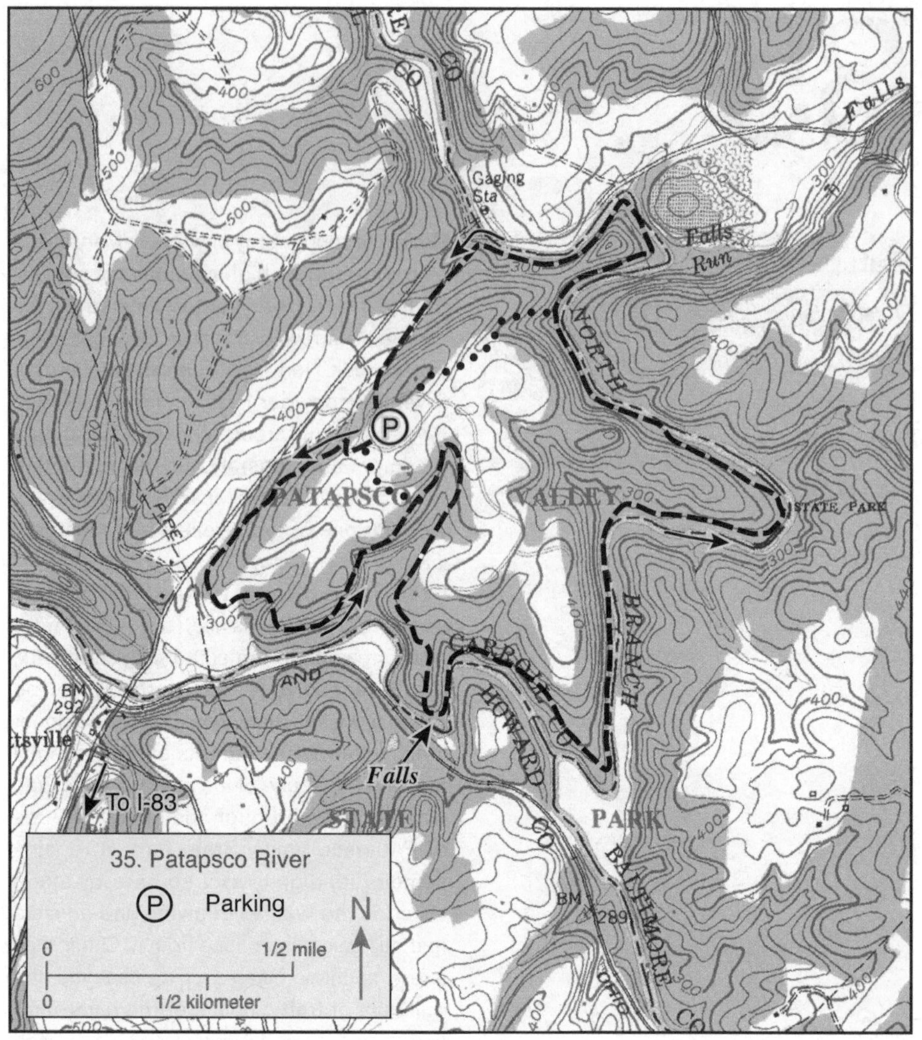

Walk back along the entrance road from the parking lot and turn onto the white-blazed Switchback Trail. In just a few feet, bypass the old road/trail to the left that is open only to hikers. (You will pass by a number of intersecting trails throughout the hike, and will take one of them, but always stay on the white-blazed Switchback Trail for the first 1.2 miles.) As you begin to descend fairly rapidly, pass by spoil piles and diggings from a former flagstone mine. A major component of the rocks that were dug out is mica, whose flecks you may notice glinting in the sunlight.

With Marriottsville Road to your right, drop into the South Branch floodplain at 0.5 mile, swing left, and stay on the main route. Thick wild grapevines, whose soft bark is often used in the construction of birds' nests, drape across this bottomland forest of locust, poplar, and sycamore trees. Even in a densely packed, mixed forest you can easily spot the sycamores by the gleaming white bark on their upper portions.

At 1 mile, you will be walking along the South Branch of the Potapsco River. While the river is cleaner than it used to be before environmental regulations were put into effect in the 1960s and 1970s, it still suffers with siltation from excessive runoff and an occasional industrial accident or sewage spill.

Turn right onto a paved park road at 1.2 miles, continuing straight along the pathway when the pavement ends. Come to the constructed overlook of the South Branch Rapids at 1.3 miles. Squeezed into a narrow channel, the river makes a quick descent of 10 feet or so over a succession of small rock steps. The churning white water slows down when it hits the pool at the base of the falls.

When done viewing, take the descending orange-blazed McKeldin Rapids Trail and arrive at a small beach with the best view of the falls. (Avoid the eroded trail that goes directly down the rocks from the overlook.) Although swimming is not permitted, this is still a great place to take a break. When you tire of sunbathing, you can scoot back a few feet to take advantage of the shade provided by the large leaves of the sycamore trees. This is a put-and-take trout stream, so hopefully you have brought along your tackle.

Continue downstream on the McKeldon Rapids Trail, avoiding the pathway that ascends to the left when you come to a curve in the river at 1.6 miles. Use caution 500 feet later when you cross a (possibly slippery) rock face. After this, continue along good treadway beside heavy growths of Asiatic dayflower. A member of the spiderwort family, this plant was imported from Asia and has escaped into the wild, ranging from Alabama to Massachusetts and as far west as Kansas

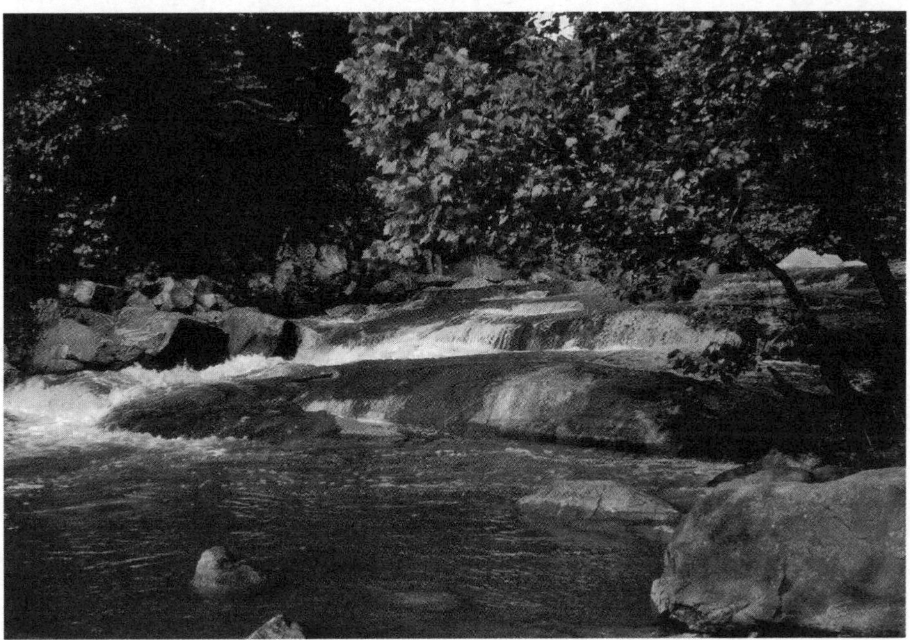

The South Branch Rapids

and Wisconsin. Its small (less than an inch wide) flower consists of two rich blue, rounded petals that last but a day.

The deep valley and the sounds of the river finally dampen the road traffic noise when you come to the confluence of the South Branch and North Branch at 2 miles, close to where the McKeldon Rapids Trail comes to an end. Join the white-blazed Switchback Trail, following the North Branch upstream and avoiding pathways that head off the main route. Great blue herons often wade the waters of this smaller, quieter, and more scenic stream. Its low water is the result of the Liberty Dam 2 miles upstream, which does not release any water. Gnawed and downed trees are indications that the beaver evidently do not mind the diminished flow.

Biologists have observed an amazing display of cooperation among beavers. They have watched young, unskilled beavers clumsily trying to build dams or lodges. When it becomes obvious that things are not going correctly, the young ones cease work, disappear, and return with older beavers, which repair and rebuild as necessary while the original workers help and learn.

The Switchback Trail is pleasant and flat at 2.3 miles and, with this easy walking, you'll possibly be lucky enough to watch an upside-down chickadee search for insects and larvae on the bottoms of twigs and branches. Because, like most other songbirds, chickadees expend massive amounts of energy by shivering in order to stay warm during the winter, their search for food is constant.

Be alert at 3.6 miles. The trail makes a sudden turn to the left and steeply ascends the hillside. (Continuing to the right would bring you to a spot blocked by a cliff that extends into the water.)

Come to the top of the rise at 3.7 miles and continue along the white-blazed pathway. Pass by a picnic shelter at 3.9 miles and begin to walk along a paved park road. Keep right at two succeeding intersections and, in order not to walk on pavement more than needed, turn left through the playground area and return to your car at 4.3 miles.

36

Soldiers Delight

Total distance (circuit): 6.0 miles

Hiking time: 2 hours, 50 minutes

Vertical rise: 640 feet

Maps: USGS 7½' Reistertown

Looking at the types of vegetation in central Maryland today, it may be hard to imagine that grasslands once spread across tens of thousands of acres of this landscape. Prior to colonial settlement, much of Baltimore and Harford Counties and adjacent counties in Pennsylvania were covered by open spaces not unlike the prairies found in the Midwest.

In order to provide prime habitat for their favorite game animals, Native Americans had burned these areas on a regular basis for hundreds of years, keeping them free of trees. Because colonists did not continue the practice, forests replaced the grasslands, and only on dry and nutrient-poor soils did the prairielike zones persist. Lamentably, the modern world has destroyed most of those by mining and development.

As in a number of other, now protected areas profiled in this guidebook, it was private citizen organizations that worked hard to make certain that the largest remaining serpentine grasslands in the state, Soldiers Delight, was preserved. (Never underestimate the power of one voice or group to affect policies or opinions.) The word *serpentine* is believed to be in reference to a snake that lives in a similar type of soil in Italy. The 2,000-acre tract harbors approximately 40 rare, endangered, or threatened plants, as well as rare insects, rocks, and minerals.

With only minor ups and downs, this circuit hike enables you to experience this exceptional province without having to expend a great deal of effort or energy. It consists of two loops, with your parked car being in the middle, so you could decide to do the loops

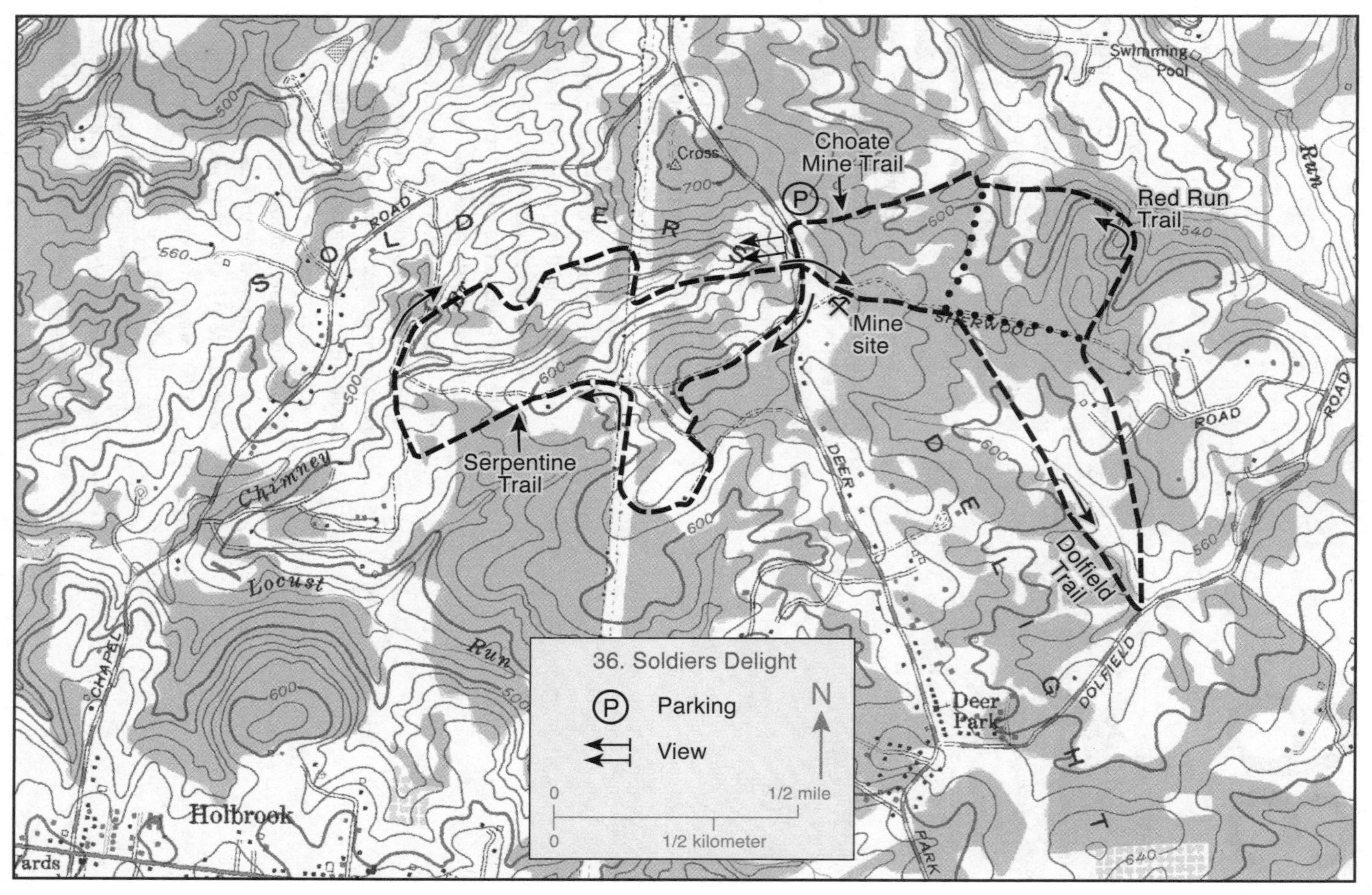

36. Soldiers Delight
Parking
View
N
0
1/2 mile
0
1/2 kilometer
Choate Mine Trail
Red Run Trail
Mine site
Serpentine Trail
Dolfield Trail
Swimming Pool
Cross
Deer Park
Holbrook
SOLDIERS DELIGHT
ROAD
SHERWOOD
DEER
DOLFIELD
PARK
CHAPEL
ROAD
Chimney
Locust
Run
Run

on two separate occasions if you do not have the time or inclination to do the entire outing all at once.

The natural environment area may be reached by leaving I-695 (Baltimore Beltway) west of Baltimore at exit 18 and heading westward on MD 26 (Liberty Road). Approximately 5 miles later, turn right onto Deer Park Road and continue for another 2.3 miles, bypassing the entrance road to the visitors center and leaving your car in the gravel parking area on the left. The trails are open from sunrise to sunset; pets must be on a leash.

Looking out at the view, the hike begins by taking the white-blazed Serpentine Trail from the left side of the parking lot. Walk along the shoulder of the road for a few feet before bearing right to enter the pines. Turn right onto a woods road at 0.2 mile and come into an open barrens, your first chance to study one of the area's special plants.

Once spread throughout the Coastal Plain, sandplain gerardia is now confined to the serpentine grasslands of Baltimore County and is possibly the last naturally occurring population in the world. Its funnel-shaped pink flowers bloom from August to October on a stem that grows to be less than a foot tall. An annual, its numbers in the area vary widely depending on each year's environmental conditions. At times, observers have found more than 10,000, while in other years there were fewer than 200.

Stay on the woods road as you walk to the right of the visitors center (worth a visit if it is open) and to the left of the abandoned, native stone Red Dog Lodge, built in 1912. The view beside the lodge provides a glimpse of the terrain through which you will be walking and provides insight into the area's name. Local lore states that soldiers stationed here were "delighted" that the open nature of the landscape lessened the possibility of being surprised by the enemy.

You must be very alert at 0.6 mile. The main road you have been following swings to the left, but your route now makes a right to follow a track along the edge of the open field, next to the trees. If you are hiking here in mid- to late summer, you might be wading into shoulder-high grass that almost obliterates the route. As you walk through it, and the tiny yellow Indian grass blossoms cling to your clothes and skin, remember that this is what thousands of acres of Maryland (and the Midwest) looked like at one time.

Be alert again at 0.8 mile; turn right to walk underneath a humming high-voltage power line (and try not to think about studies that have uncovered the possible harmful effects such lines have on the human body).

At 1.3 miles, enter a forest of Virginia pine that is becoming overgrown with greenbrier. Possibly more than anything else, the invasion of this pine tree and the eastern red cedar is the greatest threat to the grasslands. Being sun-tolerant, Virginia pines are the forest pioneers, growing taller than the grasses and providing the shade needed by many deciduous trees. In an effort to halt their spread, volunteers and state employees spend many hours every year cutting down the conifers and transporting them off-site. When conditions are right, these areas are then burned in the hope of restoring the barrens.

Swing right at 1.6 miles, where a grassy road comes in from the left. Cross a couple of open areas populated by blaze star, another plant characteristic of prairie lands, at 1.7 miles. Blooming into October, its purple flowers are a welcome bit of color amid the swaying brown grass fronds of autumn.

Cross a small creek and rise into another barrens where, if you look closely, you should be able to find a few blossoms of sandplain gerardia. If you find them, you will also be

Sandplain gerardia

looking at little bluestem, a prairie grass always found in association with the flower. Although the relationship is not clear, it is believed that the gerardia parasitizes the roots of the grass.

Pass through a small wooded plot to swing right under the power lines at 2.4 miles.

The trail swings to the left along tiny Chimney Branch and goes upstream into a near jungle of greenbrier. Within the moister setting of the environment in this area, this is the only known population of fringed gentian in Maryland. One of the last flowers to bloom in late summer and early fall, its whorl of rich blue petals opens each morning with the rising sun and closes when the sun disappears beyond the western horizon.

Switch over to the right side of the water run and rise to the overlook parking area at 2.9 miles. If this is all the time you have, drive home with plans to do the rest of this outing another day. If not, take a short break and enjoy the snacks and drinks you left stashed in the car.

When ready to resume, cross the paved Deer Park Road diagonally to the right and enter a pine forest on the red-blazed Choate Mine Trail. Come to the Choate Mine site at 3 miles, where the opening of the mine, held up by old log supports, is still visible. Active for most of the 18th century and again during World War I, the mine produced more than 3,000 tons of chromite, used to produce chromium chemicals, paint pigments, and dyes.

Continue on the main route, coming to a four-way intersection at 3.3 miles. The Choate Mine Trail goes left, the orange-blazed Red Run Trail straight, and the yellow-blazed Dolfield Trail–the one you want to follow–turns right. Blaze star flourishes in the sunny spots next to the trail, but because the forest–with its shade–is encroaching, the flowers may not last here much longer.

Cross a small water run and an open area at 3.7 miles. An abundance of flowers grows near the next water run you cross at 4 miles. Be on the lookout for blaze star, sandplain gerardia, aster, goldenrod, and even some Queen Anne's lace. Soon after this you must be alert to leave the water run and turn left.

Cross the paved Sherwood Road at 4.4 miles and continue through the pink-tinged grass of late summer. Be alert at 4.5 miles. In order to avoid walking directly behind a housing development, turn left under utility lines and descend for a short distance, soon passing through a young pine plantation.

Come to an old woods road at 4.6 miles and turn right, almost immediately swinging onto the orange-blazed Red Run Trail. Descend into a deciduous forest, listening to the chattering of squirrels–which have been conspicuously absent throughout most of this hike.

Swing left at 5 miles and begin to walk upstream beside a small creek. Cross an open barrens area full of blaze star, serpentine aster, and fameflower. The latter is found almost exclusively in serpentine outcrops. Bees are attracted to its small, star-shaped pink flowers, which open only for a few hours on sunny days.

Come to a T intersection where the red-blazed Choate Mine Trail goes left and right. You want to bear right, soon crossing a small water run, swinging left, and rising. Another mine site is to the right of the trail at 5.6 miles; after walking through more pines, turn left along the shoulder of Deer Park Road, cross the pavement, and end the hike at 6 miles.

37

Oregon Ridge

Total distance (circuit): 4.3 miles

Hiking time: 2 hours

Vertical rise: 500 feet

Maps: USGS 7½' Cockeysville; park map

Oregon Ridge is an excellent model of a county or regional park that has been able to meet many of the diverse recreational needs of the local population yet still keep the vast majority of the land undisturbed. Within the park's 1,036 acres are tennis courts, picnic areas, a dinner theater and lodge, an outdoor stage (the summer home for the Baltimore Symphony Orchestra), a swimming lake and sandy beach, and a bathhouse and snack bar. A nature center, with exhibits that relate to the local natural and human history, sponsors one of the best and most active interpretive programs available anywhere in Maryland–pick up a schedule and take part in an activity.

A network of marked pathways meanders through the undeveloped part of the park, rising to the main forested ridgeline and descending into a narrow creek valley. Of course, nearly every bit of land in Maryland has gone through countless changes as the result of uses by the human race, and this area is no exception. During the mid-1800s there was an active iron ore and marble mining operation located on what are now park lands, and even though nature has done a remarkable job of reclamation, you will see numerous reminders of those days.

Driving to the park is easy. Take I-83 exit 20 (about 5 miles north of I-695, the Baltimore Beltway) and head westward along Shawan Road for 1 mile. Make a left onto Beaver Dam Road and immediately bear right, headed toward the lake and the nature center. Leave your car in the nature center parking lot in an additional 0.4 mile.

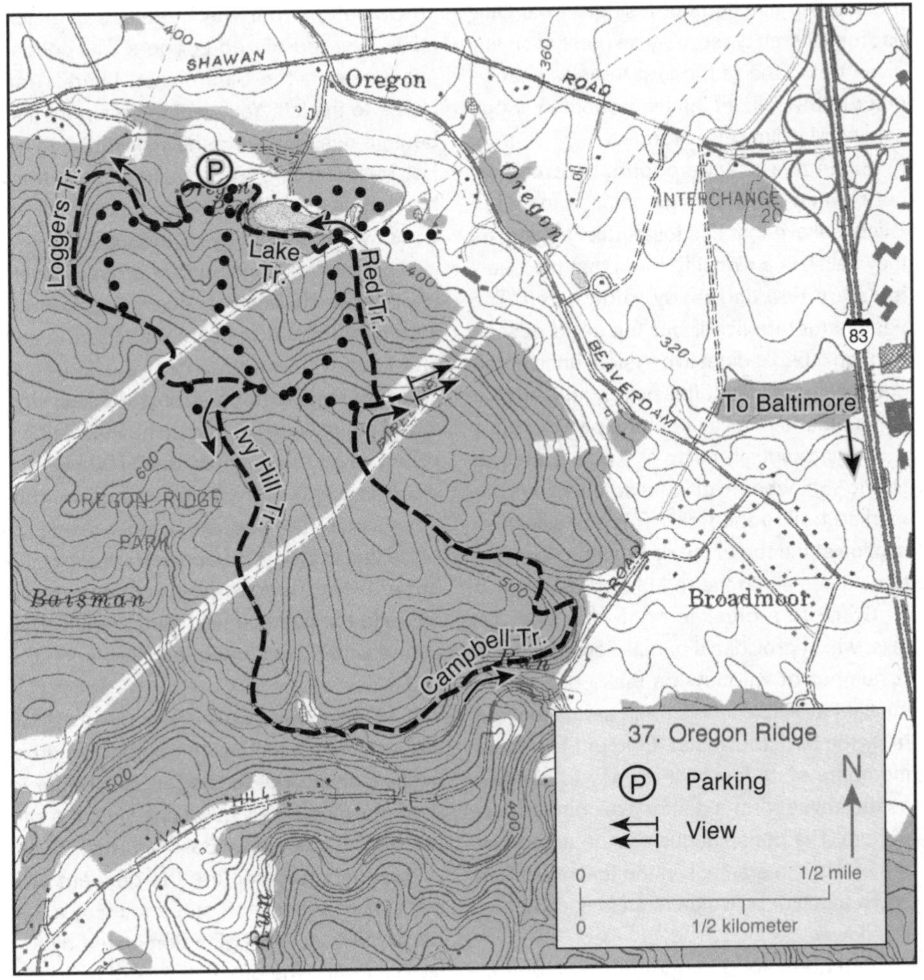

Walk from the parking lot to the nature center and take the trail to the left of the building to cross the bridge over a deep ravine. This is not a natural cavity in the earth, but the remnants of an open pit mine dug in the 1840s to remove goethite, a shiny black ore used in the manufacture of pig iron. The nature center is built atop the soil that was removed from the ravine over a number of decades.

Turn right at the far side of the bridge onto the red-blazed Loggers Trail. Keep to the right when the tan-blazed Ridge Trail heads off to the left at 0.2 mile. The next pathway to the right is the Handicap Trail; stay left on the red-blazed route in a forest of mountain laurel, sassafras, and young oak and maple trees. Identifying sassafras can be difficult at times. Its leaves may be one of three different shapes: three lobes, two lobes (resembling a mitten), or a single lobe. Only one, or all three types, may be present on any given tree. One of the first trees to change color in the fall, its leaves become various shades of yellow and orange.

Since this change occurs before many nut-bearing trees change color, some naturalists believe that this foliar fruit flagging, as they call it, is a signal to birds that the tree's fruits are ripe and ready to be eaten. The flesh is metabolized, but the seed passes through a bird's digestive system unchanged and may germinate after being deposited at some other site away from the parent tree.

Begin gradually rising at 0.5 mile, staying to the left whenever you come to an unmarked trail to the right. There is a T intersection at the top of the rise; bear to the right to continue along the red-blazed pathway.

Come to a pipeline right-of-way at 0.9 mile, which provides a partial view to the left. A number of wildflowers make use of the sunlight available in this open area, most notably the birdsfoot violet. One of the largest members of its family, it is easy to identify, as its leaves form a distinctive "bird's foot" pattern. The conspicuous orange anthers at the end of the stamens in the flower's throat add a touch of brilliance to an already attractive flower.

Turn right along the right-of-way, only to bear left off it just a few hundred feet later and reenter the woods. Avoid the Short-Cut Trail that heads to the right at 1 mile and continue through the forest, whose undergrowth is being overtaken by a number of fast-growing vines such as greenbrier. Its numerous thorns may keep you at bay, but various bird species are adept at avoiding them in order to consume the plant's numerous berries. Also seemingly oblivious to the danger, white-tailed deer and rabbits munch on the leaves.

Come to a four-way intersection at 1.2 miles: The red-blazed Loggers Trail continues straight; the blue-blazed Laurel Trail heads to the left. You want to bear right and begin a descent along the yellow-blazed Ivy Hill Trail. The Short-Cut Trail comes in from the right at 1.3 miles. Continue to the left on a pathway bordered by partridgeberry.

This plant is an important ground cover; its roots are shallow but intertwining, forming a compact mat that helps stabilize the soil and keep it from washing away. Its genus name, *Mitchella,* honors John Mitchell, who saved countless lives during the Philadelphia yellow fever epidemic of the 1700s by developing a way to treat victims stricken with the disease. The species name, *repens,* reflects that the plant creeps or trails along the ground. Partridgeberry's common name refers to the fact that wild partridge (in addition to wild turkey and quail) feed upon the fruit.

Cross another pipeline right-of-way at 1.6 miles. Amid a small patch of rhododendron, avoid a small trail to the left and begin to drop at a moderately quick pace into the narrow hollow created by Baisman Run.

Just as you complete the descent at 2 miles, take a few short steps to enjoy a rest break inside a small glen dominated by tiny Ivy Hill Pond. The green leaves of mountain laurel and rhododendron and the needles of hemlock trees make a pleasant reflection in the water. Sadly, the hemlocks show the telltale white dots of hemlock woolly adelgid infestation.

Return to the main route and continue downstream on Baisman Run. Although still yellow-blazed, the pathway is now named the S. James Campbell Trail, which honors the man who worked diligently to raise donated funds in order to purchase land for this portion of the park.

Ivy Hill Pond

Cross the creek at 2.1 miles, but be alert just 200 feet later. Your route makes a sudden left off the old road you have been following and recrosses the stream onto a footpath. Use stepping-stones to avoid getting wet feet during two more crossings at 2.4 miles, where the run drops down a series of small, pretty cascades.

Begin to ascend at 2.6 miles; avoid taking the trail to the right. Upon reaching the top of the rise at 2.9 miles, turn right along an old road that follows the yellow blazes. The ridgeline you are walking upon (and most of the others in this region) is composed primarily of metamorphic rock that contains bits of feldspar, mica, quartz, and garnet crystals. Quartz, one of most abundant minerals on Earth and found in a number of different variations, is highly resistant to erosion. That which is found on Oregon Ridge is of the milky variety, evidenced by its white color.

Diagonally cross the right-of-way at 3.4 miles, coming to an intersection 500 feet later. The red-blazed Loggers Trail runs both left and right. Turn to the right, but almost immediately bear to the left. Stay to the right just a few feet later to enjoy the vista from the top of the ski slope.

Looking to the northwest, you can take in the green grasses of the golf course and residential yards in the foreground, while a little farther back is I-83 and the development that has grown up around its exit. The rapid transit afforded by the interstate has permitted more people to move out of Baltimore and into this once-rural landscape. It would be interesting to take a photo from this vantage point and bring it back a few years later to compare it with what would exist in the valley then.

Return to the trail and bear right, descending along the red-blazed footpath. Be alert when you come to the T intersection at 3.9 miles. With a picnic area to your right, bear left uphill along the pipeline right-of-way. Do not turn right onto the red-blazed pathway barely 100 feet beyond this point, but do turn right onto the orange-blazed Lake Trail in an additional 90 feet. Make sure that you always follow the orange blazes on the main route of this rough and rocky pathway as it bypasses a number of unmarked trails.

Begin to walk high above Oregon Lake, another depression in the ground created by mining operations, which is now filled by groundwater and used for swimming by park visitors. Make use of the log bridge to cross a ravine at 4.1 miles and continue around the lake.

Drop onto a mowed grassy area near the edge of the lake at 4.25 miles, turn left, and return to your car at 4.3 miles.

38

Big Gunpowder Falls

Total distance (circuit): 12.8 miles

Hiking time: 6 hours, 15 minutes

Vertical rise: 1,160 feet

Maps: USGS 7½' Hereford

Big Gunpowder Falls? With a name like that, this must be one heck of a rip-roaring, booming, crashing waterfall. Sorry to disappoint you, but there are no such major cascades on the rivers that bear this name. Evidently, because the streams draining this 500-square-mile watershed fell from the piedmont to the Tidewater, early settlers called the entire river system a falls. The *gunpowder* part of the name comes from the saltpeter–used to make gunpowder–found along the banks by James Denton in 1665.

What you will find on this hike, though, is a quiet and protected portion of 17,000-acre Gunpowder Falls State Park. Walking along both banks of a 5-mile stretch of Big Gunpowder Falls, you will have the opportunity to discover for yourself why the state has been acquiring land along the Big Gunpowder Falls, Little Gunpowder Falls, and the Gunpowder River Valley since 1959.

Although the Prettyboy Dam has greatly reduced Big Gunpowder Falls's unconstrained flow from 260 million gallons a day, an assured continuous supply of cold water has turned it into one of Maryland's premier trout streams. The land acquisition has kept the area in such a natural state that the beavers reintroduced here in 1950 have flourished and multiplied. Protected from development, the hillsides above the river are a rich mixture of oak, poplar, cherry, loblolly, sycamore, and river birch trees. The forest floor is lush with fern, nettle, jack-in-the-pulpit, bloodroot, spring beauty, rue anemone, and hepatica. In addition to the beaver, be on the lookout for white-tailed deer, great blue

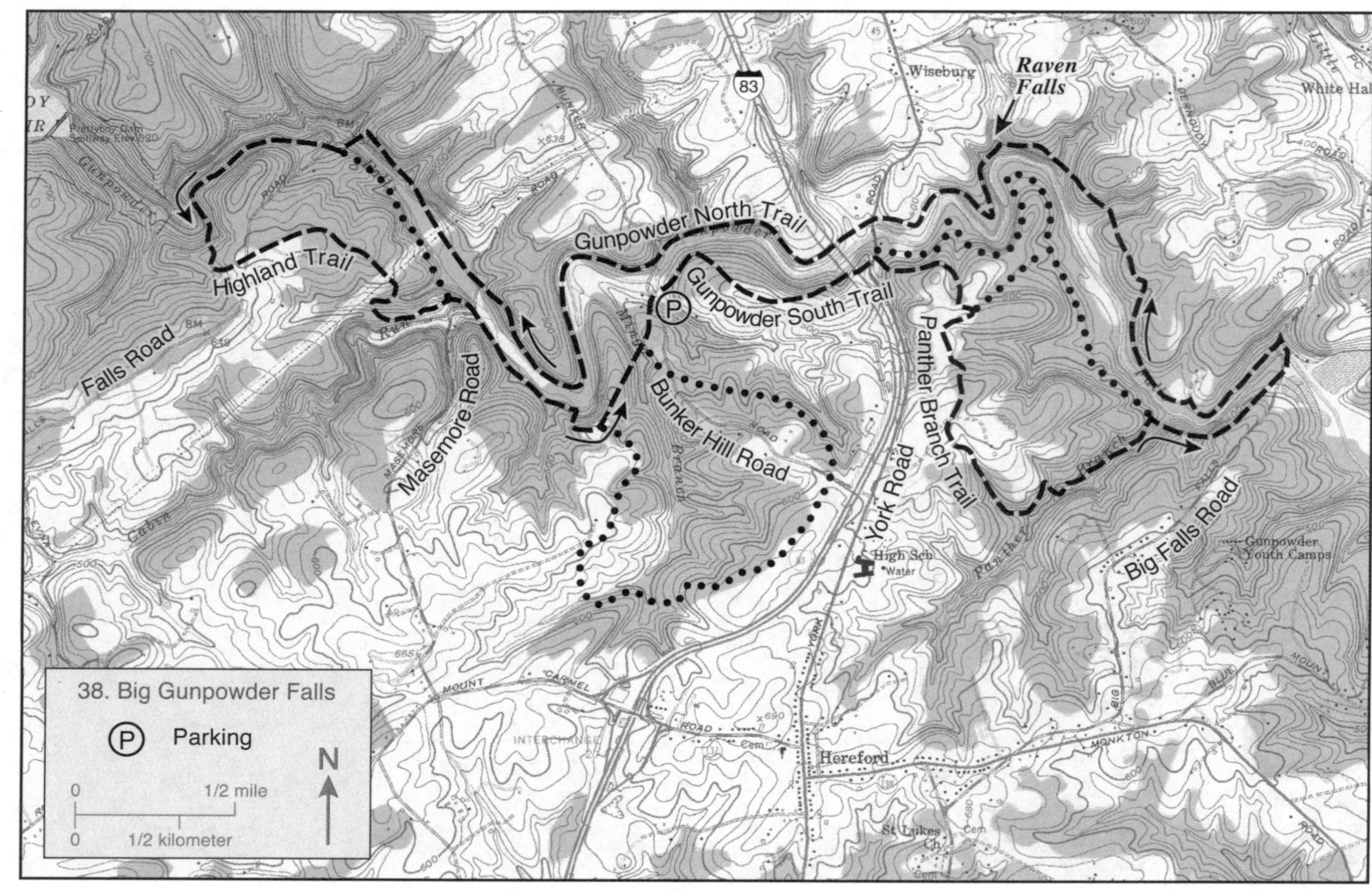
Raven Falls
Wiseburg
White Hall
83
Gunpowder North Trail
Gunpowder South Trail
Highland Trail
Falls Road
Masemore Road
Bunker Hill Road
York Road
Panther Branch Trail
Big Falls Road
Gunpowder Youth Camps
High Sch
Hereford
St Lukes Ch.
38. Big Gunpowder Falls
P Parking
0 1/2 mile
0 1/2 kilometer
N

heron, hawks, groundhog, a multitude of songbirds, and maybe a fox or two.

There are a few minor ups and downs with a couple of short, steep sections and several rocky places, but for most of this hike, the walking is comfortable and easy. Its length might be its only real difficulty, especially with the shorter hours of daylight in the winter. Whenever you go, though, just bring a supply of water, a flashlight, a good lunch, and the other items you should always carry in a day pack, and you should be all right. This is a wonderful hike–do not pass it up.

From I-83 north of Baltimore, take exit 27 and drive east on MD 137 (Mount Carmel Road). In 0.5 mile, turn left onto MD 45 (York Road), follow it northward for 0.8 mile, make a left onto Bunker Hill Road, and come to the parking area in another 1.1 miles.

Facing the river, begin the hike by taking the trail through the small field to the right. Cross a wooden bridge, swing to the left, and begin to follow the white-blazed Gunpowder South Trail, dedicated in 2012 to Maryland fishing legend Lefty Kreh. Be alert at 0.2 mile as the trail bears to the right to ascend a woods road lined by ferns. Near the top of the rise at 0.4 mile, the trail leaves the roadbed and turns left just below a pine plantation. You might notice that there are several types of ferns along the pathway now. Referred to as shade-obligates, these plants do not fully emerge in the spring until the forest's leaf canopy has developed enough to block out most of the sunlight.

The traffic along I-83 is visible through the vegetation above as you begin to descend at 0.6 mile. When crossing under the interstate at 0.8 mile, ferns are replaced by jewelweed, and trout–possibly brook, rainbow, or brown–are visible swimming through the waters of the river.

Be careful, as traffic may be heavy when you diagonally cross York Road at 0.9 mile. So as to be able to explore the hillside environment above the river, turn right and ascend the blue-blazed Panther Branch Trail, passing by bits of mountain laurel. Level out at 1.2 miles and proceed with minor ups and downs. Keep right to continue to follow the blue blazes when you come to an intersection at 1.4 miles. In quick succession, you will pass two intersections: The first is an unmarked pathway and the second is the pink-blazed Sandy Lane Trail. Stay to the right in both instances.

Be very alert at 1.6 miles. Your route makes a sudden left onto what, at first, may appear to be a lesser-used pathway. At 1.8 miles, the trail merges with and bears left onto a woods road. Soon, with an open meadow on the left and a large pine plantation on the right, it almost feels as if you are walking along an old country lane and should expect to see a horse and carriage come around a bend at any moment.

Be alert at 2 miles. The trail turns to the left, cuts across the field, and begins to descend along a tributary of Panther Branch. The water gains volume, as does the vegetation, as you continue downstream. Almost all traffic noise is blocked out once you swing left to walk through the quiet valley created by Panther Branch. The stone foundations near the trail are believed to be the remains of a gunpowder mill that blew up in the latter part of the 19th century. The cry of a red-tailed hawk is often heard above the ironwood trees of this area.

Arrive at an intersection at 3.1 miles and turn right to once again follow the white blazes of the Gunpowder South Trail. After you cross Panther Branch, avoid the trail to the right as well as the prolific growths of stinging nettle. Brushing up against the nettle will give the tiny, stiff hairs an opportunity to scratch your skin and deposit an irritant that may itch for the rest of the day. One experience of this kind will, no doubt, keep you on the watch for the nettle. The plant's tiny blossoms are so small–less than 0.1 inch–that most people do not think of it as a flowering plant.

Cross Gunpowder Falls on the Big Falls Road bridge at 3.8 miles and make an immediate left onto a private but blue-blazed gravel road. Even though you are walking along the same stretch of river, things will look different, as you are now walking upstream. Even the ripples in the water look dissimilar as the sunlight sparkles on them from a changed angle.

Be alert at 4 miles. Where the road swings to the right, the trail bears to the left to stay along the river. If you are walking here late in the season, you should be prepared to become scratched and itchy; the growth of the grasses, briers, and stinging nettles can overcome the best efforts to keep the trail clear.

Great blue herons often wade the river in search of fish and frogs. Keep close watch on one, and you may see it poke its bill into the soft mud of the bank and come up with a mouse or gopher–which it will then dip into the water so that the prey will slide more smoothly down its gullet.

Soon after entering full woods again at 4.6 miles, the trail rises on a steep switchback away from the river to avoid perpendicular terrain and possible washout areas. After several ups and downs, return to river level and take a well-deserved break where Raven Falls drops down a smooth rock face at 5.3 miles.

Leaving the falls, watch for cardinal flowers growing along the riverbank, listen for the sound of woodpecker calls, and notice that a

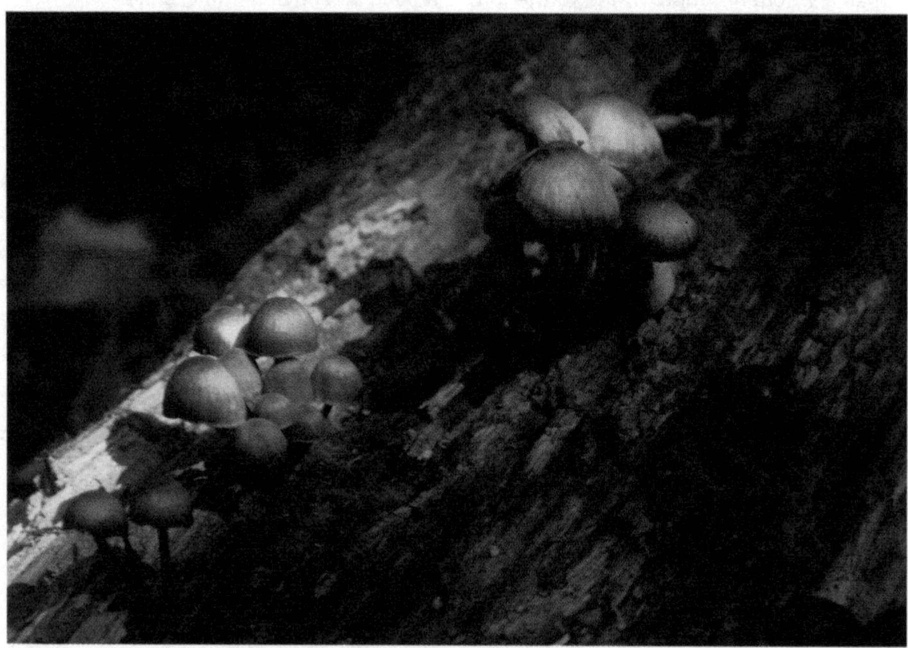

Mushrooms helping to recycle a tree

number of tree trunks have been gnawed upon by beavers. Gunpowder Falls was the first stream that the Department of Natural Resources used to reintroduce beavers back into Maryland in the 1950s, having been absent in the state for more than a century.

Rise steeply to cross paved York Road and continue to follow the blue blazes, which soon pass under I-83. There is a large pool (the result of human handiwork in building a small rock dam) at 7 miles, which is a favorite local swimming hole.

Cross paved Bunker Hill Road at 7.2 miles, continuing to follow the blue blazes, with patches of touch-me-not on both sides of the pathway. Be sure to listen closely when you see a great blue heron take off from the shallow water, and you will hear its huge wings whistle in the air. This large bird, approximately 50 inches in height, may make its summer home as far north as Ontario, Canada, but usually migrates back to coastal waters south of Massachusetts for the winter.

Cross the paved Masemore Road at 8.5 miles, follow the blue blazes into a managed hunting area, and be mindful of the extensive growths of stinging nettle. Cross Gunpowder Falls on the Falls Road bridge at 9.2 miles and turn to the right, following the white blazes of the Gunpowder South Trail.

Be alert at 9.3 miles. In order to avoid climbing over large boulders and rocks, make a sudden left turn uphill on a lesser-used pathway for a steep climb, drop back down just as steeply, and continue the upstream walk. (Actually, it is probably just as easy not to do this up-and-down, and to continue along the unmarked trail people have made over the boulders.)

The trail and footing are now rougher and rockier, and you must pick your way over one boulder after another. However, you are rewarded for this hard work, as this is, no doubt, the prettiest portion of the hike along Big Gunpowder Falls. Large boulders in the river churn the stream into white water as it drops down into quiet pools surrounded by hemlocks and other green vegetation. The scene is more reminiscent of the mountains of Western Maryland than of Central Maryland.

Be alert at 10.1 miles; the trail goes left to attain higher ground. About 400 feet later, you will leave the white blazes of the Gunpowder South Trail to bear left and ascend the blue-blazed Highland Trail to explore another hillside. Cross the paved Falls Road at 10.4 miles and gradually descend a ridgeline that, once again, has the look and feel of Western Maryland.

Pass under power lines at 10.9 miles. Soon cross a small creek, swing left, and rise to the top of the ridge, where you will bear left onto a woods road next to an old fence line and descend. Rejoin and turn right onto the white-blazed Gunpowder South Trail at 11.4 miles. Cross the paved Masemore Road at 11.5 miles, head to the upper end of the parking area, and take the wooden bridge over Bush Cabin Run.

At 11.9 miles, the trail turns right along a side creek, which it soon crosses to pass through a glen of hemlocks. (Do not go left to return to the river.) At the intersection at the top of the rise, the blue-blazed Mingo Forks Trail goes right; keep to the left along the ridge and eventually descend.

Cross small Mingo Branch at 12.6 miles and keep to the white blazes (do not turn left) immediately after the creek. Near the top of the rise, the blue-blazed Bunker Hill Trail comes in from the right. Keep left and descend to your car at 12.8 miles.

39

Northern Central Railroad Trail

Total distance (one-way): 18.8 miles

Hiking time: 8 hours

Vertical rise: 20 feet

Maps: USGS 7½' New Freedom (MD/PA); USGS 7½' Hereford; USGS 7½' Phoenix; USGS 7½' Cockeysville

The Rails-to-Trails Conservancy, the association generally recognized as spearheading the nationwide movement to convert abandoned railroad rights-of-way into trails, was formally organized in 1986. Nearly a decade before that, though, the state of Maryland, Baltimore County, and a group of local citizens were already laying the groundwork for the Northern Central Railroad Trail.

From 1838 to 1972, the Northern Central Railroad connected Baltimore with York, Pennsylvania, providing a major link for small communities along the way. Union troops made use of the railroad during the Civil War, and Abraham Lincoln traveled it on his way to deliver his famous Gettysburg Address. The construction of the interstates–and the resulting increase in truck and automobile transportation–marked the railroad's decline. Floods from Hurricane Agnes in 1972 dealt the final blow by washing out trestles and miles of track.

After years of negotiation, a corridor from Ashland to the Pennsylvania border was purchased from the railroad in 1980. Following a series of public meetings, during which the pros and cons of the trail were debated, volunteers began working on the pathway, with the Ashland to Monkton section opening to the public in 1984. Administered by Gunpowder Falls State Park, the rest of the trail was dedicated in 1989. Since that time, other rail-trails have opened throughout the state, including the Baltimore and Annapolis Trail, the Capital Crescent Trail, and the Western Maryland Trail.

While all are worthy projects and good trails in their own way, there is no doubt that the Northern Central Railroad Trail is the most enjoyable and scenic. (Although renamed, in 2007, the Torrey C. Brown Rail Trail after the third Secretary of the Maryland Department of Natural Resources, most people still refer to it by its original name.) Almost always within sight of a stream, it runs for nearly 20 miles, passing by open farmland and natural meadows, through lush forests and rural landscapes, and into small, historic communities dating from the railroad's heydays of the late 19th and early 20th centuries.

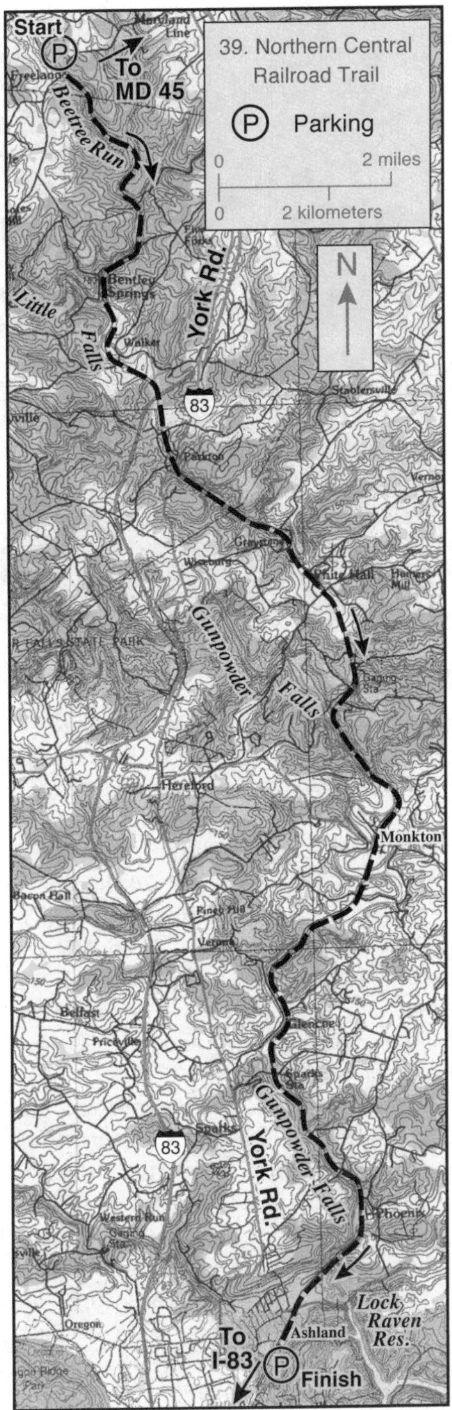

Never far from civilization, yet with long stretches of detachment from the humanized world, this is a great pathway on which to introduce people to the joys of outdoor walking without subjecting them to the rigors, and fear, of a harsh or isolated terrain. The pathway is level (even with a slight downhill trend if walked in the direction described), and road crossings are fairly frequent if the need for help should happen to arise. In addition, public restrooms are situated at seven sites, with drinking water available beside three of the road crossings. The historic aspects of the railroad are an added bonus. Be aware that this is a multiuse trail that is also open to bicyclists and equestrians, so always walk to the right and avoid walking two abreast. Pets must be on a leash.

Since this is a one-way hike, a car shuttle will be necessary. Take I-83 exit 20 (about 5 miles north of I-695, the Baltimore Beltway) and drive eastward along Shawan Road for 0.8 mile. Turn right onto York Road (MD 45), follow it for an additional 0.3 mile, and turn left onto Ashland Road. Be sure to stay on this roadway for 0.4 mile, turn right into Ashland at the Hunt Valley housing development, and continue straight for another 0.25 mile to the trailhead parking. (Some people may

Little Falls

advise you to park along Paper Mill Road, about 0.3 mile up the trail, but the only available space is on the highway shoulder.)

Having left one car and returned to the interstate, continue northward for approximately 16 miles, take exit 36, and head westward along Old York Road (MD 439). In 0.3 mile, turn right onto York Road (MD 45), follow it for 1 mile, and turn left onto Freeland Road (MD 108). The parking lot for the trail will be on your right in an additional 1.9 miles (restrooms available).

Walk southward from Freeland Road, getting used to the crushed-rock railbed that will be under your feet for the rest of the day. The clapboard houses of the small settlement date from the beginning of the 20th century, when Freeland was a popular retreat destination. By time you have walked 0.5 mile, the trail feels as if you are passing through deep woods. Just south of that, sun-loving flowers such as daisies, goldenrod, evening primrose, Queen Anne's lace, knapweed, and coneflower populate the open areas along Beetree Run.

With similar purple flower bracts, knapweed is often misidentified as a thistle, just as coneflower is often mistaken for black-eyed Susan. All four of these flowers belong to the composite family, whose members typically have rays of petals that surround a center disk of small, tubular flowers. The rays are actually sterile flowers whose main purpose appears to be to serve as a landing pad and an attractant to the insects that will visit and pollinate the fertile disk flowers.

Evidence of beaver is visible along the stream at 1 mile, while a wetlands at 1.2 miles has alders growing above skunk cabbage and a variety of ferns. This is also the home of the bog turtle, found in widely scattered, small populations from North Carolina to southern New England. It was once thought to be an endangered species, but research has shown that it is just so secretive that it is rarely seen. One of the smallest turtles in the world, it quickly burrows into mud or debris when disturbed and spends the winter buried deep in the mud and muck of underground waterways.

The landscape closes in on the trail around 2.2 miles, where the railroad bed has been cut through rock. These narrow spots are always more shaded than the rest of the trail, and you will immediately feel a drop in temperature as soon as you enter them.

A wide variety of ferns grows in these darker areas and along the length of the trail. Rarely will you get a chance to see so many different kinds of ferns on just one hike, so be sure to bring along an identification guide. So far on my outings here, I have been able to pick out Christmas, hay-scented, cinnamon, New York, royal, and bracken ferns, and there are still more that I have yet to identify.

The trail crosses Bentley Road (restrooms available) at 2.9 miles as you walk through the former resort town of Bentley Springs, named for its waters, which were once believed to be a cure for an assortment of illnesses. Little Falls, which has its origins in southern Pennsylvania, joins with Beetree Run at 3.4 miles, where the work of beavers can be seen on the land above their confluence.

The river, now known simply as Little Falls, swings to the east and crosses the trail at 3.7 miles and again at 4 miles near Walker, site of a former mill. Pass under I-83 at 5 miles, coming into Parkton at 5.8 miles. (A hunting and fishing outfitter next to the trail sells limited snacks and drinks.) During the boom days, this little town was so busy it had five local trains running between it and Baltimore daily. (The commuter train made its last run in 1959.) Parkton was also the transshipment center for the dairy products produced on nearby farms.

South of town, the hillsides close in on both sides of the trail, and Little Falls becomes a fast-flowing stream, swirling around huge boulders and rolling down small cascades. If you don't want to make a detour onto one of the short side trails to enjoy this spectacle, at least stop for a short break to admire the waterfalls at 6.4 miles.

Second Mine Branch joins Little Falls just as you come to the parking area in White Hall at 7.8 miles (water and restrooms available). Beyond the village, the terrain opens up for views of the rural landscape. Joined by numerous tributaries, Little Falls continues to increase in size.

A short distance south of Bluemont is the confluence of Little Falls and Big Gunpowder Falls, at 9.7 miles. Downstream from this point, the waterway is referred to as simply Gunpowder Falls on some maps, while others identify it as the Gunpowder River, and yet another labels it the Gunpowder Falls River.

Monkton, at 11.2 miles, is a definite rest-break spot. The refurbished railroad station houses a railroad museum, an information center, restrooms, and drinking water. The small grocery store, housed in the former Monkton Hotel across the trail, offers sandwiches, snacks, drinks, and ice cream (usually open only on the weekends).

Continuing southward, your vistas will expand as the valley becomes even wider and more rolling. The river swings back and forth, crossing the trail at 11.4 miles and 12.6 miles. Benches and picnic tables are placed at strategic spots to enjoy the most scenic views. Restrooms are located near the parking lot at 14 miles in Glencoe, a former resort town, while drinking water is available beside the Sparks Road crossing at 14.7 miles. The historic stone bank building to the left of the trail here is now used as an interpretive center.

You have no doubt noticed that traffic along the railroad trail has increased in proportion to how close you are getting to its southern terminus. Pass by the river's confluence with Carrol Branch at 15.5 miles, walking through Phoenix, a former textile mill town, at 16.5 miles (restrooms available).

The river becomes wider around 17.2 miles as its flow begins to slow; it enters the Loch Raven Reservoir, where a concrete bridge crosses it at 17.7 miles. The final mile can be outrageously busy on nice weekends, and you may have a hard time negotiating the maze of human bodies to cross Paper Mill Road (restrooms available) and come to the end of the hike in the Ashland parking lot at 18.8 miles.

Thanks in large part to the efforts of members of the Rails-to-Trails Conservancy, the rail-trail movement has been a success across the country. If you enjoyed your hike along the Northern Central Railroad Trail, you should be heartened to know that, as the 21st century began, there were more than 1,000 rail-trails open to the public, with more than 10,000 miles of pathways to explore.

The rail trail is busy almost every day

40

Sweet Air

Total distance (circuit): 6.0 miles

Hiking time: 2 hours, 50 minutes

Vertical rise: 400 feet

Maps: USGS 7½' Phoenix; park map

Just as Schaeffer Farm (see Hike 21) is a disjunct section of Seneca Creek State Park, so too is Sweet Air removed from the main portion of Gunpowder Falls State Park. Both areas are also similar in that they allow you to walk into a rural landscape of cultivated fields and woodlots located just a short drive from major population centers.

Of the two, Sweet Air has more of a wild feel. There are no signs at each and every trail junction, and the woods seem denser and more full of animal life. The two major crossings of the Little Gunpowder Falls do not have any footbridges across them to keep your feet dry. At Sweet Air, you will need to employ one of the most basic elements of backcountry travel: fording a stream. You will, however, be rewarded with some of the best of its other elements—a sense of peace, quiet, and solitude. Because Sweet Air is in such of an out-of-the-way place, few people other than local horseback riders ever venture here, so you may have the entire tract to yourself. (Be aware that these riders have evidently created a system of unmarked trails with which only they are familiar; be sure to heed the following route description and do not venture onto any unblazed pathways.)

Sweet Air is located northeast of Baltimore and may be reached by leaving I-95 at exit 74 and driving MD 152 (Mountain Road, which later becomes Fallston Road) for 10 miles. Make a left onto MD 165 (Baldwin Mill Road), go 0.5 mile, and turn left onto Green Road. Travel Green Road for 1.2 miles and make a right turn on to Moores Road. An

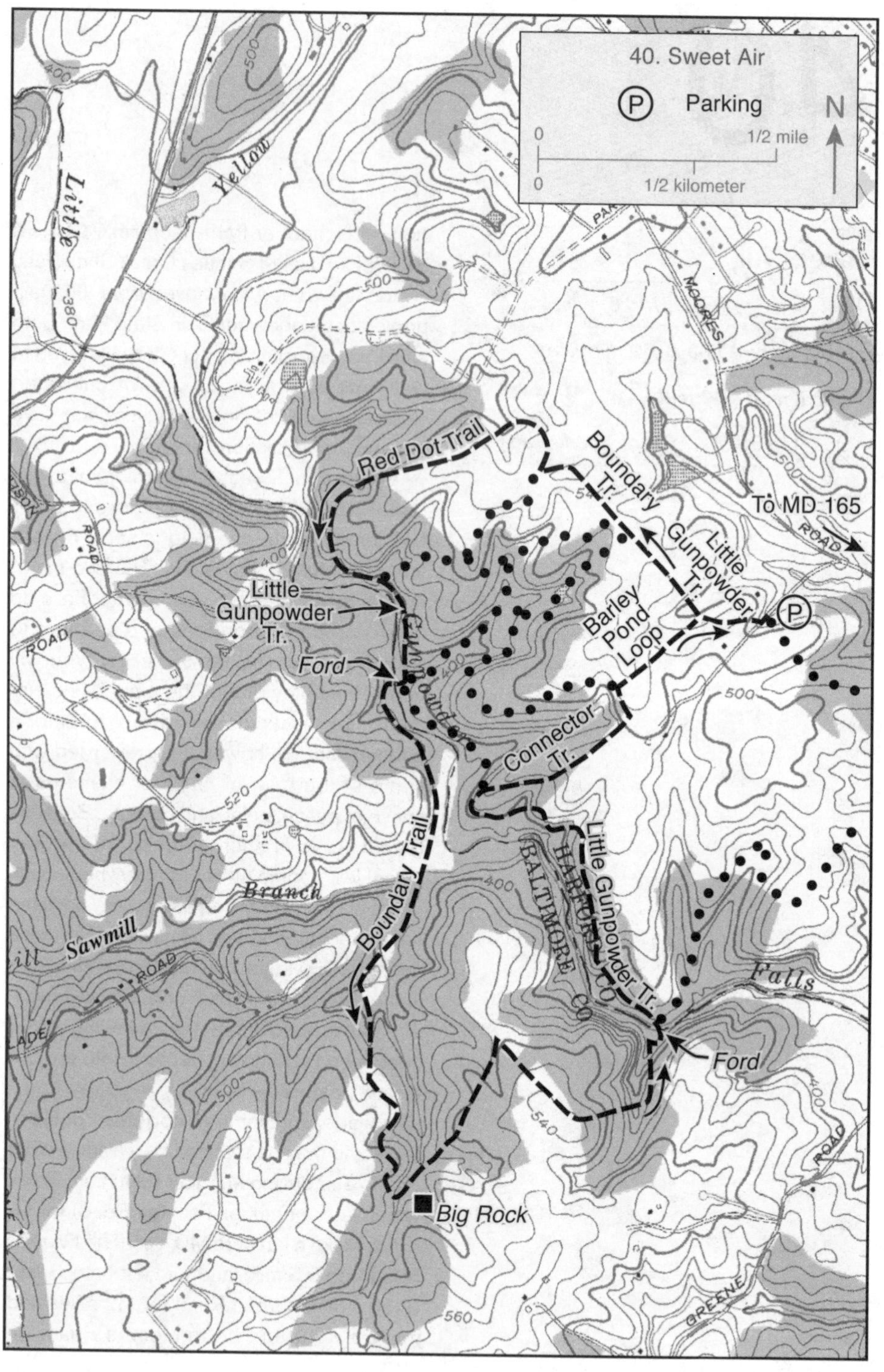
40. Sweet Air
Parking
N
0
1/2 mile
0
1/2 kilometer
Red Dot Trail
Boundary Tr.
Little Gunpowder Tr.
To MD 165
Little Gunpowder Tr.
Barley Pond Loop
Ford
Connector Tr.
Little Gunpowder Tr.
Boundary Trail
Ford
Big Rock
Little
Yellow
Branch
Sawmill
Falls
HARFORD CO
BALTIMORE CO
MOORES
ROAD
GREENE

additional 0.5 mile brings you to a left turn onto Dalton-Bevard Road. The Gunpowder Falls State Park Sweet Air parking lot is 0.2 mile down this narrow lane.

Walk from the parking area to a sign for the Barley Pond Loop Trail to begin the hike. Follow this trail to the edge of cultivated fields at 0.1 mile, where the yellow-blazed Barley Pond Loop Trail goes to the left. Keep to the right, passing through rows of planted crops. The other end of the Barley Pond Loop Trail comes in from the left at 0.3 mile; keep right on the white-blazed route and soon walk behind several private homes. Leave that pathway at 0.4 mile and turn right onto the blue-blazed Boundary Trail. Chicory and Queen Anne's lace exist in the narrow strip of soil between the cultivated crop and the edge of the woods.

Chicory's leaves have been added to salads, while its roots are dried and roasted to be used as a substitute for, or an additive to, coffee. Chicory coffee is certainly an acquired taste, being much stronger and more bitter than the ground coffee most of us are used to buying in the supermarket.

Arrive at a T intersection at 0.6 mile and turn right onto the Red Dot Trail, open only to hikers. A number of a pioneer species of trees, such as sumac and ailanthus, border the edge of the field. Enter the woods at 0.7 mile and continue to follow the Red Dot Trail to the left when it leaves the old road you have been walking upon. This is a very open forest with little undergrowth, making it easier to spot some of the white-tailed deer that make their home in the park.

Circular cavities in the tree trunks attest to an abundance of woodpeckers, which nest in them to raise their young. A hole is usually just occupied for one season, after which time the woodpecker vacates and other animals move in. Chickadees seem to prefer downy woodpecker holes, while

Little Gunpowder Falls

screech owls can be found in the former home of a pileated woodpecker. Wood ducks, prothonotary warblers, squirrels, mice, snakes, and opossums are just a few of the other creatures that take advantage of this prefabricated housing.

Begin to descend via switchbacks at 1.1 miles. As you come into the bottomland, the undergrowth becomes more lush, and the Red Dot Trail comes to an end at 1.5 miles. Bear right onto the white-blazed Little Gunpowder Trail and head downstream along Little Gunpowder Falls, where jewelweed, jack-in-the-pulpit, ironwood, and sycamore thrive in the moist soil.

Arrive at a four-way intersection at 1.7 miles. The white-blazed trail continues straight, while the blue-blazed Boundary Trail goes both left and right. You want to turn right and ford Little Gunpowder Falls (the water might be shallower a few feet downstream). Once across the stream, turn left at a T intersection, and explore the remains and stone foundations of the Stansbury Mill and Mill House a few hundred feet later. Like Big Gunpowder Falls, Little Gunpowder Falls was once used to power dozens of mills along its banks.

You will pass several unmarked trails as you walk along this bottomland forest; always continue to follow the blue blazes. After getting your feet wet from the stream ford, you are almost guaranteed to now get muddy boots, as the treadway has been churned into a turbid mixture by horse traffic.

An unmarked trail comes in from the right at 2.2 miles; stay to the left and ford Sawmill Branch. Small Green Glade Pond, at 2.4 miles, makes a nice spot for a break, where you might catch a turtle basking in the sun or watch a great blue heron troll for dinner. After eating, the great blue may do some grooming by covering itself with powder down, which comes from special feathers that are designed to crumble. It then smoothes the other feathers back into place using its beak or the claw of its middle toe.

Green Glade Pond

There is a Y intersection at 2.5 miles; keep right on the blue-blazed pathway and rise along a rocky roadway. Encounter a four-way intersection at 2.7 miles, where you want to turn left onto a grassy roadbed. Stay to the left when you come to the next intersection near the top of the rise at 2.9 miles and soon descend.

Cross a small tributary of Sawmill Branch at 3.1 miles, bear left at an intersection, and pass by a large boulder simply identified as Big Rock on park maps. Recross the water run and begin to ascend.

An unmarked trail heads to the right at 3.4 miles, just before you would rise into an open field. Stay to the left along the blue-blazed trail. Be alert 200 feet later; turn right along the field, pass through a row of trees, and bear left.

At 3.6 miles, swing around the edge of the next field, thinking about how quickly scenes like this are disappearing in America. Many of our ancestors went through their entire lives enjoying the wonderful landscape you are looking upon now: Fields of cultivated crops sway in the same breeze that turkey vultures use to stay aloft overhead. The tin roof of a distant farmhouse reflects the afternoon sun, and the sounds of playing children and dogs drift over the countryside to mix with the hum of summer insects.

Be alert for the trail to make a left into a grapevine-covered woods at 3.8 miles and descend. Cross a water run at 4 miles and again a few feet later. Turn right along Little Gunpowder Falls at 4.2 miles, only to turn left a few feet later and get your boots wet again by fording the river.

There may be a bit of confusion once you get across. In order to avoid the wet soil of the floodplain, the Little Gunpowder Trail has been rerouted. Do not immediately turn to the left. Continue straight for a few hundred feet along the blue-blazed Boundary Trail before turning left onto the new route of the white-blazed Little Gunpowder Trail.

This pathway will continue through the woods on an up-and-down route, soon rising high above the river and crossing a wooden footbridge at 5.1 miles.

You will return to the bottomland for just a few feet at 5.2 miles before you swing away from the river to come to an intersection at 5.3 miles. The white-blazed Little Gunpowder Trail heads left; you want to keep right and ascend along the red-blazed Connector Trail.

Coming into cultivated fields, follow farm roads to make a right onto the yellow-blazed Barley Pond Loop Trail at 5.7 miles and walk beside a row of huge evergreen trees.

Intersect the white-blazed Little Gunpowder Trail, turn right, and return to your car at 6 miles.

41

Gunpowder Falls State Park

Total distance (circuit): 9.25 miles

Hiking time: 4 hours, 30 minutes

Vertical rise: 680 feet

Maps: USGS 7½' White Marsh

Cool, shaded spots by a small swimming hole. Wildflower and pine fragrances wafting through the air. Owl hoots breaking the stillness of early evening. Muskrat and raccoon paw prints stamped into soft mud. Hazy silhouettes of deer foraging in the morning mist.

These are not descriptions of things you must travel to Western Maryland to enjoy but rather are some of the delights to be found just a short drive from Baltimore, within a portion of Gunpowder Falls State Park.

The hike may be reached by taking I-695 (Baltimore Beltway) exit 32 and traveling northward along US 1. The trailhead parking lot is on the right 5 miles later, just after crossing the Big Gunpowder River. Trails are open from sunrise to sunset; pets must be kept on a leash. This hike consists of two loops, with your parked car being in the middle, so you could decide to do the loops on two separate occasions if you don't have the time or inclination to do the entire outing all at once.

Walk toward the river from the parking lot and turn right to pass through the tunnel under US 1. Do not take the white-blazed walkway immediately on the other side of the tunnel that crosses the river to the Big Gunpowder Falls Trail. Rather, keep straight, enter the woods, turn right to ascend the pink-blazed Wildlands Trail, and pass over an underground cable right-of-way. Reach the top of the rise at 0.25 mile and continue with minor ups and downs through a forest of tall, straight, exceptionally large beech trees; abundant jack-in-the-pulpits; and the occasional flash of a deer's white tail.

The beech family of trees, which includes

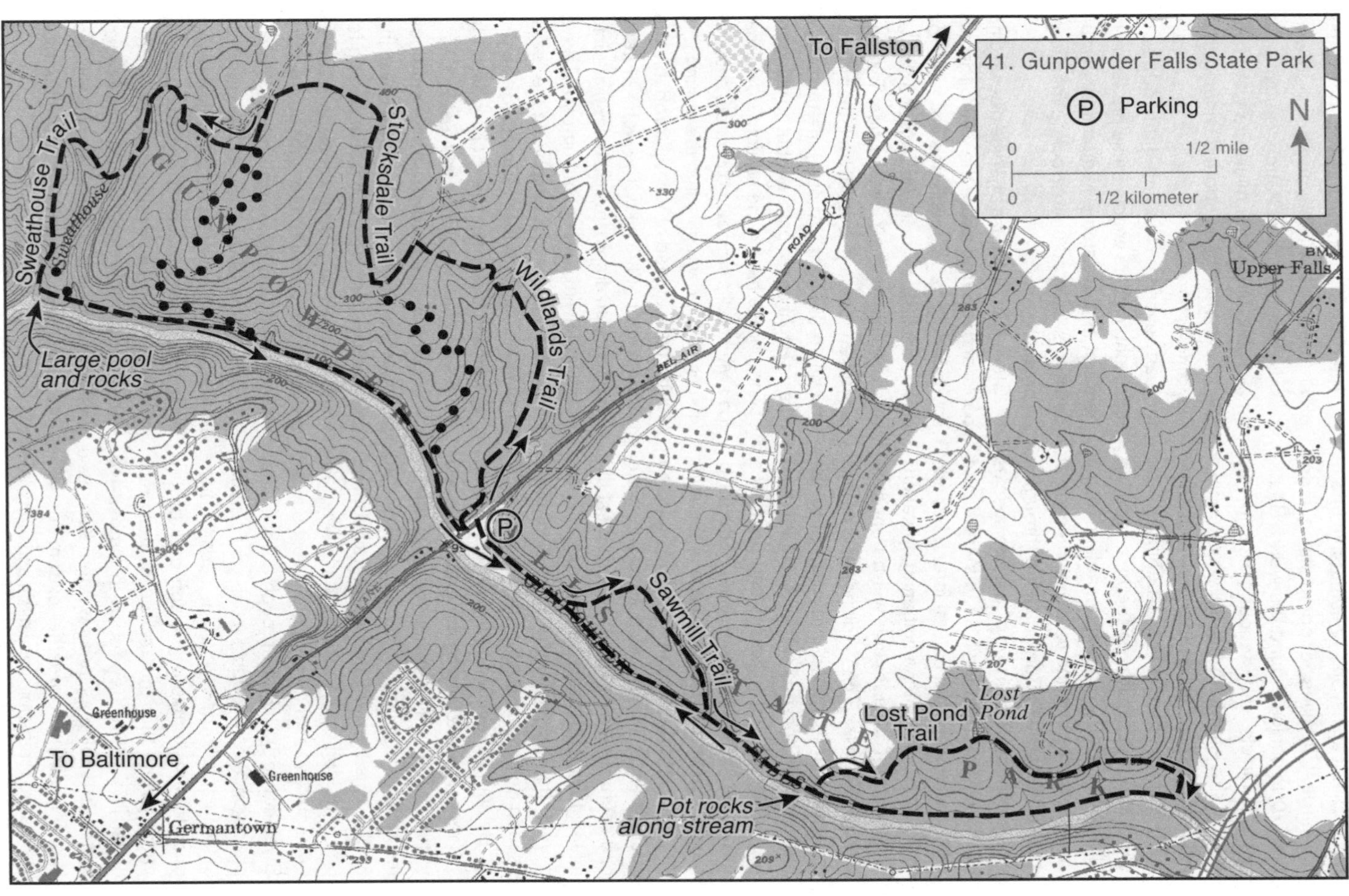
41. Gunpowder Falls State Park
Parking
0
1/2 mile
0
1/2 kilometer
N
To Fallston
To Baltimore
Sweathouse Trail
Sweathouse
Stocksdale Trail
Wildlands Trail
Large pool and rocks
Sawmill Trail
Lost Pond Trail
Lost Pond
Pot rocks along stream
Upper Falls
Greenhouse
Greenhouse
Germantown
BEL AIR
ROAD

oaks, chinquapins, and chestnuts, is one of the largest families, encompassing more than 700 species around the world. Bears, birds, squirrels, and raccoons all enjoy the nuts of the American beech, which, unlike most trees, keeps its smooth bark as it ages.

The road sounds finally begin to fade away about 0.7 mile into the hike, and the bird calls become more noticeable. Cross a creek at 0.9 mile, come to a T intersection at 1.2 miles, and turn right, passing through a pine plantation. Neat rows of just one species of even-aged trees such as this are a sure sign that this is not a natural forest, but one that was planted after a timbering operation.

Another T intersection will be encountered at 1.4 miles. The Wildlands Trail comes to an end, and you will turn right onto the blue-blazed Stocksdale Trail. Avoid the faint trail to the right at 1.7 miles and pass by a few large-leaved pawpaw trees. The pawpaw is almost out of place here in the mid-Atlantic region, as all of its relatives in the custard apple family–such as sugar-apple and soursop–are found in more tropical climates. In fact, its name comes from *papaya,* a word the Arawak Indians of the Caribbean used to describe a totally different fruit.

Be sure to keep left at the intersection at 1.9 miles, as the land to the right is closed to hikers. The same directions apply to the intersection at 2 miles.

The blue-blazed Stocksdale Trail continues to the left at 2.1 miles, but you want to turn right and ascend onto the yellow-blazed Sweathouse Trail. Pass through a small pine plantation, then through a much younger forest with smaller trees, such as cedar. Squirrels often make use of the soft bark of the cedar to line their nests. The eastern red cedar is a native tree found in almost 40 states, extending as far as western Kansas. Highly resistant to weather extremities, its berries are forage for many birds and animals.

The descent quickens as you reenter the older forest at 2.4 miles and begin to walk beside Sweathouse Branch, enjoying its small pools, riffles, and miniature waterfalls. Owls have often been spotted winging their way among the tree branches of this area in the early evening. The soft, fluffy edges of their flight feathers enable these predators to be silent and undetected when they swoop down to snatch an unsuspecting mouse or chipmunk.

Cross a stream, pass by some nice wading pools, and rise high above the water. There is a wonderfully large beech tree just after you cross a small side stream. Be alert at 3.2 miles when you come to a Y intersection. Take the unmarked but authorized trail that drops steeply to the right. (At one time this was a nicely switchbacked pathway, but so many uncaring people have gone straight down that the switchbacks are now obliterated, and erosion has cut a deep gully into the ground.)

You have arrived at what is probably the prettiest spot of the hike. The water of Long Green Stream drops down in noisy riffles into an inviting swimming or wading pool. Take a break, cool your feet, sunbathe on the rocks, or sit in the shade of the oak trees. (See if you can find the fissure in the rocks where the water flows upstream for a few feet.)

When you are ready to leave, continue downstream on the unmarked trail, walking by fronds of false Solomon's seal arching toward the pathway. You will soon need to avoid the small trail to the right so that you will continue along the main route.

The yellow-blazed Sweathouse Trail comes in from the left at 3.4 miles; keep right, cross Sweathouse Branch, and begin to walk downstream beside Big Gunpowder Falls in a lush bottomland forest. The Stocksdale Trail comes in from the left at 3.8 miles; stay along the river, now following the blue blazes.

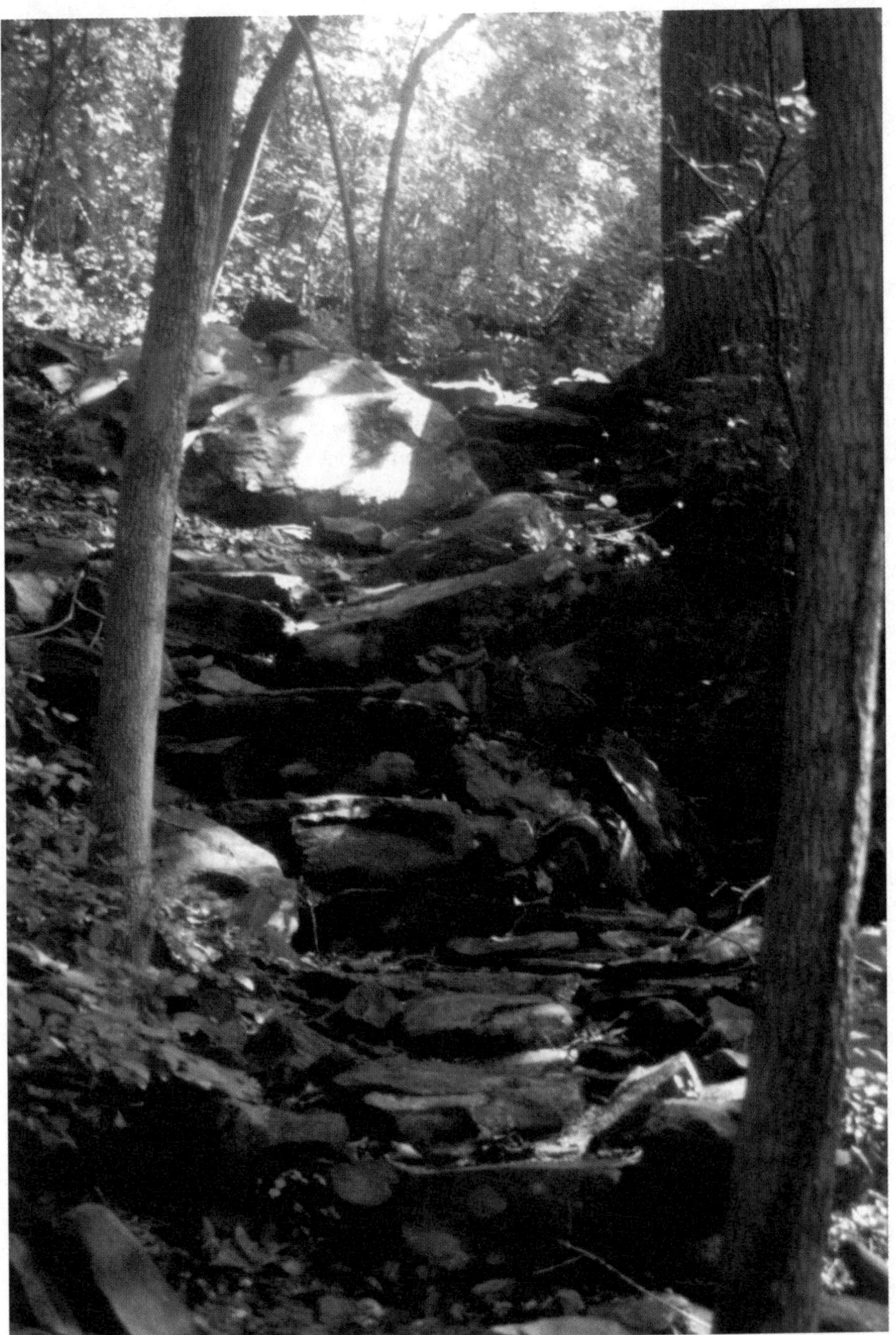

Steps of the Lost Pond Trail

The other section of the Stocksdale Trail comes in from the left at 4.4 miles, and the Wildlands Trail at 4.6 miles; keep along the river at both intersections. Walk through the tunnel under US 1 and to your car at 4.7 miles. If this is all the time you have, drive home with plans to do the rest of this outing another day. If not, take a short break and enjoy the snacks and drinks you left stashed in the car.

When ready to begin again, walk to the far end of the parking lot and enter the woods on the blue-blazed Lost Pond Trail. Within a few feet, the route will bear to the right and parallel Big Gunpowder Falls, often the site of great blue herons wading in its shallower waters.

Turn left at 5.1 miles and ascend along the yellow-blazed Sawmill Trail. The chances are good that the scat with large pawpaw seeds in the middle of the trail is from a raccoon. Because they can adapt to just about any kind of habitat, raccoons are one of the most widespread mammals in the United States, living near fields, in the forests, next to housing developments, and throughout the mountains. Their scat, which is cylindrical like a dog's and resembles that of the opossum or skunk, is often found on logs, stones, and large tree limbs. Break the scat open with a stick, and you will find evidence of what the raccoon has recently eaten–maybe seeds, nuts, corn or other garden crops, insect wings, fur, or bits of bones.

Begin to descend at 5.3 miles and avoid an unmarked trail to the left about 400 feet later. The small stream you are walking beside has pretty pools, ripples, and small waterfalls. At 5.5 miles, the pathway overlooks the ruins of the Carroll Sawmill, which operated during the early 1800s.

Turn left onto the blue-blazed Lost Pond Trail at 5.7 miles and cross Broad Run. The red berries at the end of the false Solomon's seal stems brighten the undergrowth in late summer. Keep left at 6 miles, ascend the rock steps marked as leading to Lost Pond and Overlook, and enjoy the view of the river 200 feet later.

Although there has been no indication that you were this close to farmland, you will unexpectedly walk beside a field planted in crops at 6.1 miles and bypass a red-blazed trail that descends to the right. Keep right at the next two intersections, where pathways come in from the left and the traffic noise of I-95 becomes very audible.

Lost Pond, at 6.7 miles, lives up to its name. It is quickly disappearing, being filled in by excessive siltation and runoff from the terrain above it. Beyond the pond, make sure to stay on the blue-blazed route and not inadvertently wander onto other pathways. Keep right when an unmarked trail comes in from the left at 7 miles.

Cross No Name Stream at 7.1 miles and be alert to turn right and follow the blue blazes back upstream. Walnut trees, becoming more rare because we humans so highly value the wood, have dropped enough nuts on the trail to almost make it difficult to walk in places. Continuing along the river, look for muskrat tracks in the mud. Both the front and hind paws have five toes, but the inner toe of the forepaw is so small that it often does not show in prints. The 2-inch to 4-inch hind print can be ahead of, be behind, or sometimes overlap the shorter and narrower foreprint. Occasionally the mark of a dragging tail is also visible.

Just after passing pot rocks–circular depressions made in the rock by swirling river water–at 8.1 miles, you will have returned to the junction marked Long Pond and Overlook; keep left along the river.

Cross Broad Run at 8.4 miles and bypass Sawmill Trail, which heads off to the right. Pass by the other entrance of the Sawmill Trail to the right at 8.8 miles, stay along the river, and return to your car at 9.25 miles.

42

Susquehanna State Park

Total distance (circuit): 4.9 miles

Hiking time: 2 hours, 40 minutes

Vertical rise: 840 feet

Maps: USGS 7½' Aberdeen; park map

The waters of the Susquehanna River rise in Otsego County, New York, and flow for more than 400 miles to empty into the head of the Chesapeake Bay, close to where the river separates Central Maryland from the Eastern Shore. Protecting a portion of the river's drainage just before it meets the bay is 3,600-acre Susquehanna State Park.

A network of pathways enables you to explore this varied topography of riverside vegetation, heavy forest cover, lightly flowing brooks, rock outcrops, and interesting history. In addition, the park offers a campground with restrooms and hot showers, a picnic area, boat-launch facility, a number of historic structures, and evening interpretive programs around a campfire.

The park may be reached northeast of Baltimore by taking I-95 exit 89 and driving west on MD 155 for 0.7 mile. Make a right onto Earlton Road and then, 0.6 mile later, turn left onto Quaker Bottom Road. You will drive by the privately run Steppingstone Museum (worth a visit if it is open) 1.2 miles later, but continue on Quaker Bottom Road for an additional 0.6 mile to make a right onto Rock Run Road. Stay to the right in another 0.5 mile, following signs to the historic area and leaving your car 0.2 mile later in the parking lot above the river.

Before beginning the hike, take a few minutes to look out across the river. One of the longest rivers in the East, the Susquehanna drains 42 percent of the Chesapeake Bay watershed and has an average flow of close to 20 million gallons per minute. More than likely you will see an angler or two casting a

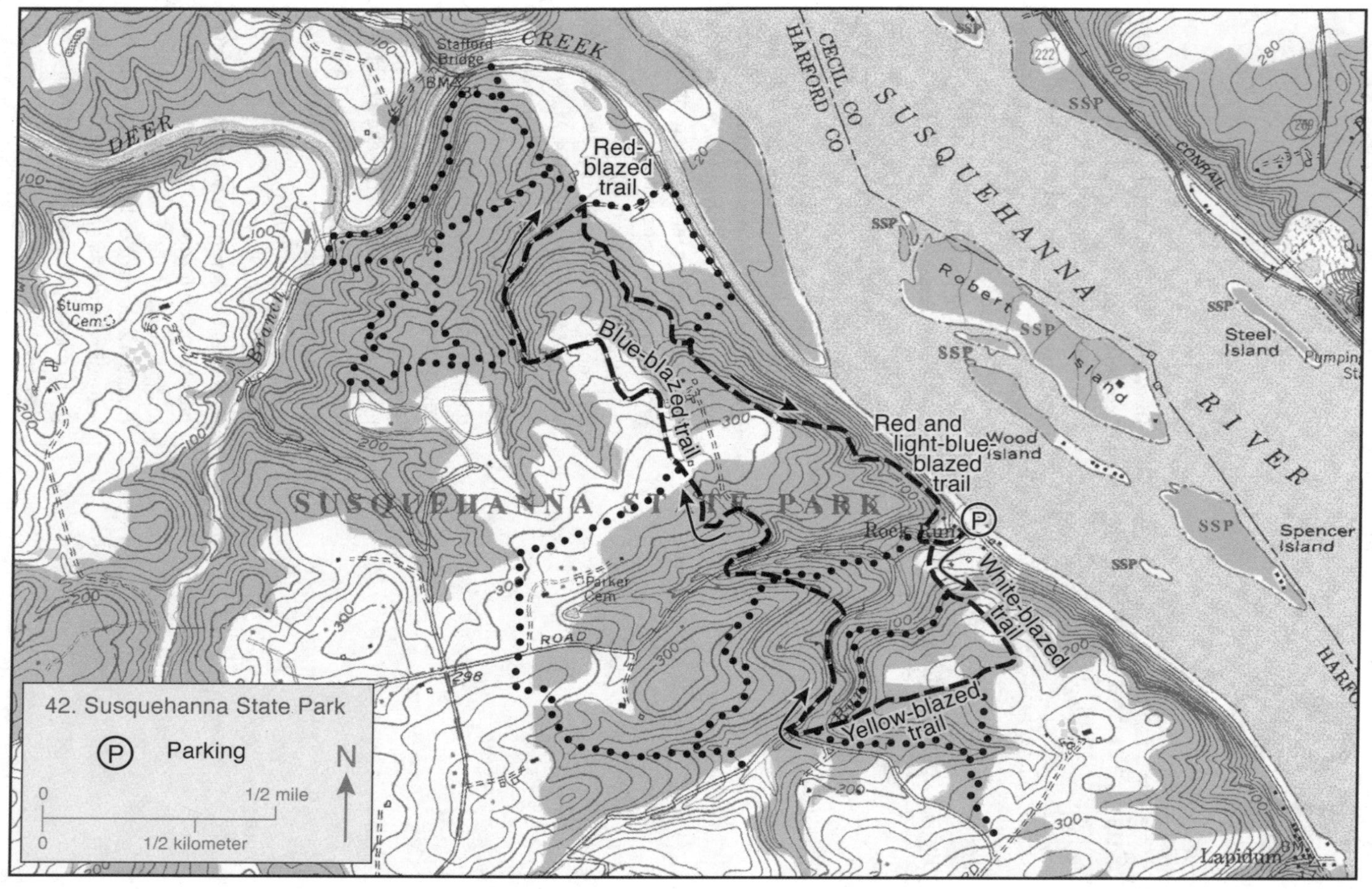
42. Susquehanna State Park
Parking
0
1/2 mile
0
1/2 kilometer
N
Red-blazed trail
Blue-blazed trail
Red and light-blue-blazed trail
White-blazed trail
Yellow-blazed trail
SUSQUEHANNA STATE PARK
SUSQUEHANNA RIVER
DEER CREEK
CECIL CO
HARFORD CO
Stafford Bridge
Robert Island
Wood Island
Steel Island
Spencer Island
Rock Run
Parker Cem
Stump Cem
Branch
ROAD
CONRAIL
Lapidum

line for striped bass, perch, catfish, walleye, carp, or bluegill. Also in search of the same catch may be osprey, kingfisher, heron, and, increasingly common, bald eagle.

The building to the left of the parking area is the Jersey Toll House, built for the toll collector of the Susquehanna River Bridge. The bridge was destroyed by ice floes in 1856. The tollhouse is now a visitors center for the park. The building to the right is the Rock Run Grist Mill, built by John Stump in the late 1700s. The mill still works, and grinding demonstrations are presented on a scheduled basis (check for times at the visitors center).

When ready to begin the hike, walk back up Rock Run Road to the entrance to the historic mansion and begin to follow the trail behind the HORSES PROHIBITED sign. With a few pawpaw trees bordering the route, the trail rises on steps to the left at 0.2 mile. (Before going up them, though, stop a few moments to enjoy the water falling over the Rock Run Dam.)

After rising on the steps, you can rest on a bench at 0.25 mile before you continue to ascend along the white-blazed Land of Promise Trail. Cross over another pathway and, a few feet later, an old stone wall, with piles of rock scattered throughout the woods. Even though you are in a forest, these stones are evidence that the land must have been cleared at one time. The walls were either boundary markers or fences for livestock, while the piles of stones grew larger as the farmers removed the rocks from the ground while plowing to plant crops.

Be alert when you come to the top of the rise at 0.6 mile. Continuing straight into the meadow would bring you to the Steppingstone Museum, but you want to turn right onto the woods road. Swing left along the edge of an overgrown meadow (which may be woods by time you hike here) at 0.7 mile and reenter the woods. Be sure to stay to the right on the descending, yellow-blazed Rock Run Y Trail, bordered by grapevines, raspberry bushes, and brier patches. The raspberries that grow here are commonly called wine berries and are very tasty.

Come to an intersection with an old trail at 0.9 mile and keep to the left. Just a short distance later, the yellow-blazed pathway splits and heads both left and right. You want to bear left and continue to descend, passing by a small grove of pines and walking along a stone wall.

Cross the street at 1.1 miles, turn right onto the paved Quaker Bottom Road, and make another right onto Rock Run Road at 1.2 miles. Where the road curves to the right at 1.4 miles, take the blue-blazed Farm Road Trail as it ascends the steps into the woods on the left and levels out amid the large leaves of pawpaw trees at 1.6 miles.

Continue straight when you intersect an orange-blazed pathway at 1.7 miles, where the forest is made up of many tall, straight-trunked poplar trees. You will cross a small stream and paved Wilkinson Road at 1.8 miles and continue to follow the blue blazes uphill along an old roadbed. Signs announce that you are entering a managed hunting area at 2 miles, where grapevines heavily cover the trees.

Come to an intersection in an open meadow at 2.2 miles. Turn slightly left, then right, and walk along the right side of the meadow. It is time to sit down, take a break, and appreciate this setting, with wonderful views across the meadow to the surrounding rural countryside. The soft breeze will help cool you, while the sun passes across a bright blue sky in which swallows, hawks, eagles, and vultures may be sailing.

The most frequently seen soaring bird all across the United States is the turkey vulture, whose 6-foot wingspan gives it a majestic look and a V-angled silhouette when seen circling high above. The lack of feathers on their red heads enables them to more

The Susquehanna River

easily extract themselves from inside the body cavities of the carrion they feed upon. Ranging only from Florida to the southern portion of New Jersey, black vultures, which are not uncommon here, have short black tails and must flap and glide a bit more than the turkey vulture to maintain a soaring flight.

Continue on your gently sloping route until a silver-blazed trail comes in from the right at 2.4 miles; you want to keep left and follow the blue blazes through a row of trees and down the middle of another meadow. Reenter the woods at 2.75 miles, pass by several large beech trees, and parallel a small stream, looking for joe-pye weed in the sunny spots.

Be very alert at a confusing intersection as you come into an overgrown meadow at 3.2 miles. Pay close attention: You want to take the very first red-blazed trail that goes to the right. (If you continue straight just a few more feet, the pathway that swings left to cross a wooden bridge enters the picnic area. The route straight ahead comes to a dead end at a forest buffer demonstration area, while the trail to the right that runs along the left side of the meadow eventually merges onto Stafford Road.)

Winding along the side of the ridge, a silver-blazed connector trail rises from the road to intersect your route at 3.8 miles. Keep right, gradually ascending on the now combined red- and light-blue-blazed trail, which has good wintertime views of the river. This pathway you are following is a part of the Mason-Dixon Trail and the Lower Susquehanna Greenway. The latter is a route that runs from the Concord Point Lighthouse at the Chesapeake Bay to the Conowingo Dam, a few miles upstream from where you are now standing.

Keep left when you come to the next intersection at 4.1 miles. Reach the high point at 4.2 miles and begin to descend, crossing the creek and turning left on the paved road at 4.7 miles, returning to your car at 4.9 miles.

V Eastern Shore

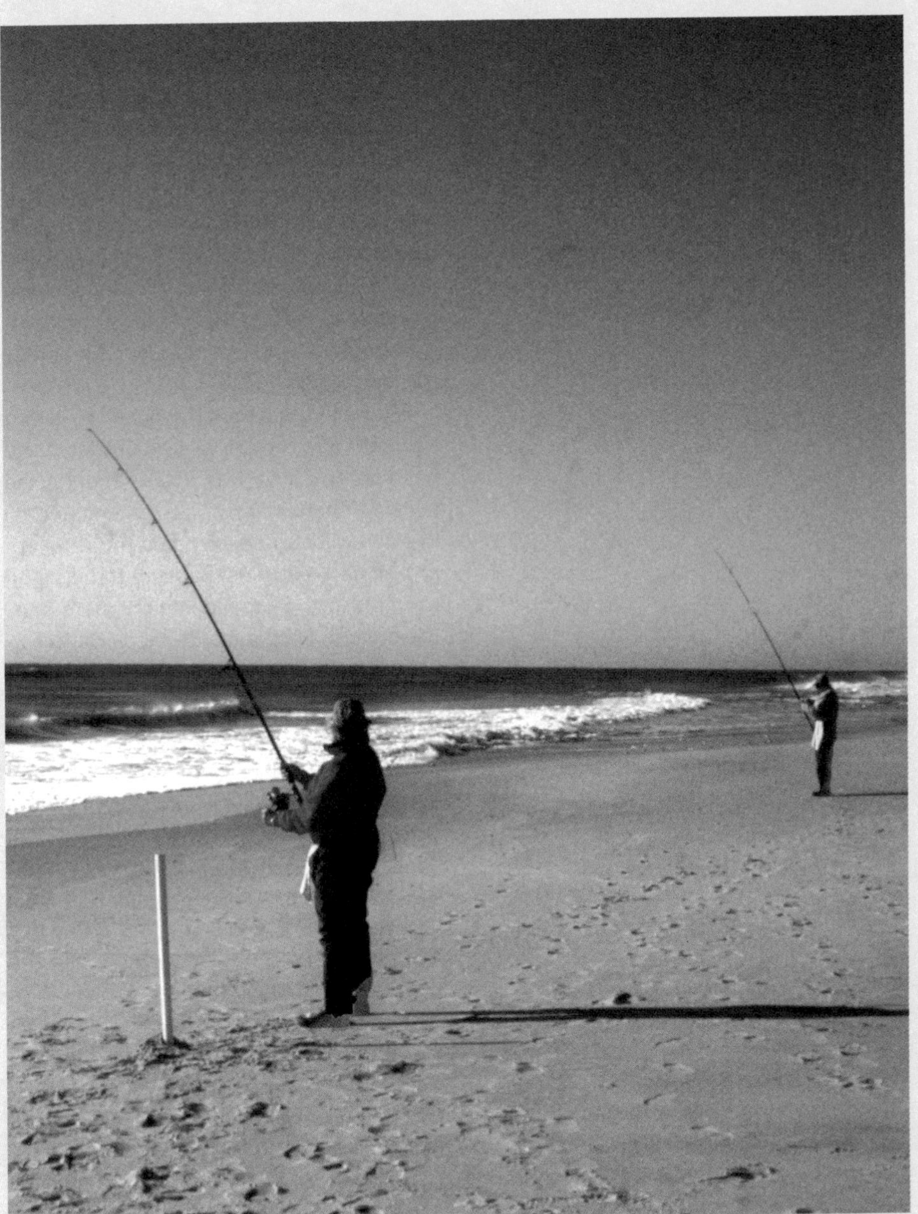

43

Turkey Point on Elk Neck

Total distance (round-trip): 2.0 miles

Hiking time: 1 hour

Vertical rise: 100 feet

Maps: USGS 7½' Spesutie; park map

Save this outing for a day when you are willing to awaken while it is still dark outside and be out on the highway long before most other people have begun to think about getting out of bed. The reason you do this is so that you can be on Turkey Point–at the very tip of Elk Neck, jutting into the Chesapeake Bay–just as the first rays of golden-pink sunlight brighten the water and spread across the narrow point.

Elk Neck State Park is reached by taking I-95 exit 100 (a few miles west of Elkton) and heading south on MD 272. Although the name of the road changes, its number designation will stay the same as you drive approximately 10 miles, passing through the town of North East and into the state park. (Near North East is the Elk Neck State Forest, with a few miles of trails and primitive camping.) Keep driving through the state park and the Chesapeake Isle housing development to where the road ends in a dirt and gravel parking area.

Hopefully you have timed it right so that the eastern horizon is just beginning to glow a bit as you walk along the gated road from the parking area, listening to the sound of a heron or two taking flight over the bay or a deer dashing behind the cover of the pawpaws' large leaves. The grapevines at 0.2 mile cover the trees so extensively that it almost looks like you are farther south in Virginia or North Carolina, where kudzu creeps over entire forests. The aroma of rotting bananas that permeates the air here in late summer is coming from the ripening fruit of the pawpaw trees.

The open meadow at 0.3 mile has a number of bluebird boxes placed around it. Due to loss of nesting cavities and competition from European starlings and house sparrows, eastern bluebird populations had been steadily declining during the middle part of the 20th century. In 1978, after the formation of the North American Bluebird Society, enthusiasts began to place nesting boxes in the bluebird's natural habitats, and, as a result, the populations have begun to recover. The male of most bird species is almost always the more colorfully plumed, but the upper parts of the female bluebird can be as deeply blue as those of her male counterpart.

Swing right into a wooded area at 0.5 mile, only to break out into another open field where a few wild turkey, more than a dozen deer, and just as many rabbits can be found browsing in the early-morning fog—an added bonus for having gotten out of bed so early.

Keep to the left when you come to the Y intersection at 0.6 mile, reenter a small woods, and arrive at the abandoned lighthouse on Turkey Point at 0.8 mile. There is absolutely no better way to greet a new dawn than to be sitting on one of the benches next to the lighthouse and watch the source of Earth's warmth rise inch by inch into the eastern sky. Things that were dark silhouettes just moments ago begin to take on the three-dimensional shapes of trees and bushes, casting long shadows upon the grass in front of you. The lights of oceangoing vessels on their way north to the Chesapeake and Delaware Canal are turned off just about the time watermen, in their much smaller boats, begin their daily chores. Although abandoned, the lighthouse still stands like a beacon, its white paint gleaming in the sun.

The hawks, eagles, and other large birds that soar above the bay at Turkey Point can be an almost never-ending source of entertainment. Found throughout the year are harrier hawks, turkey and black vultures, and peregrine, merlin, and kestrel falcons. Migrating to the south in mid-September are ospreys, followed later in the month by northern goshawks and sharp-shinned hawks. Red-tailed, red-shouldered, broad-winged, and rough-legged hawks wing by in late October, while the golden and bald eagles head south sometime in early November.

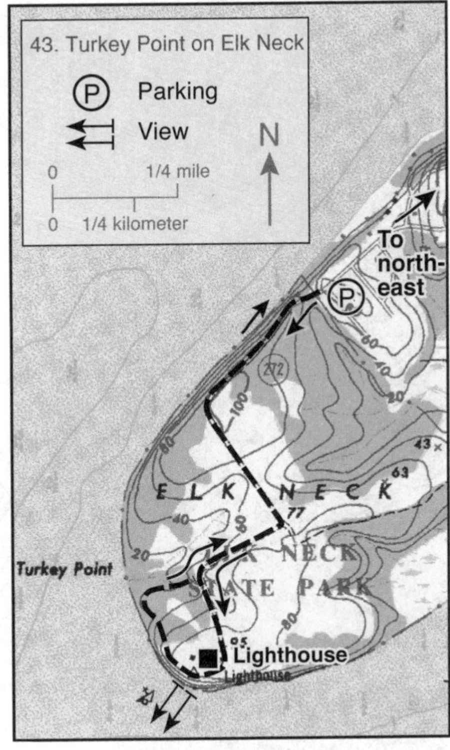

The golden eagles, possibly hatched in the spring on the tundra around Canada's Hudson Bay, are somewhat of a mystery in the East. Once thought to exist only in the West, they were first sighted in Pennsylvania in the 1930s. Since then, their numbers have not increased greatly, but every year they are seen winging their way southward. Some have even been found spending the

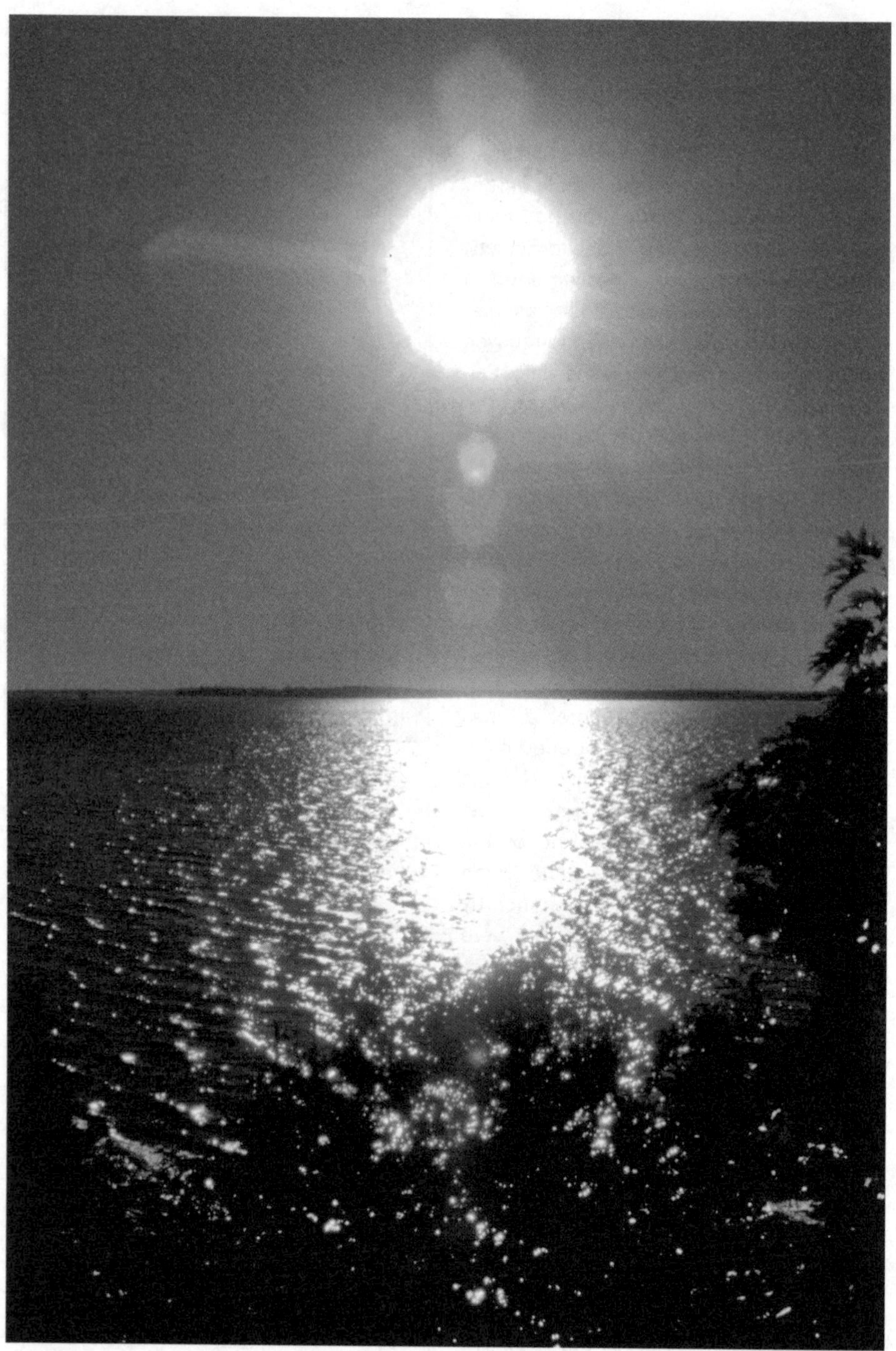

Early morning on Turkey Point overlooking the bay

winter with bald eagles near Conowingo Dam on the Susquehanna River (see Hike 42) and others in the Blackwater National Wildlife Refuge (see Hike 47) on the Eastern Shore.

Walk around and spend as much time as you can on Turkey Point, but when you are ready to leave, swing westward (that would be to the right of the lighthouse when you first encountered it) and walk to the far end of the field. Reenter the woods at 0.9 mile on a pathway to the right.

This route will bring you almost to the water's edge in an open area at 1.1 miles, where it swings to the right into the woods. (Before making this right turn, you should enjoy the shoreline for a while by walking along the flat, grassy shelf just above the boulders of the riprap.)

Continuing with your walk along the main trail, return to the Y intersection at 1.4 miles and retrace your steps back to the parking area at 2 miles.

Since you have so much of the day left, maybe you should drive back to the main part of the state park and hike one of its other pathways. The easy, 1.2-mile Mauldin Mountain Trail passes through a forest of beech, tulip poplar, and red, white, and chestnut oak. A dike along the 1-mile Pond Trail overlooks a small lake and a marsh. The 2-mile Beaver Marsh Trail provides access to the shoreline of the Elk River, where you could take a swim. The Ravines Loop Trail is only 0.75 mile long, with an interpretive booklet available at the park store.

In addition to these pathways, the state park offers picnic areas, a boat launch (bring your own vessel), fishing, a naturalist program, rental cabins, and a campground with bathhouses. Consider this: If you stayed in the campground the night before, you wouldn't have to get up so early in the morning to enjoy the hike.

44

Eastern Neck

Total distance (round-trip): 1.7 miles

Hiking time: 45 minutes

Vertical rise: 0

Maps: USGS 7½' Langford Creek; refuge map

Eastern Neck National Wildlife Refuge has what you could call an abundance of big birds–and *abundance* is almost an understatement. From October through mid-March, thousands of migratory waterfowl winter in the Chesapeake Bay region, many of them on the 2,285-acre refuge. As an example, the most common species that have been documented here include as many as 20,000 Canada geese, more than 7,000 tundra swans, more than 15,000 canvasback ducks, and an assortment of thousands of others, such as mallards, widgeons, pintails, and buffleheads. Not occurring in quite as many numbers but seen throughout more of the year are great blue and green-backed herons, great and snowy egrets, turkey and black vultures, ospreys, and bald eagles.

Remember, those mentioned so far are just some of the largest of the birds to be seen on the island. Refuge personnel and ornithologists have identified close to 250 other species, ranging from the common, such as bluebirds and chickadees, to the rarely observed, like peregrine falcons and American woodcocks.

So, if you don't happen to be a bird enthusiast, why should you come here? How about the chance to see white-tailed deer, diamondback terrapins, muskrats, beavers, red foxes, eastern gray squirrels, and the endangered Delmarva fox squirrel? Or you could sift your hands through mounds of huge shells and imagine what it would have been like to be one of the Native American inhabitants who shucked those oysters more than

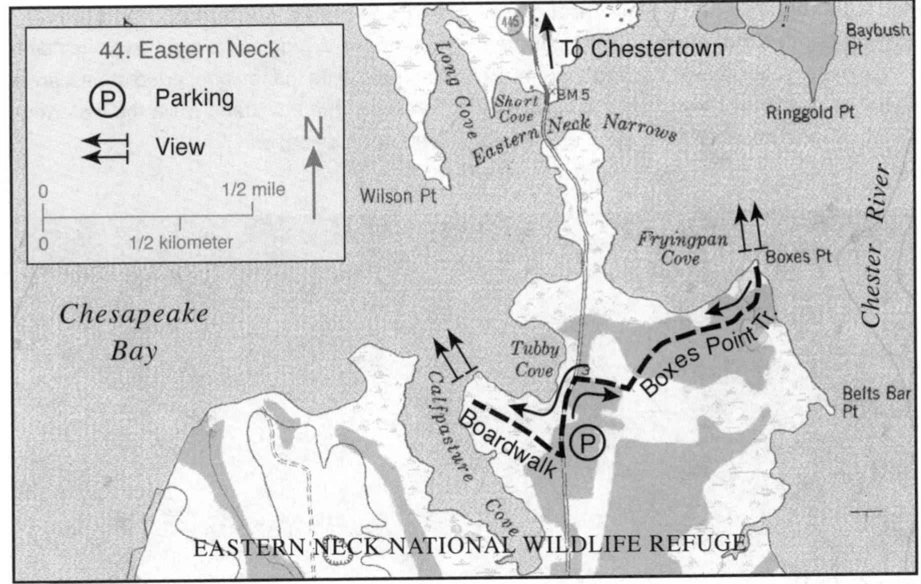

a millennium ago. Then again, you could come to the refuge just for the simple joy of the quiet beauty of a typical Chesapeake Bay landscape of marshes, croplands, hardwood and loblolly forests, and grass fields surrounded by sun-speckled water.

Getting to Eastern Neck National Wildlife Refuge by car can be an enjoyable outing in itself–the Maryland government considers the drive to be so picturesque that it has designated it a State Scenic Route. The island may be reached by leaving MD 213 in Chestertown and driving south on MD 20 for nearly 13 miles to the town of Rock Hall. Turn left (southward) on MD 445 and cross the bridge onto the island 6 miles later. Continue for an additional 0.8 mile to leave your car in the Tubby Cove parking area on the right.

Mosquitoes, chiggers, and ticks can be abundant, so bring along repellent. Also be aware that hunting is permitted during certain days in the fall, and that pets must be kept on a leash at all times.

Begin the hike by walking back up the road on which you just drove and turn right onto the Boxes Point Trail at 0.1 mile. (This pathway is sometimes closed to protect nesting bald eagles.) Turkey vultures are often seen soaring over the vegetation of sweetgum, holly, and cedar trees, some covered by the intertwining vines of poison ivy.

Poison ivy leaves grow alternately spaced along the vines and are usually unevenly notched, a good trait to help identify it. Most other plants have leaves that are symmetrical off the center vein, but one side of a poison ivy leaf may have only one or no teeth, while the other side may have a number of teeth.

With an open field to your right, swing left at 0.3 mile to enter a deeper forest, with stinging nettle now mingling with the poison ivy. Marshes are soon visible through the trees on both sides of you. Snakes, turtles, frogs, mice, voles, muskrats, and more make their homes in these wetlands and survive by dining on the marsh plants, such as cattails and salt-marsh cordgrass. The tubers of three-square, a grasslike plant given its name because of its triangular-shaped stems, are a favorite of the muskrats, while the waterfowl feed upon its seeds.

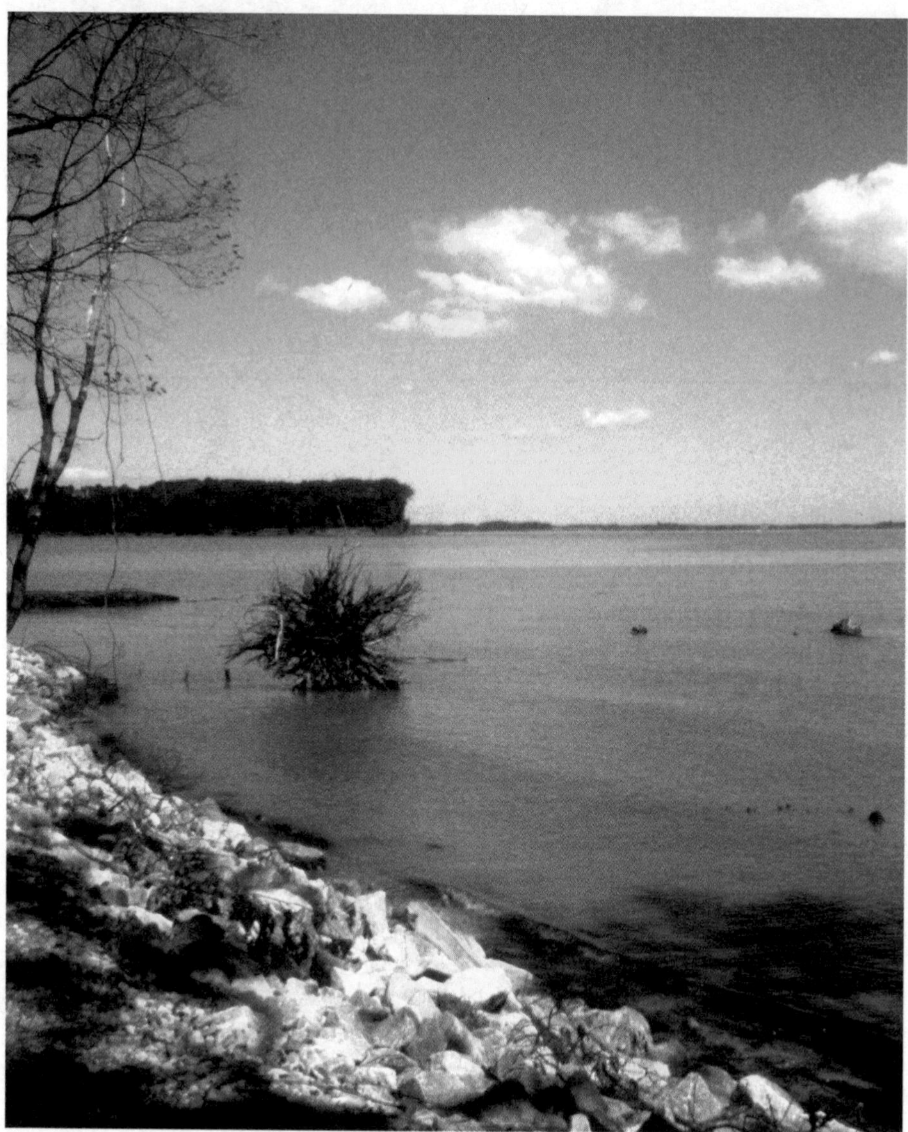

Boxes Point overlooking the Chester River

Loblolly pine trees make an appearance at 0.5 mile, and soon afterward you will walk by a pond that provides an unobstructed view onto the mouth of the Chester River.

You have reached the end of the land when you come to Boxes Point at 0.65 mile. This is the time to just sit and take in all that surrounds you. The Chester River is about 2 miles wide at this point, and you may see some rather large ships headed upstream to Chestertown. Myriad shells, including many large oyster shells of a size that Chesapeake Bay oysters no longer attain, are scattered in the sand at your feet. Long-legged herons may be standing motionless in the shallow water close to shore, hoping to spear unwary fish with their beaks. If you are lucky, you might spot a diamondback terrapin–whose powerful jaws are designed for crushing snail, crab, and mollusk shells–basking in the sun when you take the short trail that heads left (northward) to another vantage point.

When ready to leave, retrace your steps and return to the parking lot at 1.3 miles. However, before getting into your car, take the boardwalk pathway across the marsh directly in front of you. Although some people just see mud, muck, and unusable property when looking at marshes, wetlands such as this are possibly the most important areas on Earth. They produce more organic material than any other topographic feature–almost 10 tons per acre per year. The grasses that dominate them decay and, along with other material, are washed into the rivers and bays. This material, known as detritus, reaches far out into the ocean and is one of the first links in the chain of food upon which we humans depend.

You will enter a stand of evergreens at 1.4 miles. Just before rising up the ramp of the duck blind 200 feet later, take the faint trail to the left and climb the steps into the observation tower. (By the nature of its design, the duck blind would probably provide you with a better bird-watching experience, but the observation tower affords a much wider vista.)

Taking in the sweeping panorama, you can see farmland to the north in Kent County, the colorful sails of boats crossing the bay to the west, and the water of Calfpasture Cove cutting into Eastern Neck Island to the south. On clear days, you might even be able to make out some of the industrial buildings of Baltimore on the distant horizon.

If you are here during the colder months of the year, you will hopefully see some of those thousands of Canada geese. Their distinctive color patterns make them hard to misidentify. The head, back, neck, feet, and tail are black, while the white cheek patches are the most easily recognized characteristic. The average Canada goose weighs somewhere around 10 pounds and has a wingspan of 5 to 6 feet. They employ their characteristic V formation to save energy on long migratory flights. Each bird flies in the updraft of the goose's wings in front of it, thereby gaining an extra bit of lift. The strongest birds take turns being the leader, which, of course, has no such advantage and must work harder.

Retrace your steps and return to your car at 1.7 miles. Yet, you still shouldn't leave this great place. There are three other short pathways in the refuge, and all are worth walking. The Wildlife Trail is a circular pathway through a hardwood forest, the Duck Inn Trail is a route to another small beach along the Chester River, and the Bayview Butterfly Trail–really just a few steps long–leads to one of the best views of the Chesapeake Bay.

You should also consider driving to the end of the refuge road and visiting the Wickes Historic Site to gain some insight into the human history of the island.

45

Wye Island

Total distance (round-trip): 6.6 miles

Hiking time: 3 hours

Vertical rise: 6 feet

Maps: USGS 7½' Queentown

Unlike Janes Island (see Hike 48), which provides the opportunity to study the Chesapeake Bay landscape left in its natural state, Wye Island Natural Resources Management Area gives you the chance to explore an island that has been used for agricultural purposes for three centuries.

In the 1770s, John Beale Bordley gave up his law practice to spend his time farming his half of the island south of Dividing Creek. Under his tutelage, the inhabitants of the island became self-sufficient, growing their own wheat and establishing vineyards, orchards, textile production, a brick factory, and even a brewery. Bordley produced salt by processing the waters of the Wye River.

Some time after this, the island was sold off into individual tracts, yet the farming families still worked together, making it one of the most productive agricultural areas in Maryland. The people who possibly had the biggest impact on turning the island into what it looks like today were Glenn and Jacqueline Stewart. Ultimately able to purchase eight large farms, they created a cattle ranch on most of the island's 2,800 acres. When they reached an age at which they no longer wanted to care for the ranch, they sold the largest percentage of their land to the Hardy brothers.

Once under their control, the brothers participated in two controversial plans for the island in the early 1970s. One was to create a planned community complete with stores, marinas, public utilities, and cluster housing, and the other was to subdivide the island into 10- to 20-acre parcels. Both ideas ran

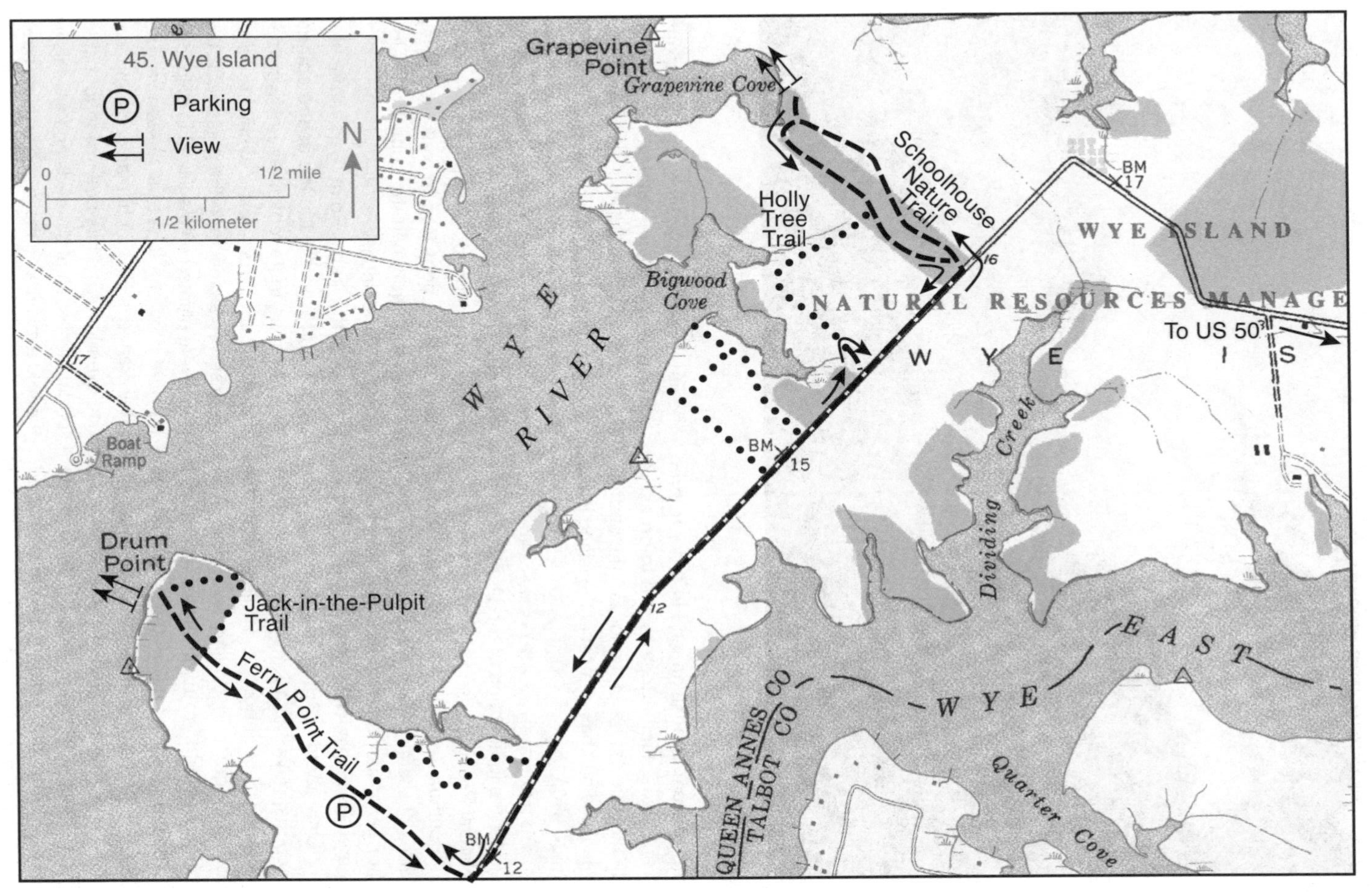
45. Wye Island
Parking
View
0
1/2 mile
0
1/2 kilometer
N
Grapevine Point
Grapevine Cove
Schoolhouse Nature Trail
Holly Tree Trail
Bigwood Cove
WYE RIVER
WYE ISLAND
NATURAL RESOURCES MANAGE
To US 50
W Y E I S
Dividing Creek
BM 17
BM 15
BM 12
Boat Ramp
Drum Point
Jack-in-the-Pulpit Trail
Ferry Point Trail
EAST WYE
QUEEN ANNES CO
TALBOT CO
Quarter Cove

The view from Drum Point

into severe opposition, and in order to prevent future such attempts and to preserve the unique nature of the locale, the state of Maryland purchased most of the island in the mid-1970s.

Approximately 2,450 acres are now under the jurisdiction of the Department of Natural Resources and are still managed for agricultural uses. The island has about 30 miles of shoreline, while virgin stands of timber serve as prime habitat for the endangered Delmarva fox squirrel.

Only about a 30-minute drive from Annapolis, Wye Island may be reached by leaving US 50 (about 12.5 miles east of the Bay Bridge) and driving south on Carmichael Road. You will cross the bridge onto the island 5.1 miles later, staying to the right at the first major intersection in an additional 1.1 miles (the management area office is to the left). Stay straight when the road becomes unpaved 0.4 mile beyond the intersection, passing by all parking areas and making a right onto Ferry Point Road 2.3 miles later. The Ferry Point Trailhead parking is 0.3 mile down this road. Be aware that controlled hunting is permitted on the island at certain times. Pets must be leashed. If at any time you feel like exploring beyond the description of the hike that follows, you are permitted to walk the grassy buffer strips between the cultivated fields and the woodlands.

Taking the Ferry Point Trail, enter the woods and walk beside the osage orange trees, whose fruits look like crinkly grapefruits. Brought from Texas, where rows of them served as fences in the grasslands, the trees were planted on the island to help form barriers between livestock meadows. The pithy orange is unfit for human consumption, and even though it has been used for cattle fodder, almost all of the birds and animals in the wild avoid it. Gumballs and walnuts have fallen to the ground beside this odd-looking fruit.

The route swings a bit to the right at 0.4 mile and enters a deeper woods. If you are here in the early morning, you might catch a few watermen or recreational anglers beginning their day on the Wye River once you break out of the forest and onto Drum Point at 0.6 mile. A few homes are visible across the water on Bennett's Point.

After enjoying this view for a while and maybe watching the acrobatics of a few osprey, you could take the circular Jack-in-the-Pulpit Trail (and add less than 0.5 mile to the hike), but on this hike I will instruct you to retrace your steps back into the woods. A road cuts through this narrow forest to connect to cultivated fields on both sides of the woods at 1 mile. For a change of scenery, you could walk along the edge of either field and return to your car at 1.2 miles.

Forsaking motorized transportation, walk along Ferry Point Road and turn left onto the island's main road. The openness of fields alternately planted in corn and soybeans provides the opportunity to enjoy a large expanse of blue sky, dotted with the black, soaring bodies of crows and turkey and black vultures.

Members of the corvidae family, which also includes jays, magpies, and ravens, crows can be found almost everywhere across America. They have such a high reproductive rate, most ornithologists believe they are more numerous now than when the colonists first arrived. In fact, there are some places where more than 500,000 crows have been seen roosting together. Although they are more or less omnivorous, a main part of their diet consists of insects, such as cutworms and grasshoppers, that are considered pests by farmers.

Pass by a parking area at 2.4 miles and turn left onto the Holly Tree Trail at 2.9 miles. Cross over a footbridge and follow the white-blazed route along the left side of the field. At 3 miles you will be standing in front of what is undoubtedly the largest holly tree you have ever seen. To truly appreciate the immense proportions of this tree, which is believed to be more than 250 years old, walk all the way around it. After that, pass through the fence and walk into, and under, the boughs of the tree, looking upward along its trunk. Trees of this magnitude are certainly rare in the eastern part of America.

Although the Holly Tree Trail continues beyond the tree, on this hike you will retrace your steps back to the road at 3.1 miles and turn to the left, making another left into the Schoolhouse Nature Trail parking area at 3.4 miles. Pick up a brochure, which is keyed to numbered stops along the way, and enter the woods. This trail was improved, and the brochure written, by the Centreville Middle School Ecology Corps.

You will pass by a small swampy area to the right at 3.6 miles in which copious amounts of poison ivy and jack-in-the-pulpit grow. The American strawberry bushes, whose bright orange capsules break open to reveal deep red seeds, are probably escapees from someone's ornamental plantings. This deep forest is the place to watch for a Delmarva fox squirrel. See Hike 47 for a discussion about these endangered creatures.

You will cross the horse trail at 3.8 miles, where there are so many gumballs on the ground that it may be hard to keep your balance. There is an intersection just 200 feet later, and you want to take the right pathway onto the footbridge that crosses a marshy, backwater area. Arrive at a small cove of the Wye River, Grapevine Cove, at 3.9 miles and take a break. Although you can see a few homes on Bennett's Point, this is a quiet area where you can watch ducks swim around or a heron or two walk stiff-legged through the shallow water.

Return to the intersection and bear right, gaining a perspective onto a different environment. The trees stop growing where they meet the tidal salt marsh. Swing to the left at 4.1 miles and walk along the edge of the field, soon passing by the Holly Tree Trail that comes in from the right.

Along the way, you will walk past loblolly trees, which adapt well to poorly drained, heavy soils, and are the most common pine tree found on the Eastern Shore. Growing straight and tall, with scales that become larger and smoother as the tree ages, the loblolly can be identified by its deep green needles that grow in bunches of three. Pitch pine needles also grow in bunches of three but are more of a yellow-green. The needles of the Virginia pine are in bundles of two.

Pass by a few older holly trees at 4.4 miles and return to the parking area at 4.6 miles.

Turn right and retrace your steps along the roadway, passing by the Holly Tree Trail at 4.9 miles and returning to your car at 6.6 miles.

46

Tuckahoe State Park

Total distance (round-trip): 3.7 miles

Hiking time: 2 hours

Vertical rise: 200 feet

Maps: USGS 7½' Ridgely

Bordered by tranquil wooded swamplands, Tuckahoe Creek forms the dividing line between Queen Anne's and Caroline Counties. Just as it has done with many of its other streams and rivers (see Hikes 34, 35, 38, 40, and 41), the state of Maryland has wisely protected much of this riparian habitat by establishing a state park. Although one of the smallest of those, Tuckahoe State Park still encompasses more than 3,700 acres.

Within this tract is a campground with modern facilities, a 60-acre lake that provides fishing and canoeing opportunities (canoe rentals available), a ball field, an archery range, and two picnic areas. Naturalist programs are available throughout the spring and summer. All of this is centered in the northern section of the park, which leaves the southern portion, where the majority of the pathways are undeveloped and natural.

The park may be reached by leaving US 50 (just east of Wye Mills and about 15 miles north of Easton) and heading east on MD 404 (Queen Anne Highway) for almost 7 miles. Turn left on Ridgely Road (MD 480), but make another left onto Eveland Road in just another 300 feet. When this roadway comes to an end (about 5 miles later), turn left onto Crouse Mill Road and leave your car in the Tuckahoe Lake parking lot on the right less than 1 mile later. Be aware that hunting is permitted in designated areas, and pets must be kept on a leash at all times.

The journey begins by walking toward the lake from the parking lot, turning left at its edge, and crossing Crouse Mill Road. Head

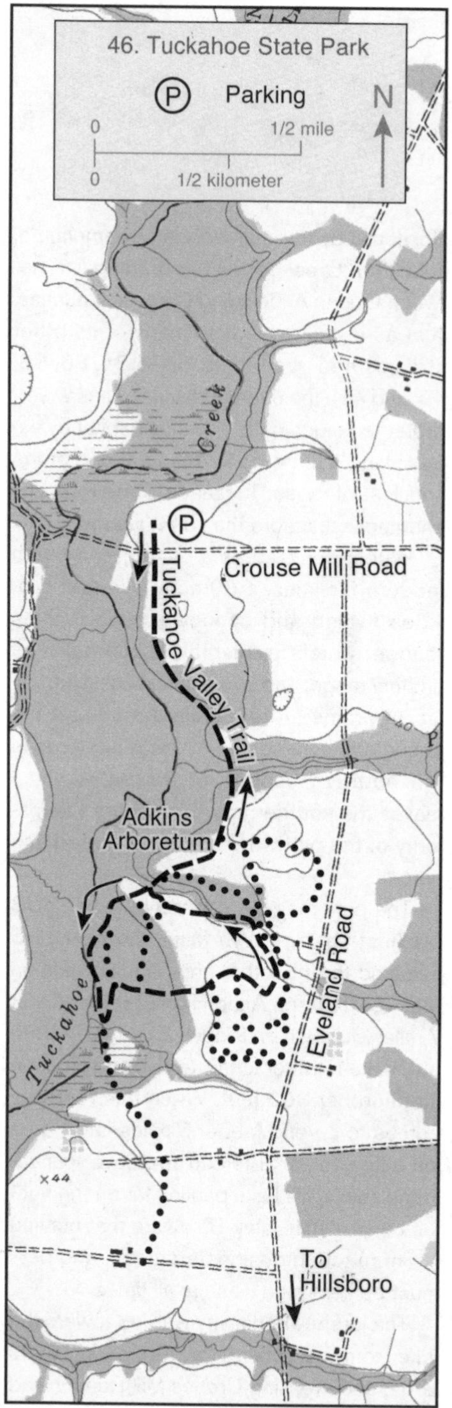

just a few feet to the left before turning right into the woods on the blue-blazed Tuckahoe Valley Trail. Greenbrier, grape-vine, and poison ivy are abundant and drape themselves in luxuriant patterns across some of the juniper trees and other vegetation.

Skirt the edge of an overgrown field for a few feet at 0.3 mile. The openness provides you with the opportunity to watch a number of turkey vultures circling overhead, while at your feet, the tentacles of Virginia creeper are skulking farther and farther into the field. An Adirondack-style shelter for long-distance travelers on the American Discovery Trail, which passes through the park, is a few feet to the left at 0.4 mile.

With more than 6,000 miles of pathway, the American Discovery Trail stretches across the country from Cape Henlopen, Delaware, to Point Reyes, California. Conceived by the American Hiking Society and *Backpacker* magazine in 1989, it connects large cities, small towns, and suburban areas to mountains, forests, deserts, plains, and natural areas by incorporating local, regional, and national trails. Along the way it passes through Washington, D.C., St. Louis, Denver, and San Francisco and leads to 14 national parks, 16 national forests, and more than 10,000 historical, cultural, and natural sites of significance. Although the trail was not officially dedicated until 2000, Bill and Laurie Foot of Lynchburg, Virginia, became the first people to traverse its entire distance in 1997–98. It is certainly an adventure worth thinking about. (More information may be obtained from the American Discovery Trail Society, P.O. Box 20155, Washington, DC 20041-2155.)

Be sure to follow the blue blazes of the Tuckahoe Valley Trail as it continues through a woods that is popular with songbirds early in the morning. Within this forest, vireos, wood thrushes, blue jays, cardinals, gold-finches,

Tuckahoe Lake

nuthatches, wood ducks, catbirds, and towhees have been seen. It is interesting to note that the word *towhee* was once used in Western Maryland and Virginia as somewhat of a derogatory term for people who lived in the mountains, while the mountain folk retaliated by calling the flatlanders "tuckahoes."

Come to a four-way intersection at 0.6 mile; continue straight. There will be another intersection, this one with a grassy road that goes both left and right, just 400 feet later. Bear to the right, only to leave the road and continue to follow the blue-blazed route by turning right onto a pathway in an additional 200 feet.

Cross the tea-colored water of Piney Branch on a footbridge at 0.8 mile and enter the grounds of the Adkins Arboretum. Occupying 400 of the park's acres, the arboretum, within a natural setting, showcases the trees, shrubs, and other plant life typical of the coastal plain.

Be on the lookout for snapping turtles in and near the water throughout this hike. Endowed with powerful jaws, they can grow up to 18 inches in length and weigh more than 40 pounds. Their sawtoothed tails may be as long as their tan to dark brown carapace, which is serrated toward the rear. Underwater, snapping turtles usually do not bite, but on land they can become mean and aggressive, with even hatchlings snapping wildly at objects perceived as intruders or threats.

Pass through a pine plantation at 1 mile, where the vines have wrapped themselves so tightly around the ironwood trees that the trunks have grown in spirals. Come to a T intersection at 1.2 miles and bear to the right, continuing to follow the blue blazes. Benches along the trail invite you to take a break for a few moments.

An unmarked pathway comes in from the left at 1.3 miles. Stay to the right and, now enjoying a slightly different environment, turn right a few feet later onto the Tuckahoe Creek Walk. Walk along the creek, looking for the beaver-gnawed trees. The trails you see leading to the creek and down its banks are the result of the beavers dragging branches into the water to replenish their food supply or repair their homes.

The dark color of the creek is produced by tannin, a substance released by the leaves and bark of some of the trees. It retards the growth of bacteria and slows the decomposition of organic material. Water dock, a member of the buckwheat family, grows along the edges of the creek and has very small green flowers that bloom in June and July.

Intersect the blue-blazed Tuckahoe Valley Trail at 1.6 miles and turn left (going right would eventually bring you to the park office). Bear right onto the Upland Walk when you come to the T intersection at 1.7 miles, keeping right again just 400 feet later when the Ridge Walk heads uphill to the left.

Swing left along the edge of the meadow on the South Meadow Loop as you emerge from the deep forest at 1.9 miles. You may squint in the bright sunlight, but be prepared for your heart to skip a beat or two when a quail you scared out of the underbrush suddenly comes flying upward.

The Adkins Arboretum Visitor Center is several hundred feet directly ahead of you at 2 miles and is definitely worth a visit if it is open. However, the route you want to follow turns off of the South Meadow Loop before you would reach the visitors center. Take the trail marked WOODLAND WALKS; enter a swampy, forested area; and cross a wooden bridge. Immediately turn left onto the Blockston Branch Walk and read the signs along the self-guided pathway to gain a better knowledge of the natural history you are experiencing.

Soon after crossing over a very tannin-stained stream, come to a T intersection at 2.5 miles and turn right. Do the same only 100 feet later, but be aware that only 50 feet after that, you will need to turn left onto the blue-blazed Tuckahoe Valley Trail to begin to retrace your steps back to the lake.

Even though you are walking the same route, keep your eyes and ears open for things you may have missed on the way out, such as prothonotary warblers. Fond of swampy, wooded areas like the one you are walking through, their bright, golden-orange heads and chests make them easy to spot against the forest's dark foliage. Arriving from the south around April, these are the only eastern warblers to nest in cavities. Amazingly, the young are capable of swimming, certainly an important skill when born within a swampy environment.

Continuing along, you might hear a pair of barred owls, some of the most vocal of owls, alternate calling back and forth to each other, even during midday. Their *who-cooks-for-you, who-cooks-for-you-all* cry can carry for more than a mile.

The hike comes to an end when you return to your car at 3.7 miles.

47

Blackwater National Wildlife Refuge

Total distance (round-trip): 2.9 miles

Hiking time: 1 hour, 30 minutes

Vertical rise: 5 feet

Maps: USGS 7½' Blackwater River; refuge map

In Virginia, it is almost common knowledge that if you want a guarantee of seeing a white-tailed deer, you should go to Shenandoah National Park. In Maryland, just about every citizen knows that Blackwater National Wildlife Refuge, in the late fall and early winter, is the place to be if you want to observe hundreds, even thousands, of migratory waterfowl; especially Canada geese.

An important resting and wintering area for birds that travel the Great Atlantic Flyway from Canada to the Gulf of Mexico, the 23,000-acre refuge was established in 1933. The area is composed primarily of rich tidal marshes characterized by fluctuating water levels and variable salinity, mixed in with evergreen/deciduous forests, freshwater ponds and impoundments, and some cropland. As with other national wildlife refuges (see Hikes 28 and 44), Blackwater is managed for the protection of wildlife and wildlife habitat.

This emphasis on protecting wildlife and disturbing it as little as possible has resulted in only a few pathways being built on the refuge. Because of the lack of trails to be explored by foot, I almost decided that the refuge was not an appropriate destination to include in this guidebook. Yet, since there are very few other places in Maryland where you can reap such a marvelous and rewarding payback for the small amount of energy you will expend, it would have been erroneous not to tell you about this exceptional place. The two trails I direct you to were chosen because they are so representative of what the refuge has to offer–marsh and

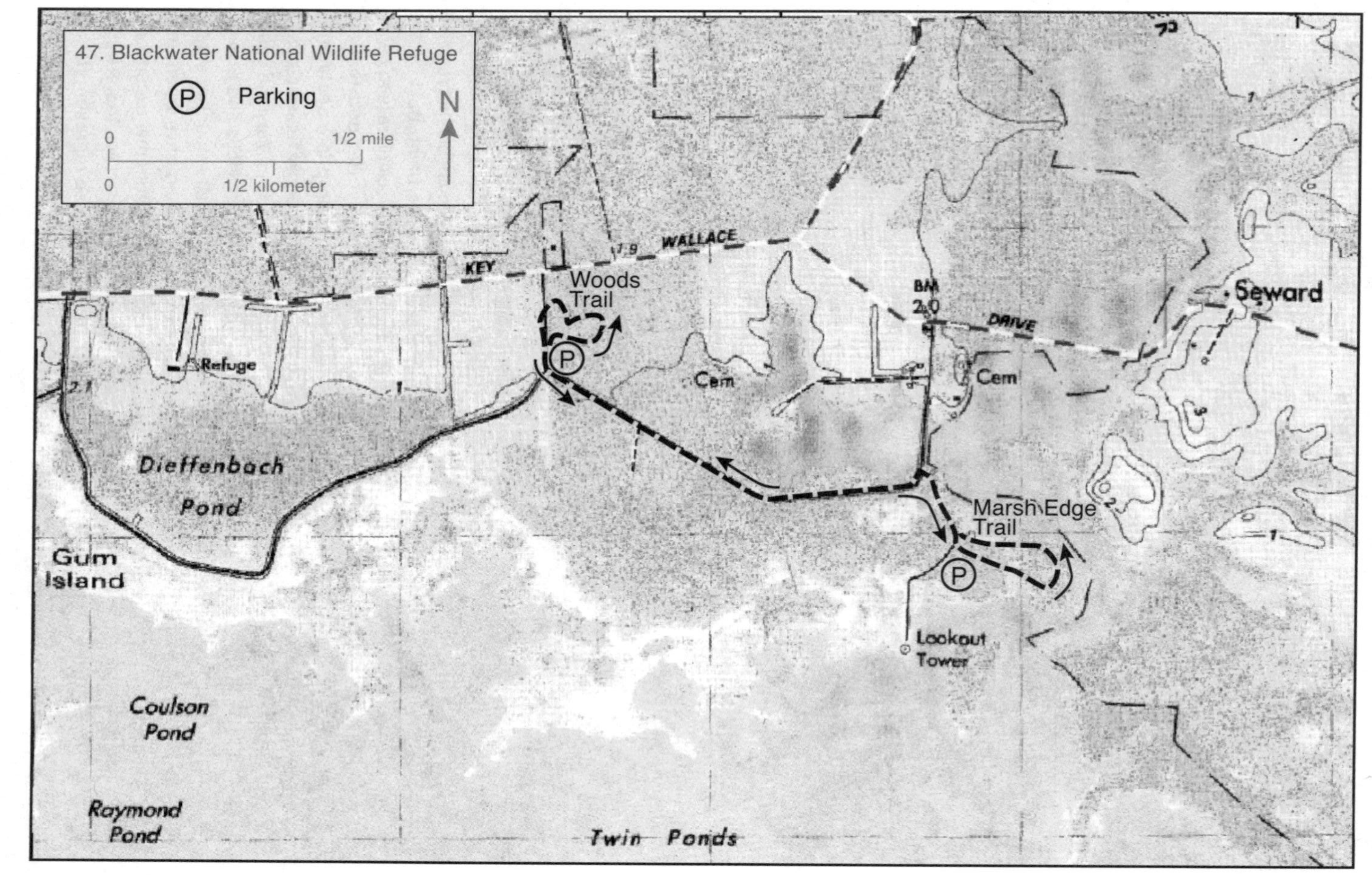
47. Blackwater National Wildlife Refuge
P Parking
N
0 1/2 mile
0 1/2 kilometer
KEY
WALLACE
DRIVE
Woods Trail
Marsh Edge Trail
Seward
BM 2.0
Cem
Cem
Refuge
Lookout Tower
Dieffenbach Pond
Gum Island
Coulson Pond
Raymond Pond
Twin Ponds

water views, deep woodland forests, and the opportunity to observe the waterfowl. If you find the hike too short, you can always walk the refuge's other two pathways. (Information is available at the visitors center.)

The refuge may be reached from the intersection of US 50 and MD 16 in Cambridge. Drive MD 16 west for 7.5 miles and, in the small village of Church Creek, turn left onto MD 335. An additional 3.8 miles will bring you to another left turn onto Key Wallace Drive. Just 1 mile beyond this, turn right and make a stop at the refuge's visitors center to look over the displays, pick up a few informative pamphlets, and watch any of a number of films about the area's natural history. You can also pay your entrance fee here.

Return to Key Wallace Drive, turn right, and drive 1.6 miles to make a right onto Wildlife Drive. Keep left at the intersection in another 0.3 mile and bypass, for now, the Marsh Edge Trail parking lot. This is so that you can drive out to the Observation Site at the end of the road.

This windswept point overlooks the thousands of acres of wetlands through which the Blackwater River flows and onto the flocks of waterfowl floating upon it. During each winter season for the past several years, approximately 35,000 Canada geese and more than 15,000 ducks of more than 20 different species have been seen on the refuge.

Drive back to the Marsh Edge Trailhead, read the displays on the bulletin board, and pick up a brochure as you begin your walk. The blacktop pathway brings you into a woods populated by loblolly pine, sweet gum, holly, and maple trees, with an occasional northern bayberry (also known as wax myrtle) bush as part of the undergrowth. The latter's berries begin to form in August and develop a white, waxy dust on them, which was used in former times to make bayberry candles. It is not just the berries, though, that have the pleasant scent. Rubbing just about any part of the plant will produce the familiar fragrance. Birds will feed on the berries when all other food sources have been depleted.

It only takes 0.1 mile of walking to bring you alongside marshland inhabitants such as common reeds, three-square, bulrushes, and cattails. A few feet beyond, a bench overlooking the Blackwater River and an osprey nest built upon a platform in the water allow you to take several moments of contemplative rest.

Ospreys usually mate for life and return to the same nest site year after year. Offshore structures, such as the one at which you are looking, offer protection from predators (like raccoons) that hurt the young birds, born in May or June. These sites also allow rapid detection of and escape from danger, provide distance from most human activities, and keep the ospreys close to their food supply.

There is always a cool breeze coming off the water, so stay here in this quiet place a bit longer, maybe even losing track of time and letting the cares of your everyday world disappear for a while.

Continuing along the pathway, there is another bench at 0.25 mile, this one looking out across the marsh and the Little Blackwater River to Barbados Island, where bald eagles have been known to nest. The refuge and the lands that surround it support one of the largest concentrations of bald eagles along the Atlantic coast, with an average of nearly 60 that use the refuge year-round.

About 200 feet beyond the second bench, a boardwalk stretches onto the watery marsh, bringing you into more intimate contact with this environment. Stay here for a while, and you are almost guaranteed to catch the natural world going about its business. Turkey and black vultures may soar overhead, egrets and herons might wade in close to the shore, and some V-shaped waves may spread across the surface of the water–indicating a muskrat or nutria is on its way back home.

Larger than a muskrat, the nutria is sometimes mistaken for a beaver. Introduced from South America in the mid-1900s for its fur, it has no natural predators, and its numbers continue to rise, causing increasing amounts of damage to the wetlands. Burrowing into the soil, the nutria feed upon the roots of the marsh plants, causing the plants to die before being able to reproduce. Large mudflats where these rodents have destroyed the vegetation are visible at low tide throughout the refuge.

At 0.35 mile, turn right off the blacktop onto a narrower pathway to enjoy the softness underfoot that comes from years of pine needles dropping onto the ground. As it swings left away from the water, the pathway becomes narrower yet, but it does bring you back to the parking area at 0.45 mile.

You could get in your car and drive to the next trail, but to continue to interact with the elements, walk out of the parking lot and turn right onto the road, passing by grasses and other wetland vegetation. To the left are open views across a couple of small ponds.

Bear left at 0.6 mile onto the main portion of Wildlife Drive. The first part of this road walk is beside a couple of ponds that are drained in the summer to permit the growth of moist-soil plants. They are allowed to refill when the fall rains arrive. This manipulation helps ensure that migrating birds will have nesting sites and food sources available to them throughout much of the year.

Soon after the trees close in on both sides of the road, turn right at 1.45 miles, take the Woods Trail, and keep to the right at the first intersection. This forest, dominated by loblolly pines, is prime habitat for the endangered Delmarva fox squirrel. At one time it was found in southeastern Pennsylvania, the Delmarva Peninsula, and possibly in southern New Jersey. Today it only exists within a few small, protected pockets of Maryland's Eastern Shore.

Intensive lumbering, coupled with habitat destruction through development, is the greatest cause for this decline. The timber industry cuts trees as soon as they are marketable and long before they develop into good fox squirrel habitat. The forest then becomes an environment better suited to the eastern gray squirrel, with which the fox squirrel must compete for food and homesites.

You will pass some decaying machinery at 1.5 miles; keep to the right at the intersection at 1.6 miles. So many pine needles have dropped off the upper branches of the loblolly that they give the understory a brown, shadowy effect. The eccentric call of a pileated woodpecker adds to this ghostly feeling.

Keep right at the next intersection and return to the Woods Trail parking lot at 1.9 miles. Turn left, retrace your steps along Wildlife Drive, and return to your car at 2.9 miles.

Before leaving this area, I suggest you drive slowly along the whole of Wildlife Drive, watching for turkey vultures to land in tree snags just a few feet away from your car or an osprey swoop into the water to catch dinner. Even when you are done with this, do not head home yet–return to the visitors center, pick up a bike map, and drive the suggested 25-mile loop. Driving along small country lanes, passing over a wide stretch of the Blackwater River, and maybe stopping in at one of the small country stores is a great

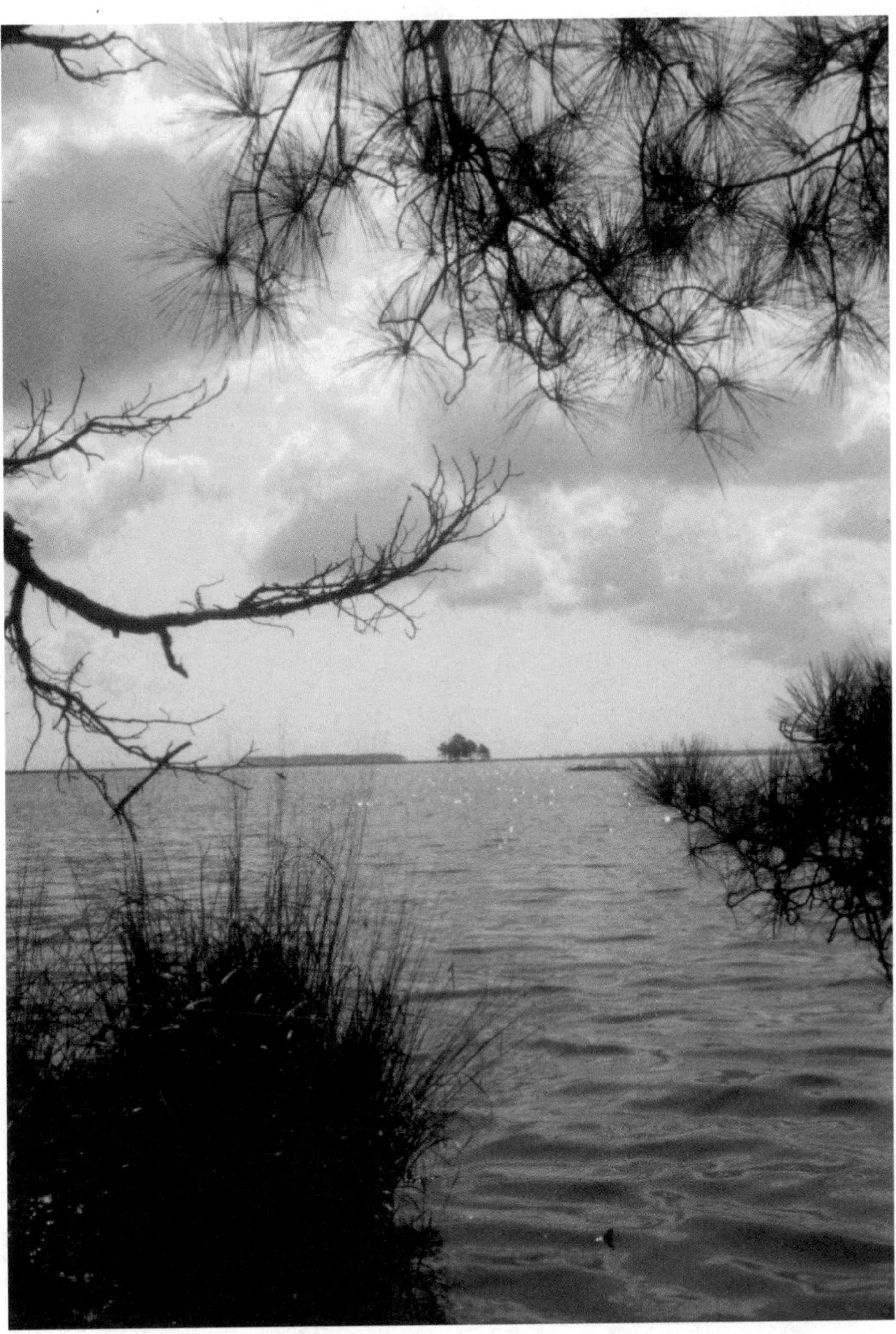

Overlooking the Blackwater River

way to become even better acquainted with what it is that draws so many people to the Eastern Shore.

Hopefully, you will have ended up dawdling so much that the sun will soon be setting by the time you return to the visitors center. This is the best time of day to once again be on Wildlife Drive, a witness to flocks of geese returning for the night, their black and white feathers standing out in contrast to the sun's crimson rays reflecting on the water.

48

Janes Island

Total distance (round-trip): 3.2 miles

Hiking time: 1 hour, 30 minutes

Vertical rise: 2 feet

Maps: USGS 7½' Marion; USGS 7½' Terrapin Sand Point; USGS 7½' Great Fox Island (MD/VA); USGS 7½' Crisfield (MD/VA)

This hike has a bit of a twist to it: You need a boat in order to reach it. At one time, state park personnel provided a free ferry on a small pontoon boat, but today you need to have your own method of water transportation or rent one in the park (available during the warmer months).

Janes Island State Park is divided into two areas: the 300-acre Hodson Memorial Area on the mainland and, separated from it by the Daugherty Creek Canal, Janes Island itself. Within the memorial area are a marina with boat-launch capabilities, a 104-site campground with modern amenities, picnic areas, and rental cabins. Although this area has two hiking trails, each a mile in length, it is the 3,000-acre island that is most worth spending your foot-travel time upon.

Except for a small boat dock and some ruins of a former fishing village on its southern end, Janes Island is completely undeveloped. Bordered by Tangier Sound, it is the quintessential Chesapeake Bay island, with a landscape barely above sea level. You will find windswept beaches, salt marshes, ponds, low-growing vegetation, and an assortment of creatures that exist only in this type of environment. To come here is to be brought back in time, to what many of the islands looked like when Capt. John Smith made his famous exploration of the bay in the 1600s.

The state park may be reached by driving southward from Princess Anne on US 13 for 3.5 miles and turning right onto MD 413. Continue for 11 more miles to the small town of Hopewell and turn right onto Plantation

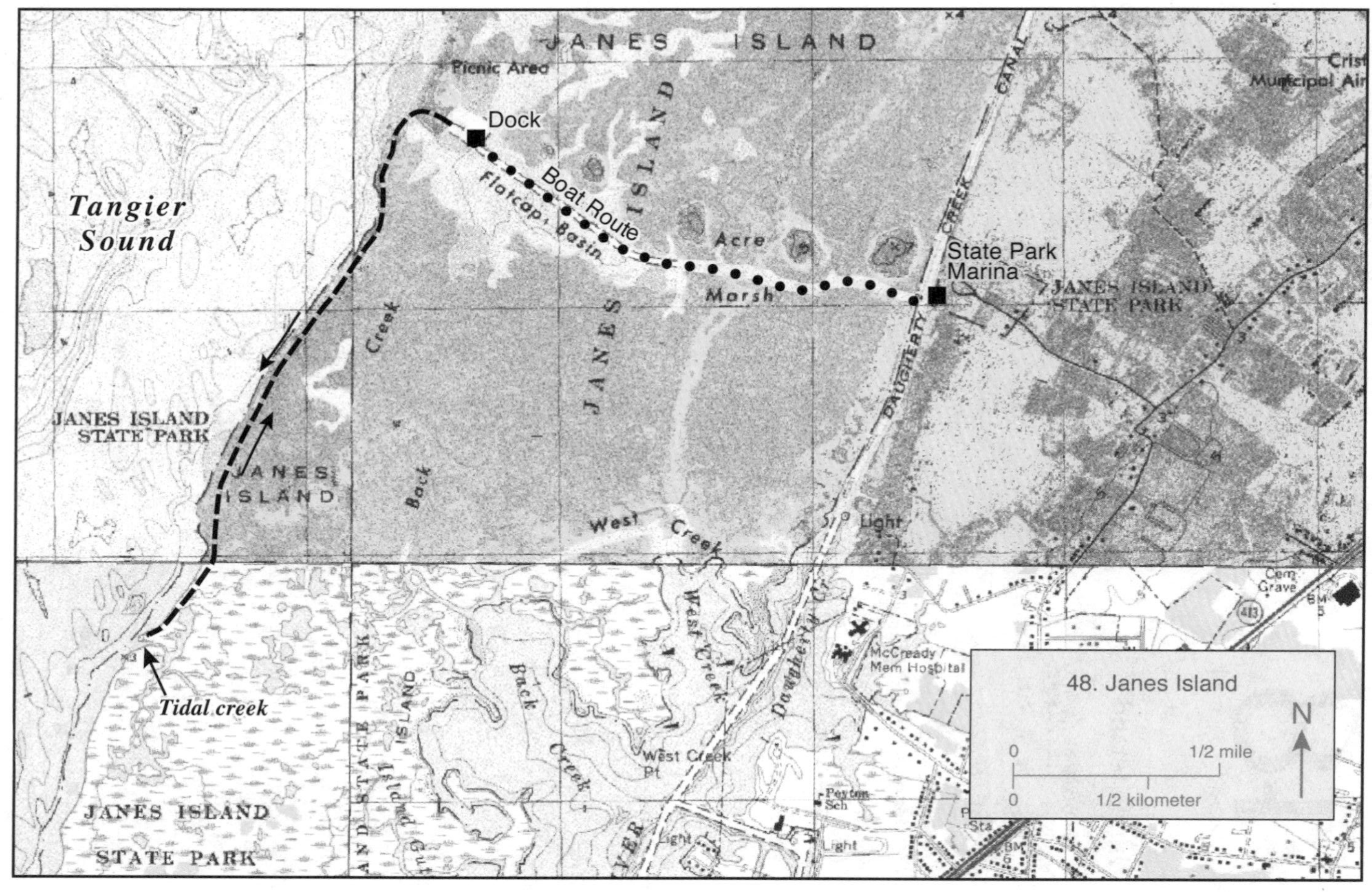

48. Janes Island
N
0
1/2 mile
0
1/2 kilometer
Tangier Sound
Dock
Boat Route
State Park Marina
Tidal creek
JANES ISLAND
Picnic Area
Flatcap Basin
Acre
Marsh
JANES ISLAND STATE PARK
DAUGHERTY CREEK CANAL
West Creek
Back Creek
Light
McCready Mem Hospital
West Creek Pt
Peyton Sch
Cem Grave
Municipal Air

Road (a sign for the state park is at this junction). Swing left onto Jacksonville Road less than 1 mile later. Within an additional 1 mile, turn right into the state park, and stop at the camper registration office to obtain a map and the information needed to make sure your boat trip to the island is a safe one.

You will be on an uninhabited island; be sure to bring plenty of food and water. Shade is unavailable, so carry sunscreen and coverups. The most important thing for comfort, though, is insect repellent. Although the breeze along the beach may keep their numbers down for short periods of time, be ready to be attacked time and again by mosquitoes, deerflies, and a particularly ornery fly, the greenhead.

This adventure actually begins as you launch your boat from the marina and head directly west, being mindful of the many swiftly moving pleasure craft running up and down the canal on busy summer weekends. Enter Ward Creek and proceed westward, with the water becoming ever wider as you continue into Flat Cap Basin and aim toward the dock at its far western edge.

After securing your boat, take the slightly defined pathway across the ripples of sand, moist spots, and salt-marsh grasses to reach Flatcap Beach in a few hundred feet. If you are on the island when no one else is, you may experience a great sense of isolation as you step onto the sand. The beach to the south runs to a far horizon faintly dotted by the short skyline of Crisfield, while just 0.5 mile or so northward, tidal waters indent the island at a point known as Rock Hole. The waters of the bay stretch out before you, uninterrupted by any land. (On extremely clear days you might be able to make out a bit of

The coast of Janes Island

Smith Island in the middle of the bay.) If you are going to take a swim, this is probably the best place to do it, as much of the water at other spots along the shore has entangling grasses in it. (There are no lifeguards, so remember that you swim at your own risk.)

When ready to explore, walk the beach southward, enjoying the ever-present breeze, looking out across the water, and finding treasures in the sand. The bubbles you see coming up just after a wave has receded are made by mole crabs. If you dig into the sand where a bubble appeared, you are almost certain to uncover one. Burrowing backward into the sand, they send up feathery, antennalike food-gathering organs to filter microorganisms out of the water. Interestingly, their eyes are attached to other antennae, a feature that allows them to stay buried yet still be able to see what is going on above.

The body parts of blue crabs, by far the bay's most important commercial product, are scattered about on the sand. Being scavengers, blue crabs will eat just about anything they come in contact with, dead or alive. Be careful if you happen to see one of them alive; their claws are powerful and can inflict a lot of pain when grabbing onto a finger or toe.

The shells of oysters, at one time at least as important a harvest of the bay as the blue crabs, are also found strewn upon the shore. These bivalves attach themselves to a solid underwater surface and grow into bars that have been known to become as large as the coral reefs found in the tropics. In fact, in past centuries, some of these bars were so extensive that they were hazardous to ships trying to navigate the bay. Due to overharvesting, disease, and pollution, the numbers of oysters began to decline in the late 1900s, and appear to be continuing today. This decline has had an effect on the entire bay. Being filter feeders, the oysters consumed large amounts of phytoplankton, which now grows almost uncontrolled, reducing the oxygen needed by other bay inhabitants.

It is hard to describe what the exact nature of the shoreline will be as you continue walking southward. As with all islands, it is always in a state of flux, changing with the whims of the weather and the effects of constant exposure to wind and water. The sandy beach will be wide and relatively flat in some places, while in others it may be narrow and drop quickly into the water. This is part of what makes Janes Island a different experience each time you visit.

The water of the marshes rules the inland portions of the island. Fiddler crabs are seen crawling onto the mudflats around these wetlands. The males have one large claw and one small claw, which make it easy to identify them. The larger claw is good neither for defense nor for eating–in fact, it hinders eating. The females, which have two normal-sized claws, are able to consume more food in less time. This crab received its name from the early settlers, who observed the male waving the large claw back and forth like a fiddler would move a bow across violin strings. They do this in order to attract females for mating.

Approximately 1.6 miles of walking will bring you to where a strong-flowing tidal creek, which drains the island's interior, has cut a wide, deep break into the beach. People have made their way across this stream, but recent storms have deepened and widened the channel, and it is suggested that this be the point at which you turn around to retrace your steps.

As you walk back up the beach, consider the body of water next to you. The Chesapeake Bay's name comes from the Native American word *Tschiṣwapeki,* which has been translated variously as "great waters," "great shellfish bay," and "mother of waters." This is the largest estuary in North America, measuring 200 miles long and averaging 15 miles wide. More seafood is harvested from it than from any of the other 800 or so estuaries in the United States. A fact that would surely be hard for the original Native American inhabitants to accept is that out of more than 4,600 miles of shoreline around the bay, less than 2 percent is accessible to the public. The rest is privately owned. Maybe we should utter a word of thanks that Janes Island is here for all to enjoy.

Your 3.2-mile exploration comes to an end as you return to your boat. If you have used a little foresight, you have rented a cabin, or your tent is already set up in the campground so that you can just relax and watch the day end while the sun drops into the bay.

49

Bald Cypress Nature Trail

Total distance (circuit): 0.9 mile

Hiking time: 20 minutes

Vertical rise: 25 feet

Maps: USGS 7½' Girdletree (MD/VA); USGS 7½' Snow Hill

Bald cypress is an oddity within the world of trees. It is coniferous, which means that it develops cones like pines, firs, and hemlocks—all trees with evergreen needles. Yet, while they may look like needles, the leaves of the bald cypress drop off as the weather turns colder, just as those on deciduous trees do. In addition, even though it is called a cypress, the bald cypress is actually a member of the redwood family. It is also a tree more common to the swamps of the South, just barely able to survive here at its very northern limits on the Eastern Shore.

Only about a 30-mile drive from Ocean City, the Bald Cypress Nature Trail in the Pocomoke River State Park is the place to take the kids after they have had enough of sun, surf, and sand and are badgering you about what to do next. The park may be reached by taking US 50 westward from the ocean for 7 miles and turning south along US 113. Once you are in Snow Hill, about 16 miles later, drive northward on MD 12 (Snow Hill Road) for 1.2 miles. Turn left onto Nassawango Road, making sure to stay on it for 6.7 miles as it twists and turns through a number of intersections. Make a left turn into the state park, follow the main road for 0.8 mile, and turn right onto the road with a sign pointing to the nature trail and boat-launching ramp. Bear left in an additional 0.4 mile and come into a large parking area several hundred yards later. Leave your car in the upper end of the lot near the trailhead.

Walk into a forest of sweetgums, oaks, Virginia and loblolly pines, maples, and poplars. Keep to the right when you come to the circuit trail intersection 300 feet later (you will return via the route to the left). Some beech trees grow amid the other trees of this forest, but, being more suited to well-drained soils, they are few in number. On the other hand, the ironwood (also called American hop hornbeam), which enjoys the moist bottomland, thrives here. Its numbers are limited only because it is a low-growing tree that must make do with the sunlight that is able to penetrate the forest canopy.

Cross a park road at 0.2 mile and note that, as you get closer to the swamp at 0.3 mile, there is an increase in the types of plants, such as willow oak, that are capable of surviving in the moist, poorly drained soil. Although willow oak is an oak that bears the familiar acorns so well liked by squirrels, its long, narrow, light green leaves make it look more like a willow tree.

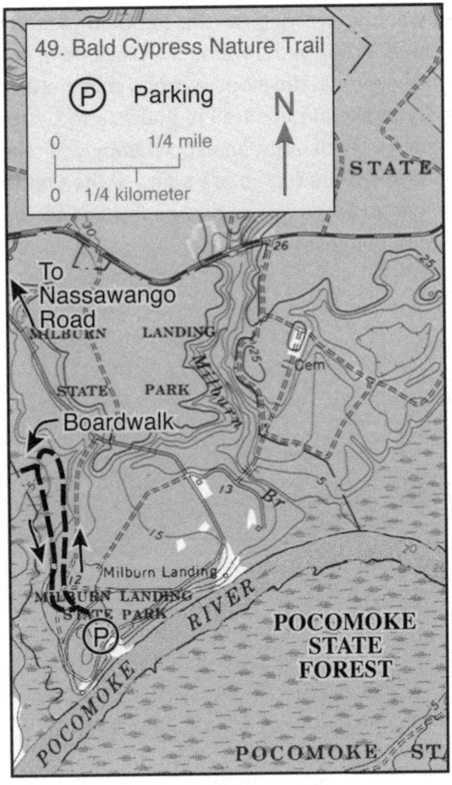

Swinging along the edge of the swamp just a few hundred feet later, you will find strange-looking, woody projections mixed in with the arrowhead-shaped leaves of the swamp vegetation. These are known as cypress knees and are part of the bald cypress tree's root system. There is still some disagreement as to the purpose of these knees. The most common theory is that the trees send them up in order to draw oxygen out of the air and back to the roots. Notice that some knees appear to be growing not in the water, but on dry land close to the trail. The swamp has evidently extended to these points at times, because the tree will not send up the knees unless its roots are underwater.

Your best views of the swamp and the bald cypress trees come after you have been walking for 0.5 mile. Close to the water's edge you will find Indian pipe and pinesap, two plants that lack chlorophyll. Although there has been recent research that suggests Indian pipe is in a symbiotic relationship with its host, the plant has historically been recognized as being saprophytic, gaining its nourishment from decaying matter through osmosis aided by a soil fungus. Although it contains a poisonous substance, Indian pipe has been used in the treatment of eye problems, fevers, spasms, and fainting spells.

Take the boardwalk to the right, which reaches into Cottingham Mill Branch. Freshwater fish live in this stream, but it is so close to the Chesapeake Bay that it is under the influence of the tides, and its water level fluctuates daily.

Return to the main route and bear right, passing by sweetbay and black gum. Also known as tupelo, the latter is usually found on the edges, or even in the middle, of the swamps, growing next to the bald cypress trees. When in the water, the black gum, like the cypress, develops a broad base; a theory to explain this trait is that it is to better anchor itself in the moist, swampy soil. The leaves of the tupelo are some of the first to change in the fall and range from deep red to bright yellow.

Turn right when you come a T intersection at 0.7 mile and cross a park road 200 feet later. Bear to the right when you return to the circuit trail intersection beside dogwood and red maple trees. The walk comes to an end when you reach your car at 0.9 mile. Maybe it's time to take the kids for some ice cream.

50

Assateague Island

Total distance (one-way): 25.0 miles

Hiking time: 2 days

Vertical rise: 36 feet

Maps: USGS 7½' Tingles Island; USGS 7½' Whittington Point (MD/VA); USGS 7½' Chincoteague East (VA)

A barrier island, Assateague Island is the farthest east you can go to take a hike in Maryland. Formed by sand that constant waves have raised from the gently sloping ocean floor, a string of such islands extends along the East Coast from Plum Island, Massachusetts, to Padre Island, Texas. Being prime beachfront property, many have been heavily developed and turned into typical high-rise resort areas.

The same thing almost happened to Assateague Island. Having purchased the largest majority of it in Maryland, the Ocean Beach Corporation began to subdivide the island into small plots in the 1950s. Within a few years, there was a paved road running down the interior of the island, electric lines had been installed, close to 6,000 plots had been sold, and a number of houses were already built.

In a perfect fulfillment of the famous lines of a Robert Burns poem, "The best laid schemes o' mice an' men gang aft agley, an' lea'e us nought but grief an' pain," a northeaster struck the island in March 1962. The most destructive storm of the 20th century (much more so than any hurricane), it drove the ocean completely across the island in several places. Almost every house was demolished, the power lines were downed and severed, and the road was destroyed, with most of its pavement washed away. Realizing the enormous costs of trying to maintain a modern way of life on the island, private investors began to shy away, and the federal government was able to establish Assateague Island National Seashore in 1965.

Today the entire island is public land and is administered as a national seashore by the US National Park Service, Assateague State Park, under the jurisdiction of the Maryland Department of Natural Resources and, on the Virginia side of the island, Chincoteague National Wildlife Refuge, within the auspices of the US Fish and Wildlife Service. What this means to you is that the island's 37-mile beach has been left gloriously undeveloped, with just a few minor amenities concentrated in two small areas.

The park service has established several oceanside and bayside backcountry campsites in Maryland, enabling you to complete a 25-mile, two-day hike along the most isolated part of the island. You can walk the beach, free of nearly every vestige of civilization, and see and learn about the marvels of the natural world as it plays out its daily dramas unhindered by human influences. This is by far one of the most primitive hikes in all of Maryland; do not miss it.

However, do not underestimate the difficulty of walking on 25 miles of sand, which is certainly more fatiguing than any other surface. Also be aware that the isolation of this place puts the responsibility for your personal safety on you. There are no places to obtain any potable water on the entire hike, not even at the campsites. Most authorities say to carry at least 2 quarts of water per person per day. I suggest 3 quarts—you can work up quite a thirst walking on a shadeless beach whose sand intensifies the heat of the sun. In the cooler temperatures of winter, your body needs even greater amounts of water not to become dehydrated. In order not to have to use any of your water for cooking, consider having canned tuna or chicken sandwiches for lunch and dinner; you are only out for one night.

A tube of sunscreen of the highest SPF you can find is also a must, as are light clothing to protect you from the sun and a heavier layer for when the wind turns chilly. Of course, a hat and sunglasses should be a part of any walk on the beach. Mosquitoes, sand fleas, ticks, and a variety of flies, including the nasty biting greenheads and deerflies, make insect repellent an essential item in the pack.

The tent pegs you use in the mountains just won't do here. The strong winds coming off the ocean will lift the short ones out of the soft sand in no time. Your pegs should be at least 15 inches long, but don't expect to find any branches or downed wood around the campsite to use. Beach tent pegs can be purchased at a number of stores near the island.

This is a one-way hike, and a 100-plus-mile round-trip car shuttle is necessary. Allow a minimum of 2½ hours for the shuttle. From the intersection of US 50 and US 113 near Berlin, drive south on US 113 for approximately 16 miles to Snow Hill, where you will turn onto MD 12 and continue south. An additional 12.3 miles brings you into Virginia, where the roadway becomes VA 679. Keep going for another 7.5 miles and make a left onto VA 175 in Wattsville. You will be on Chincoteague Island in an additional 7.9 miles; continue following signs to the Toms Cove Visitor Center. Obtain an overnight parking permit and leave one car where personnel direct you.

Retrace the route back to Berlin, where you need to leave US 113 and turn east onto MD 376. This road comes to an end in 4 miles; turn right onto MD 611 and continue for a little more than 3 miles onto Assateague Island. Turn right at the first intersection (straight leads to the state park) and continue to the North Ocean Beach parking lot on the left. The required over-night parking and backcountry permits can be obtained at the ranger station. You will be provided with a list of regulations, the main ones being that camping and fires are permitted only at designated sites. Also be aware that the only facilities at the campsites are picnic tables and chemical toilets. Pets are prohibited at the backcountry campsites.

DAY ONE

Total distance (one-way): 12.4 miles
Hiking time: 5 hours, 15 minutes
Vertical rise: 18 feet

This singular adventure begins by walking from the parking lot across the dunes on the boardwalk and turning right along the beach. The ranks of swimmers, sunbathers, and sight-seers will thin quickly as you continue southward.

One of the first things you may notice on this flat landscape is that distances can be deceiving. Objects that appear to be close to you seem to take longer to reach than you had originally thought.

Most of the sunbathers will have been left behind by time you come to the ORV (called OSV–over sand vehicles–on the island) access road at 1.5 miles. Although weekends may bring out a few people who want to just drive up and down the beach, most of the people in the vehicles are here to do some surf fishing. With their huge rods and reels, these folks are hoping to catch, among others, croaker, kingfish, rockfish, and shark.

The fin you may happen to spot from the beach most likely does not belong to a fish, but to a mammal–the bottle-nosed dolphin. They are often seen traveling in small groups during the summer, and their range reaches from Nova Scotia to Venezuela.

You will walk by the sign for the crossover to one of the bayside campsites, Tingles Island, at 2.25 miles. These sites are located among trees that provide shade, but the insects are considerably greater in number than those around the oceanside sites.

The first oceanside campsite, Little Levels, is passed at 4 miles, and the trail to the Pine Tree Campsite is at 5.1 miles.

Maybe it is time to take a short break from dedicated hiking and just saunter a bit, doing the favorite activity of beachcombers everywhere–hunting for shells. You can find the brightly colored shells of the Florida coquina at the water's edge. Living in colonies just below the surface of the sand, they follow the tides in and out, filtering food from the water. The Atlantic jingle shell is translucent with a waxy surface. The hole in the flat, lower shell is where the live jingle attached itself to solid surfaces.

Pass by the trail to the Green Run Campsite at 9.6 miles.

If you are here at a time when the biting insects are at their peak, you might find some of Assateague's famous wild ponies on the beach, hoping that the winds will help keep the insects at bay. Legend has long held that the ponies are descendants of mustangs that swam ashore after a Spanish ship wrecked off the coast in the 16th century. Most likely, the ponies' ancestors were placed on the island by mainland owners wanting to avoid taxation and the expense of putting up fencing.

The route to the Pope Bay Campsite is at 11.7 miles, and your home for the night, State Line Campsite, is behind the primary dune at 12.4 miles.

Sitting on the beach after the sun has gone down just may be the best part of this journey. There are no artificial lights to brighten the eastern horizon (Europe being quite some distance away), so the stargazing will be as good as it is ever going to get. Since most meteor showers emanate from the east, this is the place to be for one. Some of the more intense annual showers are Perseids, around August 12; Geminids, around December 12; and Quadrantids, near the first of every year.

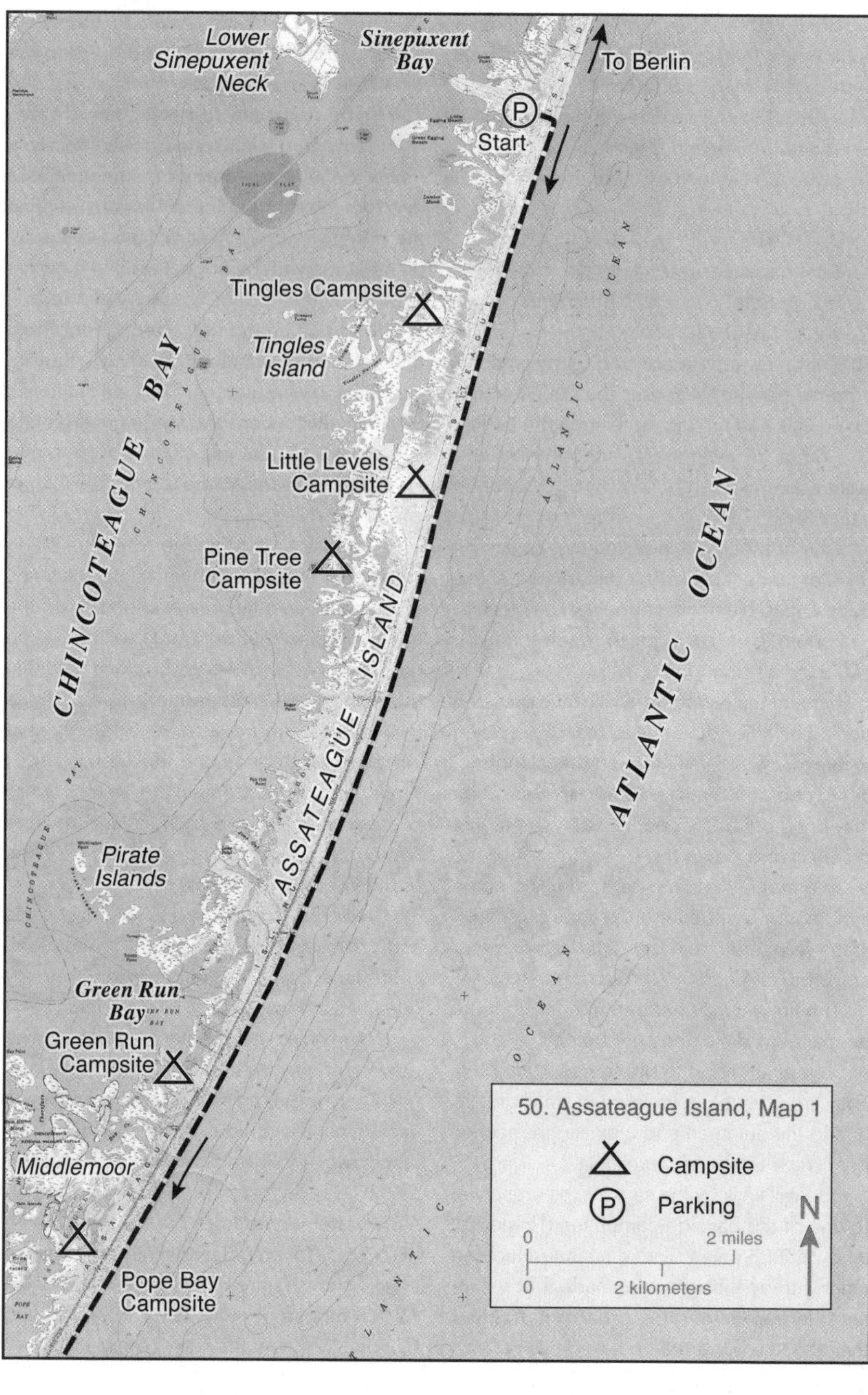
Lower Sinepuxent Neck
Sinepuxent Bay
To Berlin
Start
Tingles Campsite
Tingles Island
CHINCOTEAGUE BAY
Little Levels Campsite
Pine Tree Campsite
ASSATEAGUE ISLAND
ATLANTIC OCEAN
Pirate Islands
Green Run Bay
Green Run Campsite
Middlemoor
Pope Bay Campsite
50. Assateague Island, Map 1
Campsite
Parking
N
0
2 miles
0
2 kilometers

DAY TWO

Total distance (one-way): 12.6 miles
Hiking time: 5 hours, 30 minutes
Vertical rise: 18 feet

You watched the stars fill the night sky, so now wake up early enough this morning to catch the upper curvature of the sun creep above that narrow line in the east where the ocean appears to meet the sky. After packing up and making sure you have left no trace of having been here, resume your southbound seaside pilgrimage.

Even though it is the same beach, it has a different feel to it once you pass through the fence into Virginia and the Chincoteague National Wildlife Refuge at 1.3 miles. No vehicles (except those of refuge personnel) are permitted on the sands, and since you are miles from any road access point, you may well be the only person for miles around. It seems ironic that the land farthest to the east–some of the land that the early settlers would have most likely encountered first–is the place in which you can be the most isolated in all of eastern America.

As the sun climbs higher into the sky and you get about 3.5 miles from the State Line Campsite, the curving shoreline far to the south can almost look like it is cut off from the mainland and appear to be an island. Terns dive for fish, and gulls and sandpipers wander the beach. If you are hiking in late summer, watch for migrating shorebirds.

Since there are so few people here, you will find an abundance of whelk (sometimes mistakenly called conch) shells, many of them in near-perfect condition. The snail-like whelk rasps the edge of a bivalve's shell with its radula (a "tongue" that has minute teeth on its back surface) until it can force apart the two shells and get at the meat on the inside. As you look over at a platform that becomes visible behind the primary

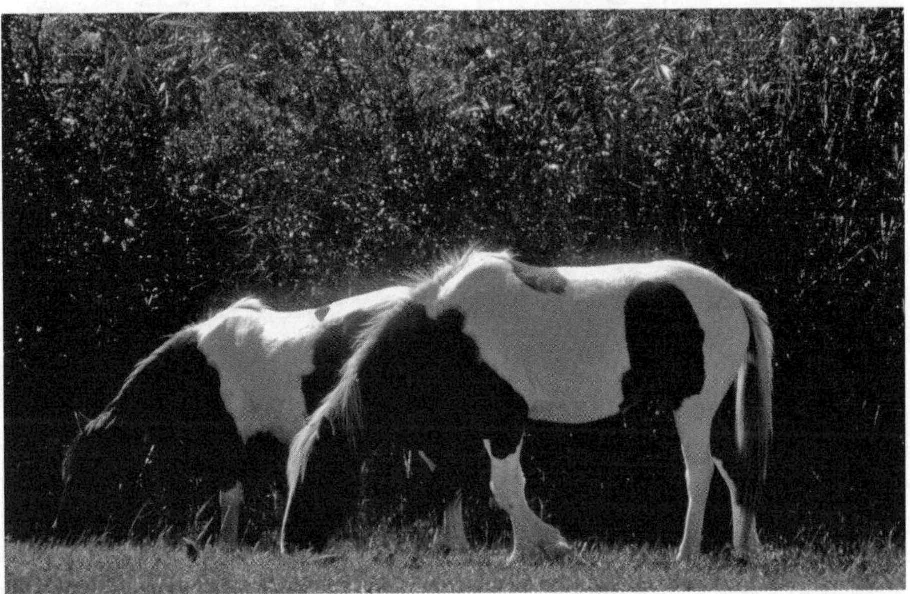

The wild ponies of Assateague

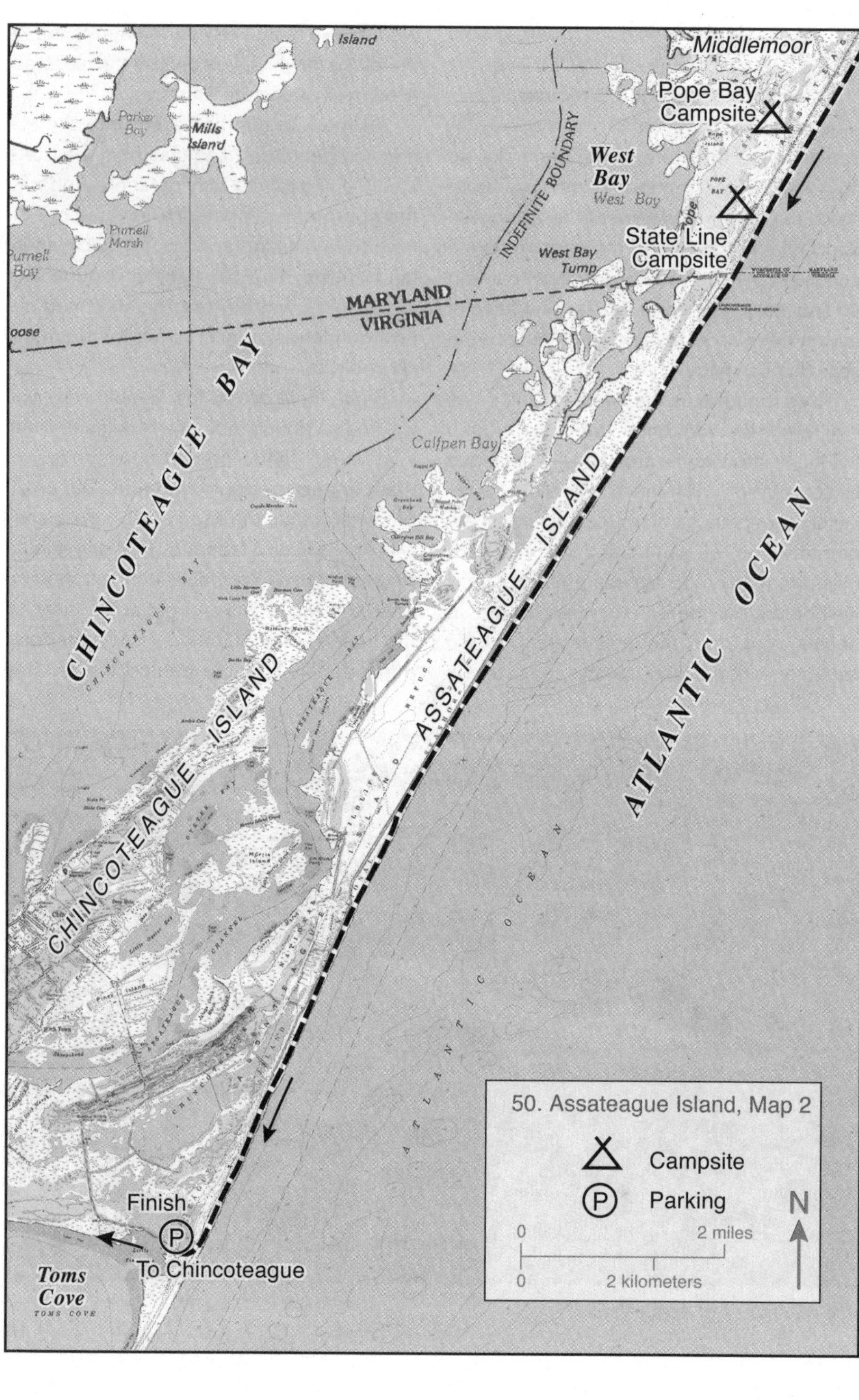
Middlemoor
Pope Bay Campsite
West Bay
State Line Campsite
West Bay Tump
MARYLAND
VIRGINIA
INDEFINITE BOUNDARY
Mills Island
CHINCOTEAGUE BAY
Calfpen Bay
ASSATEAGUE ISLAND
CHINCOTEAGUE ISLAND
ATLANTIC OCEAN
Finish
To Chincoteague
Toms Cove
50. Assateague Island, Map 2
Campsite
Parking
0
2 miles
0
2 kilometers
N

dune at 8.3 miles, you might notice the shell of a horseshoe crab washed up on the beach. Despite its fearsome appearance, the horseshoe is harmless, mostly using its long, pointed tail to turn itself back over when flipped up onto the beach. Its importance to the environment and to humans is just now being discovered. The juveniles of a threatened species, the Atlantic loggerhead turtle, feast on horseshoe crab eggs, as do northward-migrating shorebirds. Humans have historically used the crabs as fertilizer and feed for livestock, but recently it has been found that a compound in the crab's blood can be used to maintain drug quality and even test pharmaceutical and medical devices for the presence of a fatal bacterium. The compound is easily harvested from the horseshoe crabs, which can be returned to the water unharmed afterward.

There is access to a service road just after you pass a fence line, which may be buried in drifted sand by time you walk here, at 9.7 miles. For a change of pace, you could walk the service road–just be aware that you will probably encounter more insects. As compensation, though, you might see a white-tailed or Nippon sika deer, which were introduced a number of decades ago. By now you may possibly be encountering some folks along the beach, and, at about 12 miles, you can start to make out the flags flying above the Toms Cove Visitor Center.

Take the authorized pathway across the dune at 12.5 miles and come to the end of the hike as you reach the road and the developed area at 12.6 miles. Your shuttled car sits in the parking lot, ready to whisk you away to your next exploration of the outdoor world. Happy trails.

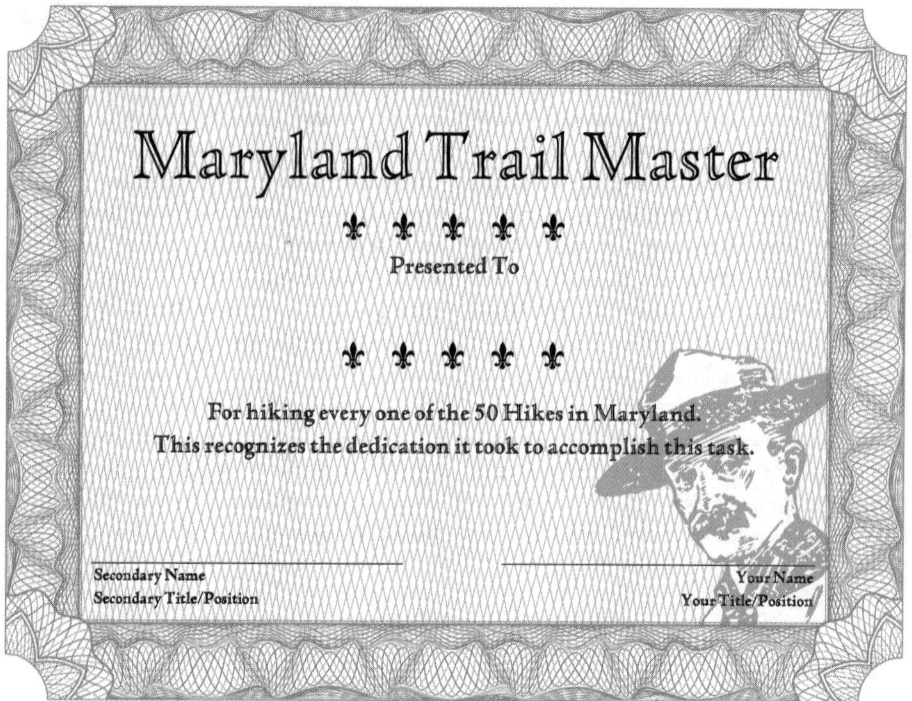
Maryland Trail Master
Presented To
For hiking every one of the 50 Hikes in Maryland.
This recognizes the dedication it took to accomplish this task.
Secondary Name
Secondary Title/Position
Your Name
Your Title/Position

Become a recognized Maryland Trail Master by hiking every one of the *50 Hikes in Maryland.* Simply keep a record of the date of each of your hikes and write a report (doesn't need to be more than one or two sentences) for each trail, providing your feelings about the hike, its condition, and if anything has changed since this book was published. In return, receive the suitable for framing Maryland Trail Master certificate of recognition. Join a very elite club–as of the publication of this book, the author, Leonard M. Adkins, is the only person to have reported having done all of the hikes. Send reports to habitualhiker@verizon.net.